DEATH ACROSS OCEANS

DEATH ACROSS OCEANS

*Archaeology of Coffins and Vaults
in Britain, America, and Australia*

EDITED BY
HAROLD MYTUM
AND
LAURIE BURGESS

A Smithsonian Contribution to Knowledge

Smithsonian Institution
Scholarly Press

Washington, D.C.
2018

Published by
SMITHSONIAN INSTITUTION SCHOLARLY PRESS
P.O. Box 37012, MRC 957
Washington, D.C. 20013-7012
https://scholarlypress.si.edu

Compilation copyright © 2018 by Smithsonian Institution

All rights reserved. No part of this publication may be reproduced, stored in a retrieval system, or transmitted in any form or by any means, electronic, mechanical, photocopying, recording, or otherwise, without the prior permission of the publisher.

Cover image: Sterling silver–plated brass single-lug coffin handle from the Coombe vault in Washington, D.C. Photo by Chip Clark. Courtesy of Smithsonian Institution.

Library of Congress Cataloging-in-Publication Data:
Names: Mytum, H. C., editor. | Burgess, Laurie E., editor. | Smithsonian Institution Scholarly Press, publisher. | Smithsonian Institution.
Title: Death across oceans : archaeology of coffins and vaults in Britain, America, and Australia / edited by Harold Mytum and Laurie E. Burgess.
Other titles: Archaeology of coffins and vaults in Britain, America, and Australia
Description: Washington, D.C. : Smithsonian Institution Scholarly Press, 2018. | Series: A Smithsonian contribution to knowledge | Copyright 2018 by the Smithsonian Institution. | Includes bibliographical references and index.
Identifiers: LCCN 2017045419 (print) | LCCN 2017047244 (ebook) | ISBN 9781944466169 (ebook) | ISBN 9781944466152 | ISBN 9781944466152(hardcover) | ISBN 9781944466169(ebook)
Subjects: LCSH: Funeral rites and ceremonies—Great Britain—History. | Funeral rites and ceremonies—North America—History. | Funeral rites and ceremonies—Australia—History. | Human remains (Archaeology)—Great Britain—History. | Human remains (Archaeology)—North America—History. | Human remains (Archaeology)—Australia—History. | Burial—Great Britain—History. | Burial—North America—History. | Burial—Australia—History. | Coffins—Great Britain—History. | Coffins—North America—History. | Coffins—Australia—History. | Tombs—Great Britain—History. | Tombs—North America—History. | Tombs—Australia—History.
Classification: LCC GT3150 (ebook) | LCC GT3150 .D396 2018 (print) | DDC 393.09—dc23 | SUDOC SI 1.60:D 34
LC record available at https://lccn.loc.gov/2017045419

ISBN-13: 978-1-944466-15-2 (print)
ISBN-13: 978-1-944466-16-9 (ebook)

Printed in Canada

♾ The paper used in this publication meets the minimum requirements of the American National Standard for Permanence of Paper for Printed Library Materials Z39.48–1992.

Contents

Chapter 1	United In Death? A Comparative Introduction to Historic Mortuary Culture *Harold Mytum*	1

Attitudes and Practices

Chapter 2	Candied Fruit or Carrionlie Carkase? Beliefs about the Dead Body in Early Modern Britain *Sarah Tarlow*	23
Chapter 3	Dressing for the Grave: The Archaeological Evidence for the Preparation and Presentation of the Corpse in Post-Medieval England *Annia Kristina Cherryson*	37
Chapter 4	In the Footsteps of Thomas Hardy: Archaeology and Exhumation at St. Pancras Burial Ground, London *Phillip A. Emery*	57
Chapter 5	Explaining Stylistic Change in Mortuary Material Culture: The Dynamic of Power Relations between the Bereaved and the Undertaker *Harold Mytum*	75

Material Culture and Classification

Chapter 6	Remember Man Thou Art Dust: A Retrospective on North American Hardware Traditions *Michael Trinkley and Debi Hacker*	97
Chapter 7	A Preliminary Seriation of Coffin Hardware in Nineteenth- and Twentieth-Century Georgia: Thirty Years Later *Patrick H. Garrow*	109
Chapter 8	The Need for Greater Precision in Mortuary Hardware Terminology *Roderick Sprague*	123
Chapter 9	Eighteenth- and Nineteenth-Century Coffin Furniture from St. George's Crypt, Bloomsbury, and the Churchyard and Crypt of St. Luke's, Islington *Louise Loe and Ceridwen Boston*	129
Chapter 10	Burial at the Edge of the Empire and Beyond: The Divergent Histories of Coffin Furniture and Casket Hardware *Megan E. Springate and Hilda Maclean*	165

| Chapter 11 | "Making a Box Worthy of a Sleeping Beauty": Burial Container Surface Treatments in the United States during the Nineteenth and Early Twentieth Centuries
Jeremy W. Pye | 177 |

Protecting the Body

Chapter 12	Body Snatchers and Mortsafes: An Archaeology of Fear *Harold Mytum and Katie Webb*	227
Chapter 13	Death, Dogs, and Monuments: Recent Research at Washington's Congressional Cemetery *Laurie Burgess and Douglas W. Owsley*	249
Chapter 14	Lost Governors, Iron Coffins, and Driven Descendants *Charles R. Ewen and Sheri B. Crane*	263

Conclusions

| Chapter 15 | Where Now? Future Agendas in Historic Mortuary Culture Studies
Harold Mytum and Laurie Burgess | 285 |

| About the Contributors | 303 |
| Index | 307 |

CHAPTER 1

United in Death? A Comparative Introduction to Historic Mortuary Culture

Harold Mytum

For tens of thousands of years, cultures have confronted death in unique ways that inform archaeologists about beliefs, social structure, economy, and a wide range of cultural practices. Some modes of body disposal, such as excarnation or placing in water, may leave little trace; others such as cremation transform the evidence (Thompson, 2015). In the historic period, however, most mortuary practice has centered around interment, which often provides the archaeologist with the greatest potential for data recovery and analysis. The acquisition of mortuary data from the historic period raises a number of ethical and practical issues that are similar to some ethnographic contexts but also unique because of the range of interested parties and the prospect for alternative data sets such as images, oral history, and documents that might suggest that scientific investigation of the relatively recently deceased is unnecessary. Ethical issues remain, as briefly discussed below, but studies of human remains and the insights they have provided on past health and life experiences and the analysis of cultural data that is the focus of this volume have indicated the rich potential of mortuary data. To date, historical archaeologists have tended to concentrate on either the biological remains from burials or the aboveground commemorative monuments, with relatively few studies of the coffins and their fittings and the structures designed and constructed to protect burials such as vaults and mortsafes. It is the purpose of this volume to address this imbalance by providing the first publication to offer a wide-ranging and comparative perspective on these important aspects of past material culture and the practices and attitudes that they represent. Historic skeletal studies have recently been reviewed elsewhere for a range of perspectives (Sofaer, 2006; Blau and Ubelaker, 2009; British Association of Biological Anthropology and Osteoarchaeology, 2010; Renshaw and Powers, 2016), and similarly, gravestones have likewise attracted synthetic works on both sides of the Atlantic (Mytum, 2004; Veit and Nonestied, 2008; Baugher and Veit, 2014). In contrast to these relatively well studied aspects of mortuary practice and culture, the contributors to this volume consider other material aspects that have received only cursory attention or have not been placed in their wider comparative context.

Of the few exceptions, many of the most significant scholars (Hacker-Norton and Trinkley, 1985; Garrow, 1987; Tarlow, 1999; Sprague, 2005) have here contributed updates to their earlier work. Sadly, many discoveries, including even those involving large data sets, have been reported only through gray literature reports in all parts of the globe; this limited distribution of results has impeded sharing of discoveries and recognition of patterns across time and space, and this lack of accessibility needs to be addressed (see Mytum and Burgess, this volume).

The first substantial studies of coffins and their fittings took place on both sides of the Atlantic in the 1980s, but the types of available evidence and approaches taken to the data have varied significantly. In Britain the most influential were Litten's (1985) summary of types of burial vaults and the clearance of the crypt of Spitalfields church, London (Adams and Reeve, 1987; Reeve and Adams, 1993). In North America the seminal studies were from New England by Bell (1990) and in the southeast by Hacker-Norton and Trinkley (1985) and Garrow (1987). Sufficient material was available by the early 1990s, largely from North America, for a substantial annotated bibliography to be published (Bell, 1994); in Britain a more historical synthesis was provided (Litten, 1991). The most important data from North America came from earth-dug graves and extended chronologically into the early twentieth century, but most British data were of the late eighteenth and first half of the nineteenth centuries, and that which could be securely dated was largely from crypts and vaults.

In the following couple of decades, several more crypt clearances have been undertaken in Britain (Boyle et al., 2005; Boston et al., 2009), and they have been augmented by substantial excavations of churchyards (Brickley and Buteux, 2006; Miles et al., 2008; Emery and Woodbridge, 2011; Rodwell et al., 2011). Nonconformist burial grounds, including those of Quakers, have also been studied (Bashford and Sibun, 2007), although many of these sites are individually small (McCarthy et al., 2012). Some significant institutional and nondenominational burial grounds have also been excavated and researched (Fowler and Powers, 2012; Miles and Connell, 2012). Many smaller-scale projects have also augmented the data sets, although with varying degrees of preservation, especially of fittings associated with earth burials, and some major projects have yet to enjoy the level of post-excavation study that they deserve. A recent review of historic burial excavation in Britain and Ireland has revealed the extent of excavation to date and provides an important preliminary overview of the evidence, although much further analysis remains to be done (Cherryson et al., 2012). Methodological advances have led to protocols for large-scale work that often has to be completed within the conflicting demands of tight development schedules and the ethics of exhumation and data recovery (Emery and Wooldridge, 2011; Advisory Panel on the Archaeology of Burials in England, 2013).

In North America, most investigation of historic burial grounds has taken place in advance of major infrastructural development, although some research investigations have been undertaken, for example, at Jamestown, in advance of conservation projects (Riordan, 2009; Riordan and Mitchell, 2011; Burgess and Owsley, this volume) and after requests by descendants, especially on small family burial grounds on private ground (Little et al., 1992; Ewen and Crane, this volume). Baugher and Veit (2014:18–34) provide a useful historiographical review of excavation and study of historic burial and pay particular attention to both the Native American Graves Protection and Repatriation Act (NAGRPA) and the African Burial Ground in New York. Excavations within churches have been relatively rare, although they have occurred at a few sites such as Jamestown, St. Mary's City (Miller et al., 2004), and Halifax (Williams et al., 2001). Some contract archaeology projects have been large-scale clearances, often exclusively or with a large

African American component (Davidson, 1999; Mack and Blakey, 2004), although others have had an institutional context (Bell, 1990). Large archaeological excavations of vaults or crypts have not taken place within churches in North America, but one of the largest was at Spring Street Presbyterian Church, New York City, with over 200 individuals (White and Mooney, 2010) with four vaults noted. Three brick-lined shafts with barrel-vaulted roofs were investigated at the Little Dutch Church, Halifax (Williams et al., 2001). Although in Britain historic earth-cut graves within churches were popular into the nineteenth century, they seem to be common in only the earliest periods in North America; a mass burial found at Halifax took place prior to the construction of the church, rather than within it, although it may have been deliberately placed over the burial place (Williams et al., 2001:32). Burial grounds associated with churches have been excavated not only at early colonial sites but also from nineteenth-century sites; in some, such as Belleville, Ontario, where 579 graves were investigated, coffin hardware survived in good condition and could be analyzed in detail (McKillop, 1995).

In North America, many excavated burial grounds either were established as serving a rural farmstead or were community burial grounds associated with (but often distant from) a particular place of worship. Although many sites of these types are known, mapped, and, to varying degrees, protected, many more are not known or have no protection. These latter sites are the ones that have often been subject to excavation in advance of development and cover the whole of the historic period and a range of ethnicities and denominations. There have also been major urban cemetery clearances, of which Philadelphia (Crist et al., 1997) and Dallas (Davidson, 2007) are among the best known.

Therefore, some significant sample differences exist between the data sets available for analysis on each side of the Atlantic. In British colonial contexts, such as Australia, the scale of investigation thus far has often been small (Birmingham and Liston, 1974), and where this investigation has taken place on any scale, it has been reported only in gray literature (Higginbotham, 2002). No large-scale crypt clearances have been published from North America, in contrast to Britain, but chronologically, the British data are relatively limited. Early burials in Britain have largely been disturbed by the continued use of burial grounds causing intercutting and redeposition of earlier interments, with the result that few intact earth burials before the eighteenth century have been found. In contrast, sites used for only a limited period in areas such as the Chesapeake have yielded valuable seventeenth-century assemblages. Moreover, the dates of excavated burials in North America continue right through the nineteenth century and into the twentieth century, unlike the British sample, which is very sparse from the middle of the nineteenth century onward because later burials are generally well protected or are cleared by commercial clearance without any archaeological component; for the challenges of working with exhumation contractors in Britain, see Emery and Wooldridge (2011). Rather more coffin fitting producer catalogs survive for North America (Springate, 2015) than Britain (Mytum, 2016), although these are important for research everywhere. Nevertheless, some important trends can be discerned that indicate similarities and divergences and how other English-speaking contexts such as Australia also sit within these developing traditions (Maclean, 2015).

The studies within this volume examine particular issues and data sets to reveal the complexity, potential, and cultural insights that studies of mortuary culture can bring to historical archaeology. This chapter provides a comparative chronological and geographical synthesis that identifies, for the first time, broad trends across time and space that the research to date reveals. There has been little comparative consideration of aboveground mortuary monuments and the belowground data regarding both graves and tombs, on the one hand, and the body container and its fittings, on the other hand (Mytum, 2004; this volume). Most studies have tended to concentrate on site-based analysis with an emphasis on description and typological classification. This single site focus has been exacerbated by the constraints imposed by developer-funded archaeology, which has meant that most relevant reports have been disseminated only through gray literature reports, although some of them have been extremely valuable for providing comparanda for other researchers.

Some of the classificatory issues are still central to the research focus and are pushed forward in this volume (Garrow, this volume; Sprague, this volume), but the studies here also develop the interpretive aspects of the research in relation to pricing (Trinkley and Hacker, this volume), and some highlight the diverse ways in which mortuary archaeology uniquely links to the interests of descendant communities of all ethnicities (Emery, this volume; Ewen and Crane, this volume). This chapter provides the background context and a wide comparative analysis against which the individual chapters reveal deeper focus on particular issues. The prospects for further research and the key directions that it should take are discussed in the final chapter.

Ethics and Field Practice

The ethics of burial archaeology are relevant to all periods and places (Sayer, 2010) but have a particular relevance in historic mortuary studies because descendant communities are temporally close and can be closely related. Moreover, in some cases the remains can be identified as documented individuals with their own known beliefs, which adds a further ethical dimension (Beaudry, 2009). This volume is not concerned with forensic archaeology (Crist, 2001), although that contributes to issues of taphonomy (Reeve and Adams, 1993; Nawrocki, 1995) and ethics. Most debate regarding ethics has related to excavation and analysis of human remains, but there are also issues linked to curation and conservation (McGowan and LaRoche, 1996). Retention for further study can sometimes be arranged instead of reburial; how collaboration with state or church authorities can produce solutions has been considered in Britain (Mytum, 1997; Giesen, 2013) and has also been approached in similar ways in Australia (Anson and Henneberg, 2004). Material culture associated with burial is often discarded or reburied with the human remains, usually because it is poorly preserved but also because its potential value is not appreciated and its independent status as a resource that could be retained is rarely considered. It is hoped that this volume, highlighting the potential of such data, will encourage those involved in the setting of project briefs and curation policies to actively consider how the retention and discard policies could be disentangled from those for the human remains; this subject is discussed further in the final chapter.

Although the excavation of mortuary material culture is intimately associated with human remains, it is largely only the issues associated with the latter that have been discussed at length, and not the associated artifacts. This focus on the biological evidence is because the central concern of national and sometimes other levels of legislation is on human remains, linked to issues of health, crime detection, and public decency. Burial structures, body containers and fittings, and the cultural contents of containers such as textiles are, in contrast, rarely given any statutory protection. Some upstanding features may have some prominence in heritage management, which is the case for some high-status tombs and mortsafe structures in Britain, for example, and some historic burial grounds have forms of landscape protection. In England, some cemeteries are registered under parks and gardens (English Heritage, 2013), and others form elements of conservation areas. Under certain circumstances in the United States cemeteries and burial grounds can be placed on the National Register of Historic Places or designated National Historic Landmarks (Potter and Boland, 1992), but these regulations only indirectly protect cultural resources. In Australia, burial ground conservation awareness is relatively well developed, but again, the emphasis is on aboveground features and landscape character (National Trust of Australia (NSW), 2009).

Whether investigation of historic burials should take place, and to what extent that should involve study of the cultural evidence associated with the human remains, has attracted some discussion. Occasionally, a research question, sometimes raised initially by the descendants, prompts demands for investigation (Ewen and Crane, this volume), but investigation is normally prompted by some form of development. In Britain the archaeological clearance of the crypt of Christ Church Spitalfields, London (henceforth Spitalfields throughout this volume), during the early 1980s led to the first published comments on this topic. Although many crypts in London and some elsewhere had already been cleared by commercial exhumation companies without any archaeological recording or even comment from the heritage sector, this detailed investigation revealed so much about past lives and practices that it raised ethical and practical issues (Cox, 1994, 1997; Morris, 1994; Cox and Kneller, 2001). The clearance of human remains could be reconciled by the needs of the present, but the study of the remains and associated artifacts was seen by some as prying into a past that was still too recent; strangely, the far less respectful commercial clearance was not seen as problematic by some. Although archaeology, combined with historical sources, throws light on past attitudes and expectations regarding the dead (Cherryson, this volume; Tarlow, this volume), the views of the deceased are rarely brought to bear in ethical discussions of present practice. The archaeological justification of the Spitalfields project was clear once publication began to set out the advances in understanding that allayed fears of voyeurism (Adams and Reeve, 1987; Reeve and Adams, 1993) and also generated a great deal of interest among the descendants of the Huguenot community strongly represented by those investigated by the project (Molleson and Cox, 1993; Cox, 1996). Similar descendant interests are demonstrated from another London burial ground by Emery (this volume), in this case leading to reinterment in a different country, and in Washington, D.C., in the context of monument conservation (Burgess and Owsley, this volume). Indeed, the sensitivity in the treatment of human remains by archaeologists and the ways in which these remains shed light on past individuals and populations have increasingly led to archaeologists' involvement in British clearance operations and, in some cases, taking them over completely from exhumation companies.

In North America and Australia there is less published literature indicating any archaeological concerns with investigating historic European burials, perhaps in part because an emotional link with early European settlement provides a reason that does not require further justification. Moreover, current overt separation of state and federal law from religious belief may cause utilitarian ethics to be applied without challenge, although what standards should apply to archaeological clearance of human remains has been considered (Garman, 1996). In the case of African American burial grounds, complex sociopolitical structures and attitudes have affected and, indeed, continue to influence choices made by developers, planners, and heritage professionals, including field archaeologists.

The American cause célèbre that stimulated debate was that of the New York African Burial Ground (Harrington, 1993; LaRoche and Blakey, 1997; Mack and Blakey, 2004), which revealed different perceptions and expectations and also highlighted how collaboration with descendant communities could be part of the development process, which would include archaeology. Given that most disturbance is not initiated by archaeologists, often, the information retrieved that provides new insights into forgotten or poorly remembered generations and even whole communities is often much appreciated if both gathered and presented in a collaborative and open way (Roberts and McCarthy, 1995), even if this positive reactive behavior may not address all issues (Leone et al., 2005).

The specialist range of material culture that was developed by the funeral industry and that is recovered by archaeologists requires a specialist range of descriptive terms. Many items have been given numerous different names both by different companies in their catalogs and by archaeologists reporting their discoveries. Gradually, however, some level of standardization has been achieved, although the British and North American terms are often different (Table 1). These two different traditions have been recognized within this volume, and others elsewhere have used terms linked to particular catalogs that seem to have been those used to identify items recovered. How far the specialist terminology of the catalogs was used outside the profession is hard to estimate, but probably for many clients these definitions were unimportant, and a suitably priced but seemly funeral package is what was required, with little detailed considerations of style and content except at a generalized level (Mytum, this volume). Certainly, some of the most variable patterning, such as the arrangements of pins on coffin lids and sides and the size and symbolism of lid motifs, indicate a wide range of choices that would never have been individually named. Indeed, many catalogs used names for general styles and numbers and/or letters for individual items. This convention was in part because it made ordering these items easier, as undertakers had to obtain them from distant suppliers after the shift from the use of furniture hardware on coffins to that of customized funerary items in the later eighteenth century.

Contexts of Disposal and Recovery

Contexts of historic interment vary significantly between countries, in part because of the role of the church and the nature of legislation relating to burial at the time of death. Britain, like much of Europe, had laws whereby the state denomination controlled burial in terms of location and the rites associated with the interment. Even in European countries such as France where the state took the place of religious bodies, the same types of limited choice were offered. The established church in England and Wales (the Anglican denomination) and the established denomination in Scotland (Presbyterianism) set the rules regarding place and type of burial from the Reformation into the early nineteenth century. Alternative burial areas were established by some nonconformist sects, such as Quakers (Stock, 1998), but where possible the established churches restricted these alternatives as they reduced income for clergy derived from burial fees. Only a few powerful individuals could escape from these constraints beginning in the early eighteenth century, the first in England being at Castle Howard with its elaborate mausoleum and estate landscape setting, although even there strong relationships with churches within the estate were maintained (Mytum, 2007). Only social outcasts such as criminals, suicides, and drowning victims might otherwise be interred other than in community burial grounds (Cherryson et al., 2012).

Table 1. Terminology in Britain and its empire and North America as used by archaeology. British twentieth-century catalog terms are in square brackets.

British term	North American term	Description
Coffin furniture	Coffin hardware	
Coffin, hexagonal/single break	Coffin, hexagonal	Body container, widest at the shoulders
Coffin, rectangular/casket	Casket/coffin	Parallel-sided body container
Pin	Tack	Round-headed upholstery pin used to decorate coffins and, if cloth covered, hold cloth in place; may also have a decorative white-metal head that makes the tack appear like a coffin screw when in use
Breastplate/depositum plate	Coffin plaque/coffin plate	Key details of the deceased are inscribed or painted onto these sometimes large and elaborately shaped and/or decorated plates set on the lid just below its widest point
Lid motif/decoration [Head/foot ornament]	Plates (with text)/ornament	Large decorative pressed-metal designs placed above the breastplate and/or near the foot of the lid
Grip [Handle]	Handle	Handles, often decorative, placed on the sides and sometimes the ends of the coffin
Grip plate	Lug/ear/backing plate	Backing plate behind the handle, often significantly larger and may be decorative in shape or with motifs
Escutcheon/drop	Stud	Small decorative pressed-metal designs placed on the lid and/or sides
Lace	Lace	Decorative strip of metal, usually elaborately perforated, placed along the edges of the coffin lid, serving the same function as the pin/tack
[Screw]	Coffin screw	Iron shank with decorative white-metal heads
[Screw]	Thumbscrew	Later period fixings for lid, often with elaborate decorative heads
[Washer]	Escutcheon/screw plate/diamond plate	Decorative plates through which thumbscrew/stud was inserted
[Screw cover]	Screw caps/diamond caps	Decorative cover for screw
Clip	Box corners	Right-angled fitting fixed onto the lid and side of the coffin/reused shipping box
	Caplifter	Substantial screw with decorative head used to lift the lid before final closure.

In colonial contexts some alternatives to the ecclesiastical domination model could be explored. In North America, many different religious groups were able to establish their own burial grounds, even in states such as Virginia, where the Anglican church had aspects of the established role confirmed by law until late in the eighteenth century. However, the most notable difference was that family burial grounds on private land, usually farms, were commonplace. This diversity of burial location—and many different sizes of burial grounds with varied life spans—has created a far more dispersed pattern of burial (Sloane, 1991:4–5) and many more burial grounds that are either completely undocumented or poorly recorded. This lack of documentation means that many more of these burial grounds are encountered unexpectedly during development or the scale of the burial component is unknown before on-site evaluation. The disappearance of aboveground evidence of many such burial grounds also inhibits mitigation strategies avoiding these areas during development, with the result that these invisible sites are the ones most frequently investigated and represented in the gray literature. This same pattern is the case in Britain, where undocumented or poorly recorded burial areas of nonconformist sects are relatively far more frequently excavated than others. In Australia, early settlement included casual burial in a diverse range of locations close to the site of death, but farm burial plots were also established, although they were subsequently closed as church influence grew during the first part of the nineteenth century.

Only in the nineteenth century did private and then municipal cemetery locations become important as state legislation relaxed church control in those countries that had this, and internal church burial and, later still, urban churchyard burial were stopped, ostensibly for health reasons. This shift to cemetery burial can be seen across North America, Britain, and Australia (Sloane, 1991; Martin, 2004; Mytum, 2004). Most major cemeteries have remained in use, albeit sometimes in a poorly maintained state, so relatively few opportunities for archaeological investigation have taken place, although in North America some filled with lower-status individuals, without influential descendants to protect the sites from developers, have been investigated, as with the Freedman's Cemetery in Dallas, Texas (Davidson, 2007).

Small-scale work in many British churchyards, often linked to building conservation or introduction of infrastructure such as heating, lighting, and toilet facilities, has led to the collection of small assemblages of fittings, although they are often undated or in poor condition. The same limitations often apply to North American farmstead family cemeteries, although a significant number of burial grounds with several hundred interments have been recovered during CRM mitigations.

Before the shift to urban cemetery burial, churchyards and church crypts were the major recipients of human remains, the latter increasingly popular as graveyards became overcrowded. Crypts were constructed beneath a few North American city churches, but family burial vaults were also erected in many burial grounds. The different types of burial location affected investment in that part of the funeral process, as the costs of the options varied widely in price, but such decisions also greatly affected the chances of survival of intact burials and also the preservation of the body containers and fittings and thus their availability for study. The diverse forms of burial context have already been discussed under terminology; the important point here is that these contexts often present better opportunities for intact coffins with all the fittings in situ, in better condition having not been buried in earth, and often in association with wood and textiles. However, the very presence within a vault or crypt suggests higher disposable income, so although there may be a wide array of material culture, emphasis on vault burial encourages a focus on the more affluent within society. Some counterbalance is provided by investigations at institutional burial grounds such as workhouses and hospitals (Bell, 1990; Fowler and Powers, 2012).

Trends in Material Choice

The earliest phases of widespread coffin use in the English-speaking Atlantic world indicate similar practices everywhere. During the seventeenth century shroud burial was replaced by coffined interment for a substantial section of society. The use of communal coffins for funerals that were not left in the grave (Litten, 1991) meant that although coffin use appeared almost universal to contemporaries during the funeral ceremony, it was only by the early nineteenth century that everyone was provided with their own coffin, even the destitute.

Some of the earliest coffins were made from lead, and the known English examples have been usefully reviewed by Litten (2009). These were expensive items of funerary consumption and were usually, although not always, chosen by those who could also afford a brick or stone family vault. These coffins were anthropoid in form, with the earliest known examples being royal interments of the early sixteenth century but being more widely used among the aristocracy and upper gentry through the seventeenth century. Some have faces moulded onto the heads of the coffins and may have a limited amount of other decoration. Many display no text, but others have text incised into the lead or on a plaque or with applied lead letters. Lead trapezoidal coffins, tapering toward the feet, also appear from slightly later within the seventeenth century, often encasing a wooden coffin. In some cases the lead lid was formed in a mold that could produce whatever decoration or text was desired. The quality of production and variability in the technical details suggest that local plumbers were employed, rather than there being any specialist trade; a significant number of the known coffins are of infants and children, as well as adults. The earliest known lead coffins in North America are seventeenth-century examples recovered from a vault within Brick Chapel, St. Mary's City (Miller et al., 2004), where the lead encased wooden coffins; one was of a child, and there were two for adults.

Wooden coffins of the early period were of a variety of forms and are best known from North America for a variety of reasons (see above) and even then from few sites. Tapered and rectangular coffins are the most common in St. Mary's City, with the hexagonal form widest at the shoulders becoming dominant in the later seventeenth century (Riordan, 2009), although early examples of this form and the short-lived anthropomorphic shapes are known from early seventeenth-century Jamestown. The hexagonal shape was almost exclusively used throughout the Atlantic world in the eighteenth century, remained the dominant form in Britain for most of the nineteenth century, and sustained high levels of use through the twentieth. Some of the Chesapeake excavations have produced evidence for gabled lids, which also can have distinct patterns of coffin nails (Riordan, 2009). The gabled coffin is known from Britain only through illustrations, although these occur in a range of media, including paintings and funerary sculpture (Llewellyn, 1991). The distribution of such images suggests that it was a common choice across Britain and Ireland, and it is likely that they will be identified archaeologically in due course. All these early wooden coffins have no metal fittings or texts, although it is possible that some were incised or painted with such details, and only constructional nails are found with the coffin stains.

It is during the seventeenth century that the use of metal fittings on wooden coffins becomes widespread in Britain and subsequently appears in North America, although

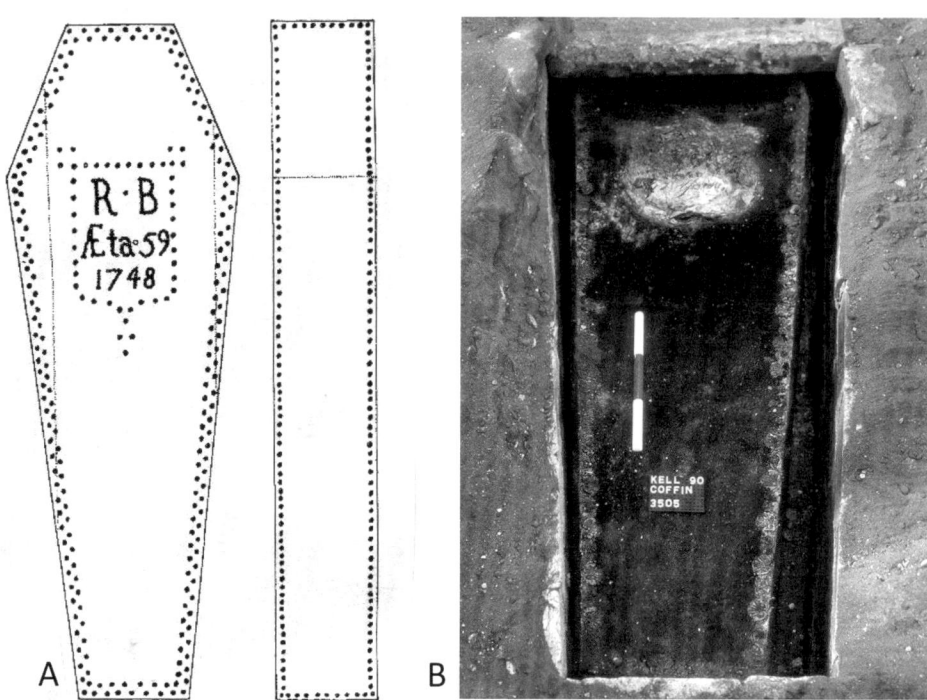

FIGURE 1. British coffins. (A) Coffin of Ramsden Barnard with initials and year of death in pins, North Dalton, East Yorkshire. Adapted from Mytum (1988). (B) Coffin with breastplate and coffin lace in brick-lined grave, Kellington, West Yorkshire. Photo by author.

perhaps not until from the mid-eighteenth century, when they are found from Florida to New England (Springate, 2015:56). Handles of forms available because of their use on a variety of items of furniture could be fixed to the sides or ends and mark a phase when fittings were required but there was no specialized production; there was as yet no clearly defined undertaking profession that would be the primary market for producers, although elite members of society could have fittings commissioned in silver. The handles come in a range of designs but are all bail handles with two lugs that fix the handle to the coffin. Copper alloy and sometimes iron pins, as used in upholstery work, were arranged to form initials and year of death of the deceased (Figure 1A), sometimes within a frame or with a heart motif (Bashford and Sibun, 2007). This method of elaboration may be an archaeologically visible manifestation of a tradition previously marked on the wooden lid in some other way, or it could be a wider cultural spread of the identifier tradition seen in some of the earlier lead coffins. It is likely that this demand for naming and dating increased during this period, as it is also seen across a range of material culture and coincides with the first appearance of external burial markers (Mytum, 2007). This wider trend towards naming and dating material culture therefore suggests that the first appearance of coffin fittings does not indicate investment primarily for display but as an indicator of personal identity and place in time and social context. This form of elaboration was not employed on all coffins (although it occurs on both sides of the Atlantic), but it continues until the appearance of specialist coffin hardware in the second half of the eighteenth century, when the use of pins for text and symbol is rapidly abandoned. Instead, pins held cloth covering the coffin in place and were applied in a wide variety of arrangements that complemented the fittings in creating degrees of elaboration (Reeve and Adams, 1993; see Mytum, this volume, fig. 4).

The development of mass-produced coffin fittings from the later eighteenth century allowed funerary display with a wide range of levels of investment. Although there were very many different designs produced, their aesthetic variation was relatively restricted, being largely based around neoclassical symbols, cherubs, and foliage (see Loe and Boston, this volume; Mytum, this volume). The fittings were manufactured in the metal-bashing workshops of the Midlands and London and used across Britain and Ireland, as well as being exported to colonies and North America (Church and Smith, 1966). One of the most popular grip and grip plate designs (CCS 4 and CCS 3, respectively; see Loe and Boston, this volume, fig. 2) has been found across England and in Philadelphia's and New York's African American burial grounds (Springate, 2011). The bail handle was still the popular form, although now made with many elaborate designs as well as various plain forms. Pins were also replaced during the middle of the nineteenth century with metal strips perforated with designs, termed lace, that ran around the edge of the top and sides of the coffin (Figure 1B). The range of breastplates, escutcheons, and other forms of decorative hardware proliferated, produced by many different manufacturers but often with similar designs, such as an urn with flowers or flames emanating from the top (Figure 2; see Loe and Boston, this volume, fig. 6).

During the early nineteenth century more of the working class could afford coffins with fittings, and exports to the British Empire rose, judging by catalog requests (Maclean, 2015; Springate and Maclean, this volume). In Britain, protection of the body was largely against body snatchers who supplied the medical schools with cadavers, but this practice was far less of a concern among those who could have afforded such protection in North America, where the weak legal and social status of African Americans meant that their remains could be relatively easily obtained (see Mytum and Webb, this volume). The development of body protection measures in North America, which intensified as the nineteenth century passed and are perhaps best exemplified in the relative popularity of the Fisk cast-iron coffins (Owsley et al., 2006), was therefore more associated with social attitudes to the body than actual threat of disturbance.

In the middle of the nineteenth century, in North America the drop handle, with a single lug, becomes an alternative to the bail form (Springate, 2015:17–18), as local mass-produced coffin hardware begins to become available. Another form that appears at this time is the short bar handle, with a straight rod handle held between two brackets by two tips, the whole assembly fixed to lugs attached to the coffin. At the same time as these new handle forms emerged, the rectangular form of burial container—the casket—also becomes an alternative to the hexagonal coffin. The flat-sided design allowed the parallel development of the long bar handle, which had several brackets holding the rail along the side of the casket (see Garrow, this volume, fig. 4; Trinkley and Hacker, this volume, fig. 1). The type of wood and its finish still created various options in coffin style for the middle classes, with the cheapest coffins made from any available supplies, including reused materials; by the late nineteenth and early twentieth centuries textile coverings, some elaborate, were also available (Pye, this volume). British coffins only rarely had viewing panels, and no hinged lids are known for this period; coffins were not cloth covered in Britain by this time; some children's coffins could be painted white, continuing an earlier tradition that was sometimes selected, but even here many were simply polished.

The new drop and short bar handle forms are known from British catalogs from the late nineteenth century (Figure 3) but are still in a minority compared with bail forms. When the new forms began to be used in Britain is not known because substantial

FIGURE 2. Urn with flowers lid motif, St. Pancras, London. Copyright HS1 Ltd/Ramboll UK Limited.

archaeological assemblages and trade catalogs of the mid-nineteenth century are not available. Those few excavated burials from the middle of the century generally show maintained popularity of earlier forms, although there are indications that as the second half of the century went by, some simpler fittings designs and more restrained use of decoration became more dominant. During this time cloth covering, and the attendant use of pins, was abandoned in Britain. The variety of timber species and whether they were polished created complex pricing options, with historical associations evoked by the names used in the catalogs (Mytum, 2016). The casket seems to become a regular alternative to the hexagonal coffin only very late in the nineteenth century, along with some hinged

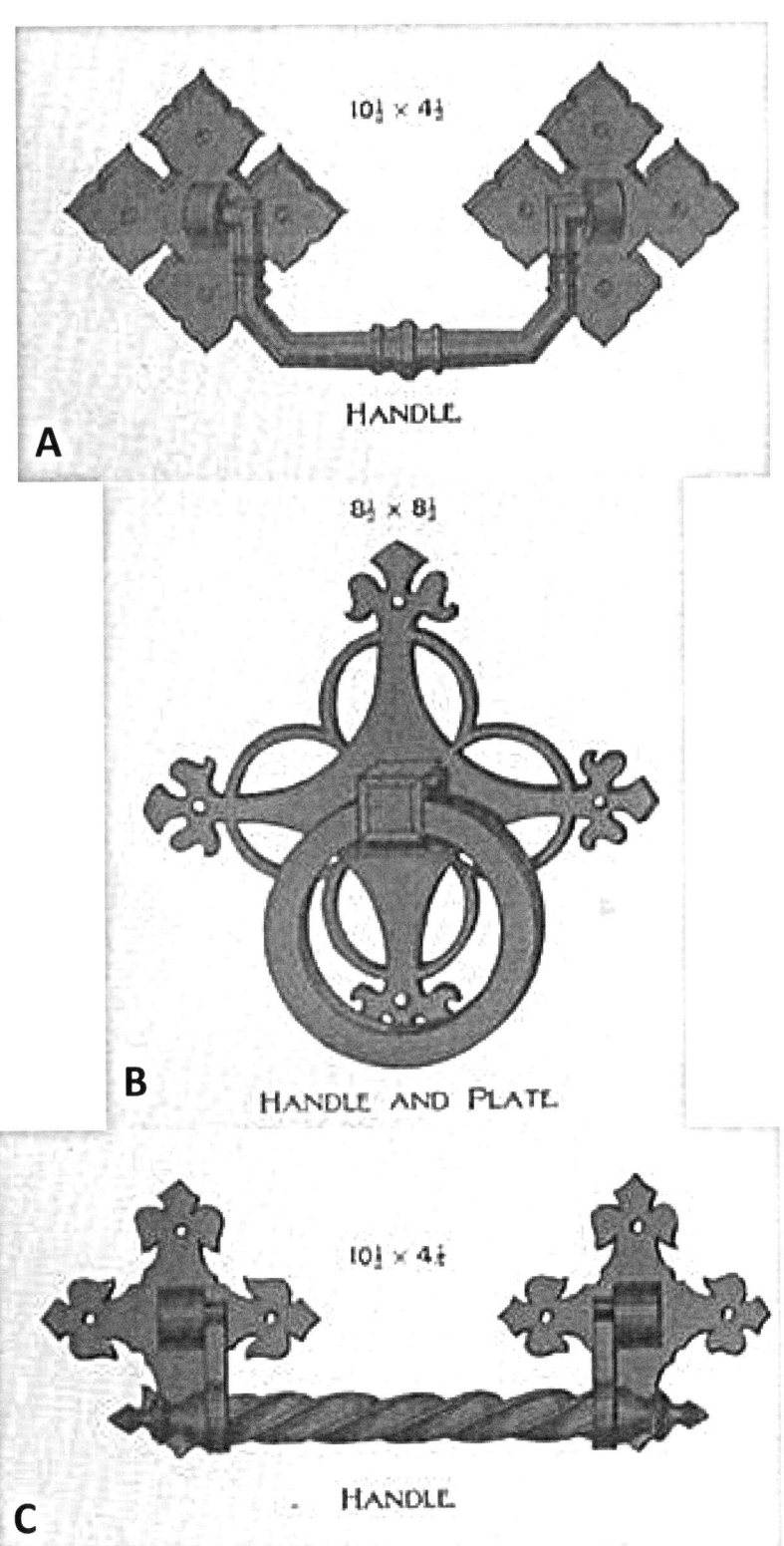

FIGURE 3. Coffin fittings from the late nineteenth- and early twentieth-century Dottridge Brothers (London and Birmingham) catalog. (A) Bail handle, (B) drop handle, and (C) short bar handle. Courtesy of the Beamish Museum.

lids for viewing, but the long bar handle is not offered in the extant late nineteenth- and early twentieth-century catalogs in Britain. It may be assumed that these changes were influenced by North American fashions, although the attitudes to the body that became so elaborate and included embalming never became as popular in Britain.

The overall trends suggest that North America develops its own pattern of burial container and fittings from the middle of the nineteenth century, whereas the British market continued with earlier styles (including those very similar to the late eighteenth-century designs) for some time. The greater popularity of caskets and long bar handles in North America is also distinctive, as is the extent of the use of textiles (Pye, this volume). The relative frequency of glass viewing windows and hinged lids reflects different expectations and practices during the period prior to the funeral and, together with the greater propensity to embalm the body, suggests different anxieties surrounding the dead. Although more severe climatic conditions may have been a factor, the ways in which burial ground and cemetery design and management also differed in emphasis on each side of the Atlantic are notable. The divergence on either side of the Atlantic suggests that more distinctive and deep-seated attitudes to the body, the funeral, and commemoration seem to have developed during the nineteenth century. It is noteworthy that even in a very different set of environmental conditions, the Australian choices mirrored those of Britain (Springate and Maclean, this volume), further emphasizing cultural over climatic factors.

Conclusions

Distinctly different current legal, cultural, and taphonomic conditions occur on either side of the Atlantic and in British colonial contexts that affect what we have available for study and how we might approach such data. However, the research outlined in this volume reveals a shared mortuary tradition in the seventeenth and eighteenth centuries in which variation in preferences was largely caused by different densities of population, differential access to traded products such as hardware, and the exigencies of creating infrastructures in an era of expanding European settlement. British industrial production of domestic furniture and coffin hardware created a wide range of options available to those disposing of the dead that were suited to different economic and religious circumstances, and these products were consumed at home and exported widely across the English-speaking world. Most excavated evidence for this period comes from London, but sufficient evidence has been recovered from the rest of Britain and in North America to demonstrate this pattern archaeologically, although the regional and religious variations in stylistic choice implied by some of the documentary sources have yet to be explored because of the limited sample size of the recovered material evidence.

The nineteenth century saw a clear divergence of trajectory between the two sides of the Atlantic in which North America developed distinctive industries, a trend also seen in other areas of production such as ceramics, glass, and gravestones. North America (both the United States and Canada) developed particular designs of coffins and hardware and in funeral direction that both reflected and created distinctive attitudes to death, the body, its containment, and its disposal. Britain and most of its colonies continued existing styles even as the undertaking professions adapted to changing technologies in production and distribution. Gradually, some of the shifts seen in North America were adopted, although never to the same degree and always selectively. The extent to which this was emulation or parallel changes caused by similar wider cultural shifts is at present uncertain, in part because of the paucity of all forms of evidence in Britain for much of the second half of the nineteenth century (Cherryson et al., 2012), in contrast to the wide range of sources, both archaeological and archival, available from North America for that period.

The twentieth century changes reveal adaptation to different technologies of body disposal such as coffins and fittings designed for cremation, but they are not explored in this volume. Likewise, recent global trends in "green" coffins of cardboard and basketry reveal wider cultural shifts that indicate that the funeral industry continues to react to changing societal attitudes to death and body disposal. Every generation has to grapple with the disposal of loved ones; their choices reveal much about their aspirations, attitudes, and beliefs through the funerary practices and material selections they prefer. The chapters in this book offer important new data, interpretations, and methodologies for the study of below-ground mortuary material culture that will form a secure basis for further exploration of this important aspect of the human life cycle.

Acknowledgments

I thank all those with whom I have discussed coffin fittings and mortuary archaeology, most recently Megan Springate, Louise Loe, Ceridwen Boston, and Laurie Burgess, although the views expressed here are mine and they may not subscribe to them all. Julian Litten supported my first research interests in this field, and David Gaimster and Lawrence Butler encouraged continued involvement in below- as well as aboveground mortuary material culture.

References

Adams, M., and J. Reeve. 1987. Excavations at Christ Church, Spitalfields 1984–6. Antiquity, 61(232):247–256.

Advisory Panel on the Archaeology of Burials in England. 2013. Science and the Dead: A Guideline for the Destructive Sampling of Archaeological Human Remains for Scientific Analysis. London: English Heritage Publishing.

Anson, T. J., and M. Henneberg. 2004. A Solution for the Permanent Storage of Historical Skeletal Remains for Research Purposes: A South Australian Precedent That Keeps Scientists and the Church Community Happy. Australian Archaeology, 58:15–18.

Bashford, L., and L. Sibun. 2007. Excavations at the Quaker Burial Ground, Kingston-upon-Thames, London. Post-Medieval Archaeology, 41(1):100–154.

Baugher, S., and R. F. Veit. 2014. The Archaeology of American Cemeteries and Gravemarkers. Gainesville: University Press of Florida.

Beaudry, M. C. 2009. "Ethical Issues in Historical Archaeology." In International Handbook of Historical Archaeology, ed. T. Majewski and D. Gaimster, pp. 17–29. New York: Springer.

Bell, E. L. 1990. The Historical Archaeology of Mortuary Behavior: Coffin Hardware from Uxbridge, Massachusetts. Historical Archaeology, 24(3):54–78.

Bell, E. L. 1994. Vestiges of Mortality and Remembrance: A Bibliography on the Historical Archaeology of Cemeteries. Metuchen, N.J.: Scarecrow Press.

Birmingham, J., and C. Liston. 1974. Old Sydney Burial Ground 1974. Studies in Historical Archaeology 5. Sydney: Australian Society for Historical Archaeology.

Blau, S., and D. H. Ubelaker, eds. 2009. Handbook of Forensic Anthropology and Archaeology. Walnut Creek: Left Coast Press.

Boston, C., A. Boyle, G. Gill, and A. Witkin. 2009. "In the Vaults Beneath": Archaeological Recording at St. George's Church, Bloomsbury. Oxford Archaeology Monograph 8. Oxford: Oxford Archaeological Unit.

Boyle, A., C. Boston, and A. Witkin. 2005. The Archaeological Experience at St. Luke's Church, Islington. Oxford: Oxford Archaeology.

Brickley, M., and S. Buteux. 2006. St. Martin's Uncovered: Investigations in the Churchyard of St. Martin's-in-the-Bull Ring, Birmingham, 2001. Oxford: Oxbow Books.

British Association of Biological Anthropology and Osteoarchaeology. 2010. Association of Biological Anthropology and Osteoarchaeology: Code of Practice. http://www.babao.org.uk/index/ethics-and-standards/ (accessed 4 June 2017).

Cherryson, A., Z. Crossland, and S. Tarlow. 2012. A Fine and Private Place: The Archaeology of Death and Burial in Post-Medieval Britain and Ireland. Leicester Archaeology Monograph 22. Leicester: School of Archaeology and Ancient History, University of Leicester.

Church, R. A., and B. M. D. Smith. 1966. Competition and Monopoly in the Coffin Furniture Industry. Economic History Review 19: 612–641.

Cox, M. 1994. On Excavating the Recent Dead. British Archaeological News, 18(November):8.

Cox, M. 1996. Life and Death in Spitalfields 1700 to 1850. York: Council for British Archaeology.

Cox, M. 1997. Crypt Archaeology after Spitalfields: Dealing with Our Recent Dead. Antiquity, 71(271):8–10.

Cox, M., and P. Kneller. 2001. Crypt Archaeology: An Approach. Technical Paper 3. Reading, UK: Institute of Field Archaeologists.

Crist, T. A. J. 2001. Bad to the Bone?: Historical Archaeologists in the Practice of Forensic Science. Historical Archaeology, 35(1):39–56.

Crist, T. A. J., D. G. Roberts, R. H. Pitts, J. P. McCarthy, and M. Parrington. 1997. "The First African Baptist Church Cemeteries: African-American Mortality and Trauma in Antebellum Pennsylvania." In In Remembrance: Archaeology and Death, ed. D. A. Poirer and N. P. Bellantoni, pp. 19–50. Westport, Conn.: Bergin and Garvey.

Davidson, J. M. 1999. Freedman's Cemetery (1869–1907): Establishing a Chronology for Exhumed Burials from an African-American Burial Ground, Dallas, Texas. African Diaspora Archaeology Newsletter 6(4).

Davidson, J. M. 2007. "Resurrection Men" in Dallas: The Illegal Use of Black Bodies as Medical Cadavers (1900–1907). International Journal of Historical Archaeology, 11(3):193–220.

Emery, P. A., and K. Wooldridge. 2011. St. Pancras Burial Ground: Excavations for St. Pancras International, the London Terminus of High Speed 1, 2002–3. London: Gifford Monograph.

English Heritage. 2013. Landscapes of Remembrance. London: English Heritage.

Fowler, L., and N. Powers. 2012. Doctors, Dissection and Resurrection Men: Excavations in the 19th Century Burial Ground of the London Hospital. London: Museum of London Archaeology.

Garman, J. 1996. "This Church is for the Living": An Assessment of Archaeological Standards for the Removal of Cemeteries in Rhode Island and Massachusetts. Northeast Historical Archaeology, 25(1):1–12.

Garrow, P. H. 1987. A Preliminary Seriation of Coffin Hardware Forms in Nineteenth and Twentieth Century Georgia. Early Georgia, 15(1/2):19–45.

Giesen, M., ed. 2013. Curating Human Remains: Caring for the Dead in the United Kingdom. Woodbridge, UK: Boydell Press.

Hacker-Norton, D., and M. Trinkley. 1985. Remember Man Thou Art Dust: Coffin Hardware of the Early Twentieth Century. Chicora Foundation Research Series 2. Columbia, S.C.: Chicora Foundation.

Harrington, S. P. M. 1993. Bones and Bureaucrats. Archaeology, 46(2):28–38.

Higginbotham, E. (ed.). 2002. Report on the Archaeological Excavation of the Cadia Cemetery, Cadia Road, Cadia, New South Wales 1997–1998. Volume 1. Main Report. Prepared for Cadia Holdings Pty. Ltd..

LaRoche, C. J., and M. L. Blakey. 1997. Seizing Intellectual Power: The Dialogue at the New York African Burial Ground. Historical Archaeology, 31(1):84–106.

Leone, M. P., C. J. LaRoche, and J. J. Babiarz. 2005. The Archaeology of Black Americans in Recent Times. Annual Review of Anthropology, 34:575–598.

Litten, J. 1985. Post-Medieval Burial Vaults: Their Construction and Contents. Bulletin of the CBA Churches Committee, 23:9–17.

Litten, J. 1991. The English Way of Death: The Common Funeral Since 1450. London: Robert Hale.

Litten, J. 2009. The Anthropomorphic Coffin in England. English Heritage Historical Review, 4:73–83.

Little, B. J., K. M. Lanphear, and D. W. Owsley. 1992. Mortuary Display and Status in a Nineteenth-Century Anglo-American Cemetery in Manassas, Virginia. American Antiquity, 57(3):397–418.

Llewellyn, N. 1991. The Art of Death: Visual Culture in the English Death Ritual c. 1500–c.1800. London: Reaktion Books.

Mack, M. E., and M. L. Blakey. 2004. The New York African Burial Ground Project: Past Biases, Current Dilemmas, and Future Research Opportunities. Historical Archaeology, 38(1):10–17.

Martin, S. K. 2004. Monuments in the Garden: The Garden Cemetery in Australia. Postcolonial Studies, 7(3): 333–352.

Maclean, H. 2015. Funerary Consumption in the Second Half of the 19th Century in Brisbane, Queensland. Ph.D. thesis, University of Queensland, St. Lucia.

McCarthy, R., S. Clough, A. Boyle, and A. Norton. 2012. The Baptist Chapel Burial Ground, Littlemore, Oxford. Post-Medieval Archaeology, 46(2):281–290.

McGowan, G. S., and C. J. LaRoche. 1996. The Ethical Dilemma Facing Conservation: Care and Treatment of Human Skeletal Remains and Mortuary Objects. Journal of the American Institute for Conservation, 35(2):109–121.

McKillop, H. 1995. Recognizing Children's Graves in Nineteenth-Century Cemeteries: Excavations in St. Thomas Anglican Churchyard, Belleville, Ontario, Canada. Historical Archaeology, 29(2): 77–99.

Miles, A., and B. Connell. 2012. New Bunhill Fields Burial Ground, Southwark: Excavations at Globe Academy, 2008. Archaeology Study Series 24. London: Museum of London Archaeology.

Miles, A., N. Powers, and R. Wroe-Brown. 2008. St. Marylebone Church and Burial Ground: Excavations at St. Marylebone School, 1993 and 2004–6. Museum of London Archaeology Service Monograph 46. London: Museum of London Archaeology Service.

Miller, H. M., S. D. Hurry, and T. B. Riordan. 2004. The Lead Coffins of St. Mary's City: An Exploration of Life and Death in Early Maryland. Maryland Historical Magazine, 99(3):351–373.

Molleson, T., and M. Cox. 1993. The Spitalfields Project. Volume 2: The Anthropology. The Middling Sort. York; Council for British Archaeology Research Report 86.

Morris, R. 1994. Examine the Dead Gently. British Archaeological News, 17(October):9.

Mytum, H. 1988. A Newly Discovered Burial Vault in North Dalton Church, North Yorkshire. Post-Medieval Archaeology, 22:183–187.

Mytum, H. 1997. Reinterment of Human Remains: The Kellington Solution. Church Archaeology, 1:50–51.

Mytum, H. 2004. Mortuary Monuments and Burial Grounds of the Historic Period. New York: Kluwer Academic/Plenum.

Mytum, H. 2007. Materiality and Memory: An Archaeological Perspective on the Popular Adoption of Linear Time. Antiquity, 81:381–396.

Mytum, H. 2016. "The Artefacts of Mortuary Practice: Industrialisation, Choice, and the Individual." In Nineteenth-Century Material Culture Studies from Britain, ed. A. Brooks, pp. 274–304. Lincoln: University of Nebraska Press.

National Trust of Australia (NSW). 2009. Guidelines for Cemetery Conservation. Sydney: National Trust for Australia.

Nawrocki, S. P. 1995. "Taphonomic Processes in Historic Cemeteries." In Bodies of Evidence: Reconstructing History through Skeletal Analysis, ed. A. L. Grauer, pp. 49–66. New York: Wiley-Liss.

Owsley, D. W., K. S. Bruwelheide, L. W. Cartmell Sr., L. E. Burgess, S. J. Foote, S. M. Chang, and N. Fielder. 2006. The Man in the Iron Coffin: An Interdisciplinary Effort to Name the Past. Historical Archaeology, 40(3):89–108.

Potter, E. W., and B. M. Boland. 1992. Guidelines for Evaluating and Registering Cemeteries and Burial Places. National Register Bulletin 41. Washington, D.C.: National Park Service.

Reeve, J., and M. Adams. 1993. The Spitalfields Project. Volume 1: The Archaeology: Across the Styx. CBA Research Report 85. York: Council for British Archaeology.

Renshaw, L. and Powers, N. 2016. The Archaeology of Post-Medieval Death and Burial. Post-Medieval Archaeology, 50(1):159–177.

Riordan, T. B. 2009. "Carry Me to You Kirk Yard": An Investigation of Changing Burial Practices in the Seventeenth-Century Cemetery at St. Mary's City, Maryland. Historical Archaeology, 43(1):81–92.

Riordan, T. B., and R. M. Mitchell. 2011. Eighteenth-and Nineteenth-Century Brick-Lined Graves: Their Construction and Chronology. Historical Archaeology, 45(4):91–101.

Roberts, D. G., and J. P. McCarthy. 1995. "Descendant Community Partnering in the Archaeological and Bioanthropological Investigations of African American Skeletal Populations: Two Interrelated Case Studies from Philadelphia." In Bodies of Evidence: Reconstructing History Through Skeletal Analysis, ed. A. L. Grauer, pp. 19–36. New York: Wiley-Liss.

Rodwell, W., C. Atkins, S. Badham, and T. Waldron. 2011. St. Peter's Barton-upon-Humber, Lincolnshire: History, Archaeology, and Architecture. 2 vols. Oxford: Oxbow Books.

Sayer, D., 2010. Ethics and Burial Archaeology. London: Duckworth.

Sloane, D. C. 1991. The Last Great Necessity: Cemeteries in American History. Baltimore: Johns Hopkins University Press.

Sofaer, J. R. 2006. The Body as Material Culture: A Theoretical Osteoarchaelogy. Cambridge: Cambridge University Press.

Sprague, R. 2005. Burial Terminology: A Guide for Researchers. Lanham, Md.: AltaMira Press.

Springate, M. E. 2011. Coffin Handles from the African Burial Ground, New York City: Notes on Their Source and Context. African Diaspora Archaeology Newsletter 14(2).

Springate, M. E. 2015. Coffin Hardware in Nineteenth-Century America. Walnut Creek: Left Coast Press.

Stock, G. 1998. "Quaker Burial: Doctrine and Practice." In Grave Concerns: Death and Burial in England 1700 to 1850, ed. M. Cox, pp. 129–143. CBA Research Report 113. York: Council for British Archaeology.

Tarlow, S. 1999. Bereavement and Commemoration: An Archaeology of Mortality. Oxford: Blackwell.

Thompson, T., ed. 2015. The Archaeology of Cremation. Oxford: Oxbow Books.

Veit, R. F., and M. Nonestied. 2008. New Jersey Cemeteries and Tombstones: History in the Landscape. New Brunswick, N.J.: Rutgers University Press.

White, R. L. and Mooney, D. B. 2010. Stories from the Rubble: Analysis of Mortuary Artifacts from the Spring Street Presbyterian Church Vaults. Northeast Historical Archaeology, 39(1): 40–64.

Williams, P. B., P. Erickson, and L. Niven. 2001. "Retrieving History: The 18th Century Mortuary History of the Little Dutch Church, Halifax." In A Collection of Papers Presented at the 33rd Annual Meeting of the Canadian Archaeological Association, ed. J-L. Pilon, M. W. Kirby, and C. Thériault, pp. 24–41. Ottawa: Canadian Archaeological Association and Ontario Archaeological Society. http://freepages.genealogy.rootsweb.ancestry.com/~richmond/documents/lockman/Old_Dutch_Church.pdf (accessed 23 June 2017).

Attitudes and Practices

CHAPTER 2

Candied Fruit or Carrionlie Carkase? Beliefs about the Dead Body in Early Modern Britain

Sarah Tarlow

What did people really believe about the dead body in the sixteenth and seventeenth centuries? Reading the works of theologians who wrote popular manuals instructing people how to prepare for death, in the ars moriendi tradition, or ruminated on the nature of the resurrection, one answer seems to dominate:

> Is not this Body wherein now I dwell,
> Nought But my Vassall, Casket, House or Shell?
> Compact of dust and Ashes, things most base

asks the Soul in William Prynne's poem "The Soule's Complaint against the Body" published in 1641.

"So soone as my soule shall bee delivered out of the *prison* of this my body, it shall straight wayes possesse the blessed inheritance of the heavenly kingdome," wrote Thomas Becon in 1568 (112–3; italics added). In 1629, Zacharie Boyd, another theologian, looked forward to the death of Christians as the "translation of their Soule from a prison to a Palace." He went on to ask, rhetorically, "Is it not your greatest desire to flitte from this bodie which is but a Booth, a shoppe, or Tabernacle of clay? Is not your Soule wearie to sojourne into such a reekie Lodge?" (1629:84). In his "Dialogue between bodie and soule," Boyd describes the body as a "carrionlie carkase" (1629:1143).

William Sherlock, over a century later, went further. For him the body was, at best, "a litle organized and animated clay" (1690:36), at worst, just a "dead Carkase." Echoing Becon, he says our bodies are prisons, and we look out from them as through a grate (1690:50–51). Once the soul has gone, the dead body, Sherlock believes, is just food for worms; the life of the body, with its appetites, its lumpishness, its hungers and lusts, is totally opposed to the pure spirit. For Sherlock, the death of the body is a rebuke to sinful, lustful, greedy, undisciplined humanity. Although he believes in the resurrection of the body, it is a far different body than the one we inhabit during life:

> Such gross earthly Bodies, as we now carry about with us, cannot
> live and subsist in those pure regions of light and Glory, which

God inhabits; no more than you can lodge a Stone in the air. We should, therefore, he says, accustom ourselves

> to live without our Bodies now, as much as possibly we can . . . to have but very little commerce with flesh and sense; to wean our selves from all bodily pleasures, to stifle its appetites and inclinations, and to bring them under perfect command and government. (1690:53)

Although he sometimes took politically controversial positions, Sherlock was not considered theologically extreme. He was an establishment figure—Dean of St. Paul's—and his discourse concerning death was a seventeenth-century bestseller (Somerville, 1976). Death for Sherlock is a mocking reminder of the worthlessness of the flesh, a rebuke to our vanity. The best death is "freely to give up our Bodies to the Stake, or to the Gibbet, to wild Beasts, or more savage Men. This vindicates our Bodies from the natural shame and reproach of Death; what we call a natural death is very inglorious, it is a mark of dishonour, because it is a punishment of Sin" (1690:67).

In early modern Britain Sherlock's sentiments were not at all unusual. Alicia Woodforde, wife of the diarist Samuel Woodforde, died following the birth of her second child in 1664. Because she was afraid of being buried alive, she had asked to be left in bed for two or three days before being laid out, a fairly common request at the time. But after one day her body smelled so bad and her stomach had swollen so much that it had to be bound to stop it bursting. Her distraught husband Samuel exclaimed in his diary, "Oh God, what things are wee when once thou callest for our Breath into thyne owne hands" (quoted in Houlbrooke, 1998:229).

Common to all these discourses is a more or less explicit contrast between the body and the soul. Whereas the soul is eternal, glorious, divine, beautiful, and pure, the body is ephemeral, material, lowly, mundane. Time and care spent on attending to the needs of the body are vain, futile, and misguided. To return to Prynne's "Soule's Complaint," the soul rebukes us for wasting such time caring for the body, buying clothes and wigs,

> Spending more time, craft, thoughts on excrement,
> Than upon Mee mans onely ornament,
> What is the belly but a filthy sinke,
> Jakes which engenders nought but dung and stink?

> . . . yea let mee once withdraw
> My selfe from the most faire corps, eyes ere saw,
> It's beauty fades, it's flesh to rottennesse
> is turned, and all abhorre it's loathsomenesse.

Theology

The Protestant rejection of the body is theologically coherent. Given a dualistic understanding of human nature where the principal distinction is between body and soul, the one being temporary and worldly, the other divine, it makes sense to value the soul more highly and to value the body principally because it is the container for the soul; a "temple" is among the more positive metaphors regularly used. But when the soul leaves the body, it is no longer a temple but a "jakes" (toilet) or even just a piece of stinking, nasty meat. It is of no particular worth or value. There was no unanimity about the exact nature of the bodily resurrection: the main division was between those who thought that the resurrected body would be just like the earthly one, individuated in the same ways and recognizable but transformed like, as John Bunyan evocatively expressed it, candied fruit, where the fruit itself is still recognizable but made bright, sweet, and fragrant, and those who believed the resurrected body would be of an altogether different nature to the cloddish earthly one. However, the treatment of the body at death matters not at all to the future fate of the soul, say early modern Protestant theologians, in a rare example of consensus. They do not agree about exactly what our resurrected bodies will be like, but they all concede that God will be able to reconstitute the bodies of the righteous for resurrection, no matter what kind of funerary rites they have received. "Vile, or no exequies at all hinder nothing the sepulture of the poore saints," wrote Becon. Even if evil people, said Oxford preacher Thomas Beconsall, "tear Infants from the Womb, to sacrifice to Wolves and Tygers; yet after Wit and Malice, and Cruelty have spent themselves, there will still be Materials enough for Omnipotence to perfect his own Designs, in a glorious and triumphant Resurrection" (1697:23). Beconsall has a forensic approach to the mechanics of bodily resurrection, in which he concludes that God will reform the body out of whatever particles of it can be found, even "those fleeting Particles . . . that are carried off by more nice and delicate sorts of Evacuation."

Treatments of the Body: the Archaeology

The actual treatment of dead bodies at this time, however, is not consistent with the rejection of the soulless body by so many theologians and philosophers. Repeated use of a register of stink, filth, and worthlessness is belied by the evidence of care taken to inter the corpse and often also, particularly in the case of the well-off, to preserve both body and memory.

Bodies of the rich were often painstakingly embalmed. In the early seventeenth-century *Description of Leicestershire* William Burton describes the opening of the coffin of Thomas, Marquis of Dorset, who had died in 1530. He had been buried at Astley in Warwickshire and would not have been disturbed but that the old church had fallen down in 1608 and a new chancel was being built. Thomas's wooden coffin was discovered and "at the curious desire of some, and the earnest motion of others" opened. Inside, the body of the marquis was found wrapped in a cerecloth. When the cerecloth (fabric impregnated with wax) was cut the body was "perfect . . . nothing corrupted" even after 78 years, but looked like a recently interred corpse (Burton, 1622:51). Burton wondered if the exceptionally good preservation was evidence that the corpse had been embalmed (1622:52), which might well be the case. Additionally, however, the dry conditions of a vault burial probably impeded decay, and the effects of the cerecloth would also reduce microbial action on the body. Thorough washing of the corpse before it was wrapped in cerecloth would not prevent decay from the inside but would severely restrict access to the outside of the body by airborne bacteria and those on the skin. Generally, the cerecloth was wrapped around the body before it had hardened so that it would conform to the shape of the corpse and fit as a close, relatively airtight layer around it.

The use of lead coffins or sheets of lead wrapped around the body as shrouds would have had similar anaerobic effects. Lead coffins were usually enclosed within outer wooden coffins that were sometimes covered in velvet. Because of the cost, lead coffins were generally the preserve of the wealthy. The Cavendish vault at Derby Cathedral contained 35 coffins of the seventeenth to early nineteenth centuries, most of which had identifiable lead inners. The coffin of Elizabeth, Countess of Shrewsbury ("Bess of Hardwick"), who died in 1607, was a large rectangular chest (Butler and Morris, 1994:19). The vault also housed two drums containing two sets of embalmed entrails; their former owners have not been identified, but they probably died during the seventeenth century. Similar attention to the dead body was observed in the vault at Kedington, where even the children's burials were in lead coffins (Barnardiston, 1918).

All the rhetoric applied to the body by early modern Protestant theologians might lead one to predict a decrease in the amount of care and attention given to the preparation of the dead body and its disposal. It would also be consistent to expect the abandonment of the crowded churchyard and the hard-to-access under-floor space within the church itself since the belief that any part of the ground was more holy than any other or that burial close to saints or churches would in any way enhance your prospects of redemption was seen at the time as popery of the worst kind. The Church of Scotland even officially banned burial beneath the church, John Knox memorably admonishing his people "defile not Christ's kirk with your carrion."

But the archaeological evidence of Christian burial in the sixteenth and seventeenth centuries tells a very different story. The amount of care and money spent on the preparation and disposal of the average dead body, if anything, increased after the Reformation. The use of coffins, usually the preserve of the well-to-do and elite clergy in the late medieval period (Gilchrist and Sloane, 2005), became widespread and normative in many parts of Britain, even for the burials of the poor. Vanessa Harding's (1994) examination of the parish records of St. Bride's in London, not a wealthy part of town, shows that in the mid-seventeenth century even burials at parish expense were generally provided with individual coffins; only the great volume of plague deaths caused the vestry to suspend this practice for a few months in 1665. The cemetery at Abingdon, Oxfordshire, in use in the mid-seventeenth century, was excavated to reveal 26 individuals, buried in three neat rows, most of the graves having nails or stains indicating that they had been buried in coffins (Norton et al., 2005). This treatment of the dead bodies is all the more remarkable if, as the excavators surmise from the restricted age profile, the pathology, and the absence of either intercutting or grave markers, the cemetery represents the burial of the victims of an epidemic of a lethal infectious disease. Even if the bodies of those buried at Abingdon were possibly quite unpleasant to look at or smell and were contaminated with disease, their relatives and friends took care to lay them out, coffin them, and inter them singly, rather than piling corpses into a pit. In fact, Harding says that even in London, the number and use of "plague pits" in the early modern period has been much exaggerated in London folklore. Most of the sixteenth- and seventeenth-century plague dead were accommodated in parish burial grounds and usually in single graves. At the height of plague mortality in the late summer and autumn of 1665 mass graves were used, but these were overwhelmingly dug within parish churchyards, and the dead were individually shrouded. There were only a couple of overflow burial grounds—most famously the New Churchyard, founded in the sixteenth century, and Bunhill Fields, enclosed during the great plague, and only Bunhill Fields really fits the mold of unconsecrated waste ground used for mass pit burials. In September 1665, when the plague deaths were at their very peak, the city ordered the keeper of the New Churchyard only to dig single graves, and later records confirm that he did so.

At Hemingford Grey, in Cambridgeshire, a late seventeenth-century dissenter cemetery eschewed the conventions of west–east burial, still an almost universal custom in

Anglican graveyards. However, the bodies of the dead were still treated with care, being dressed specially for the grave in lace-up shrouds of the nightdress variety, attested by the presence of copper alloy aglets (lace ends) in the coffined burials (McNichol et al., 2007).

In a vault at Blandford parish church one of the five early modern coffins, apparently of sixteenth- or early seventeenth-century date, contained the skeleton of a child and several twigs of bay and rosemary (Goodall, 1970:155). There is widespread evidence throughout the British Isles of continuing care in dressing and preparing the body and, most abundantly, in its placement.

Documented Attitudes to the Body

Before the Reformation wills usually asked that the body of the testator be buried in consecrated ground, often, in the case of the wealthy, within the church. The most important people and senior clergymen might specify the location of their burial more closely: close to the high altar, in a particular chapel, or adjacent to another burial, for example (Houlbrooke, 1998:111). After the Reformation the vast majority of will preambles did not mention the fate of the dead body at all. Rather, it was the destination of the soul (to God alone and not, as was previously customary, to Mary and the Company of Heaven as well) that occupied the mind of testators. Increasingly, the location of the burial of the body was left to executors; people affected indifference to the treatment of their own corpses (Houlbrooke, 1998:125). By 1640 over 60% of Berkshire wills specified no particular place of burial. In Norwich 84% of wills registered in 1649 did not say where the body should be interred (Houlbrooke, 1998:125, 385).

In tracing the history of attitudes toward the body, however, the picture suggested by wills is not fully borne out by the archaeological evidence. Testators' professed indifference to the fate of their earthy husk seems to bear little relation to the remarkable continuity in their places of burial. Pre-Reformation individuals commonly asked for burial not only in consecrated ground but actually beneath the floor of the church itself. Catholics of the time attributed superior sanctity to certain material objects, in particular, saints' relics, holy water, and the furnishings and substance of the church itself. Through a principle of contagious sanctity, the places in contact with or proximity to those especially holy substances were more holy than elsewhere. Thus, the churchyard was more sacred than the unconsecrated profane land that surrounded it; the church was more sacred than the churchyard, and the chapels housing relics and the high altar were more sacred than the nave. According to Protestant doctrine, however, no ground or thing was more imbued with the spirit of God than any other. There was therefore no spiritual advantage in being buried beneath the altar or, indeed, within the church at all. Devotional literature suggests that this point was frequently made. In the 1629 ars moriendi text *The Last Battell of the Soule in Death*, Zacharie Boyd has the dying man visited by a "carnall Friend" who asks whether he would like to be buried in a church. The sick man—who at this point in the book has been largely redeemed thanks to more than a week's worth of improving talk with his pastor—emphatically rejects the suggestion:

> Wherefore should I make the glorious House of my God a flesh pot of corruption? Fye upon our folie : should it be convenient that my stinking bones cast up anie noysome vapours, for to trouble the living at the service of the everliving?

> What advantage shall it be to my Soule to come and fetch this bodie out of a Church more than out of a Church-yard? . . . Let no man mak me an evill example after my death. (Boyd, 1629:1043)

Nevertheless, in England there was no noticeable change during the Reformation away from church burial and toward burial outside or even, as the logic of Protestant doctrine would seem to indicate, in unconsecrated land altogether. As a pious Glaswegian, Boyd was probably firmer in his resolve upon this issue than many of his Church of England counterparts. In Scotland, unlike England and Wales, intramural burial (interment under the church building) was actually forbidden by the reformed church in the first Book of Discipline, and this prohibition was reinforced by several additional orders of the Church of Scotland. Andrew Spicer (2000:149) records the inscription on the mausoleum of Sir James Melville at Halhill, Fife, who died in 1609. The relevant parts read

> Repent amend on Christ the burden cast
> Of your sad sinnes who can your sauls refresh
> Syne raise from grave to gloir your grislie flesh
>
> Defyle not Christ's kirk with your carrion
> A solemn sait for God's service prepar'd
> For praier; preaching and communion
> Your byrial should be in the kirk yard

In Scotland the construction of mausoleums or burial aisles, such as Melville's, permitted the continued erection of intramural types of commemorative memorials and distinguished those buried in them from those in the rest of the kirkyard. Despite the firmness of the Scottish Church's resolve to prevent church burial as a potentially superstitious action, there is considerable evidence of continuing adherence to the practice. Spicer (2000) cites a number of early post-Reformation aristocratic sources who attached importance to burial in the same place as one's ancestors, even when that meant that the corpse had to undertake a journey of many miles (this significance attached to place of burial also sheds some light on the continuing practice of the predominantly Catholic and continental custom of heart or entrail burial [Weiss-Krejci, 2001], even in Protestant England, like Bess of Hardwick's relatives). When further burial in those places was made difficult or impossible, responses included moving the ancestral remains to a new place of burial or appropriating and walling off parts of churches to act as private mausoleums. The construction of burial aisles in kirkyards was another possible response. However, in some parts of Scotland, burial beneath the floor of the church did not end with the first Book of Discipline. For parishes, kirk burial could be a lucrative source of income, and for parishioners there were reasons other than theological ones for wanting to bury and be buried within the kirk itself. Because of the limited space available, floor space for burial was expensive and prestigious: only the best families of a parish could afford it. Commemoration within the church was more highly regarded than commemoration outside in the graveyard (in the sixteenth century there is very little evidence for any graveyard commemoration at all, especially in Scotland). Intramural monuments were highly visible and were, moreover, regularly and inevitably encountered by the rest of the parish. Both parish authorities and wealthy inhabitants were therefore often unwilling to comply with Church of Scotland dicta that could deprive them of income and opportunity for status display. Despite regular restatements of the official line, some parishes continued to offer burial "lairs" beneath the church floor. At St. Magnus Cathedral, Kirkwall, for example, church records and commemorative monuments suggest that intramural interment continued throughout the early modern period and into the nineteenth century (Tarlow, 1999). At Balmerino Abbey in Fife, excavations revealed a considerable number of post-Reformation burials beneath the floor of the nave (Kenworthy, 1980), and Glasgow Cathedral only managed to restrict burials to the nave and crossing as a concession to reformed teaching (Driscoll, 2002).

The Microcosm

But popular practice is not the only other belief discourse about the dead body. The contrast between soul and body that dominates theological discourse about the dead body is also evident in some poetical and philosophical approaches to the subject. Andrew Marvell's "Dialogue between the Soul and the Body" (1681) is an example of this; the Soul opens the dialogue employing quite anatomical imagery to complain about being imprisoned within the body:

> O, WHO shall from this dungeon raise
> A soul enslaved so many ways?
> With bolts of bones, that fettered stands
> In feet, and manacled in hands;
> Here blinded with an eye, and there
> Deaf with the drumming of an ear;
> A soul hung up, as 'twere, in chains
> Of nerves, and arteries, and veins;
> Tortured, besides each other part,
> In a vain head, and double heart? (Gardner, 1957:243)

Other written discourses present the human body not as an unworthy counterpresence to the glorious soul but as a demonstration of God's ingenuity, the form of God, the pattern of the universe. The early modern body was not the collection of biological facts that it would become in later centuries. It was an allegory of God, the universe, and the world. In 1615 Helkiah Crooke published his *Microcosmographia* a highly detailed and illustrated anatomy of the human body. The eponymous microcosm is the human body itself, frequently used in literary and philosophical texts of the period as a conceit for the whole universe (Figure 1). When John Donne referred to his body as "a little world made cunningly / Of elements and an angelic sprite" (Holy Sonnet V; compare George Herbert's line in his poem "Man" that the body is "in little, all the sphere" [Gardner, 1957:128]), he was invoking a view of the self—and the body—as a microcosm of the universe (Patrides, 1985). This microcosmic view held that the whole world was inside the body, including the presence of God. But it was not only poets who meditated on the divine in their own bodies; a study of the introductory chapters and dedicatory epistles of anatomy textbooks in the seventeenth century shows that the ultimate purpose of studying anatomy, as advanced by most of the famous anatomists, was a greater knowledge of God. At the start of the seventeenth century Anthony Nixon's anatomy text, called *The Dignity of Man, Both in the Perfections of His Soule and Bodie* (1612), describes the practice of anatomy as a meditation upon the divine. The book itself takes the form of a catechistic set of questions and answers. In response to the question "What commoditie commeth by *Anatomy of the*

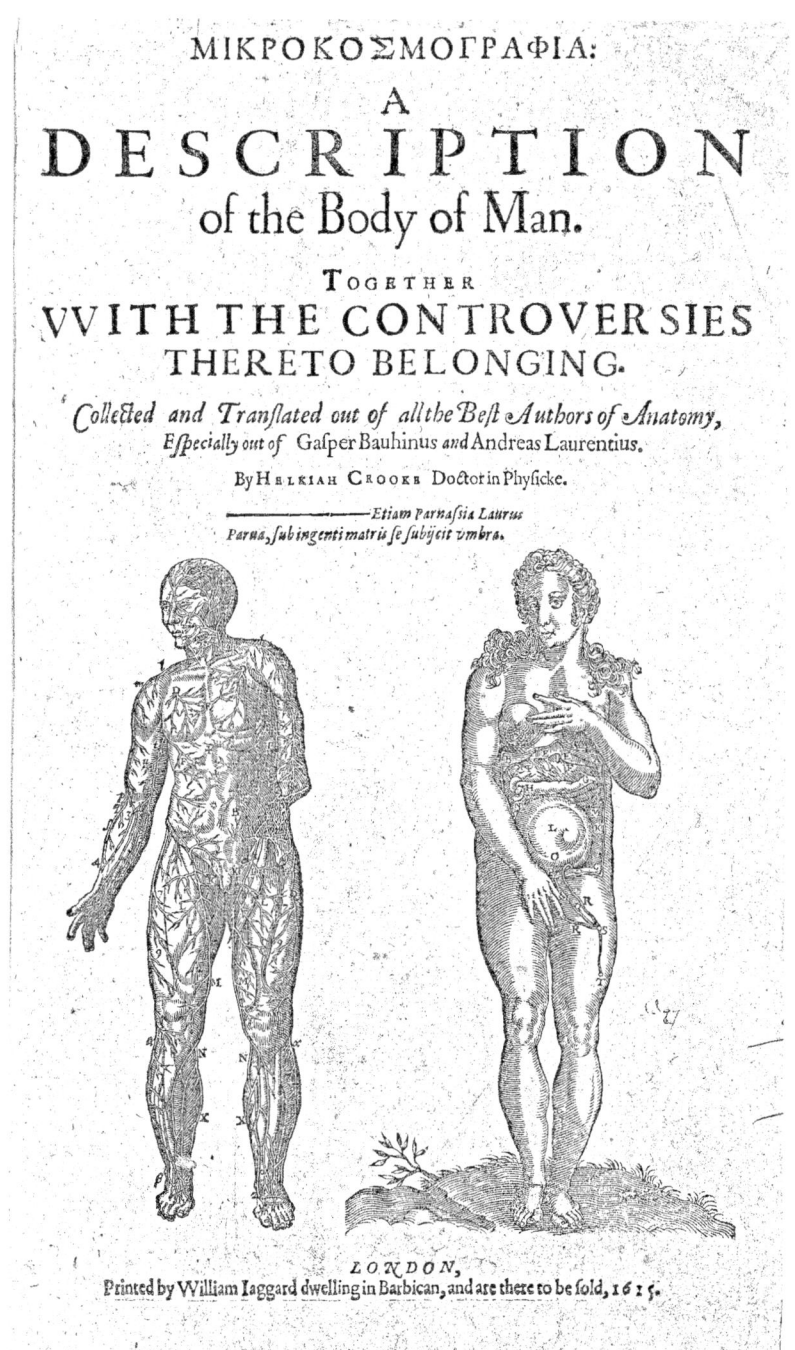

FIGURE 1. Frontispiece of *Microcosmographia* (Crooke, [1615] 1631).

body?" Nixon answers, "It puts us in minde of our mortality, and teacheth us that if the providence of God bee so wonderful in the composition of the vilest and the earthly partes, It must needes follow that it is farre more great, and admirable in the creation of the Noble parts, especially of the Soule." For Nixon and others of his time, anatomy is not primarily a practical discipline for the improvement of medicine or for the development of a scientific clarity of understanding; it is most valuable as a suitable ground for moral exegesis or poetical conceit. Helkiah Crooke says that since God can be known only by his effects, to study the wonder of the body, the architecture of the hand, for example, or the diversity of parts and substances in a body formed only from "a small quantity of Seed (the parts whereof seame to be all homogenie or of one kind) and a few drops of Blood" (1631:14), is to know God. "How profitable and helpful Anatomie is to the knowledge of God," he notes, challenging any atheist to retain his convictions after studying the workings of the brain and eye, "dumb schole-masters" to humanity (1631:15).

The other area where an attitude to the body different from that promulgated by church leaders is very evident is the treatment of the dead criminal body. Oxford Castle acted as the main prison for the city from 1578, although a jail existed on the site from the eleventh or twelfth century (Norton, 2006). A deep ditch that surrounded the original castle moat was gradually filled in from around the thirteenth century, and it was during the excavation of this ditch that 64 human burials were found by Oxford Archaeology during excavations between 1999 and 2002. The burials were in three phases and are broadly datable to between the sixteenth and the eighteenth centuries. Most of the remains belonged to young men. The burials from the castle ditch were not oriented west–east; rather, the majority were deposited along the line of the ditch. Although some were positioned for burial, with arms crossed over the chest or straightened by the sides, others have been casually placed or thrown into their graves. Some, belonging to the second phase, were buried facedown. There is also, most tellingly, abundant evidence of anatomy. Several skulls have had craniotomies; one young man had his skull sectioned on at least three different planes. Other bodies had been buried with the head removed and either nestled inside the chest cavity or placed on top of it (Norton, 2006). Although craniotomies were sometimes carried out on the bodies of respectable and high-status members of society as part of postmortem examination or the process of embalming, given the other circumstances of the Oxford Castle burials, it seems certain that these people were executed criminals whose remains were given to the university anatomists for pedagogical or research anatomy, as part of the criminal sentence.

The body, for the purposes of criminal punishment, acted as an index of the self. Up until the mid-nineteenth century the postmortem fate of the criminal body was often part of their judicial punishment. Unorthodox disposal of the body as a punishment for social deviance persisted as a sanction in popular folk practice for much longer. Execution itself sometimes involved breaking the body into pieces by removing the head (most frequently) and, in the most serious cases, the removal of intestines and partition of the body. The sentence for high treason, passed in England from the thirteenth century until 1870, was "that you be drawn on a hurdle to the place of execution where you shall be hanged by the neck and being alive cut down, your privy members shall be cut off and your bowels taken out and burned before you, your head severed from your body and your body divided into four quarters to be disposed of at the King's pleasure." There are cases of this sentence being enacted in full until the end of the eighteenth century.

Moreover, these bodily punishments often specified ways in which the dead body should be treated. Primarily, the corpses of criminals could be stigmatized by the division or segmentation of the body, by its anatomization, and by special treatment in the place and/or manner of burial. The broken bodies dumped in the ditch around Oxford Castle are the remains of criminals treated in this way. All this suggests that people cared sufficiently about their bodies for the threat of violation of the body after death to work as a deterrent or at least for contemporary legislators to assume that any such threat would have this effect. The eighteenth-century act that set forth what the treatment of the criminal corpse should be was actually called "An Act for Better Preventing the Horrid Crime of Murder." That act ruled that the body of the executed criminal should not receive a normal Christian burial. In the case of criminals the law specified that the body should either be passed to the anatomists for dissection or be gibbeted. Gibbeting involved leaving the body hanging in a cage from a tall edifice, tree, or a specially constructed gibbet until it fell to pieces and was devoured by animals and the natural processes of decay. Archaeological evidence of a former gibbet comes from Dunball Island in the mouth of the Avon, where numerous pieces of disarticulated bone were found when the pilings for the Royal Edward Dock were being sunk (Brett, 1996). Eyre Square in Galway City also produced disarticulated human bone thought to be gibbeting deposits, as well as a number of crania from just below the city walls that are likely to be the remains of heads exhibited on the walls (Lofqvist, 2004).

The bodies of criminals were alternatively given for anatomical dissection. The public dissection has been quite extensively discussed by cultural historians (e.g., Richardson, 1988; Sawday, 1995). From the Ashmolean Museum at Oxford comes a dump of anatomical specimens dating to the nineteenth-century take-over of the Ashmolean basement by chemistry, when they threw out much of the old anatomy collections. These included children's bones as well as adult ones, confirming that the collection was not entirely composed of criminal bodies (Hull, 2003). The cemetery of York prison, however, contains the bodies of adults, some of whose skeletons bear clear evidence of having been dissected (Evans, 1999). These belong to the period between the Murder Act of 1751 and the Anatomy Act of 1832. After 1832, the bodies of the "unclaimed" poor dying in workhouses, asylums, and hospitals were taken to supply the needs of anatomy.

The sanction of denying Christian burial had a long history in Britain and Ireland; archaeological evidence from early medieval sites shows that some individuals were buried outside normal churchyards, sometimes staked and sometimes prone as well. Suicides and those suspected of witchcraft were excluded from consecrated ground and were buried in the road. The bodies of suicides were buried with stakes through their abdomens. Road burial of witches is recorded in Cambridgeshire (Porter, 1969:163) in the early twentieth century and County Durham (for a suicide) in the nineteenth (Brockie, 1886:151).

The threat of having one's body subject, after death, to the intrusions of the anatomists was sufficiently powerful not only to underwrite the law but to inspire great cultural anxiety—especially in the period between the Murder Act and the Anatomy Act—about grave robbing. The fear of resurrectionists, as they were known—men who would steal the new corpse from its grave and sell it at a tidy profit to the teachers and students of anatomy—is thoroughly documented from the historical sources by Ruth Richardson (1988). But there is also archaeological evidence of the care taken to keep the body safe. However, most of the resurrectionist hysteria belongs to a later period than that discussed (see Mytum and Webb, this volume). Whatever the general wisdom might have been when discussing the relative properties of the body and the soul and the theologically coherent teaching on the vanity of caring for the body and the particular insignificance of the dead body—as a body without a soul—in fact, in other contexts or in other belief discourses, they cared very deeply about what happened to the dead body.

Conclusions

This chapter began with the question "What did people really believe about the dead body in the post-Reformation period?" The problem with the question of belief is that the moment one starts asking what people really believed, it becomes unanswerable. Leaving aside the problems of inferring belief from practice and the potentially enormous distance between what people believe and what they do or say, beliefs are so complicated, contextual, cultural, and ephemeral that such an uncompromising question has no meaning. Instead, we might ask, "In what circumstances did people participate in particular belief discourses?"

Ancient historian Paul Veyne (1983) asks us, "Did the Greeks believe in their myths?" Veyne shows us how what people believed in the classical world could be context specific and appropriate to the moment. The same men who might make devotions to household gods would also be making political strategy to promote the interests of their state. Rather than moving to condemn those people for hypocrisy or attribute their words and actions to a strategic promotion of ideological myth for personal gain, Veyne shows how multiple, and contextual, cultural truth can be. In considering beliefs about the human body I have certainly found it helpful to think of belief not as a fixed interior conviction but a set of parallel discourses and material practices that sometimes contradict each other but that can be drawn upon to provide a contextual way of doing and thinking. The theologians who apparently despised the corpse were not being hypocritical when they buried their own relatives in expensive lead-lined coffins. Rather, they were participating in different discourses with their own traditions or rules. Social belief, religious belief, scientific belief, and folk belief all coexisted in the early modern period, and most people probably participated in many of them. Even William Harvey, one of the major figures in the development of a scientific approach to the body, also participated in folk discourses of belief and recommended to one of his patients that a cancer could be cured by the application of the hand of a hanged man to the affected place (Napier, 1879:92–93). So the human body was not consistently believed to be either candied fruit or a stinking jakes. It was both.

Acknowledgments

The research on which this paper is based was funded by the Leverhulme Trust and forms part of a larger project on "Changing Beliefs of the Human Body." I am very grateful to Annia Cherryson for her work as a research assistant on this project and for her comments on this paper. The staff of Oxford Archaeology have been extremely helpful in sharing and discussing unpublished data with us. I also thank Harold Mytum for inviting me to write this paper.

References

Barnardiston, W. B. 1918. Barnardiston Vaults in Kedington Church. *Proceedings of the Suffolk Institute of Archaeology and Natural History*, 16:44–48.

Becon, T. 1568. *The Sicke Man's Salve*. London: Company of the Stationers.

Beconsall, T. 1697. *The Doctrine of a General Resurrection: Wherein the Identity of the Rising Body Is Asserted against the Socinians and Scepticks. A Sermon Preached on Easter Monday 1697*. Oxford: George West.

Boyd, Z. 1629. *The Last Battell of the Soule in Death*. Edinburgh: Heires of Andro Hart.

Brett, J. 1996. Archaeology and the Construction of the Royal Edward Dock, Avonmouth, 1902–8. *Archaeology of the Severn Estuary*, 7:115–120.

Brockie, W. 1886. *Legends and Superstitions of the County of Durham*. Wakefield: E.P. Publishing.

Burton, W. 1622. *The Description of Leicestershire*. London: John White.

Butler, L., and R. Morris. 1994. Derby Cathedral: The Cavendish Vault. *Derbyshire Archaeological Journal*, 114:14–28.

Crooke, H. (1615) 1631. *Microcosmographia: A Description of the Body of Man*. 2nd ed. London: Thomas and Richard Cotes.

Driscoll, S. T. 2002. *Excavations at Glasgow Cathedral 1988–1997*. Society for Medieval Archaeology Monograph 18. Leeds: Society for Medieval Archaeology.

Evans, D. T. 1999. The Former Female Prison "Skeletons in the Cupboard." *Archaeology in York (Interim)*, 23(1):17–22.

Gardner, H., ed. 1957. *The Metaphysical Poets*. Harmondworth: Penguin.

Gilchrist, R., and B. Sloane. 2005. *Requiem: The Medieval Monastic Cemetery in Britain*. London: Museum of London Archaeology Service.

Goodall, H. G. 1970. A 17th Century Vault in Blandford Parish. *Proceedings of the Dorset Natural History and Archaeology Society*, 92:153–155.

Harding, V. 1994. "Burial of the Plague Dead in Early Modern London." In *Epidemic Disease in London*, ed. J. Champion, pp. 53–64. Working Papers Series 1. London: Centre for Metropolitan History.

Houlbrooke, R. 1998. *Death, Religion and the Family in England 1480–1750*. Oxford: Oxford University Press.

Hull, G. 2003. The Excavation and Analysis of an 18th Century Deposit of Anatomical Remains and Chemical Apparatus from the Rear of the First Ashmolean Museum (Now the Museum of the History Science), Broad Street, Oxford. *Post-Medieval Archaeology*, 37(1):1–28.

Kenworthy, J. B. 1980. Excavations at Balmerino Abbey NE Fife. Report held by National Trust for Scotland, Edinburgh.

Lofqvist, C. 2004. Osteological Report on Human Skeletal Remains from Eyre Square, Galway City. Galway: Moore Archaeological and Environmental Services Ltd.

McNichol, D., S. Clough, and L. Loe. 2007. Hemingford Flood Alleviation Scheme, St. Ives, Cambridgeshire. Watching Brief and Excavation Report. Oxford: Oxford Archaeology.

Napier, J. 1879. *Folk Lore: or, Superstitious Beliefs in the West of Scotland within This Century*. Paisley, UK: Alexander Gardner.

Nixon, A. 1612. *The Dignitie of Man, Both in the Perfections of His Soule and Bodie*. London: Edward Allde.

Norton, A. 2006. Oxford Castle. Post-excavation Analysis and Research Design. Report. Oxford: Oxford Archaeology.

Norton, A., G. Laws, and A. Smith. 2005. Abingdon West Central Redevelopment Area, Oxfordshire. Post-excavation Assessment and Updated Project Design. Report. Oxford: Oxford Archaeology.

Patrides, C. A., ed. 1985. *The Complete English Poems of John Donne*. London: Dent.

Porter, E. 1969. *Cambridgeshire Customs and Folklore*. London: Routledge and Kegan Paul.

Prynne, W. 1641. *Mount-Orgueil. A Poem of the Soule's Complaint against the Body Hereto Annexed*. London: Michael Sparke Senior.

Richardson, R. 1988. *Death, Dissection and the Destitute*. London: Penguin.

Sawday, J. 1995. *The Body Emblazoned*. London: Routledge.

Sherlock, W. 1690. *A Practical Discourse Concerning Death*. 2nd ed. London: W. Rogers.

Somerville, C. J. 1976. Religious Typologies and Popular Religion in Restoration England. *Church History*, 45(1):32–41.

Spicer, A. 2000. "'Defyle not Christ's Kirk with Your Carrion': Burial and the Development of Burial Aisles in Post-Reformation Scotland." In *The Place of the Dead: Death and Remembrance in Late Medieval and Early Modern Europe*, ed. B. Gordon and P. Marshall, pp. 149–169. Cambridge: Cambridge University Press.

Tarlow, S. 1999. *Bereavement and Commemoration: An Archaeology of Mortality*. Oxford: Blackwell.

Veyne, P. 1983. *Les Grecs ont-ils cru à leurs mythes?* Paris: Editions du Seuil.

Weiss-Krejci, E. 2001. Restless Corpses: 'Secondary Burial' in the Babenberg and Habsburg Dynasties. *Antiquity*, 75:769–780.

CHAPTER 3

Dressing for the Grave: The Archaeological Evidence for the Preparation and Presentation of the Corpse in Post-Medieval England

Annia Kristina Cherryson

The boundaries between life and death are far from absolute. Modern medicine imposes a sharp distinction between life and death, the cessation of brain function, the failure of the heart to continue beating, and the inability of the lungs to oxygenate the blood. Yet even here the boundaries can be blurred, particularly when machines are used to support a life no longer able to sustain itself. In a social context the demarcation between life and death is less abrupt. Instead, the time between the death of the physical body and the final deposition of the corpse represents a period of transition between the living and the dead.

According to some folk beliefs, the soul was thought to linger around the body after death, at least for a short time, whereas other mores held that the actions of friends and family could influence the soul's final destination (Richardson, 1988:16; Porter, 2003:217). This period of transition was marked by a series of rituals with the cleaning, adornment and display of the corpse forming a constant component of this process throughout the historic period in England. The body of the Anglo-Saxon Saint, Cuthbert, was washed and re-dressed prior to burial in the seventh century as were the bodies of the dead during the reign of Victoria over a millennium later (Colgrave, 1940:131; Webb, 1965a, 1965b:97; Richardson, 1988:17). During this period attitudes toward the body and its role in the afterlife oscillated wildly, from the bodily resurrection of the early medieval period to the early modern concept of death marking the soul's release from a putrefying prison of flesh (Bynum, 1995:10; Tarlow, this volume). Yet throughout the last 1,400 years, regardless of contemporary eschatological beliefs, a degree of solicitude toward the corpse persisted, ensuring the corpse was washed, garbed, and usually displayed prior to interment. This in part may be explained by the fact that the corpse resembled the body of a known and often beloved individual and, as such, was due the care befitting that individual (Richardson, 1988:16; Cressy, 1997:387). Also, there appears to have been a perception that treating the dead with due respect was a means of ensuring the fate of the soul and the well-being of the bereaved (Richardson, 1988:17). Furthermore, the treatment of the deceased is not just defined by contemporary ideas about the corpse but by traditional beliefs.

Washing the dead is mentioned in some of the earliest British documentary sources and probably dates back much earlier (Webb, 1965a:181, 1965b:97). Such long-held ideas on the treatment of the corpse are deeply ingrained and unlikely to be affected by fleeting contemporary fashions. Yet although the need to prepare and display the body prior to interment remained a constant, the form that these practices took did change over time. This change was particularly true of the way the corpse was dressed for the grave, which during the post-medieval period was influenced by contemporary eschatological views, the rise of the undertaking profession, and even state legislation. This chapter examines the archaeological evidence for the preparation and presentation of the corpse in England between AD 1600 and 1900 and how these practices evolved over time and considers some of the factors influencing these changes.

Preparing the Corpse

Washing the body after death was an important and constant element of funerary rites in post-medieval England. Misson, writing in the early eighteenth century, described how it was customary to wash the body and shave it if male (1719:89). The release of the bladder and anal sphincter after death may offer a practical explanation for the practice, particularly if the body was to be viewed (Richardson, 1988:18; Janaway, 1993:104). Yet, as Kselman points out, in a period where the living bathed infrequently, the emphasis on washing the bodies of the dead cannot be attributed to reasons of hygiene alone (1993:51). It is possible that the process evoked elements of purification, with the water cleansing at more than just a physical level (Richardson, 1988:18–19). Although well attested in documentary sources, the washing of the body by its very nature has left little trace in the archaeological record.

The next stage in the preparation of the corpse, plugging of the body's orifices, usually with fabric, to prevent the release of the products of decomposition soiling the body (Richardson, 1988:17: Cox, 1998:114), also rarely leaves an archaeological trace. Only a few examples of such textiles have been recovered, and this absence is probably due to problems in the preservation and recognition of these fabrics. A pad of fabric found between the legs of one of the burials from Christ Church, Spitalfields, in London may have been used to absorb the products of decomposition and accidentally left in place (Janaway, 1993:104). Concern over the side effects of putrefaction may also explain why two individuals were interred in the nineteenth century wearing leather trusses at St. Peter's Church, Barton-upon-Humber, in Lincolnshire (Rodwell, 2007:28). Trusses were used in the treatment of hernias to avoid the protrusion of viscera (Buchan, 1789:662; Andrews, 1847:603) and were perhaps left in place on the corpses to prevent the extrusion of the viscera due to the buildup of gases as the body began to decompose.

Embalming was not routinely used when preparing the body for burial between AD 1600 and 1900. However, in some circumstances it was necessary to retard the process of putrefaction if the family had sufficient means. For example, embalming the bodies of those dying away from home allowed them to be returned for interment in the family mausoleum. Also, during the sixteenth and seventeenth centuries, elaborate funerals were essential for members of the aristocracy to maintain their families' social standing.

Embalming provided time to plan the funeral and allowed the body to be displayed some time after death (Misson, 1719:93). The bacteria contained in the intestines, which are released after death, are an important element of the process of bodily decomposition, and removal of the viscera, or "emboweling," was a virtually universal element of embalming during this period (Read, 1696:710).

Treatment of the body parts removed during the embalming process varied. Often, they were also interred in close proximity to the body, either within the coffin or in separate containers. For example, the coffin of Charles Lethieullier, who died in 1737 and was interred at St. Mary's Church, Little Ilford, accompanied by a viscera chest. When it was opened in 1984, it was found to contain the internal organs, including the heart, packed in aromatic bran (Litten, 1991:54). The repatriation of the deceased may explain the two lead drums found in the Cavendish vault in Derby Cathedral, Derbyshire, which are thought to contain the entrails of family members who died some distance away and required embalming (Butler and Morris, 1994:26). The drums are thought to contain the viscera of Mary and Henry Cavendish, who died in London and Parma in 1698 and 1821, respectively, although other possibilities include the internal organs of Colonel Charles Cavendish and the second Earl of Northumberland, both Civil War fatalities.

The late sixteenth and early seventeenth centuries saw a decline in embalming, and the procedure appears to have been performed infrequently by the early eighteenth century (Gittings, 1984:105). This decline may in part be a result of the distaste expressed by some members of the nobility at having their corpses manhandled by so many people and concerns, particularly of women, about having their body opened (Gittings, 1984:190). Also, the decline in elaborate heraldic funerals during the seventeenth century would have reduced the need to embalm corpses for display during funerals occurring many days or even weeks after death (Litten, 1991:193), although embalming would still have been required for those dying away from home but wishing burial close to their ancestors. The latter half of the eighteenth century saw changes in the nature of embalming and a new reason to embalm bodies: scientific enquiry. The application of science to the art of embalming changed not only the methods used to preserve the dead but the reasons behind such treatment. Although bodies continued to be embalmed, often by undertakers, to facilitate their transport over great distances, in the hands of the anatomist preservation of corpses became an arena for experimentation and display (Dobson, 1953; Litten, 1991:35).

There is little archaeological evidence in England for embalmed corpses from the seventeenth to nineteenth centuries. Apart from the possible examples from the Cavendish vault discussed above, other possible examples include some of the nineteenth-century burials from Ashton-under-Lyme in Lancashire, in which the bodies appear to have been embalmed by injecting formalin (Duff and Johnson, 1974:564). Liquid mercury was found at the base of one of the coffins from the vault under St. Luke's, Islington, London and below the depositum plate in a burial from the burial ground of St. Peter's Church in Wolverhampton (Boyle et al., 2005:87; Adams and Colls, 2007:87). Mercury was used in the treatment of syphilis in the eighteenth and nineteenth centuries, which may explain the metal's presence in the grave, as might the use of a popular homeopathic remedy Mercurius vivus. However, mercury is toxic to many bacteria and may have been used to retard putrefaction and thus preserve the corpse. Finally, it has been postulated that the small open-topped wooden box full of sawdust found above the feet in a coffin from the vault at Christ Church, Spitalfields, may have held viscera (Reeve and Adams, 1993:82). The absence of archaeological evidence for embalming may be a reflection of the comparative rarity of the practice, particularly in the eighteenth and nineteenth centuries. Indeed, Matthew Baillie (1812:7) stated that embalming occurred so rarely that many surgeons would not be sure how to embalm a body.

Dressing the Dead

The shroud was the standard attire for the deceased throughout the post-medieval period in England, but significant changes in the form of the shroud occurred between the seventeenth and nineteenth centuries. Textiles rarely survive from the seventeenth century, and much of the information on how the body was clad for burial during this century is derived from artistic representations of the deceased. In contrast to the tightly swaddled enshrouded corpse of the late medieval period, the shroud of the sixteenth and seventeenth centuries appears to have been a voluminous sheet. It was three times the width of the body and approximately 12 inches longer than the corpse to allow it to be tied above the head and below the feet (Litten, 1991:57, 60).

From the 1630s a cap or bonnet was added to the standard funerary attire, with increasing use of undershirts or smocks placed on the body before it was wrapped in a shroud (Gittings, 1984:112; Litten, 1991:76). During the first part of the seventeenth century shrouds were often sheets belonging to the family, although there are examples of fabric being specially purchased (Gittings, 1984:111–112; Litten, 1991:71). This changed with the passing of the Burial in Woollen Act in 1666 (Litten, 1991:74). This legislation, which required the corpse to the interred in woolen cloth, was designed to support the indigenous wool industry (Gittings, 1984:56). Initially, adherence to the legislation was poor, requiring a subsequent act in 1678 imposing a fine on those failing to adhere to the regulations (1678 30 Cha 2 CAP 3; Litten, 1991:74). An affidavit was required confirming only woolen fabrics had been used to clothe the dead, although for those with means, it was possible to purchase an exemption from the act for £5 (Gittings, 1984:113). It had been possible to procure ready-made shrouds from the mid-seventeenth century, and the restrictions on the use of certain fabrics imposed by this legislation enhanced this trade by allowing undertakers to buy large numbers of woolen shrouds in many sizes (Litten, 1991:72, 74).

Although little textile evidence exists, shroud pins have been found accompanying seventeenth-century burials. Wound wire-headed shroud pins were found with 57 burials from the seventeenth-century burial ground at Abingdon Vineyard in Oxfordshire (Allen, 2006). Copper alloy shroud pins were also found with 7 of the 16 burials in the late seventeenth- and early eighteenth-century Quaker burial ground at Hemingford Grey in Cambridgeshire (McNichol et al., 2007:5). Pins are not found with all burials, and when present, their numbers are relatively low. This rarity suggests that they were not necessarily the primary means of securing shrouds (Gilchrist and Sloane, 2005:110). Shrouds were tied above the head and below the feet during the seventeenth century, and it is possible this practice reduced or eliminated the need for shroud pins. Individuals were also known to have been sewn into shrouds, and pins may have just been used to secure fabric during this process and then removed. As such, examples found in burial contexts may have been missed when the others were removed then may have been accidentally interred with the body.

Funerary representations from the last quarter of the seventeenth century suggest a decline in the use of loose shrouds fastened at the head and feet and the increasing use of open-backed shifts with drawstrings at the wrist and neck (Litten, 1991:76). Misson, writing in the early eighteenth century, describes how the body was dressed in a garment similar to a long flannel shirt with lace or embroidery at the wrists and neck (1719:89). The length of the shirt was sufficient for the fabric to be folded over the feet and tied with woolen thread. The ensemble was completed with a cap, gloves, and a cravat. These changes in funerary attire appear to reflect changes in eschatological beliefs and funerary behavior.

The use of coffins in England did not become widespread until the latter part of the seventeenth century (Litten, 1991:86, 99). During the medieval period some individuals were interred in coffins, but many were simply carried to the grave in the parish coffin and then removed and placed in the grave in just a shroud (Litten, 1991:124; Gilchrist and Sloane, 2005:106, 111). The use of coffins as a container in which to inter the body became increasingly common during the early modern period, and by the end of the seventeenth century burial without a coffin was unusual. Thus, the shroud was no longer the only protection for the corpse within the grave. That role was now served by the coffin, freeing the shroud from its more functional role and allowing its form to be shaped by contemporary perceptions of death (Richardson, 1988:20). In the early modern period death was something to be feared—an enemy whose arrival had to be ameliorated by acts of penitence and fortitude (Porter, 2003:212, 222). During and after the Enlightenment attitudes changed, with death for many becoming the transition between two states, often seen as a final sleep. Death was no longer something to be feared, and for those reaching the end of long and painful illnesses it was often a welcome visitor (Porter, 1989:85–86; Tarlow. 1999:189). This change in attitude toward death was reflected in the shift-like form of the shroud, which mimicked contemporary nightwear (Rogers, 2006:163).

The analogies between shrouds and contemporary nightwear are very apparent in textiles recovered from the late eighteenth- and early eighteenth-century burials from Christ Church, Spitalfields, in London (Janaway, 1993). These shrouds were designed to cover the body from head to foot and had long sleeves (Janaway, 1998:26). These garments were usually of woven wool in accordance with the Burial in Woollen Act, with cotton not appearing until after the act's repeal in 1815 (Janaway, 1998:24–5). Although the textiles assemblage from Spitalfields comprises the largest known assemblage from eighteenth- and nineteenth-century England, examples of shrouds are known from other sites. Shrouds were found with the bodies of Sarah Latimer and Sarah Brook, who were interred in New Bunhill Fields, London, in 1844 and 1839, respectively (Miles, 1997:46). The remains of shrouds were also found with two child burials from the Cross Bones Cemetery in London (Brickley and Miles, 1999:27). The body of General Sir Alexander Mackenzie, who was buried at St. Nicholas Church, Bathampton, in Somerset in 1853 was found wearing a shroud with a frill on the front and a ribbon at the neck (Cox and Stock, 1994:140). Fragmentary remains of a shroud were found on the body of Catherine Harrison, who was interred at St. Philip's Cathedral in Birmingham in 1870. It was gathered at the waist using a band of cloth tied with a bow, and there was a drawstring at the neck (Patrick, 2001:22). For all their similarities to nightwear, the shrouds were attire for the dead, not the living—the garments were backless, presumably to make dressing the corpse easier. The garments were often roughly sewn with long tacking stitches, and the hems and edges were often finished with pinking shears (Janaway, 1993:110; Patrick, 2001:26, 29).

Funerary clothing was decorated with gathered cloth in the form of frills or ruffles on the chest and by the use of punched decoration, yet there was none of over sewing of the punched designs required for everyday wear, and the frills and ruffles were often pinned or tacked in place. Shrouds lacked the usual dress fastenings such as buttons and buttonholes;

instead, they were fastened using ties or copper alloy pins (Janaway, 1998:27). The poor construction and finishing of shrouds is reflective of their function; they had to look respectable for a short period of time before being consigned to the grave, and they did not have to withstand the rigors of everyday wear.

 The typical funerary ensemble of the eighteenth and nineteenth centuries was usually completed by a cap or bonnet for males and females, respectively, as well as long stockings and, occasionally, gloves. Although caps and bonnets were often made especially for the funeral, usually from the same fabric as the shroud and with similar decoration, there are also many examples of existing headwear used in a funerary context (Janaway, 1993:27). Of the 15 caps in the Spitalfields assemblage, only 10 were part of specially constructed sets of funerary attire. The remaining items, including a knitted night cap, were items of normal dress. Elsewhere, two female burials from the seventeenth- to nineteenth-century Quaker burial ground in Kingston-upon-Thames were interred with leather caps, whereas a female burial from All Saints Church, Pavement, in York was found wearing a wire-frame indoor cap of the early to mid-nineteenth century (MAP Archaeological Consultancy Ltd., 1998:94; Bashford and Sibun, 2007:121). Seven pairs of stockings of silk, wool, or cotton were found among the burials at Spitalfields (Janaway, 1993:108). Stockings were also found on the enshrouded body of Sarah Latimer, who was interred in 1844 at New Bunhill Fields, and on a male burial from St. Martins-in-the-Bullring in Birmingham, whereas a child burial from the Cross Bones Cemetery in London was wearing knitted booties (Miles, 1997:46; Brickley and Miles, 1999:27; Rogers, 2006:172). Although less common, gloves are known from burial contexts. Examples include two pairs of silk gloves and a pair of mittens, made from the same fabric as the shroud, from Spitalfields, and knitted gloves were found on the hands of a nineteenth-century female burial from the Catholic Mission of St. Mary and St. Michael (Janaway, 1998:31; Miles and Powers, 2006:22).

 Although the textiles recovered from Spitalfields and the smaller assemblages from other sites have offered invaluable insights into the funerary clothing of the eighteenth and nineteenth centuries, it is important to recognize that there are inherent biases in the evidence. The majority of evidence comes from within triple-shell coffins, often from burial vaults or brick-lined graves (Janaway, 1998:18). Triple-shell coffins were not cheap, nor was interment in a vault or brick-lined grave. Surviving textiles from such contexts, although providing insight into the burial attire of the upper and middling classes, shed little light on the funerary clothing of the poorer members of society. Moreover, the textile evidence is dominated by the Spitalfields assemblage, and it is unclear to what extent the funerary clothing of a Huguenot community of reasonable means in London can be assumed to be typical of the period in Britain as a whole. Similarities between the shrouds from Spitalfields and those from New Bunhill Fields and Bathampton do suggest a degree of standardization, probably due in part to the undertaking profession, but with such a small sample caution is necessary.

 Shrouds dominate the textile evidence from the eighteenth and nineteenth centuries, but everyday clothing has also been recovered from burial contexts indicative of low levels of clothed burial (Janaway, 1993:19). In many cases, the individual was attired as if for bed, but in their own nightclothes rather than a shroud. One nineteenth-century burial from St. Nicholas Church, Sevenoaks, in Kent was interred in a cotton nightshirt that had been darned (Janaway, 1993:29), whereas a number of individuals from Spitalfields wore linen shirts, shifts, or chemises, all of which could conceivably be worn to bed (Janaway, 1993:111). Other corpses at Spitalfields were interred in day clothing, including a jacket, a lace dress, and a silk waistcoat (Janaway, 1993:109, 1998:18). All the clothing from

Spitalfields was for the upper body; presumably, the lower body was covered by coffin sheets. However, felt trousers with an accompanying jacket were found on the remains of David Dallas, who was interred at St. Nicholas Church, Bathampton, in Somerset in 1829 (Cox and Stock, 1994:140). The trousers had metal buttons along the outside seams and may have been part of some form of uniform or livery. The remains of trousers and a shirt were found on a burial from the Cross Bones Cemetery along with a pair of leather boots (Brickley and Miles, 1999:27). Shoes were also found on one of the burials from the Catholic Mission of St. Mary and St. Michael and on a child's burial from St. Mark's Church, Lincoln, whereas a 60-year-old male interred at Spitalfields in 1798 wore slippers (Mann, 1986:41; Janaway, 1993:112; Miles and Powers, 2006:39). Footwear appears to have been a rare inclusion within burial contexts, perhaps because such items were not in keeping with the general perception of death being synonymous with sleep. Given the rarity of clothing survival, it is unclear when use of clothing belonging to the deceased began in the post-Reformation period, but the occasional presence of buttons and other fasteners from the seventeenth century onward suggests that it started at that time (Cherryson et al., 2012:29).

Even when textiles do not survive, the presence of clothing as opposed to shrouds can be inferred by the presence of dress fasteners such as buttons and wire hooks. This evidence is particularly useful for periods where little textile evidence survives. For example, seventeenth- and early eighteenth-century artistic representations of the deceased suggest the universal use of the shroud. Yet finds from the seventeenth-century cemeteries at Abingdon and the late seventeenth- and early eighteenth-century Quaker cemetery at Hemingford Grey in Cambridgeshire suggest that small numbers of individuals were interred in clothes, with the evidence from later cemeteries indicating this practice continued throughout the eighteenth and nineteenth centuries (Table 1).

Although it is possible that the buttons found at the necks and wrists of some eighteenth- and nineteenth-century burials may be from shrouds, the evidence from Spitalfields suggests that buttons were rarely used (Janaway, 1998:27); instead, woolen ties or copper alloy pins fastened the garments. Yet not all shrouds were commercially produced, and even if the shrouds were supplied by an undertaker, widespread chronological and geographical uniformity should not be assumed. Thus, small glass, bone, shell, and even mother-of-pearl buttons often found at the wrist and necks are probably from shifts, shirts, chemises, or nightgowns, although it is possible that a few may be from shrouds (Cowie, 2002:38). More elaborate buttons made from metal or cartwheel buttons are unlikely to be from shrouds. For example, the five plain copper alloy buttons found in the grave of Richard Gideon Hand, who was interred at 2-4 Church Street, Chelsea, in London, are thought to have come from a jacket (Cowie, 2002:38). The seven copper alloy buttons from a burial at St. Benet Sherehog burial ground are also likely to have originated from clothing, as is the row of wire circles found overlaying the ribcage of a young woman interred at St. Nicholas, Forest Hill, in Oxfordshire (Boston, 2004:21; Miles and White, 2008:68). The position of the buttons may also indicate the use of clothing as opposed to shrouds. For example, the bone buttons recovered from the abdominal area of a nineteenth-century burial from York Prison are likely to have been from trousers (York Archaeological Trust, 1998:13).

Interment in clothes did not necessarily preclude the use of a shroud, and there are of burials from Spitalfields that have a shroud covering day clothes (Janaway, 1993:108). The clothed burials of this period can be attributed to several factors. The buttons found with interments from the prison burial grounds at Launceston and York may be indicative of a lack of care toward the deceased, with the authorities simply depositing prisoners in the

Table 1. Examples of buttons and dress fittings found associated with seventeenth- to nineteenth-century burials.

Site	Date	Dress fittings	Reference
Abingdon Vineyard, Oxfordshire	Seventeenth century	Three lace chapes	Allen (2006)
Abingdon West, Oxfordshire	Seventeenth century	Five hook and eye fasteners from one burial	Norton et al. (2005:14)
Hemingford Grey, Cambridgeshire	Late seventeenth century and eighteenth century	Two copper alloy aglets	McNichol et al. (2007:28)
St. Benet Sherehog burial ground	Seventeenth to nineteenth century	Seven copper alloy buttons with one burial	Miles and White (2008)
2–4 Church Street, Chelsea, London	Late seventeenth to mid-nineteenth century	Five plain copper alloy buttons from a single grave; shell buttons	Cowie (2002)
Quaker burial ground, Kingston-upon-Thames	1664–1814	Leather ties in area of sternum of one burial; cuff links found with another	Bashford and Sibun (2007)
Launceston Castle (prison burial ground)	Eighteenth century	Buttons of copper alloy and iron; copper alloy lace tags	Saunders (2006:161, 164)
Baptist burial ground, King's Lynn	1773–1841	One cartwheel button	Boston (2005:146)
Catholic Mission of St. Mary and St. Michael, London	1843–1854	Glass and shell buttons, wire hooked fasteners	Miles and Powers (2006:34)
St. Marylebone Church, London	Eighteenth to nineteenth century	Copper alloy buttons, livery button	Miles et al. (2008:53)
Bow Baptist Church Burial Ground	Circa 1810–1837	Copper alloy, bone, shell, and glass buttons; copper alloy rings, probably eyelets	Miles and Powers (2007:29)
St. Nicholas Church, Forest Hill, Oxfordshire	Post-medieval	Buttons of copper alloy, mother-of-pearl, enamel, and wire circles from cloth or cartwheel buttons	Boston (2004)

Table 1.
(*Continued*)

Site	Date	Dress fittings	Reference
Carver Street, Sheffield	1805–1855	Buttons, often of bone	McIntyre and Willmot (2003)
Ebenezer Chapel, Leicester	Nineteenth century	Buttons	Jacklin (2006a:5)
Bond Street Congregational Chapel, Leicester	1824–1892	Buttons	Jacklin (2006b:3)
Sheffield Cathedral	Eighteenth to mid-nineteenth century	Buttons of bone, shell, and copper alloy	Symonds and Sawyer (2001:4, 6)
St. Martins-in-the-Bullring, Birmingham	Eighteenth to nineteenth century	Buttons of bone and copper alloy	Rogers (2006:183)
Southwark Cathedral, London	Eighteenth century	Copper alloy and ivory buttons and a copper alloy hook and eye	Divers (2001:108–109)
York Prison	Nineteenth century	Bone and copper alloy buttons	York Archaeological Trust (1998:13–14)
Newcastle Infirmary	Nineteenth century	Buttons of bone, pewter, and shell	Nolan (1998:58)

clothes in which they died (York Archaeological Trust, 1998:13–14; Saunders, 2006:161, 164). Similar circumstances may account for the buttons found with burials in Newcastle Infirmary's burial ground. Another possibility is that death resulting from an infectious disease might necessitate rapid interment or result in an unwillingness to wash and re-dress the body prior to burial (Nolan, 1998:58). Infectious disease was not confined to hospitals, and fear of contagion may also account for some of the examples of clothed burials found in churchyards and nonconformist burial grounds. Both of the seventeenth-century cemeteries in Abingdon have been linked to the English Civil War, and the disruption caused by the conflict may have prevented adherence to the usual funerary conventions. However, many examples of clothed burial result from choices made by individuals prior to their deaths or by their families, with the corpse interred in garments that had a personal significance to the deceased or the bereaved.

Arranging the Dead

The corpse was not just dressed but arranged prior to display—the limbs were straightened, and the eyes and mouth were closed; evidence for this process survives in the archaeological record. Unlike the winding sheets and tightly bound shrouds of the early modern period, the looser funerary attire of the eighteenth and nineteenth centuries allowed the body to move around within the coffin (Janaway, 1993:95). From the eighteenth century onward, ties were used to secure the limbs and hold the body in place during viewing. Examples of textiles were found securing the legs of a number of burials at Christ Church, Spitalfields, either by binding the ankles or tying the big toes together (Janaway, 1993:104, 1998:24). The ties were often commercially produced ribbons, but strips of torn fabric were sometimes used instead. Although less common, fabric securing the arms to the torso was also encountered.

The presentation of the face was important, especially during the nineteenth century with the increased emphasis on the beautification of the corpse and the use of drawings and photographs of the deceased, sometimes in the coffin, for commemorative purposes (Jalland, 1996:288; Tarlow, 1999:194). Coins were sometimes necessary to hold the eyes closed if rigor had set in (Richardson, 1988:19), and the archaeological evidence suggests that they were not always removed prior to interment. At Spitalfields, a two-year-old infant who died in 1826 was found with pennies over the eyes (Cox, 1998:115), as was an adult male (Figure 1) from the nineteenth-century nonconformist burial ground at Ebenezer Chapel in Leicester (Jacklin, 2006a:5). Two George III halfpennies dating to 1799 and 1806–1807 had been placed over the eyes of a three-year-old child buried at St. Marylebone Church, London (Miles et al., 2008:50). The two coins found stacked to the right of the skull of the burial at the eighteenth- to nineteenth-century Baptist burial ground in King's Lynn, Norfolk, may have originally been placed over the eyes but then removed prior to interment and placed next to the head (Boston, 2005:146).

Preventing the mouth from gaping open was also important and was addressed in a number of ways. Ties attached to the funerary bonnets or caps would, in many cases, have been sufficient to prevent the jaw dropping (Janaway, 1998:24). Other options included securing the jaw with silk ribbons or the use of a jaw cloth that was pinned to a cap or bonnet. Surviving jaw cloths include examples from Spitalfields where triangular pieces were wrapped around the head and jaw and then tied below the chin with a cap or bonnet used to obscure the jaw cloth, whereas Colonel John Hume, who was interred at Bathampton in Somerset in 1815, had his jaw strapped up (Cox and Stock, 1994:140).

Concerns over the appearance of the face and the increasing emphasis on the beautification of the corpse during the eighteenth and nineteenth centuries may also offer an explanation for individuals interred wearing full sets of dentures, as this would have masked the hollowing out of the lower face of edentulous individuals. Examples of burials with in situ dentures are known from a number of sites, including Christ Church, Spitalfields; St. Nicholas Church, Bathampton; St. Pancras Old Church, London; St. Martins-in-the-Bullring, Birmingham; St. Andrew Holborn, London; and St. George's Church, Bloomsbury (Cox and Stock, 1994:141; Boston et al., 2006:99; Brickley, 2006:140; Miles, 2006:33; Powers, 2006:460–461). Why an individual interred at St. George's Church, Bloomsbury, wearing a full set of dentures had a second identical set placed in his coffin is not clear, nor are the reasons for the inclusion in 1785 of two sets of dentures, neither being worn by the occupant, in a lead coffin from St. Nicholas Church in Sevenoaks in Kent (Boyle and Keevil, 1998:92). Dentures in the eighteenth and nineteenth centuries were custom-made and expensive, and this availability only to the wealthy is reflected in the high-status funerary contexts from which most examples were recovered. Their cost may also account for their comparative rarity in burial contexts, and it is possible that in some cases dentures were removed immediately prior to burial (Molleson and Cox, 1993:54).

FIGURE 1. Burial from Ebenezer Chapel with coins over the eyes. Copyright University of Leicester Archaeological Services.

Care in the preparation of the corpse was not confined to just the body. Simple combs found accompanying four eighteenth- and nineteenth-century burials from St. Martins-in-the-Bullring in Birmingham are thought to have been used to comb the hair of the corpse prior to burial (Brickley and Buteux, 2006:180). A reticence to retain items intimately associated with the preparation of the corpse may explain the inclusion of the combs in the coffin. The almost ubiquitous funerary cap or bonnet by its very nature to a great extent negated the need to recreate in death the elaborate hairstyles favored by women in the eighteenth and nineteenth centuries. Moreover, the analogies between death and sleep reflected in funerary attire were likely to have extended to the way the hair was dressed.

Just as elaborate coiffures were not appropriate when retiring for the night, similarly simple styles were likely to have been favored for those going to their final rest. Yet there is some evidence that at least a few women went to the grave with elaborate hairstyles. The survival of hair is not uncommon in more recent burials, and occasionally, the level of preservation is sufficient to determine how the hair was styled. A 13- to 18-year-old female interred in the Catholic Mission of St. Mary and St. Michael's burial ground in London during the nineteenth century had her hair arranged in a bun held in place with hair grips (Miles and Powers, 2006:22).

Tortoiseshell combs used to support elaborate hairstyles were found in burials from St. Martins-in-the-Bullring in Birmingham and the nineteenth century Bow Baptist Church Burial Ground in London (Brickley and Buteux, 2006:180; Miles and Powers, 2007). Another burial from the former site contained a decorative bone comb. A pad of fabric used both to support and add volume to a hairstyle was found with a tortoiseshell comb among the hair of a burial from the Quaker burial ground at O'Meara Street in London during the site's clearance in 1860 (Brickley and Miles, 1999:51). Wigs and hairpieces were often worn during the eighteenth- and nineteenth-centuries, and wigs, hairpieces, wig bases, and a queue recovered from contemporary burials from Christ Church, Spitalfields, indicate that on occasion they were worn in death (Janaway, 1993:109). One elderly lady was interred in a wig of long dark hair at Spitalfields, whereas Anna Barnard was buried in 1792 in the Quaker cemetery in Kingston-upon-Thames wearing a blonde hairpiece (Bashford and Sibun, 2007:111).

The analogies between death and sleep extended to the corpse's surroundings, and during the nineteenth century the body was often displayed on a bed before being placed in a coffin (Jalland, 1996:214). Moreover, once in the coffin, the textiles around the body were arranged to mimic bedding (Litten, 1991:79). The all-encompassing winding sheets of the early modern period were all but replaced by the 1770s by coffin sheets that were wrapped around the corpse in a manner akin to sheets on a bed to suggest that the dead were simply sleeping (Litten, 1991:214; Janaway, 1998:25). Examples of coffin sheets from the burials at Christ Church, Spitalfields, were plain woven fabrics of wool or cotton with pinked or scalloped edges and punched decoration. The analogies between death and sleep are continued in some burials with the use of pillows, often decorated with ribbons and bows, to support the head (Rogers, 2006:163). Pillows, stuffed with a variety of materials, including wool, feathers, and hay, were recovered from Spitalfields (Janaway, 1993:103). Other examples include pillows stuffed with animal hair and straw from the eighteenth- and nineteenth-century Backchurch Lane burial ground in London (Watson, 1993:17) and a pillow stuffed with wood shavings from the nineteenth-century Bond Street Congregational Chapel burial ground in Leicester (Jacklin, 2006b:3). In some cases the analogies between bed and coffin were taken still further, with the corpse placed on a mattress within the coffin, as seen in some of the eighteenth- and nineteenth-century burials from St. Nicholas Church in Bathampton, Somerset, and St. Luke's, Islington, in London (Cox and Stock, 1994:139; Boyle et al., 2005:87).

Adorning the Dead

Personal adornment in the form of jewelry was a rare inclusion in seventeenth- to nineteenth-century burials, suggesting that it was not considered an appropriate addition when preparing the body for burial, although it has occasionally been found in situ. Finger rings are the most common form of adornment encountered, with gold wedding rings with eighteenth- and nineteenth-century burials from Christ Church, Spitalfields, in London; St. Martins-in-the-Bullring in Birmingham; and St. Peter's Church, Barton-upon-Humber, Lincolnshire (Reeve and Adams, 1993:89; Bevan, 2006:179; Rodwell, 2007:28). Wedding rings tend to be associated with female skeletons, although one ring from St. Martins-in-the-Bullring was found on the remains of a male. This ring was very thin and worn, leading to suggestion that it may represent a memento.

The absence of any seventeenth-century wedding rings may simply be the result of the skewed distribution of burial evidence across the period under consideration but could also be a reflection of changing mores. Wedding rings were in common use by the early modern period, although the Puritans tried to abolish them in the seventeenth century, deeming them symbols of popery (Oman, 1974:35). However, the practice of continuously wearing a wedding ring did not become commonplace until the eighteenth century, and this is perhaps reflected in the burial evidence (Bury, 1984:15). Yet even among burials of the eighteenth and nineteenth centuries wedding rings are rare, with only three examples found at St. Martins-in-the-Bullring among 857 burials (Bevan, 2006:179). The very scarcity of such finds in burial contexts suggest that that wedding rings were routinely retained by the family of the deceased as mementoes or heirlooms rather than being consigned to the grave with the corpse. Indeed, the gold ring found on the left hand of Eliza Haines, who was interred at St. Martins-in-the-Bullring in 1904, bore an 1842–1843 hallmark indicating it had been made some years prior to her birth and was probably a family heirloom (Bevan, 2006:179). The occasional finds of wedding rings in burial contexts appear to represent a conscious decision to inter the body with the ring for personal reasons, although in a few instances the inability to remove the band from the finger may also be a factor.

The use of jewelry, especially rings, as a means of commemorating the deceased was a common practice during the post-medieval period (Oman, 1974:71), and it was not just confined to the bequeathing of jewelry owned by the deceased (Jalland, 1996:295). During the early modern period money was left in wills for specially commissioned rings. These took a variety of forms, some having inscriptions or symbols appropriate to their function, whereas others bore little evidence of their significance. These "mourning" rings became increasingly popular during the eighteenth and nineteenth centuries and were commissioned in batches with the advent of mass production in the latter part of the eighteenth century (Bury, 1984:47). The rings were given out at funerals and worn to commemorate the deceased during and after the period of formal mourning (Jalland, 1996:298). Occasionally, these commemorative items are themselves found in burial contexts. A ring commemorating the death of Thomas Martin in 1808 was found with the burial of a middle-aged male at St. Martins-in-the-Bullring in Birmingham, and another enshrining the memory of Judith Mesman, who died in 1763, was found with a burial at Christ Church, Spitalfields (Reeve and Adams, 1993:89; Bevan, 2006:179).

Jewelry during this period was not only used to signal marital state or mourning but could also be an indicator of faith. Pendants depicting religious figures were found with four burials from the Catholic Mission of St. Mary and St. Michael's burial ground in London (Miles and Powers, 2006:34). The mission lay in a part of London with large numbers of Irish immigrants. Several graves from the same site contained rosaries with wood or glass beads, whereas other burials contained copper alloy crosses worn on chains. A rosary was also found with the body of an eighteenth-century French prisoner of war (Figure 2) buried at Portchester Castle in Hampshire (Cunliffe and Garratt, 1994:119).

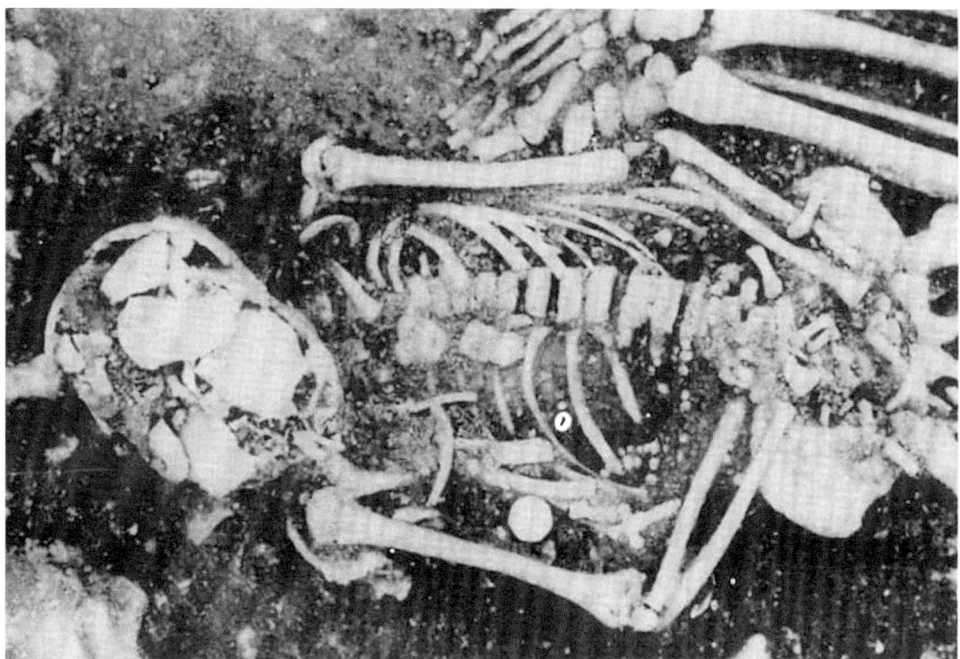
FIGURE 2. Burial from Portchester Castle with rosary. Image courtesy of the Institute of Archaeology, Oxford University, 2017.

Jewelry did not have to be a functional symbol of marriage, mourning, or faith to be included in a burial context. A few decorative rings of gold or copper alloy have been recovered from eighteenth- and nineteenth-century burials, including examples from St. Nicholas Church, Bathampton, in Somerset; the Catholic Mission of St. Mary and St. Michael's burial ground in London, St. Peter's Church, Barton-upon-Humber; Sheffield Cathedral; and St. Peter's Church, Wolverhampton (Cox and Stock, 1994:141; Symonds and Sawyer, 2001:9; Miles and Powers, 2006:35; Bevan, 2007:35; Rodwell, 2007:28). Although rings are rare finds in burial contexts of this period, other forms of jewelry are even more infrequent. Individuals wearing a pair of gold earrings have been found at a few sites, including Christ Church, Spitalfields, and St. Peter's, Wolverhampton (Reeve and Adams, 1993:89; Bevan, 2007:35). A female burial from St. Marylebone burial ground was interred with a pair of copper alloy earrings (Miles et al., 2008:65). Another burial at St. Peter's contained just a single earring, as did a burial from the Catholic Mission of St. Mary and St. Michael, and a burial from St. Luke's church in Islington, London, contained fragments of an earring (Boyle et al., 2005:100; Miles and Powers, 2006:35). Bead necklaces were found with two burials from St. Martins-in-the-Bullring, and two bracelets of glass beads were recovered during the excavations at Sheffield Cathedral (Bevan, 2006:180; Ponsford, 2006:376).

The very low incidence of jewelry in seventeenth- to nineteenth-century burials implies that such items were not considered appropriate or necessary for inclusion in the grave. Nor do they appear to have been important in the display of the deceased prior to burial, although the possibility that items used to adorn the corpse were removed prior to interment cannot be completely excluded. Jewelry belonged to the living, not the dead, with pieces owned by the deceased becoming heirlooms and mementoes, passed on and used in commemoration. When jewelry is recovered from a burial context, its inclusion was probably the result of specific wishes of the deceased or the bereaved, although accidental inclusions, perhaps due to the item being overlooked during the preparation of the body, may account for a few occurrences.

Conclusion

The corpse lies at the center of any funerary process. Initiated by the death of the body, the primary function of the funeral is the disposal of the mortal remains of the deceased. Given the centrality of the corpse to mortuary practices, the care lavished on the remains of the deceased is in many ways understandable. As with the centerpiece in any important social event or ritual, the body must be appropriately prepared and presented. Yet although the need to prepare the corpse for the grave remains constant through time, some aspects of the form that preparation takes, particularly how the body is presented, do change over time. This is well illustrated by changes in the form of shrouds during the post-medieval period.

During the early medieval period the shroud was a voluminous sheet fastened at the head and foot, but by the eighteenth century it had become a more tailored and decorated garment resembling contemporary nightwear. This change can, in part, be attributed to changes in attitudes toward the body of the deceased, from the decaying flesh of the post-Reformation period to beautified sleeping corpse of the nineteenth century (Tarlow, 1999, 2002, this volume). The voluminous shrouds of the seventeenth century would have obscured all recognizable features of the individual, with the body then increasingly hidden from view within a coffin—a fitting treatment for a rotting corpse. By the eighteenth century, attitudes toward death and the corpse had changed. Death was a less fearsome prospect, simply a transitional phase akin to going to sleep, and this change was reflected in the form of the shroud. Instead of the voluminous seventeenth-century garment obscuring the body, the shroud now resembled nightclothes, with the coffin often made up like a bed (Tarlow, 2002:87).

Eschatology was not the only factor to influence the design of shrouds; the development of less substantial examples in the eighteenth and nineteenth centuries was made possible only by the virtually universal use of coffins by this time. The shroud was no longer the corpse's sole protection from the earth of the grave, and the loss of this role allowed a greater flexibility in design. The post-medieval period also saw increasing regulation of burial as the state, as opposed to ecclesiastical authorities, had a direct impact on funerary attire through the Burial in Woollen Acts. This legislation also proved advantageous to the fledgling undertaking profession, allowing bulk purchases of woolen shrouds in a variety of sizes and removing the requirement to provide funerary attire in a variety of fabrics.

By the nineteenth century, the body had also become a focus of both mourning and remembrance (Tarlow, 2002:87). The impression of the body when viewed by loved ones for the final time was increasingly important, and this last view of the body, sometimes in a coffin, could be preserved for posterity in photographs and drawings as an additional means of commemorating the deceased. Care was taken in the presentation of the corpse to make the body beautiful, as seen in the archaeological record with hair combs, wigs, hair pieces, and false teeth, as well as decorative bows, rosettes, and ribbons on shrouds and coffin pillows. In contrast, the rarity of jewelry in burial contexts implies that such items were not considered appropriate adornment for the corpse.

Acknowledgments

The author is grateful to the following individuals and institutions that have generously provided information on unpublished sites: Birmingham Archaeology Unit; Ceri Boston; Harriet Jacklin; Louise Loe; Museum of London Archaeological Services; Oxford Archaeology; Natasha Powers; Duncan Sawyer; University of Leicester Archaeological Services. Thanks must also be extended to Barry Cunliffe and Richard Buckley for allowing the reproduction of the images used in this paper. I also thank to Harold Mytum for the invitation to write this paper and Sarah Tarlow for her advice and comments. This research, which is part of a larger project on "Changing Beliefs of the Human Body," was funded by the Leverhulme Trust.

References

Adams, J., and K. Colls. 2007. *"Out of Darkness, Cometh Light": Life and Death in Nineteenth-Century Wolverhampton*. British Archaeological Reports (British Series) 442. Oxford: Archaeopress.

Allen, T. 2006. Abingdon Vineyard. Unpublished manuscript held at Oxford Archaeology, Oxford.

Andrews, T. 1847. *A cyclopedia of domestic medicine and surgery; being an alphabetical account of the various diseases incident to the human frame; with directions for their treatment, and performing the more simple operations of surgery. Also instructions on administering the various substances used in medicine; for the regulation of diet and regimen; and the management of the diseases of women and children.* Glasgow: Blackie and Son.

Baillie, M. 1812. On the Embalming of Dead Bodies. *Transactions of a Society for the Improvement of Medical and Chirurgical Knowledge*, 3:7–23.

Bashford, L., and L. Sibun. 2007. Excavations at the Quaker Burial Ground, Kingston-upon-Thames, London. *Post-Medieval Archaeology*, 41:100–154.

Bevan, L. 2006. "Jewellery and Other Personal Items." In *St. Martin's Uncovered: Investigations in the Churchyard of St. Martin's-in-the-Bull Ring, Birmingham, 2001*, ed. M. Brickley and S. Buteux, pp. 179–184. Oxford: Oxbow Books.

Bevan, L. 2007. "Small Finds." In *"Out of Darkness, Cometh Light": Life and Death in Nineteenth-Century Wolverhampton*, ed. J. Adams and K. Colls, p. 35. British Archaeological Reports (British Series) 442. Oxford: Archaeopress.

Boston, C. 2004. St. Nicholas', Forest Hill, Oxfordshire: The Human Skeletal Assemblage. Report. Oxford: Oxford Archaeology.

Boston, C. 2005. "Appendix 10: Human Bone – Baptist Inhumations." In *Vancouver Centre and Clough Lane Car Park, Kings Lynn. Post-Excavation Assessment and Updated Project Design*, ed. R. Brown, pp. 121–159. Report. Oxford: Oxford Archaeology.

Boston, C., A. Boyle, G. Gill, and A. Witkin. 2009. *"In the Vaults Beneath": Archaeological Recording at St. George's Church, Bloomsbury*. Oxford Archaeology Monograph 8. Oxford: Oxford Archaeological Unit.

Boyle, A., C. Boston, and A. Witkin. 2005. The Archaeological Experience at St. Luke's Church, Old Street, Islington. Report. Oxford: Oxford Archaeology. https://lso.co.uk/images/pdf/Oxford%20Archaeology%20Report.pdf (accessed 26 November 2017).

Boyle, A., and G. Keevil. 1998. "'To the Praise of the Dead, and Anatomie': The Analysis of Post-Medieval Burials at St. Nicholas, Sevenoaks, Kent." In *Grave Concerns: Death and Burial in England 1700–1850*, ed. M. Cox, pp. 85–99. CBA Research Report 113. York: Council for British Archaeology.

Brickley, M. 2006. "The people: Physical Anthropology." In *St. Martin's Uncovered: Investigations in the Churchyard of St. Martin's-in-the-Bull Ring, Birmingham, 2001*, ed. M. Brickley and S. Buteux, pp. 90–151. Oxford: Oxbow Books.

Brickley, M., and S. Buteux, eds. 2006. *St. Martin's Uncovered: Investigations in the Churchyard of St. Martin's-in-the-Bull Ring, Birmingham, 2001*. Oxford: Oxbow Books.

Brickley, M., and A. Miles. 1999. *The Cross Bones Burial Ground, Redcross Way, Southwark, London: Archaeological Excavations (1991–1998) for the London Underground Limited Jubilee Line Extension Project*. MoLAS Monograph 3. London: Museum of London Archaeological Service.

Buchan, W. 1789. *Domestic Medicine, or a Treatise on the Prevention and Care of Diseases by Regimen and Simple Medicines with an Appendix Containing a Dispensatory for the Use of Private Practioners*. London: W. Strahan.

Bury, S. 1984. *An Introduction to Rings*. London: Her Majesty's Stationery Office.

Butler, L., and R. Morris. 1994. Derby Cathedral: The Cavendish Vault. *Derbyshire Archaeological Journal*, 114:14–28.

Bynum, C. W. 1995. *The Resurrection of the Body in Western Christianity, 200–1336*. New York: Columbia Press.

Cherryson, A., Z. Crossland, and S. Tarlow. 2012. *A Fine and Private Place: The Archaeology of Death and Burial in Post-Medieval Britain and Ireland*. Leicester Archaeology Monograph 22. Leicester: School of Archaeology and Ancient History, University of Leicester.

Colgrave, B. 1940. "Anonymous Life of Sty. Cuthbert." In *Two Lives of Saint Cuthbert*, ed. B. Colgrave, pp. 59–139. Cambridge: Cambridge University Press.

Cowie, R. 2002. 2-4 Church Street, Chelsea, SW3. Royal Borough of Kensington and Chelsea. A Post-Excavation Assessment and Updated Project Design. Report. London: Museum of London Archaeological Service.

Cox, M. 1998. "Eschatology, Burial Practice and Continuity: A Retrospection from Christ Church, Spitalfields." In *Grave Concerns: Death and Burial in England 1700–1850*, ed. M. Cox, pp. 112–125. CBA Research Report 113. York: Council for British Archaeology.

Cox, M., and G. Stock. 1995. Nineteenth Century Bath-Stone Walled Graves at St. Nicholas's Church, Bathampton. *Proceedings of Somerset Archaeology and Natural History Society*, 138:131–150.

Cressy, D. 1997. *Birth, Marriage and Death: Ritual, Religion and the Life-Cycle in Tudor and Stuart England*. Oxford: Oxford University Press.

Cunliffe, B., and B. Garratt. 1994. *Excavations at Portchester Castle*. Volume 5: *Post-Medieval 1609–1819*. London: Society of Antiquaries.

Divers, D. 2001. Assessment of an Archaeological Excavation at Southwark Cathedral, London Borough of Southwark SE1: Phases 1 & 2. Pre-construct Archaeology Ltd Report. London: Pre-construct Archaeology Ltd.

Dobson, J. 1953. Some Eighteenth Century Experiments in Embalming. *Journal of the History of Medicine and Allied Sciences*, 8:431–441.

Duff, E. J., and J. S. Johnson. 1974. Some Social and Forensic Aspects of Exhumation and Reinterment of Industrial Revolution Remains. *British Medical Journal*, 1:563–567.

Gilchrist, R., and B. Sloane. 2005. *Requiem: The Medieval Monastic Cemetery in Britain*. London: Museum of London Archaeology Service.

Gittings, C. 1984. *Death, Burial and the Individual in Early Modern England*. London: Routledge.

Jacklin, H. A. 2006a. Ebenezer Chapel: The Human Remains and Burial Archaeology. Draft Report. Leicester, UK: University of Leicester Archaeological Service.

Jacklin, H. A. 2006b. Bond Street Congregational Chapel: The Human Remains and Burial Archaeology. Draft Report. Leicester, UK: University of Leicester Archaeology Service.

Jalland, P. 1996. *Death in the Victorian Family.* Oxford: Oxford University Press.

Janaway, R. 1993. "The Textiles." In *The Spitalfields Project.* Volume 1: *The Archaeology: Across the Styx*, ed. J. Reeve and M. Adams, pp. 92–119. CBA Research Report 85. York: Council of British Archaeology.

Janaway, R. 1998. "An Introductory Guide to Textiles from 18th and 19th Century Burials." In *Grave Concerns: Death and Burial in England 1700–1850*, ed. M. Cox, pp. 17–32. CBA Research Report 113. York: Council for British Archaeology.

Kselman, T. A. 1993. *Death and the Afterlife in Modern France.* Princeton, N.J.: Princeton University Press.

Litten, J. 1991. *The English Way of Death: The Common Funeral Since 1450.* London: Robert Hale.

Mann, J. 1986. "Small Finds." In *St. Mark's Church and Cemetery*, ed. B. J. J. Gilmour and D. A. Stocker, pp. 41–42. Archaeology of Lincoln 13, 1. London: Council for British Archaeology for the Trust for Lincolnshire Archaeology.

MAP Archaeological Consultancy Ltd. 1998. All Saints Church, Pavement–York. Archaeological Excavations, Phases I and II, Interim Report. North Yorkshire, UK: MAP Archaeological Consultancy Ltd.

McIntyre, L., and H. Willmot. 2003. Excavations at the Methodist Chapel Carver Street Sheffield. Report. Sheffield, UK: Archaeological Research and Consultancy at the University of Sheffield.

McNichol, D., S. Clough, and L. Loe. 2007. Hemingford Flood Alleviation Scheme, St. Ives, Cambridgeshire. Watching Brief and Excavation Report. Oxford: Oxford Archaeology.).

Miles, A. 1997. New Bunhill Fields Burial Ground, Gaskin Street, Islington Green, London N1, London Borough of Islington. An Archaeological Watching Brief. Report. London: Museum of London Archaeology Service.

Miles, A. 2006. The Crypt of St. Andrew, Holborn London EC4. An Archaeological Assessment and Updated Project Design. Report. London: Museum of London Archaeological Service.

Miles, A., and N. Powers. 2006. Bishop Challener Catholic Collegiate School, Luken Street, London E1. Borough of Tower Hamlets. A Post-Excavation Assessment and Updated Project Design. Report. London: Museum of London Archaeology Service.

Miles, A., and N. Powers. 2007. Bow Baptist Church Burial Ground, 2-25 Payne Road, London, E3. Report. London: Museum of London Archaeology Service.

Miles, A., N. Powers, and R. Wroe-Brown. 2008. *St. Marylebone Church and Burial Ground: Excavations at St. Marylebone School, 1993 and 2004–6.* Museum of London Archaeology Service Monograph 46. London: Museum of London Archaeology Service.

Miles, A., and W. White. 2008. *Burial at the Site of the Parish Church of St. Benet Sherehog before and the after the Great Fire.* Museum of London Archaeological Service Monograph 39. London: Museum of Archaeology Service.

Misson, H. 1719. *M. Misson's Memoirs and Observations in His Travels over England: With Some account of Scotland and Ireland. Dispos'd in Alphabetical Order.* London: D. Browne, A. Bell, J. Darby, A. Bettesworth, J. Pemberton et al.

Molleson, T., and M. Cox. 1993. *The Spitalfields Project.* Volume 2: *The Middling Sort: The anthropology.* CBA Research Report 86. York: Council for British Archaeology.

Nolan, J. 1998. The Newcastle Infirmary at the Forth, Newcastle upon Tyne. Volume 1: The Archaeology and History. Report. Newcastle, UK: Northern Counties Archaeological Services.

Norton, A., G. Laws, and A. Smith. 2005. Abingdon West Central Redevelopment Area, Oxfordshire. Post-Excavation Assessment and Updated Project Design. Report. Oxford: Oxford Archaeology.

Oman, C. 1974. *British Rings 800–1914*. London: B. T. Batsford.

Patrick, C. 2001. Churchyard of St. Philips's Cathedral, Birmingham. An Archaeological Watching Brief. Report. Birmingham, UK: Birmingham University Field Archaeology Unit.

Ponsford, M. 2006.Post-Medieval Fieldwork in Britain and Northern Ireland. *Post-Medieval Archaeology*, 40:316–410.

Porter, R. 1989. "Death and the Doctors." In *Death, Ritual, and Bereavement*, ed. R. Houlbrooke, pp. 77–94. Routledge: London.

Porter, R. 2003. *Flesh in the Age of Reason*. London: Penguin.

Powers, N. 2006. Archaeological Evidence for Dental Innovation: An Eighteenth Century Porcelain Dental Prosthesis Belonging to Archbishop Arthur Richard Dillon. *British Dental Journal*, 201:459–463.

Read, A. 1696. *Chirurgarum comes, or the whole practice of chirurgery. Began by the learned Dr Read; continued and completed by a member of the Royal College of Physicians in London. To which is added by way of an appendix, two treatise, one of venereal disease, the other concerning embalming*. London: Hugh Newman.

Reeve, J., and M. Adams, eds. 1993. *The Spitalfields Project*. Volume 1: *The archaeology: Across the Styx*. CBA Research Report 85. York: Council of British Archaeology.

Richardson, R. 1988. *Death, Dissection and the Destitute*. London: Penguin.

Rodwell, W. 2007. "Burial Archaeology." In *St. Peter's, Barton-upon-Humber, Lincolnshire: A Parish Church and Its Community*. Volume 2: *The Human Remains*, ed. T. Waldron, pp. 15–32. Oxford: Oxbow Books.

Rogers, P. W. 2006. "Textiles." In *St. Martin's Uncovered: Investigations in the Churchyard of St. Martin's-in-the-Bull Ring, Birmingham, 2001*, ed. M. Brickley and S. Buteux, pp. 163–178. Oxford: Oxbow Books.

Saunders, A. 2006. *Excavations at Launceston Castle, Cornwall*. Society for Medieval Archaeology Monograph 24. Leeds: Maney Publishing.

Symonds, J., and D. Sawyer. 2001. Data Structure Report. Excavation of Skeletons from Sheffield Cathedral. Sheffield, UK: Archaeological Research and Consultancy at the University of Sheffield.

Tarlow, S. 1999. "Wormie Clay and Blessed Sleep: Death and Disgust in Later Historical Britain." In *The Familiar Past? Archaeologies of Later Historical Britain*, ed. S. Tarlow and S. West, pp. 183–198. London: Routledge.

Tarlow, S. 2002. "The Aesthetic Corpse in Nineteenth-Century Britain." In *Thinking through the Body: Archaeologies of Corporeality*, ed. Y. Hamilakis, M. Plucienik, and S. Tarlow, pp. 85–97. New York: Kluwer Academic/Plenum Publishers.

Watson, B. 1993. 109–153 Back Church Lane, London, E1. London Borough of Tower Hamlets. An Archaeological Evaluation. MoLAS Report. Lavenham, UK: Museum of London Archaeological Services

Webb, J. F. 1965a. *Eddius Stephanus: Life of Wilfred*. In *The Age of Bede*, ed. D. H. Farmer, pp. 105–184. London: Penguin.

Webb, J. F., trans. 1965b. *Bede's Life of Cuthbert*. In *The Age of Bede*, ed. D. H. Farmer, pp. 41–104. London: Penguin.

York Archaeological Trust. 1998. Former Female Prison, Castle Yard, York. Report on an Archaeological Evaluation. York Archaeological Trust Report 26. York: York Archaeological Trust.

CHAPTER 4

In the Footsteps of Thomas Hardy: Archaeology and Exhumation at St. Pancras Burial Ground, London

Phillip A. Emery

On 14 November 2007 St. Pancras International was opened as the new London railway terminus for High Speed 1 (formerly known as the Channel Tunnel Rail Link) following major development at the historic St. Pancras Station (Figure 1; Bradley, 2007). To make way for construction of an extended platform deck to accommodate the 400-meter-long Eurostar trains, the southern part of the former burial ground of St. Pancras Old Church, which had been buried beneath the existing railway embankment, was cleared by an exhumation contractor under the provision of Schedule 11 of the Channel Tunnel Rail Link Act 1996. These works were undertaken in 2002 and 2003, with a team of archaeologists in attendance to record the burials. Gifford Ltd. (now Ramboll UK Limited), the archaeological contractor appointed to undertake the investigation at St. Pancras Terminus and King's Cross Lands, assembled a multidisciplinary team to suit the requirements of this complex and challenging project, which culminated in publication of the site report as a book entitled *St. Pancras Burial Ground* (Emery and Wooldridge 2011).

The buried population housed within the St. Pancras cemetery was unusually diverse in terms of class, religious persuasion, and nationality, reflecting its location on the edge of the growing metropolis at a time of dramatic urban growth and industrialization (Figure 2). Many burials were of refugees from the French Revolution, including aristocrats and churchmen. The discovery of these remains, and the research questions arising from their analysis, provided an important Anglo-French dimension to the project.

High Speed 1 was not the first railway scheme to disturb this famous burial ground—indeed, it remained intact for scarcely a decade after its closure in 1854, when burial within the heart of London itself was ended, with consequent relocation of interment activity to new municipally owned suburban cemeteries, including St. Pancras and Islington at East Finchley. Crossing the disused burial ground posed a challenge for the builders of the Midland Railway and the then new St. Pancras station in the 1860s, and the treatment of human remains during their preliminary excavations caused much controversy. The Bishop of London, Archibald Tait, made representation to the Home Secretary on behalf of the vicar of St. Pancras, who had observed skulls and thigh bones

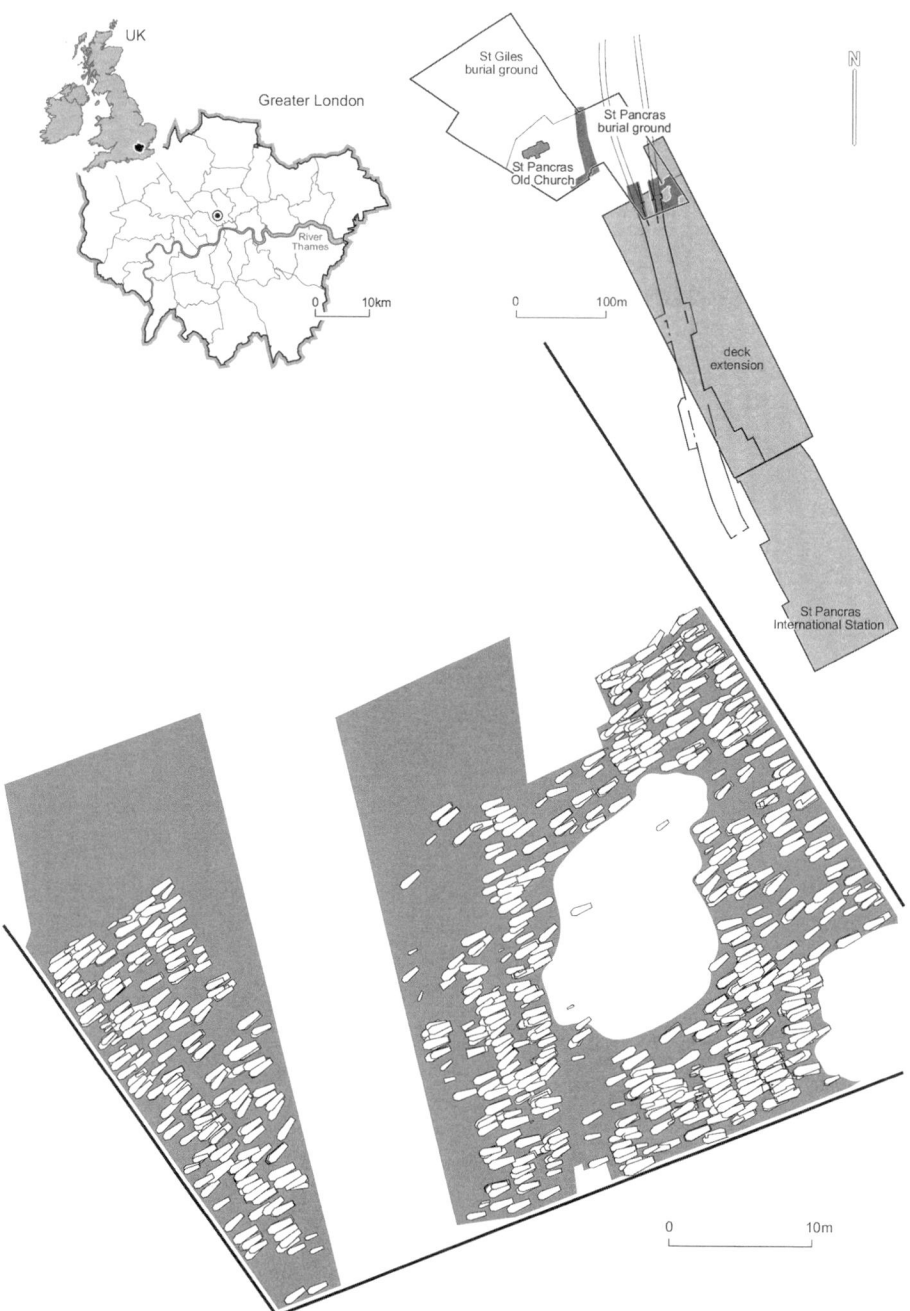

FIGURE 1. Site location plan. Copyright HS1 Ltd./Ramboll UK Limited, drawing by Carlos Lemos.

scattered "heedlessly about." A burial pit 40 feet deep was excavated on the site of the present-day Coroner's Court for the reinterment of the remains of over 7,000 individuals. These graphic scenes made a deep impression on one of nineteenth-century England's greatest writers. As a young architecture student working under Arthur Blomfield (clerk of works appointed by Bishop Tait and himself the fourth son of Tait's predecessor, Charles

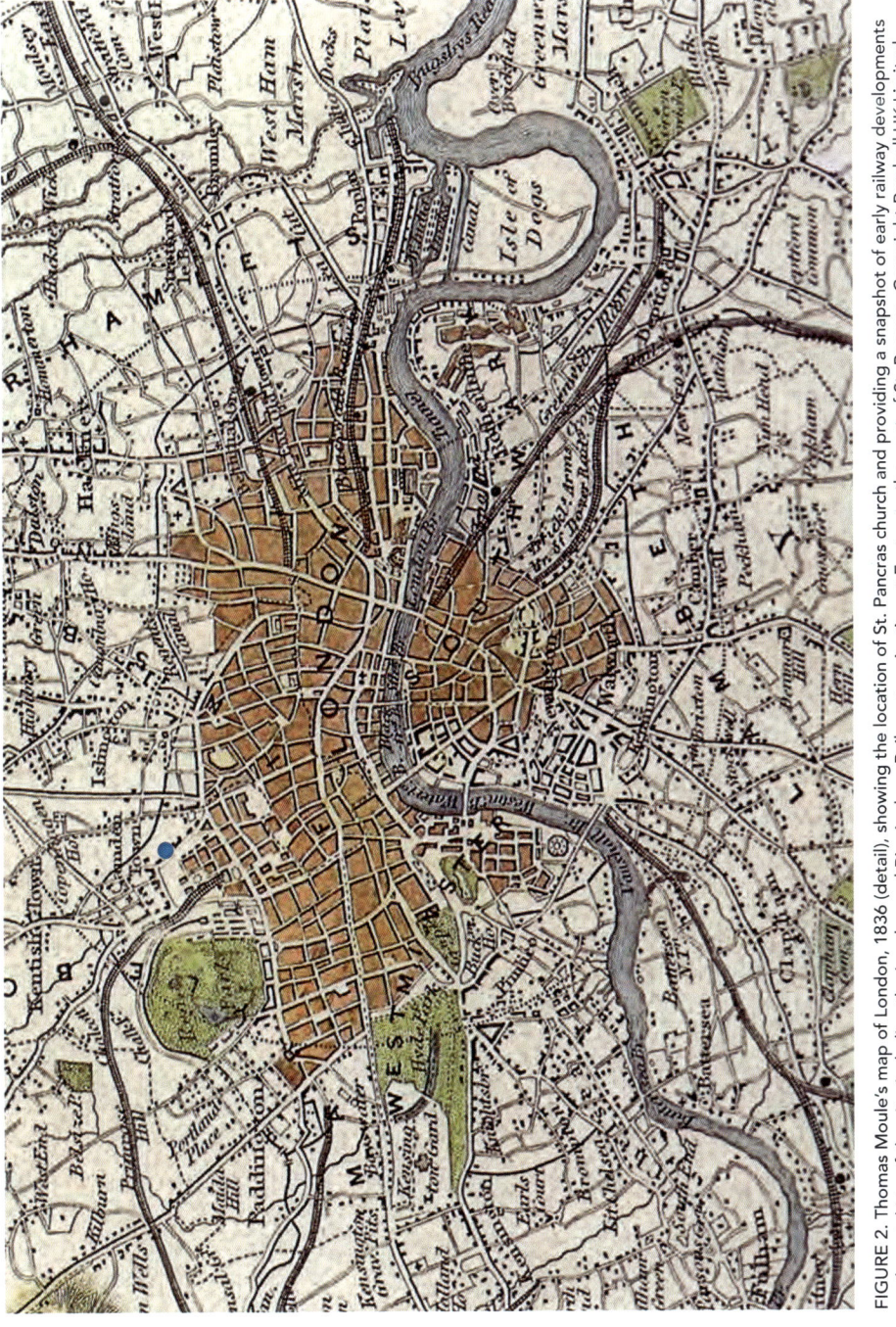

FIGURE 2. Thomas Moule's map of London, 1836 (detail), showing the location of St. Pancras church and providing a snapshot of early railway developments on the outskirts of the city, including the London and Birmingham Railway terminating at Euston to the west of St. Pancras. Copyright Ramboll UK Limited.

Blomfield), Thomas Hardy oversaw the exhumation works at St. Pancras (Tomalin, 2006:80–81). In 1882, some 16 years later, Hardy—by now a celebrated novelist and poet—was moved by his experiences to write a poem entitled "The Levelled Churchyard," the second verse of which reads

> "We late-lamented, resting here,
> Are mixed to human jam,
> And each to each exclaims in fear,
> 'I know not which I am!'"

Excavation Methodologies

Some 135 years later, controversy was to return to St. Pancras burial ground when archaeological attendance on cemetery clearance operations was suspended under pressure from the demanding railway construction program. The situation that led to this suspension had a complex history. The exhumation works by Burial Ground Services (UK) Ltd. (BGS) had begun in February 2002, their scope constrained by the need to maintain various operational railways crossing the site both above- and below-ground. In order to work within these restrictions, it had been decided to expose coffins by mechanically excavating a series of deep shafts separated by baulks in the natural clay. The archaeological drawbacks of this methodology were manifold: Coffins were frequently exposed only partially with elements of burials continuing into the baulk. Access for archaeological staff was seldom permissible for safety reasons, so that remains could only be loosely provenanced and often became separated from their coffins before confident identification could be made from coffin plates. In addition, the absence of direct archaeological supervision led to concerns that the integrity of individual skeletons was not always maintained during lifting.

The project managers (Rail Link Engineering) recognized the flaws in the methodology and so concentrated the archaeologically monitored exhumation into two mutually exclusive operations that were separated spatially on site. While BGS continued to recover coffins, assisted by machine, across a large proportion of the site, the archaeologists were redeployed within a sample area where detailed stratigraphic excavation and recording were undertaken. Even this compromise proved unsustainable in the face of the pressures arising from the project timetable, however, and consequently, on 15 November 2002 all archaeological work on site was suspended. For two days mechanical exhumation by BGS continued without archaeologists in attendance, provoking widespread concern and objections from the Church of England, English Heritage, the Council for British Archaeology, and Rescue (the British Archaeological Trust), as well as the general public and news media (Emery, 2006). It was universally recognized that meaningful engagement by the archaeological team was essential to the successful delivery of the construction project.

The archaeologists proposed an integrated procedure for exhumation and archaeological recording that could be accommodated within the existing groundworks program, with mechanical removal by the exhumation contractor of shallow spits to expose coffins, which were then archaeologically surveyed (Figure 3). Accurate surveying with total station theodolite was the cornerstone of the revised methodology—doubts about the precise three-dimensional location of burials would have undermined any attempts at reconstructing the superimposition of coffins during post-excavation analysis. Horizontal errors of only 300 mm, for example, could have introduced stratigraphic confusion between

FIGURE 3. General view (looking north) of mechanical excavation in spits by exhumation contractor. Copyright HS1 Ltd./Ramboll UK Limited.

adjacent stacks of coffins. For individual burials selected for osteological study in accordance with the agreed sampling strategy (below), four corners of the coffin were surveyed. For skeletons excluded from the recovered sample, only two points were taken, located centrally at each end of the coffin.

Each coffin was digitally photographed in situ following opening. Metal coffin fittings were detached and retained for analysis. Sampling of burials was structured with respect to observable characteristics of the coffin and human remains. As disproportionate emphasis on recovery of ornamented coffins could lead to a bias in the osteological sample toward individuals of higher socioeconomic status, a corresponding sample of individuals occupying plain coffins was also retrieved. A statistically significant sample of subadults was prioritized for study, and the implications for biasing the overall age profile were explicitly acknowledged during subsequent analysis. Skeletons exhibiting interesting pathologies were also targeted for recovery, but many of the coffins were filled by groundwater, which hindered the consistent application of this selection criterion. A total of 780 burials were taken to the laboratory for processing, of which 715 underwent the full program of analysis. Soft-tissue survival on several of the skeletons, particularly within the brain cavity, was detected only during washing. Health and Safety and public health protocols required the immediate reburial of such remains by the exhumation specialist.

The quality of preservation of wooden coffins, metal coffin fittings, and human bone was exceptional because of the clay soil in which the remains were buried. Although coffins in the upper, drier levels of the burial ground were in relatively poor condition, those at depth were generally complete and retained their structural integrity. However, ground pressure had caused some to collapse inward, so that they occupied only a fraction of their original width. Decorative coffin fittings, fabricated in thin iron sheet and often coated in tin, had remarkable preservation given their ephemeral nature, reflecting the brevity of the period of mourning for which they were intended to be visible. The collection comprises over 1,100 items and is now permanently retained for specialist reference at the Museum of London. The unusual survival of legible inscribed coffin plates proved to be one of the most valuable facets of the St. Pancras data set as it provided a vital link with the parish burial registers and all of the biographical detail that could be accessed via documentary research (Figure 4). Burial clothes and textile coffin linings were also found. In two coffins, those of Mrs. Mary Arrit (died 1795, aged 55) and Rebecca Maskoll (died 1806, aged 62), plant remains consisting of box and bay indicated the presence of floral tributes.

Direct on-site recording of stratigraphic relationships between individual burials and soil layers was beyond the scope of the integrated exhumation and archaeological process. To compensate for this omission, the three-dimensional survey data were analyzed using a modeling program allowing reconstruction of coffin-stacking sequences. Post-depositional lateral compression of coffins was taken into account to ensure that the full original extent of successive burials could be overlaid for comparison, and the stratigraphic principle of superimposition was applied to infer relationships between coffins. Following initial manipulation in AutoCAD, the data from the survey of burials were imported into Google SketchUp for three-dimensional viewing (Figure 5). In this model, each burial was represented by a three-dimensional coffin-shaped template of standardized proportions. This template was scaled to fit the length of the coffin recorded in the ground and was centered on its longitudinal axis. This manipulation allowed the configuration of recorded coffins in three-dimensional space to be analyzed, with a view to determining sequence of deposition. Comparison of levels taken on the lids of successive coffins within particular grave plots allowed the extent of vertical compaction to be determined. In some cases the model illustrated graphically how one coffin had sunk into another immediately below.

The accurate location of named burials provided the crucial platform for integrated study embracing archaeological data and documents to elucidate the management of the cemetery and the identities of specific burials (Emery, 2007). The parish burial registers contained entries for the period 1793 to 1804, which included alphanumeric grave plot references, but no key plan survived. Of the 119 recorded burials identified by coffin plate inscriptions, 26 could be matched with register entries for which a plot reference was given.

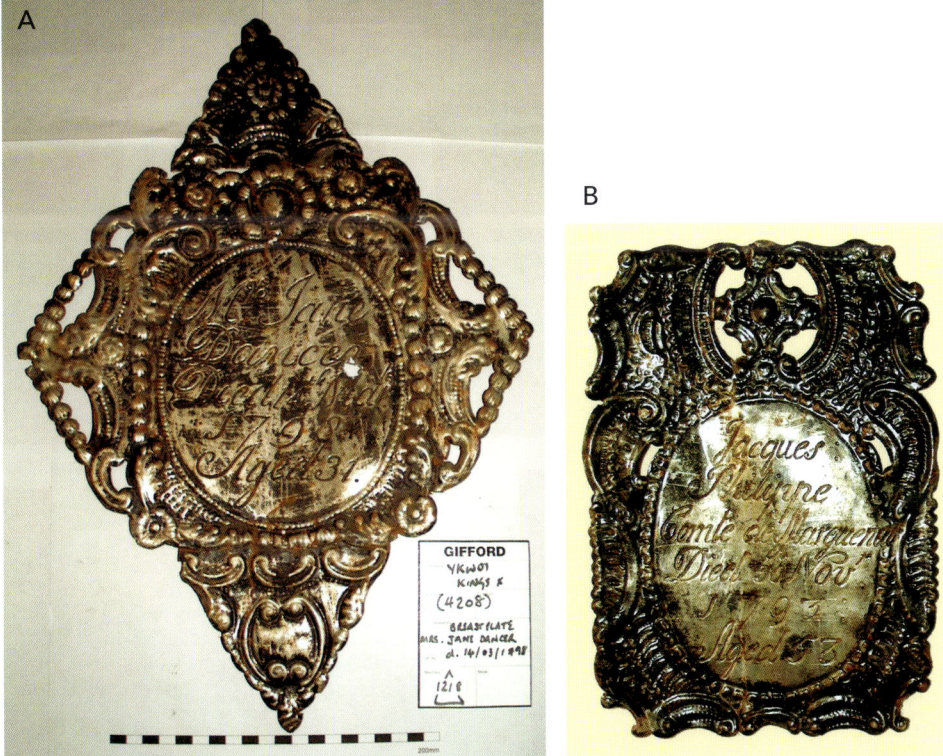

FIGURE 4. Breastplates. (A) Lozenge form identifying the coffin of Mrs. Jane Dancer (1766/1767–1798). (B) Rectangular form identifying the coffin of Jacques Philippe, Comte de Marguenat (1739/1740–1793). Copyright HS1 Ltd./ Ramboll UK Limited.

This matching allowed the spatial referencing scheme to be decoded: rows of graves apparent in the archaeological record could thus be reconciled with those historically conceived by the cemetery administrators.

A total of 647 headstones and 88 structural elements of tombs originating from both St. Pancras and the adjacent St. Giles burial grounds were recorded during the works. Most of these had been incorporated into a dry-stone wall and railway embankment to the east of the church, probably in the first decade of the twentieth century. Others had been laid horizontally to form a pavement between the pier bases of the original railway viaduct built in 1866. The date range of the memorials, derived from inscriptions recorded off site, was 1708–1862. Unfortunately, none of the St. Pancras memorial stones could be attributed to individual burials recorded during the exhumation, probably reflecting their origin in other areas of the cemetery. Nonetheless, their examination in tandem with that of the metal coffin fittings allowed a comparative investigation of stylistic development between the two forms of funereal ornament. Archaeological recording of memorial stones (Rendall, 2011a, 2011b; Wooldridge and Rendall, 2011) was based upon techniques and typologies developed by Mytum (2000).

The analysis of memorial stones to certain individuals about whom biographical information could be discovered often generated further insights into the relationship between social and religious background and funerary practice. One individual commemorated in stone had a notable American connection. Benjamin Woolsey Muirson died as a local

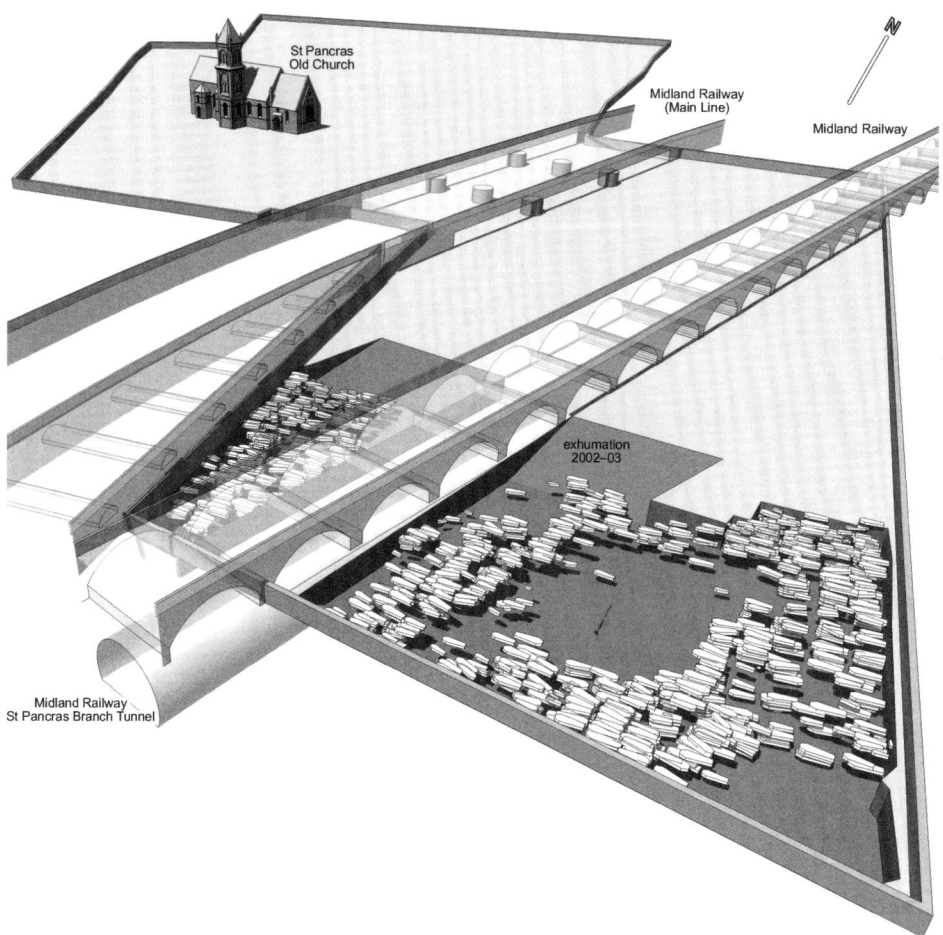

FIGURE 5. Three-dimensional model of buried coffins. Copyright HS1 Ltd./Ramboll UK Limited, drawing by Carlos Lemos.

resident in 1809, aged 52, but was the eldest son of Dr. George Muirson of Brookhaven in New York province, who was a prominent supporter of Crown forces at the outbreak of the American Revolution in 1776. As a consequence of his allegiance, the family's land and property were confiscated by the New York Assembly in 1779 (Phillpotts, 2011:109–110). Another headstone with a transatlantic association bore a simple Latin inscription recording the grave of Joseph Littee (died 1798), once curator of the vacant estates in the department of the Stewartry of Martinique in the French West Indies, where he was born in 1749 (Phillpotts, 2011:106–107).

The results of the osteological study (Powers, 2011:127–153; White, 2011:112–117) were made all the more significant by the very heterogeneous population buried at St. Pancras, ranging from French aristocrats and prelates to paupers who died in the local workhouse. Recorded diseases reflected the changing behaviors and stresses of life in a rapidly urbanizing and industrializing environment, including syphilis, known to contemporaries as the "French disease" (Powers and Emery, 2007). The demographic pattern of those affected by enamel hypoplasia indicated that those who suffered a "stressful" childhood were less likely to survive into adulthood than those who did not, but evidence of healed rachitic changes in the adult population showed that some were able to survive such an onslaught, probably reflecting the variety within the population buried here. The overall high rates of tooth enamel hypoplasia, a relatively high infant mortality rate, and evidence of growth retardation support suggestions that this was a predominantly poor urban population. However, a below-average prevalence of cribra orbitalia, a high prevalence of diffuse idiopathic skeletal hyperostosis (a condition associated with being overweight and therefore with easy access to food), and a high proportion of older adults with diseases of old age, such as osteoporosis and osteoarthritis, appear to contradict this characterization. The population also had a low prevalence of fractures, suggesting a commensurately low risk lifestyle. An apparent sharp increase in the prevalence of caries in the last years of the eighteenth century may reflect an increase in the consumption of sweetened foods as refined sugars became more widely available (Powers, 2011:152), the bulk of this commodity by this time being shipped to Europe across the Atlantic from plantations in the British and French colonies in the West Indies. Poor dental health seems to have been endemic, and the varied response, including the ownership of expensive, bespoke dentures (see below), further confirms the mixed nature of the group. Indications of other infectious diseases were also lower than might be expected in a poorer, urban group. It is unfortunate that we cannot tell what proportion of the burials was of victims of the series of cholera epidemics that had such an impact upon nineteenth-century London since illnesses of this kind leave no skeletal trace. Evidence of early nineteenth-century autopsy was recorded on several coffined skeletons. Given the likely moderate status of these individuals (inferred from the presence of coffin plates), some of these autopsies may have been occasioned by "enlightened" families seeking scientific answers for the death of their loved ones. Anatomical study or medical instruction, by contrast, may have motivated the dissection of both arms of Ann Hart (died 1798, aged 19), who came from the nearby St. Pancras Smallpox Hospital, the humeri, radii, and ulnae of her skeleton all having been sawn through at the midshaft. The Anatomy Act of 1832, making it easier for surgeons to acquire cadavers for dissection, was passed while the Third Ground at St. Pancras churchyard was in use. Contemporary accounts suggest that inmates of the nearby workhouse and executed criminals would have been prime candidates.

Intriguingly, four of the coffins were found to contain not only human bones, which had been subject to dissection, but also faunal remains (Pipe and Emery, 2011). A carapace of a tortoise was found in one of these coffins, but another contained the most curious find: eight bones from the left forelimb and left hind limb of a very large walrus. All the walrus bones are considerably larger than their equivalents at the National History Museum in London and are most likely from the same adult animal. The size suggests that this was a large male Pacific walrus, with definitely identified knife cuts signaling that they had been prepared for display and study. Alongside the walrus remains were dissected human bones representing at least eight individuals, including three human skulls exhibiting cranial autopsy. The interment of human and animal bone together would seem to reflect a common source and their pragmatic disposal. The coffins were located within the mass burial trenches that were prevalent in the southern part of the Third Ground sometime after November 1822. On 8 November 1853, within the date range of the St. Pancras find (1822–1854), a Professor Richard Owen recorded the dissection of a 1.22-m-long walrus in his paper entitled "On the Anatomy of a Walrus," which was published in the *Journal of Zoology* (Owen, 1853:103–106). The animal had come to the Zoological Society of London with a ship under the command of Captain Henry von Peterhead, which had been hunting seals around Svalbard (Svanberg, 2010, 123). These pioneering anatomists were polymaths, many, including the famous John Hunter, working on both human and animal subjects and gripped by a sense of scientific adventure. Owen's vivid account was published six years before Charles Darwin's *On the Origin of Species* (1859), when overarching systems for explaining human and animal evolution were still controversial. In this context it is ironic that the limbs of a walrus may have been mistaken for those of a human among the disused specimens in an anatomist's laboratory.

Documentary research into the composition of the buried population at St. Pancras revealed significant diversity. The cemetery by no means served a purely parochial community, one conspicuous element being immigrants, not only from outside the metropolis but also from abroad, the latter chiefly comprising refugees from the French Revolution who arrived as early as 1792. By the late eighteenth century London's emergence as an industrialized capital city was reflected by the increased representation of paupers and the lower working class at St. Pancras. A workhouse had existed in the parish from 1730; its successor was established in 1805 immediately to the north of the burial ground. Positive identification of pauper burials from monuments and coffin furnishings is not a straightforward matter since it appears that some parish burials made prior to the Poor Law Amendment Act of 1834 were relatively well provided for. Indeed, some even had individual memorials: Lysons (1795–1811) noted that to Eleanor Bonner from the workhouse, buried in April 1794 (Phillpotts, 2011, 109). Later pauper burials are thought to have been particularly concentrated in the Third Ground and were made in open trenches at the south end, near the charnel house, where there were fewer vaults and gravestones. This hypothesis was borne out by the occurrence in the southernmost part of the cemetery of archaeological evidence for a transition in the 1830s from grave-specific coffin stacks to the excavation of linear trenches within which coffins were laid alternately head to toe. This change in cemetery management may have been in response to increased mortality, partly resulting from the documented cholera epidemics after 1828.

Interments of French Émigrés

Twenty-four nameplates—approximately 15% of the assemblage recorded during the project—indicated that the coffins to which they were attached contained the remains of émigrés from France and her colonies. Assuming that the cemetery population as a whole included a similar proportion of French people, this suggests that approximately 200 of the 1,300 burials recorded archaeologically were French citizens. Among the burials associated with plates were those of three aristocrats: Jean Charles Julien d'Andigné (born 1749, died 1824), Jacques Philippe, Comte de Marguenat (born 1739/1740, died 1793; Figure 4B), and Paul François Marie, Comte de Monstiers (born 1760, died 1837), who was the abbé de Mérinville. In addition, a fourth individual, Charlotte Henriette de Vogué (born 1764, died 1796), may have been connected with the comtes de Vogué, seigneurs de la Rochecolombe, la Chapelle Saint-Germain, Plantade, and St. Maurice (Phillpotts, 2011:99–102).

In addition to that of Paul François Marie at least four of the coffins recorded during the exhumation works were occupied by French ecclesiastics (Phillpotts, 2011:99–106). Guillaume Alexandre Jacques Langlois (born 1721, died 1798: Bellenger, 1986:209) was a vicar from Rouen diocese, whereas Auguste Poisson (born 1743, died 1806; no further details are known) was a priest in France. Other clerical burials included those of

Pierre-Augustin Godart de Belbeuf, bishop of Avranches (born 1730, died 1808), whose coffin was uncovered in 2002. He went into exile from his diocese in 1792 but continued to regard himself as bishop of Avranches. Dying in his armchair after a painful illness on 26 September 1808, he was buried at St. Pancras on 29 September (Beaurepaire, 1935:19). In his absence, the eleventh-century Cathédrale Saint-André, which had been damaged during both the Hundred Years' War (1337–1453) and the French Wars of Religion (1562–98) and consolidated repeatedly, finally collapsed in 1796 (Nicolas-Méry, 2011:34).

The discovery of Arthur Richard Dillon, archbishop of Narbonne (born 1731, died 1806), was to arouse particular interest, in France as well as in Britain. Monsignor Dillon's coffin, exposed on 16 January 2003, was triple shelled, comprising inner and outer wooden caskets separated by an intermediate lead lining. While the inner casket bore an inscribed lead plaque, the outer coffin, which was visible at the funeral, was decorated with a breastplate, two lid motifs (a flaming urn and a crucifix), 18 escutcheons, eight grips, and eight grip plates. This burial was located in the second row from the east edge of the cemetery and overlaid the coffin of 59-year-old Mr. Joseph Hudson, who had died only 11 days before the cleric. The archbishop had been buried with his fine set of porcelain dentures, secured in the mouth by a pair of gold springs, although only one was still present. The dentures are likely to be the work of the pioneering dentist Nicholas Dubois de Chemant, who had a furnace at the Sèvres factory and obtained a royal patent for "mineral paste teeth" from Louis XVI in 1789, before leaving for England as an economic migrant in 1792 (Powers, 2006, 2011:132–134).

The St. Pancras Burial Population

A century before the advent of the French, the burial ground of St. Pancras Old Church was already favored as a resting place for Catholics, particularly for those of the upper social classes (Lysons, 1795–1811, vol. 3, 351, n32), many of them political "outsiders" who supported the exiled Catholic House of Stuart rather than the Hanoverian monarchy in the eighteenth century. Indeed, such was the enduring association between St. Pancras and Catholicism that it has been claimed that this was the last church in England where the bells were tolled for the Latin mass (Brown, 1904:10; Phillpotts, 2011). It is clear, however, that not all of the outsiders buried here were motivated by religion or royalism. Devon-born Maurice Margarot (1745–1815) was living in France at the time of the Revolution but returned to Britain in 1792 and joined the London Corresponding Society, which was inspired by Jacobinism to discuss parliamentary and constitutional reform. Following his arrest and conviction, Margarot was taken with fellow radicals Thomas Muir, Rev. Thomas Fyshe Palmer, and William Skirving to New South Wales on board the *Surprize*, which set sail in May 1794 (Phillpotts, 2011:107). The lengthy sentence of transportation that he and his wife Elizabeth, who joined him as a free settler, endured in Australia illustrates the authorities' fear and suspicion of revolutionary France—in sharp contrast to the widespread sympathy extended to anti-Revolutionary exiles on their arrival in a nation that was at war with their homeland.

Situated on the fringe of the growing metropolis, St. Pancras experienced a dramatic transition from a rural to an urban character during the eighteenth and nineteenth centuries, with all of the demographic and environmental implications of this transformation. Changes in the composition of the living population, and the conditions in which it lived and worked, have left their mark in the buried remains.

The burial ground extension of the Third Ground witnessed 61 years of sustained heavy use on a scale that was not anticipated at the time that it was opened. The late eighteenth and early nineteenth centuries saw the population of London rise in a manner that must have seemed alarming to many contemporaries. The population of the parish of St. Pancras grew dramatically in the 1780s and 1790s: between 1776 and 1801 it rose from less than 600 to 31,779 (a 53-fold increase; Phillpotts, 2011;30). It had reached 46,333 by 1811, 71,838 by 1821, 103,548 by 1831, 129,763 by 1841, and 166,956 by 1851 (Brown, 1904:7, 9, 11, 14, 19, 23, 26; Sheppard, 1971:25). The influx of immigrants from the French Revolution contributed to this explosion from the 1790s onward. By the 1840s many of the London burial grounds were in an insanitary state as they struggled to accommodate the bodies of the increasing numbers of people who died every year in the fast-growing city. The grotesque crowding of London's churchyards became a focus of hot debate, not least in the light of the cholera outbreaks that rocked the city in the years after 1828. St. Pancras churchyard came under scrutiny from those committed to the closure of London's old burial grounds and the opening of new cemeteries beyond the city limits (Phillpotts, 2011:35–40, 77–78).

Research into the number of burials recorded in the St. Pancras parish registers identified a series of peaks in 1833 (1,754), 1837 (1,653), and 1854 (1,865), with that in 1833 interpreted as resulting from a major cholera epidemic (figures based on unpublished data compiled by amateur local historian Michael Rennie). The wealth of documentary evidence testifies to the complexity and oddness of St. Pancras as a study group. For example, the intimate biographical insights that it affords reveal the importance of tradition, belief, and idiosyncratic personal choice for burial location. In this, the project provides a salutary warning of the dangers of trite or deterministic explanations of funerary practice. With numbers increasing on this scale during the period of the Third Ground's use and with so many social and cultural factors influencing the evolution of funerary practice at St. Pancras, any attempts at generalized explanation may seem unwise.

Definition of a valid sample for osteological study is inherently shaped by our understanding of the social historical questions prioritized by researchers. Although we may seek to view the archaeological evidence from the burial ground as representing the development and customs of an eighteenth- and nineteenth-century community, we need to ask what constitutes "the community" in such a diverse socioeconomic context. Not everyone buried at St. Pancras was a local resident, and the cemetery absorbed outsiders from disparate backgrounds. Social historians must play a key role in informing the archaeological research agenda; at the same time, they may have much to gain from acknowledging the value of archaeological results for this period (Harding, 1998). The specific lesson to be gained from the St. Pancras experience is that articulating the historical records with key archaeological data at an early stage can help researchers formulate and implement intelligent sampling strategies. This interdisciplinary approach to project design is important in the United Kingdom, where the scope of archaeological recording has to be justified to developers, statutory authorities, and archaeological bodies as reasonable. In preparing the project design, cemetery archaeologists can also benefit from the strategic involvement of other specialists, crucially osteologists. The discipline of osteoarchaeology is currently benefiting from rapid technical advances, for example, in the use of radiography, the study of specific pathologies, microsampling of teeth for isotope analysis, dietary insights through study of dental calculus, and sex identification of DNA samples using microfluidics.

Mediating the disparate aims of cemetery clearance and archaeological research—so often manifest on site as incompatible working methods—continues to challenge those responsible for ensuring that such projects are undertaken with academic rigor, scientific integrity, and propriety. The planning of such projects brings together a wide range of stakeholders, including clients, project managers, local authority archaeological advisors, church representatives, and a growing contingent of the general public pursuing an interest in genealogy. It is regrettable that the organizational and methodological debate in which these parties engage is sometimes revisited and reargued with each new case, leading to inconsistencies in approach and a waste of already scanty resources. Strategic uncertainty can be compounded by regulatory idiosyncrasies arising from site-specific issues of current land use and custodianship. Whatever the specific project, the operations of a cemetery clearance contractor should always be acknowledged as an integral part of the implementation of any agreed archaeological research framework. Exclusion of a cemetery population, or parts thereof, from the archaeologist's remit should reflect a conscious sampling decision guided by the research framework. Exhumation contractors provide a range of essential specialist services, particularly in cases where archaeological work is either unnecessary or inappropriate. However, in situations where there *are* aspirations for archaeological research, their activities should be embedded within an overarching archaeological framework. Archaeological curators should acknowledge the advantages of adopting this nesting of roles where burials have been defined as a potential archaeological resource, and this best practice needs to be enshrined in planning and curatorial policy. The need for the work of clearance companies to be placed "under archaeological supervision and not vice versa" has been recognized by the Advisory Panel on the Archaeology of Burials in England (2015:10) in its recently launched guidance on the sampling of large burial grounds.

Attitudes to the treatment of the dead remain mutable since they reflect contemporary concerns and mores. The history of the St. Pancras burial ground vividly illustrates how perceptions and values in this context have changed over time; forensic archaeology, through its technical advances and intimate revelations, has itself contributed to a heightened regard for past populations.

Reinterment Narratives

After osteological analysis the human remains exhumed at St. Pancras had to be returned, in batches, to the exhumation contractor for reinterment at St. Pancras cemetery in East Finchley within two months of discovery. For two individuals, however, this was not the end of the story. Letters proposing repatriation of the two prelates, Dillon and Belbeuf, had been sent to their respective modern dioceses, but the responses from each had been negative. Sensing that there might yet be community interest in seeing these exiled clerics returned home, the author made special arrangements for their reburial on 24 October 2003 in a discrete shared grave at East Finchley, which was accurately surveyed. So on 23 March 2006, when telephoned by international wine merchant Peter Darbyshire enquiring on behalf of Professor Jacques Michaud (president of the Archaeological and Literary Commission of Narbonne), the author was in a position to divulge the precise whereabouts of Monsignor Dillon. This call was just the beginning of 12 months of preparations—legal, logistical, and ceremonial—that took place on both sides of the English Channel, Monsignor Dillon's remains being reexhumed under the author's supervision on 7 March 2007 in the presence of Professor Michaud and the Honorable Mrs. Madeleine Louloudis (née Dillon).

The archbishop set off on his poignant homeward journey (on an Air France freight jet bound for Montpellier) just over 200 years after his death (Amigues and Michaud, 2007;

FIGURE 6. Funeral procession of the repatriated remains of Monsignor Arthur Richard Dillon, last archbishop of Narbonne, on 15 March 2007. Copyright Ramboll UK Limited.

Commission Archéologique et Littéraire de Narbonne, 2008). The enthusiastic welcome by the Narbonnaise during the ensuing ceremonies, culminating on 15 March 2007 in the grand funeral procession from the Canal de la Robine to the Cathédrale Saint-Just et Saint-Pasteur and a service presided over by the late Cardinal Lustiger, with the apostolic nuncio sitting on his right and the Abbot of Downside to his left, was an illustration of Monsignor Dillon's enduring civic legacy (Figure 6). The repatriation of Dillon's fellow countryman, Mgr. Pierre-Augustin Godart de Belbeuf, took place on 13 September 2009, his skeletal remains and inscribed coffin plate being returned by the author to Avranches,

FIGURE 7. Reinterment of the remains of Mgr. Pierre-Augustin Godart de Belbeuf in the basilica of Saint-Gervais, Avranches, 23 September 2011. Copyright Ramboll UK Limited.

the seat of the ancient bishopric that he had occupied when it was suppressed in 1790. The funeral service in the basilica of Saint-Gervais, two years later on 23 September 2011, was attended by family members and Jean-François Le Grand, president of Conseil Général de la Manche (Figure 7).

Dillon and Belbeuf would have been acquainted with one another in life, sharing their ordeal as refugees. Archaeological research into their émigré community, undertaken as part of this project, sheds light on the complex series of Anglo-French ties that existed despite the bitter and protracted warfare between the two countries at the time. For these two prelates in exile, regime change in 1815 came too late. It seems fitting then that the circumstances of their discovery during the building of a major high-speed railway are the consequence of enhancing the connection between England and France.

Acknowledgments

The project was funded by HS1 Ltd. Helen Glass (formerly archaeology manager, Rail Link Engineering) is acknowledged for her comments on an earlier draft. The late Trevor Ashwin assisted with recrafting sections of the text, and the late Chris Phillpotts, the project's documentary researcher, also provided helpful input. Gifford Ltd. (now Ramboll UK Limited) subcontracted Pre-Construct Archaeology Ltd. (PCA), which delivered the fieldwork under the supervision of Kevin Wooldridge, assisted by Duncan Sayer, and Museum of London Specialist Services (now Museum of London Archaeology), which was responsible for the osteological and environmental analyses, and aspects of the artifact studies, the remainder being undertaken by PCA staff. The osteological research was led by the late Bill White (Museum of London), with Natasha Powers (formerly Museum of London Archaeology) kindly assisting with the osteological element of this chapter. Michael Rennie generously allowed access to his extensive database of burial register entries. Sarah Tarlow (University of Leicester) kindly advised during the latter stages of the post-excavation work. Dom Aidan Bellenger (Abbot of Downside) provided invaluable information about the French émigré clergy. Finally, the author extends his gratitude to Roy Stephenson (Museum of London) and François Amigues, Peter Darbyshire, Mark Meyts, Jacques Michaud, and David Nicolas-Méry.

References

Advisory Panel on the Archaeology of Burials in England. 2015. *Large Burial Grounds: Guidance on Sampling in Archaeological Fieldwork Projects.* London: Historic England Publishing, in association with the Advisory Panel on Archaeology of Burials in England.

Amigues, F., and J. Michaud. 2007. *Arthur-Richard Dillon, dernier Président-Né des Etats de Languedoc, de 1793 à 1790; recueil de souvenirs publié à l'occasion du retour de ses restes découverts à Londres, Narbonne, 15 et 16 mars 2007.* Narbonne: Commission Archéologique et Littéraire de Narbonne.

Beaurepaire, C. A. de. 1936. *Monseigneur Godart de Belbeuf, dernier évêque d'Avranches.* Communication faite au Congrès de l'Association Normande tenu à Avranches en Julliet 1935. Bayeux: R. P. Colas.

Bellenger, D. A. 1986. *The French Exiled Clergy in the British Isles after 1789: An Historical Introduction and Working List.* Bath: Downside Abbey.

Bradley, S. 2007. St. *Pancras Station.* London: Profile Books.

Brown, W. E. 1904. *The St. Pancras Book of Dates of the Principal Events in the History of the Parish.* London: St. Pancras Borough Council.

Commission Archéologique et Littéraire de Narbonne. 2008. *Arthur-Richard Dillon, dernier Président-Né des Etats de Languedoc, de 1763 à 1790. Bulletin de la Commission Archéologique et Littéraire de Narbonne,* 51 (special issue).

Emery, P. A. 2006. End of the Line. *British Archaeology*, 88:10–15.

Emery, P. A. 2007. "Cracking the Code: Biography and (Reconstructed) Stratigraphy at St. Pancras Burial Ground." In *Proceedings of the Seventh Annual Conference of the British Association for Biological Anthropology and Osteoarchaeology*, ed. S. R. Zakrzewski and W. White, pp. 6–13. BAR International Series 1712. Oxford: Archaeopress.

Emery, P. A., and K. Wooldridge. 2011. St. *Pancras Burial Ground: Excavations for St. Pancras International, the London Terminus of High Speed 1, 2002–3.* London: Gifford Monograph.

Harding, V. 1998. "Research Priorities: An Historian's Perspective." In *Grave Concerns: Death and Burial in England 1700 to 1850*, ed. M. Cox, pp. 205–212. CBA Research Report 113. York: Council for British Archaeology.

Lysons, D. 1795–1811. *The Environs of London.* 3 vols. and supplement. London.

Mytum, H. 2000. *Recording and Analysing Graveyards.* York: Council for British Archaeology.

Nicolas-Méry, D. 2011. *Avranches: Capitale du pays du Mont Saint-Michel.* Cully, France: OREP Éditions.

Owen, R. 1853. On the Anatomy of the Walrus. *Proceedings of the Zoological Society of London*, 21:103–106.

Phillpotts, C. 2011. "Documentary Evidence." In St. *Pancras Burial Ground: Excavations for St. Pancras International, the London Terminus of High Speed 1, 2002–3*, by P. A. Emery and K. Wooldridge, passim. London: Gifford Monograph.

Pipe, A., and P. A. Emery. 2011. "Faunal Remains." In St. *Pancras Burial Ground: Excavations for St. Pancras International, the London Terminus of High Speed 1, 2002–3*, by P. A. Emery and K. Wooldridge, p. 157. London: Gifford Monograph.

Powers, N. I. 2006. An Eighteenth Century Porcelain Dental Prosthesis Belonging to Archbishop Arthur Richard Dillon. *British Dental Journal*, 201:459–463.

Powers, N. I. 2011. "Osteological Evidence." In St. *Pancras Burial Ground: Excavations for St. Pancras International, the London Terminus of High Speed 1, 2002–3*, by P. A. Emery and K. Wooldridge, pp. 127–153. London: Gifford Monograph.

Powers, N. I., and P. A. Emery. 2007. "The 'French Disease": Syphilis and the Burial Ground of St. Pancras." In *Proceedings of the Seventh Annual Conference of the British Association for Biological Anthropology and Osteoarchaeology*, ed. S. R. Zakrzewski and W. White, pp. 32–35. BAR International Series 1712. Oxford: Archaeopress.

Rendall, H. 2011a. "Recording Monumental Stonework." In St. *Pancras Burial Ground: Excavations for St. Pancras International, the London Terminus of High Speed 1, 2002–3*, by P. A. Emery and K. Wooldridge, pp. 18–20. London: Gifford Monograph.

Rendall, H. 2011b. "Memorial Stones and Tomb Fragments." In St. *Pancras Burial Ground: Excavations for St. Pancras International, the London terminus of High Speed 1, 2002–3*, by P. A. Emery and K. Wooldridge, CD Appendix 1. London: Gifford Monograph.

Sheppard, F. 1971. *London 1808–1870: The Infernal Wen*. London: Secker and Warburg.

Svanberg, I. 2010. Walruses (Odobenus rosmarus) in Captivity. *Svenska Linnésållskapets Årsskrift*, 2010:119–136.

Tomalin, C. 2006. *Thomas Hardy: The Time-Torn Man*. London: Viking.

White, W. 2011. "Osteological Evidence." In St. *Pancras Burial Ground: Excavations for St. Pancras International, the London Terminus of High Speed 1, 2002–3*, by P. A. Emery and K. Wooldridge, pp. 112–117. London: Gifford Monograph.

Wooldridge K., and H. Rendall. 2011. "Grave Memorials." In St. *Pancras Burial Ground: Excavations for St. Pancras International, the London Terminus of High Speed 1, 2002–3*, by P. A. Emery and K. Wooldridge, pp. 158–166. London: Gifford Monograph.

CHAPTER 5

Explaining Stylistic Change in Mortuary Material Culture: The Dynamic of Power Relations between the Bereaved and the Undertaker

Harold Mytum

The explanation of product changes in historic contexts tends to rely on one of three assertions, and these have all been emphasized within studies of British mortuary material culture. The first is that fashion is a dominant, inevitable, and inexorable force for change that can be described but not explained (Burgess, 1963; Curl ,1972; Willsher, 1985; Litten, 1991). The second is that the rise in industrial mass production led to the dominance of the producer in the creation of choices from which customers made their selection (Church and Smith, 1966; Buckham, 1999). The third is that the customers by their choices affected the success of competitive options within the range produced and so created the market within which producers operated (Cannon, 1989; Tarlow, 1999); in other words, the producers reacted to public taste rather than created it. This study examines, within the context of consumption within mortuary behavior, how the retailer (here the undertaker or mason) mediated between producer and consumer (usually the bereaved) during the late eighteenth to early twentieth century, in a dynamic relationship where the power relationships vary from one context to another. That this topic has not been explored in mortuary archaeology reflects the limited examination of this issue in historical archaeology more generally, despite the widespread interest in artifact production, on the one hand, and patterns of consumption, on the other (Mullins, 2004).

It can be argued that at different stages in the bereavement process the power relations between retailer and consumer change and also the social importance of details of style varied. It is thus possible to investigate how the dynamics of this relationship affects the rate and nature of stylistic change. Although highly contextualized, this pattern of relationships can be considered important in many other cultural contexts. This is particularly so in the case of mortuary material culture because even though the elements used such as coffin fittings or monument blanks may have been mass produced, the manufacture of the coffin and the arrangement of fittings and the further carving and inscribing of the monument remained under the control of the undertaker or mason throughout the nineteenth century. Here the producer-consumer relationship was similar to that experienced in craftsman-producer economies, although with an awareness of choices derived from an environment within which most material culture was mass produced (Mytum, 2016).

Context of Choice and Use

In the process of death, burial, and commemoration, two groups of material culture were normally consumed. The first was the coffin, with its associated furnishings and fittings; the second was the memorial, set on a grave plot. Although today undertakers may attempt to arrange for the purchase of the memorial at the same time as the funeral arrangements are made to maximize business and ensure that the bereaved family members consider all aspects of the mortuary process, that was not the case in earlier periods. Although undertakers were responsible for the funeral (Litten, 1991), the various stages in mourning dress were part of the costume and jewelry trade (Morley, 1971; Cunnington and Lucas, 1972; Taylor, 1983), and the stonemason was responsible for the monument (Burgess, 1963; Mytum, 2004a). Memorials were sometimes commissioned and produced ahead of a death, in which case the person to be commemorated could have a significant input into the design, but most were selected after the death and often six months or a year after interment. This allowed time for the grave fill to settle and also meant that the choices were made after a period of grave visiting prior to the commissioning of a memorial. Each of the two categories of material culture were therefore produced and consumed in very different relationships between consumer and producer and with the client in quite distinct emotional states.

The coffin served a functional role of containing the body during the period prior to burial, when it was viewed first in a private setting at home, although by the later nineteenth century in many contexts this viewing had been shifted to the funeral directors' mortuary chapel. The coffin was then visible in public during the journey to the church service and on to the burial ground, unless covered by a rented cloth, usually called a pall or mortcloth. Some individuals viewed the coffin up close, but more saw it only from a distance (Litten, 1991). The closer the view, the more emotionally linked and charged was the viewer. Indeed, those able to examine the coffin prior to interment were more focused on the body within it (and the style of dress and body treatment were important in this respect but are not considered here) and on their relationships with the bereaved and other visitors. By the later nineteenth century, coffins could be provided with viewing windows or hinged sections allowing the face of the deceased to be visible while the rest of the lid was in place (Mytum, 2016); earlier, the whole lid and its fittings would not be in position. This was a highly emotional context for social interaction, and the relationships, memories, and emotions shared by individuals, including those of the deceased, were dominant. The physical form of the coffin and its degree and nature of elaboration would be noted and remembered, particularly by neighbors and friends, but the details of the styles and symbols used on the fittings were arguably less socially important.

The coffin was generally seen on its own; only if several members of a family died at the same time would their coffins be displayed at home and in the church together. Comparison of one coffin with another was therefore intrinsically difficult. Moreover, each coffin was available for inspection only for a few days, and its public visibility lasted only hours at most. Whether placed in private or public vaults or in earth graves, the coffin and its fittings were disposable and served a very short term display purpose. Although concerns with maintaining the integrity of the corpse ensured that the coffin was seen to have a long-term role, this role was in time taken over by the vault or burial plot rather than the inevitably decaying wooden coffin. Cast iron and lead were used to create more permanent containers, but the former was rare in Britain, and the latter tended to be placed within a wooden case that could be covered in colored cloth and display a range of fittings. In all these cases it was the containing and protection of the body (see also Mytum and Webb, this volume) that dominated over symbolic communication. The coffin was part of the paraphernalia associated with the funeral ritual, where socially appropriate norms would be adhered to and a set of elaborations and generalized qualities of the coffin would fit the class and religious affiliation of the family, but the minutiae of the coffin design and fittings would be of lesser importance than other aspects of the funeral ritual, including behavior and dress of the bereaved, entertainment of visitors, and format and content of the funeral service, including the sermon address.

The context in which consumer choice was exercised over the coffin was an emotional and difficult one, and deciding the details of the coffin design may have been a very low priority for the bereaved. Although an early nineteenth-century hand-drawn catalog of fittings shows many individual types (Portfolio of original anonymous drawings, V&A EL1826), by the later nineteenth century catalogs show sets of fittings (Mytum, 2016), even though individual items could continue to be obtained. It would seem that the undertaker took many decisions regarding the coffin under general instructions regarding the overall elaboration and cost of the item. In this situation, the role of the consumer in determining the style and symbolic content of the overall design and of individual fittings could have been very low. The only concern may have been to largely conform, to do that which seemed proper given the family's social status and cultural context. An undated but probably early twentieth-century manual for undertakers and coffin makers emphasizes the importance of assessing the wealth and social standing of the deceased and that taking advantage of clients at an impressionable moment might create a larger sale but, as they reflect on their treatment, could create resentment and a poor reputation that would limit further business (Plume, n.d.).

The graveyard monument was selected at some other time, with due reflection on the values and sentiments that are to be expressed on it through text and decoration. This selection was usually after bereavement, but some memorials were commissioned and sometimes erected prior to death. The monument is of some lasting significance, can be studied at leisure, and can be carefully scrutinized close up or seen from a distance by many. It is also situated within an environment of other memorials already existing and with the expectation of others being erected subsequently, in a landscape of memory with its own dynamic physical and biographical history. Gravestones can also be used to commemorate more than one person and so have long-term use-lives and biographies (Mytum, 2004a); the same cannot apply to coffins. The nature of the decisions made regarding the graveyard memorial are therefore more measured, are seen in a more emotionally balanced and considered situation, and are chosen with greater regard for public comparison and display than the coffin.

Gravestone monuments are culturally and socially more significant items than coffins because they have a long-lasting public role while at the same time providing a personalized commemorative focus for family and friends (Mytum, 2004b). This dual role, and the incorporation of more choices relating to stone type and material, texts, and symbols, creates a vehicle for communication that requires many choices on the part of the commissioner.

Given the very different circumstance within which decisions were made and the type of temporal and locational contexts of their visibility and use, it is perhaps not surprising, therefore, to see a different pattern of variability in the two groups of mortuary material culture and a somewhat divergent trajectory in terms of stylistic and symbolic change. This difference reveals how the dynamics of highly unequal and more equal relationships between producer and consumer have direct effects on the scale, nature, and even direction of cultural change.

The Nature of the Sample Available for Analysis

Graveyard memorial data collected in a systematic fashion from Britain that are available in the quantities necessary for analysis date mainly from 1780, as there was an exponential rise in external commemoration that began in the later eighteenth century (Mytum, 2006a). However, not all parts of Britain saw memorials with decoration as a major feature of the designs, and even where this was the case, there can be problems in using the data for this analysis. For example, the many headstones known in Gloucestershire were of a limestone that has caused preservation of the deeply carved iconography, but the shallow-cut lettering has eroded away, so most are now impossible to date closely, although stylistically, they can largely be assigned to the later eighteenth century. In contrast, certain forms of earlier headstones, such as the Swithland slate cherubs with mortality symbols, have received more attention (Mytum, 2004c), so they have become overrepresented in the collected data. Nevertheless, the spread of dates can be appreciated, and it will be relatively straightforward, although time-consuming, to increase sample size to reinforce the patterns already becoming visible. For this analysis, however, samples from two areas of Britain, Pembrokeshire in Wales and the hinterland of York, Yorkshire, have been combined to give indications of generalized trends.

The belowground evidence, in contrast to that of memorials, belongs mainly to the later eighteenth and early nineteenth centuries. The only large, well-published assemblage of coffin material comes from Spitalfields and belongs to the period 1729–1852 (Reeve and Adams, 1993), and unfortunately, most of the other major London sites at St. Pancras and St. George's, Bloomsbury, largely do not stretch beyond the 1850s (see Emery, this volume; Loe and Boston, this volume) as this was when the crypts were closed, and most datable fittings come from these contexts rather than external earth-dug graves. However, a few excavated coffins give some indication of later patterns, such as a small number from Birmingham (Hancox, 2006) and one from St. Luke's in Islington (Boyle at al., 2005), and from the later nineteenth century there is also the valuable source of illustrated trade catalogs that, although not indicating the popularity of different styles, at least demonstrate what was on offer. These can be compared with one important early nineteenth-century illustrated catalog. Unfortunately, the period 1830–1880 is not well represented in known British catalogs, so that both surviving and recorded coffins and documented sources are limited for several decades; this lack emphasizes how archaeological study can be vital even in what might appear to be well-documented periods.

The Graveyard Monuments

By the late eighteenth century, the range of external memorial features available to consumers in any one region was very large. That had not been the case earlier, where very limited although often discrete regional schools existed, each with their own defined but limited repertoire and made from local stone (Burgess, 1963; Mytum, 2004b). There are not only headstones but also large numbers of chest and table tombs and flat ledger stones (Mytum, 2000), unlike New England and other parts of eastern North America, where headstones are the overwhelming majority of monuments for the later eighteenth and first part of the nineteenth century. Even within the headstones, there is a bewildering array of shapes, many linked to architectural revival styles such as Gothic or Egyptian. Moreover, beyond the shape comes the decoration, which is also very variable. At any one time, certain motifs or styles may be popular within a region (Mytum, 2002), but these are portrayed in many variations and change over time. Moreover, at the same time many other alternative motifs are usually available and are occasionally used, demonstrating consumer choice was wide, even if often the same forms or motifs were actually chosen by the clients.

Mortality symbols are well known as being among the earliest symbols on external commemorative monuments (Deetz and Dethlefsen, 1967). Although common on many Scottish monuments (Willsher, 1985) and in Ulster (Mytum, 2009), they are less common in large numbers in England and Wales, although unquantified research in Kent demonstrates that there may be some areas where they were at least once widespread (Benes, 1977). One English graveyard, St. Mary the Virgin, Potton, Bedfordshire, does have a significant number of mortality stones (Figure 1A, 1B). Whether this is an unusual survival or an atypical consumer choice in the eighteenth century it is at present not possible to ascertain, although a few survive in adjacent churchyards (Mytum and Chapman, 2006). Although Potton is only a single site, it is valuable because it is relatively close to London, where the coffin data have been recovered, and for a single graveyard has an unusually large number of stones with the relevant motifs (Figure 1C). Death's heads and other symbols of mortality are found alone on 11 stones in the late seventeenth to early eighteenth centuries. Slightly later but largely overlapping were four stones with both death's heads and cherubs. Cherubs alone, of which there are 74, begin from around 1720. They are most popular around the middle of the century and are gone by 1820. Thus, we can see a short phase of mortality symbols—the end of their popularity coinciding here with the earliest headstones, whereas in most English regions headstones start only after that phase is over. There is then a century over which cherubs are the preferred choice of motif, with this phase ending significantly in the early decades of the nineteenth century.

Major archaeological recording projects of graveyard monuments have been undertaken in both Pembrokeshire and Yorkshire, and data derived from these can be combined to examine both the cherub and then the urn phases of popularity, although people in these areas started erecting external memorials only after the mortality phase was over and after the use of cherubs began elsewhere. Nevertheless, it is clear that cherubs appear on memorials from the early eighteenth century (Figure 2), the first decades for monument erection in these regions. Popularity of the cherubs peaks in the 1820s in these areas, and although monument erection rates continue to increase with an exponential rise in memorial numbers through most of the nineteenth century (Mytum, 2006a), the selection of cherubs drops rapidly.

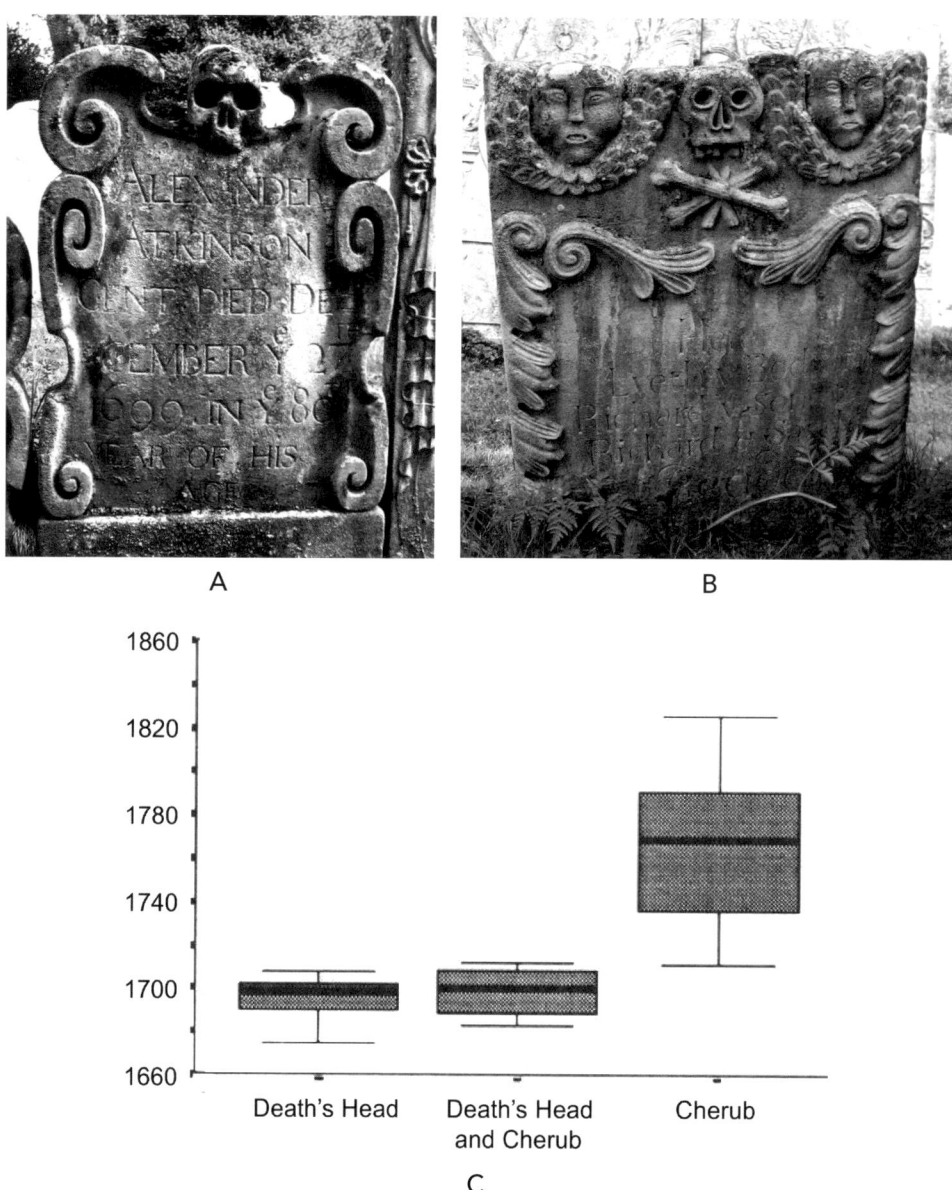

FIGURE 1. Potton graveyard. (Top left) Mortality symbols on headstones. (Top right) Mortality and cherub motifs on headstones. (Bottom) Plot of motif popularity over time. Photos by author.

The selection of urns as a symbol starts in the 1770s but also ends in the 1820s. Some memorials indeed display both cherubs and urns. The use of urns appears to be more regionally specific than that of cherubs, but it forms part of a classical revival tradition that is also indicated over a longer time period on elite internal memorials. There is some indication that nonconformist sects preferentially selected a draped-urn monument in the later nineteenth and early twentieth centuries (Mytum, 2002), but this phenomenon is quite distinct from the late eighteenth- and early nineteenth-century pattern shown here (Figure 3).

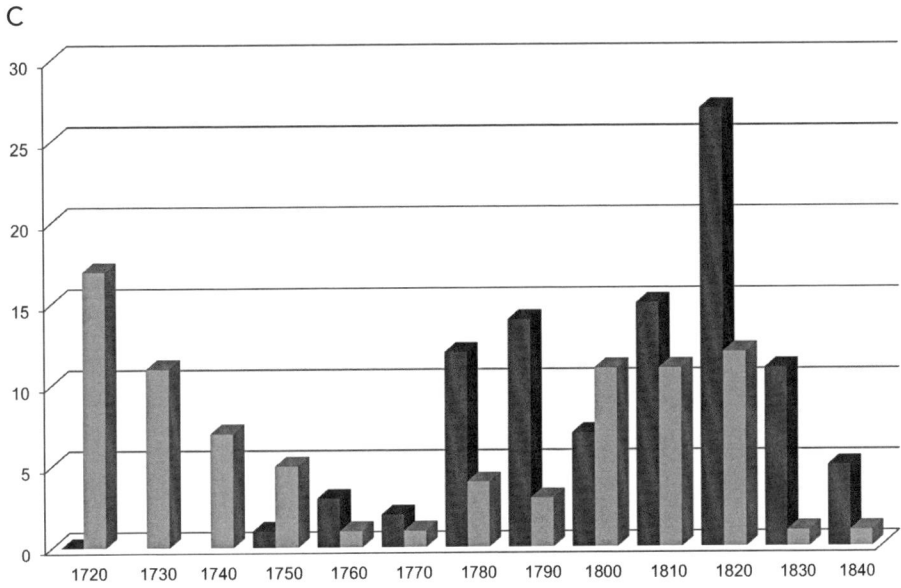

FIGURE 2. Cherubs on headstones. (A) Double cherub motif on headstone. (B) Single cherub motif on headstone. (C) Bar graph showing percentage of artifacts with cherub motif (dark gray, memorials from Yorkshire and Pembrokeshire; light gray, Spitalfields breastplates). Photos by author.

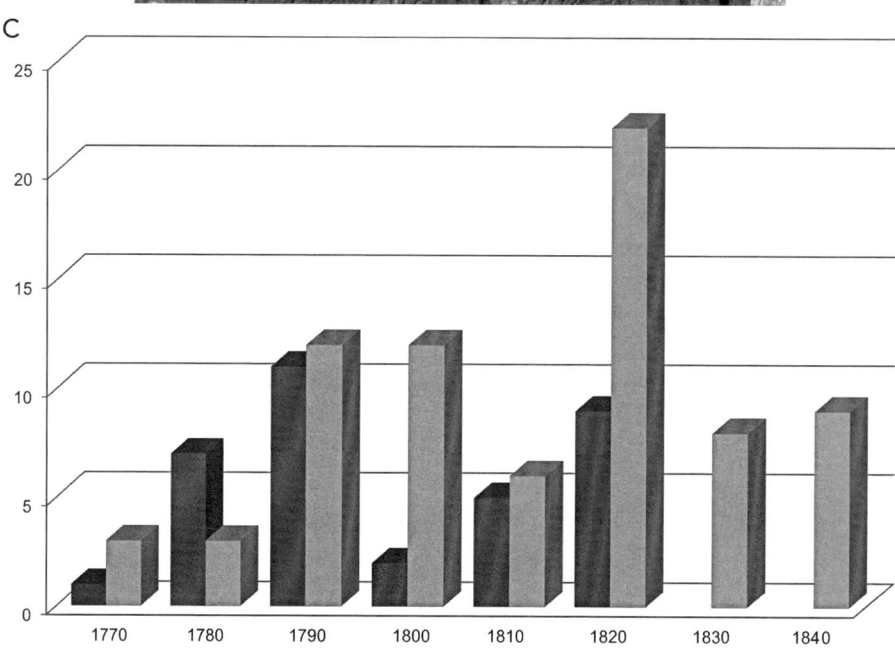

FIGURE 3. (A) Central urn. (B) Central double urn. (C) Bar graph showing numbers of artifacts with urn motif (dark gray, memorials from Yorkshire and Pembrokeshire; light gray, Spitalfields breastplates). Photos by author.

Beginning in the 1840s, the Gothic revival rapidly takes hold as a major style, and it is more uniform nationally. Many stones are still plain, but features such as tracery and trefoils are also found on such monuments, as well as flowers; the IHS symbol (originally chosen as it is the first three letters of Jesus in Greek, but with other later Christian meanings) also becomes very popular later in the century (Figure 4). Many different forms of Gothic revival monuments can be noted, not only in a range of headstone forms but also with low monuments imitating or inspired by medieval grave slabs. In some areas, the Gothic tradition begins earlier; Brooks (1989:21) notes that it becomes increasingly popular on funerary monuments from the 1800s. At St. Mary's, South Stoneham, Hampshire, 8 of the 33 stones erected in the first quarter of the nineteenth century were of Gothic revival type (Hill and Mays, 1987:72), but generally, it is a mid- and later nineteenth-century style that lasted in a simple form into the first decades of the twentieth century.

Trends in the symbols used on the memorials and changes in their form can be identified from the data and match trends in architecture and other categories of material culture. Variation is very great, even though there are regional and some national trends. The inscriptions also change in their typography and content, but those variables are not examined here. It is clear that memorials are vibrant, adaptive, active, and meaningful, as seen through decoration and form.

The Coffin: The London Evidence

The archaeological investigation of the crypt of Christ Church, Spitalfields, in London was a landmark in historical archaeology in Britain and is important here because of the large number of coffins that were recorded (Reeve and Adams, 1993). The published reports do not analyze the complex data regarding the coffins, but it is possible to review in summary the coffins and their fittings. All the designs within each category of lid motifs, breastplates, grips, grip plates, and escutcheons were numbered with the prefix code CCS and have become the standard reference for types recovered elsewhere, and the relevant numbers are used here; originally published on fiche in Reeve and Adams (1993), they are also available online through the Archaeology Data Service.

The coffins recovered from the crypt reflect only a small sample of those buried at Spitalfields; no excavation of earth burials took place, and anyway, later burial and soil conditions would have made the information recovered difficult to compare. As burial in the crypt was significantly more expensive than that in the graveyard, only the wealthier elements of the population are represented. It must be remembered that for the poorest sections of the population, coffin burial was not even the norm in the eighteenth century. However, as most poorer burials, certainly in the period to 1850, were not marked subsequently by inscribed stone memorials, there is a certain equivalence in wealth and status here between crypt burials and graveyard memorials that can make comparison valid.

It is possible that as crypt burial did not give an opportunity for memorialization (except for the most affluent and influential, who could obtain an internal wall memorial), more may have been expended on the coffin than would have been the case with an earth burial with a stone to follow. This supposition is at present impossible to assess, particularly given the consumerist tendencies of the London undertakers so well exposed by Julian Litten (1991).

The coffins were almost certainly almost all made locally; six Spitalfields undertakers were listed in Watkins London Directory of 1852 (Reeve and Adams, 1993), but the fittings

FIGURE 4. Monuments with Gothic revival designs. (A) Cross and angels. (B) IHS monogram and flowers. (C) Chest tomb with tracery. Photos by author.

could have been manufactured in either London or the Birmingham area (Church and Smith, 1966). All the coffins discussed here are of the single-break hexagonal form, and the various inner shells, including lead ones that many of the more elaborate coffins contained, are not relevant to the external appearance and style issues, although they further increased choices and options for expenditure. All the coffins were covered with upholstery, held in place by pins that also provided a decorative scheme. In total 58 different pin designs were recorded, although they can be largely described under a few broad groupings. From later in the nineteenth century onward, cloth covering of coffins was abandoned in favor of polished wood, leading to the provision of a variety of woods and finishes, with an array of designs (Mytum, 2016), some of which included paneling on the sides that mirrored the earlier stud patterns (which probably themselves reflected paneling of wood).

At Spitalfields there are plain designs, with simple lines of pins around the lid and defining panels along the sides. These are the most numerous and start the earliest. Triangles or chevrons are also popular, but they start slightly later and finish earlier, although a decade may not be significant given the numbers involved and the many undated examples (Figure 5). More intricately paneled coffins are also a significant group, and these start distinctly later than the previous two broad groups. In all cases, the theme on the top tends to be followed on the sides, although there are some examples of mixed styles. The patterns at Spitalfields show a considerable variety, in some senses similar to that expressed through variations on a theme with gravestones, but given the small number of main groupings that cover most coffins, there is not the same degree of variety shown for a period of well over 100 years.

Excavations by the Museum of London Archaeology Service at St. Saviour's burial ground, Southwark, which served a poor urban neighborhood, recovered 160 coffined burials, most of which were made from soft woods and were crudely made (Miles, 1993). Only small numbers of these churchyard burials had fittings or were decorated with patterns of studs. Those that were decorated conformed mainly to the plain category or to the triangle design. It is therefore the case that both the coffin fittings and the majority of the memorials under discussion belong to the middle classes, although the more affluent

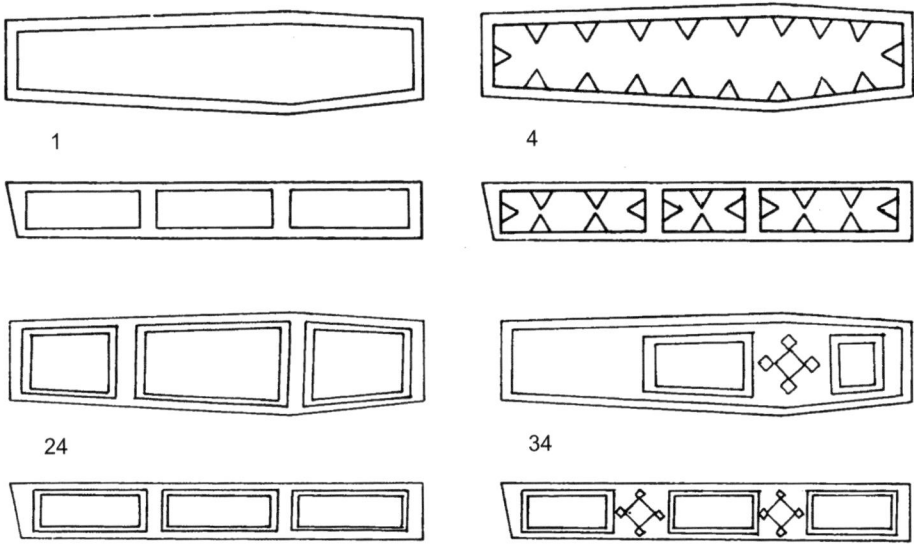

FIGURE 5. Selection of Spitalfields coffin pin designs.

FIGURE 6. Spitalfields coffin fittings with cherubs: grip plate CCS 3, grip CCS 4, and breastplate CCS 13 (not to scale).

working classes could by the end of the period considered here also participate in the mortuary trends discussed here, as evidenced from the mortuary monuments that show an increasing proportion of the population able to invest in mortuary display (Mytum, 2002). Earth burials with more elaborate coffins were recovered from St. George's graveyard in Bloomsbury, London (Boston et al., 2009), as the church served an affluent middle-class clientele and the mortuary traditions reflect this.

Onto the decorated coffins at Spitalfields were also fixed a series of fittings: grips and grip plates (the handles and the plates on which they were fixed) and lid motifs, which were decorative elements of some size and should be distinguished from the escutcheons, which were small but could be used on the lid or sides and in any number. The breastplate could also be highly decorated but also included the inscribed text identifying the deceased; it is sometimes called the depositum plate. When the designs are considered over time, it is clear that cherubs occur on one particular, extremely popular design of grips (CCS 3) from 1729 (Figure 6), and many of the grip plates often also have cherubs, but in a wider range of designs; on the grips the cherubs remained popular much later than on the gravestones, with CCS 3 now known in use as late as 1880. The evidence on the breastplates is slightly less clear because of the vast array of different designs and elements in those designs, but here also the cherubs remained popular in the 1840s and the 1850s; even though there were very few interments by that stage at Spitalfields, cherubs are now known from other London sites and Wolverhampton. In contrast, cherubs are in rapid decline and virtually disappear despite the increase in actual headstones per decade at that stage in the sample graveyard database (Mytum, 2006a). Unfortunately, the end of interments at Spitalfields in the 1850s prevents identification of how long-lived the cherub designs were, as their decline on memorials was by this stage complete, although it may be significant that the single late dated burial from St. Luke's, Islington, of 1880 still carries this design of grip plate (Boyle et al., 2005).

FIGURE 7. Spitalfields coffin fittings with urns: two grip plates, CCS 10 CCS 20, and one lid motif, CCS 2 (not to scale).

Urns first appear on coffin fittings later in the nineteenth century, as would be expected from the memorial evidence (Figure 2C). Unlike the cherub selection pattern, urn choice on breastplates matches more closely that for memorials. Moreover, use of urns is quite restricted; they are rare on the grip plates and are never used on the grips themselves; the cherubs continue in use instead, reflecting a traditionalist attitude to styles. Many of the lid motifs not only include urns but may actually be urn shaped, and the whole item is this motif (Figure 7); unfortunately, only a few of these are dated, but they are all relatively late, few being eighteenth century. Breastplates at Spitalfields include urns on quite a number of examples from 1773, but it is worth noting that all examples of breastplates with urns also have cherubs in the designs, and this combination occurs also on other categories of coffin furniture (Figure 8).

Grips could have other designs—notably flowers and, at a late date, shields. Shields also occur elsewhere within the coffin fitting repertoire, particularly on breastplates, but always at a late date. Flowers also are popular on a wide range of individually rare designs, sometimes as the major motif and in other cases as a minor space filler, so making chronological measurement of their popularity is difficult to define. However, cherubs and urns do not stop being used. An innate conservatism within the provision of coffins and their fittings can be ascribed to the limited stimulation for change by customers wishing for this aspect of the grieving process to be at the edge of fashion. The only addition of note is the shield (Figure 8), and it can be seen as much to hark back to the supposedly ancient armorial elements of the funeral than to new developments in the wider range of material culture. The eighteenth-century burials from St. Saviour's produced a few breastplates

FIGURE 8. Spitalfields coffin fittings with cherubs and urns or cherubs and shield: breastplates CCS8 and CCS 48 and lid motif CCS 24 (not to scale).

decorated with angels and urns (Miles, 1993), and at St. Mary by the Bourne, Marylebone, coffins from the 1830s had breastplates including a shield design. These albeit very small samples support the patterns identified at Spitalfields. Large samples, sadly mainly overlapping chronologically with Spitalfields, were recovered from St. Luke's, Islington (Boyle et al., 2005), and St. George's, Bloomsbury (Boston et al., 2009), and reinforce the stylistic trends seen at Spitalfields (see also Loe and Boston, this volume).

To date, coffin studies are dominated by London assemblages. Material from Penn, Wolverhampton (Loe and Boston, this volume), is contemporary with the London assemblages but does include some later material (Boyle, 2004), and Kellington, North Yorkshire, provides another small sample of later coffins and fittings from outside London (Mytum, 1993), although sadly neither is yet published in detail. These show the increased use of strip edging for the coffins and less elaborate arrangements of the coffin pins, and it would seem that elaborate patterns of coffin pins were never fashionable in the rural north as only simple designs were found in the coffins in an earlier family vault at North Dalton (Mytum, 1988). Because of the limited amount of data, regional traditions within England remain obscure at present.

Patterns and Relationships

The conservatism of the coffin fitting repertoire compared with that of memorials can be demonstrated in two ways. The first is that certain symbols or motifs are applied to coffin furniture at a later date than on memorials, and then some continue in use even though they are no longer being selected for monuments. The second is that particular categories of stud patterns continue to be placed on coffins for far longer periods than the main monument forms are in popular use.

Clear evidence shows that cherubs appear in numbers of coffin fittings only several decades after they first appear on external memorials (Figure 1C). Although the sample size for memorials from the surveyed areas of Pembrokeshire and Yorkshire is small, a significant number of the earliest external memorials in those areas have cherubs, and this trend has already been demonstrated in the case of Potton, Bedfordshire (Figure 1). Moreover, in other areas not yet systematically studied but where a greater number of early eighteenth-century stones survive, such as the Vale of Belvoir in Leicestershire and Nottinghamshire, a high proportion of memorials of the period from the 1720s to the 1740s have cherubs. It is only from the 1750s, however, that coffin fittings have this motif, and although it is documented that a cheaper method of producing stamped designs was developed in 1769 (Church and Smith, 1966:621), which may have encouraged more complex designs from that time onward, some stamped designs using other methods were already in use before that date, and motifs could have been added to earlier metalwork using other techniques if they had been required. Decorated breastplate designs such as CCS 95 and CCS 96 were produced from the 1730s and could easily have included cherubs within their decorative repertoire.

The pattern for the urn motif shows no differentiation between memorials and coffin fittings (Figure 2C), but whereas urns are accompanied by cherubs on breastplates and often on other coffin items (Figure 7), this pairing is far less common on memorials, where new fashions replace old ones rather than merely augmenting an outdated repertoire.

The period of time over which particular designs of coffin fittings remained in use is also striking. Although a few simple gravestone shapes have remained popular over long periods, as is the case also with the simplest designs of coffin fittings, that is not the case with more complex designs of monuments. Even at times with quite small samples, the date range for a coffin fitting design can be as much as four or five decades, and this information can be identified in the tables assembled by Loe and Boston (this volume, Appendix), which include some samples that run into the later nineteenth century and so can identify longer-used forms than is possible from Spitalfields alone. These data, however, are not in a format to be included in the bar charts as they are not defined by decade, and total numbers of coffins in the sample that are dated coffins to the decade need to be known. However, the sheer length of time that some designs remained in use indicates an unusual level of conservatism. Examples of breastplates with elaborate decoration that were in use for at least 50 years include CCS 6 (1783–1852; Figure 7), CCS 27 (1788–1839), CCS 31 ((1759–1821), CCS 46 (1771–1846), CCS 61 (1765–1811), and CCS 67 (1769–1826). Likewise, the most popular grip plate, CCS 3 (Figure 7), has a known use of over 110 years (1768–1880), and one of the most frequently found grips, CCS 4 (Figure 5), has an even longer spread of over 130 years (1743–1880).

Urns also demonstrate a long use-life when assemblages that extend the date range beyond that of Spitalfields are included (Loe and Boston, this volume). Examples include grip plate CCS 14 (1824–1847) and breastplate CCS 6 (1783–1852, Figure 7), but surprisingly few of the 65 designs from Spitalfields incorporated urns at all, indicating resistance to using this motif widely. Moreover, the retention of mortality symbols on coffin furniture well into the nineteenth century, albeit as minor symbols, such as on grip plate CCS 33 (1806–1828) and breastplates CCS 6 (1783–1852; Figure 7) and CCS 43 (1793–1797), when mortality symbols had disappeared from Potton memorials by the 1720s (Figure 1), reveals the tendency to retain what would be anachronistic symbols on mortuary monuments.

The conservatism in coffin furniture cannot be explained by lack of competition in the production of the items as many small manufacturers of a variety of metal items included coffin furniture in their repertoires (Church and Smith, 1966). These manufacturers did not sell direct to consumers, but to undertakers, and it is they who would seem to be the conservative brake on fashion change, whereas the customers interacting with monumental masons actively engaged with changing fashions in memorials. The explanation must partly be therefore the conservatism of undertakers, possibly because of their dominant position in controlling choice while interacting with consumers weakened in their bargaining power by grief. It may be argued that the bereaved preferred traditional designs over innovations in coffin or fitting designs in order that the funeral should appear seemly, but the use of non-matching sets (even grips were not always of the same design) suggests that the undertaker had much discretion and the bereaved were not intimately involved in the detail.

Monuments, chosen later in the grieving process, were not subject to this inequality between consumer and coffin producer. The stages of the grieving process as defined by Kübler-Ross (1969) are denial, anger, bargaining, depression, and acceptance. Although the length of time and, indeed, the linearity of these stages is far from uniform and disputed (Maciejewski et al., 2007) and may indeed have been different in the cultural setting of eighteenth- and nineteenth-century Britain, studies in recent times indicate that at the time of decisions regarding the funeral the bereaved would normally be in one of the first two stages, and most would have largely come to terms with the death by the eighth month (Hardt, 1979) or even by six months (Maciejewski et al., 2007), both well before memorials were normally chosen.

The controlling position of the undertaker was undoubtedly easier to maintain because of the rapid disappearance of the choices made beneath the ground as the deceased was interred. This disappearance meant that the old-fashioned styles could not be compared and commented upon at leisure at a later date or at the time by those not so affected by grief, which would be the case with memorials in their public space of the graveyard or cemetery.

Conclusions

The patterns revealed on coffin fittings and mortuary monuments show a disparity in the rates of stylistic change and in the variety of choices available. In both sets of data there is at one level a bewildering diversity of options in particular elements and their combination. On closer examination, however, there was a steady increase in the significant options available in the case of memorials (with aspects not discussed here including lettering styles and content of inscriptions, including epitaphs, trade and craft motifs, and other revival styles such as Egyptian and Romanesque, all more or less absent from coffin fittings). Moreover, these options were subject to limited periods of popularity. By considering the basic trends of the cherubs and urns, which can be quantified, and noting the different application of the Gothic revival in qualitative terms, it is clear that coffin furniture lagged behind in the popularity of monument styles, on the one hand, and retained older motifs for longer, on the other.

The coffin decorations—with regard to both upholstery pin designs and the various fittings—are open to very little change over long periods of time. Cherubs are dominant, whereas urns and other classical motifs have a subsidiary, although significant, role by the last quarter of the eighteenth century. Once introduced to the repertoire, there was little change in form. Not only were the motifs fixed, but in many features such as the grips, exactly the same design lasted a century. Although this lack of change could be ascribed to the mass-produced nature of these items, one would expect a more varied output and changes to the designs over time even with mass production. Although the upholstery pin designs are quite varied, this differentiation is again over a long period of time, with most being designs subsumed within three broad groupings. The later coffins from other sites do not suggest greater innovation as the nineteenth century proceeds, although the pattern books of the late nineteenth century suggest a significant shift to a different repertoire that then once more is remarkably stable through much of the first part of the twentieth century (Mytum, 2016).

Memorials, on the other hand, show enormous variation at the small-scale level and frequent and widespread changes in the popularity of shapes and design motifs over time. These trends vary from one part of the country to another (as may the use of coffin fittings and upholstery pin designs if we had enough well-preserved and dated examples outside London), but even so there is no doubt that this arena of material culture production and use was much more vibrant than that for coffins.

The explanation for the different degrees of variation and stylistic change in the two sets of mortuary material reflects the different contexts of choice in which the material is selected. In the case of the coffins, the undertakers are dominant, dealing at short notice with relatives in a state of shock, emotionally distracted and unable to greatly influence details of style. The memorial, however, is erected significantly later when the full implications of the death can be considered and the way in which memorialization and commemoration should take place can be contemplated. Here the family of the deceased has an active and powerful role in negotiating the type of memorial required; the supplier is not dominant.

The dynamics that lead to change in a consumer society can thus be seen to be driven by the interaction of consumer and producer; where that interaction is small, as with the coffin where the undertaker is dominant, the dynamics are not stimulated, and change is slow and limited. This controlling resistance to change is assisted by the limited temporal and social visibility of this category of material culture prior to burial. On the other hand, the memorial is chosen later (when the bereaved is in a more resilient state) and for a purpose of public display. In this context consumer choice is more active in creating the demand for stylistic change and a more powerful force in relation to the producer to ensure that a socially, culturally, and emotionally satisfactory monument, appropriate for its time, is erected. The nature and rate of stylistic change within a market economy can thus be shown to require sufficient power not only on the part of the producer but also the consumer, and it is this dynamic that stimulates change.

References

Benes, P. 1977. *The Masks of Orthodoxy: Folk Gravestone Carving in Plymouth County, Massachusetts, 1689–1805*. Amherst: University of Massachusetts Press.

Boston, C., A. Boyle, G. Gill, and A. Witkin. 2009. *Archaeological Recording at St. George's Church, Bloomsbury.* Oxford Archaeology Monograph 8. Oxford: Oxford Archaeological Unit.

Boyle, A. 2004. What Price Compromise? Archaeological Investigations at St. Bartholemew's Church, Penn, Wolverhampton. *Church Archaeology*, 5/6:69–79.

Boyle, A., C. Boston, and A. Witkin. 2005. *The Archaeological Experience at St. Luke's Church, Old Street, Islington.* Oxford: Oxford Archaeology.

Burgess, F. 1963. *English Churchyard Memorials.* London: SPCK.

Brooks, C. 1989. *Mortal Remains: The History and Present State of the Victorian and Edwardian Cemetery.* Exeter: Wheaton Publishers.

Buckham, S., 1999. "'The Men That Worked for England They Have Their Graves at Home.' Consumerist Issues within the Production and Purchase of Gravestones in Victorian York." In *The Familiar Past? Archaeologies of Britain 1550–1950*, ed. S. Tarlow and S. West, pp. 199–214. London: Routledge.

Cannon, A. 1989. The Historical Dimension in Mortuary Expressions of Status and Sentiment. *Current Anthropology* 30(4):437–458.

Church, R. A., and B. M. D. Smith. 1966. Competition and Monopoly in the Coffin Furniture Industry. *Economic History Review,* 19:612–641.

Cunnington, P., and C. Lucas. 1972. *Costume for Births, Marriages and Deaths.* London: Adam and Charles Black.

Curl, J. S. 1972. *The Victorian Celebration of Death.* Newton Abbot, UK: David and Charles.

Deetz, J. F., and E. Dethlefsen. 1967. Death's Head, Cherub, Urn and Willow. *Natural History,* 76(3):29–37.

Hancox, H. 2006. "Coffins and Coffin Furniture." In *St. Martin's Uncovered: Investigations in the Churchyard of St. Martin's-in-the-Bull Ring, Birmingham, 2001*, ed. M. Brickley and S. Buteux, pp. 152–160. Oxford: Oxbow Books.

Hardt, D. V. 1979. An Investigation of the Stages of Bereavement. *Omega Journal of Death and Dying,* 9(3):279–285.

Hill, J. D., and S. Mays. 1987. *Dead Men Don't Tell Tales? A Graveyard Project for Schools.* Archaeology and Education Project Report 5. Southampton, UK: University of Southampton.

Litten, J. 1991. *The English Way of Death: The Common Funeral since 1450.* London: Robert Hale.

Kübler-Ross, E. 1969. *On Death and Dying.* London: Collier-Macmillan.

Maciejewski, P. K., B. Zhang, S. D. Block, and H. G. Prigerson. 2007. An Empirical Examination of the Stage Theory of Grief. *Journal of the American Medical Association,* 297(1):716–723.

Miles, A. 1993. *St. Saviours Burial Ground, Redcross Way London Borough of Southwark: An Archaeological Excavation.* London: Museum of London Archaeology Service.

Morley, J. 1971. *Death, Heaven and the Victorians.* London: Studio Vista.

Mullins, P. R. 2004. Ideology, Power, and Capitalism: The Historical Archaeology of Consumption. In *A Companion to Social Archaeology*, ed. L. Meskell and R. W. Preucel, pp. 195–211. Oxford: Blackwell.

Mytum, H. 1988. A Newly Discovered Burial Vault in North Dalton Church, North Humberside. *Post-Medieval Archaeology,* 22:183–187.

Mytum, H. 1993. Kellington Church. *Current Archaeology* 133:15–17.

Mytum, H. 2000. *Recording and Analysing Graveyards.* Practical Handbook 15. York: Council for British Archaeology.

Mytum, H. 2002. A Comparison of Nineteenth and Twentieth Century Anglican and Nonconformist Memorials in North Pembrokeshire. *Archaeological Journal,* 159:194–241.

Mytum, H. 2004a. Artefact Biography as an Approach to Material Culture: Irish Gravestones as a Material Form of Genealogy. *Journal of Irish Archaeology,* 12/13:111–127.

Mytum, H. 2004b. *Mortuary Monuments and Burial Grounds of the Historic Period.* New York: Kluwer Academic/Plenum.

Mytum, H. 2004c. "Rural Burial and Remembrance: Changing Landscapes of Commemoration." In *The Archaeology of Industrialization,* ed. D. Barker and D. Cranstone, pp. 223–240. Society for Post-Medieval Archaeology Monograph 2 Leeds: Maney Publishing.

Mytum, H. 2006. Popular Attitudes to Memory, the Body, and Social Identity: The Rise of External Commemoration in Britain, Ireland, and New England. *Post-Medieval Archaeology,* 40(1):96–110.

Mytum, H. 2009. "Mortality Symbols in Action: Protestant and Catholic Early 18thcentury West Ulster. "*Historical Archaeology* 42(1):160–182.

Mytum, H. 2016. "The Artefacts of Mortuary Practice: Industrialisation, Choice, and the Individual." In *Nineteenth-Century Material Culture Studies from Britain.*, ed. A. Brooks, pp. 274–304. Lincoln: University of Nebraska Press.

Mytum, H., and K. Chapman. 2006. The Origin of the Graveyard Headstone: Some 17th-Century Examples in Bedfordshire. *Church Archaeology,* 7–9:67–78.

Plume, S. n.d. *Coffins & Coffin Making.* London: Undertakers' Journal.

Portfolio of original anonymous drawings of coffin fittings with prices. Undated but specimen date on drawings is 1826. V&A EL1826. Victoria and Albert Museum, London.

Reeve, J., and M. Adams. 1993. *The Spitalfields Project.* Volume 1: *The Archaeology: Across the Styx.* CBA Research Report 85. York: Council for British Archaeology.

Tarlow, S. 1999. *Bereavement and Commemoration: An Archaeology of Mortality.* Oxford: Blackwell.

Taylor, L. 1983. *Mourning Dress: A Costume and Social History.* London: Allen & Unwin.

Willsher, B. 1985. *Understanding Scottish Graveyards: An Interpretative Approach.* Edinburgh: Council for British Archaeology Scotland.

Material Culture and Classification

CHAPTER 6

Remember Man Thou Art Dust: A Retrospective on North American Hardware Traditions

Michael Trinkley and Debi Hacker

In 1984 an opportunity arose to examine a collection of late nineteenth-century coffin hardware and trimmings long forgotten at the A. L. Calhoun General Store in Clio, South Carolina, coupled with some early to mid-twentieth-century hardware and catalogs at the Sumter Casket Company in Sumter, South Carolina. Following these discoveries, catalogs ranging in dates from 1865 through 1966 were examined during a brief visit to the National Foundation of Funeral Service in Evanston, Illinois. Our resulting publication was largely descriptive, although we did attempt to relate the collections to the overall economic patterns of rural South Carolina (Hacker-Norton and Trinkley, 1984).

The Calhoun General Store collection evidenced some "stylistic lag," as we called it, containing examples of hardware that predated the store's opening in 1896 by perhaps as much as two decades. We acknowledged that it was impossible to determine if the out-of-style items in the general store were the result of Calhoun's idiosyncratic buying habits or if the antiquated styles were the result of the rural, impoverished nature of Marion County. We found it difficult, although we thought not impossible, to quantify the prevailing cultural and economic biases.

We suggested that there was a shift from the swing bail to the two-lug short bar handles around 1880 and that by 1912 the extension handles were gaining popularity. We offered similar temporal suggestions for studs, escutcheons, thumbscrews, caplifters, hinges, and related items. We also, somewhat naively, attempted to document costs and relate those costs to social status, noting that coffin hardware might reflect either "real" or "apparent" status. Distinguishing between the two might prove difficult.

Finally, remembering that our study was prepared over 30 years ago, we were also able to identify artifacts that colleagues of that time were listing as unknown, such as caplifters. And we were able to explain the "plaques" found in the thoracic region of burial. We also suggested that a more thorough knowledge of coffin hardware might help archaeologists charged with burial removals.

We were criticized—justifiably so—for overreaching, for attempting to do too much with too little. For example, Edward Bell (1987:16, 1990:55) discounts efforts to derive economic data from coffin hardware, suggesting that the "complexity of behaviors, beliefs, and material culture" are too great. Even Bell, however, comments that his Uxbridge almshouse coffin hardware was "unremarkable" and that the "minimal nature of the burials is a clear testimony of the status accorded the poor" (Bell, 1987:151), indicating some socioeconomic observations based on hardware may be possible.

A number of researchers have expanded on, refined, and vastly improved our original research. Mentioning just a very few—and intending no slight to those not included—Pat Garrow used his research at the Nancy Creek Primitive Baptist Church in Georgia to assign broad dates: swing bails were used from the 1870s to shortly after 1900; short bar handles begin replacing swing bails about 1900, and extended bar handles were noted to be a late addition (Garrow, 1987:16–17). Barbara Little and her colleagues suggested that mortuary display might be used to support a desired status, especially in the postbellum when the South's social structure was destabilized (Little et al., 1992:418–419). But perhaps most interesting is the exceptional work conducted by James Davidson (1999a, 1999b) at the Freedman's Cemetery in Dallas, Texas. Davidson went beyond simple handle styles to examine the specific embossed design motifs in order to provide very specific dating of over 1,000 burials. Using hardware catalogs and patent information, he was able to match perhaps 75% of the recovered hardware to a specific manufacturer, an incredible feat. This work was expanded and refined by Davidson (2004) in his dissertation. He also calculates wholesale costs of the hardware and coffin, using the data to document "wealth expended on a mortuary display within the Beautification of Death movement." Although a laborious process, he demonstrates that hardware can be used successfully to document change over time and offer insights on the display of wealth.

Our own research has gone down very similar paths, with very similar results. We have not focused on design motifs—a process that, however, successful is unlikely to be widely duplicated simply because of the extraordinary labor involved. We believe that the simple form of the hardware, harkening back to our original study and Pat Garrow's projections, can be used to provide a broad temporal framework. Although offering far less precision than design motifs, the form can still help to broadly date collections and burials, providing immediate assistance to coroners, medical examiners, and archaeologists faced with small collections and limited budgets.

Coffin Hardware Catalogs and a Dating Framework

When a series of 15 coffin hardware catalogs (Table 1), dating from 1875 to 1952, are examined and the handles are classified as ring bail/other (i.e., stationary), swing bail, short bar, or extension bar (Figure 1), we can see that there are relatively well defined periods of commercial availability (Figure 2A). Ring bails likely predate the mid-nineteenth century and may reflect a late eighteenth- and early nineteenth-century style from England. Swing bails, however, are a dominant style to about 1880, although clearly there were companies that continued to offer—even rely—on the public's acceptance of this style into the early twentieth century (confusing this, however, is the late use of this style on infant coffins). Although short bar handles were offered by at least 1869, they really do not appear to have made much of an impression on wholesalers until about 1880 (replacing swing bails). Extension handles were offered by a few companies as early as 1877–1880 but do not appear to have made much of an impact and disappeared from catalogs for about 20 years until reintroduced in the first decade of the twentieth century. Even then, however, they do not appear to have been particularly

Table 1. Coffin catalogs used to provide data for Figure 1.

Date	Company	Location
1875	Cincinnati Coffin Co.	Cincinnati, Ohio
1881	Cincinnati Coffin Co.	Cincinnati, Ohio
1882	Cleveland Burial Case Co.	Cleveland, Ohio
1900	Peerman Burial Co.	Richmond, Virginia
1903	National Casket Co.	Albany, New York
1911	Milwaukee Casket Co.	Milwaukee, Wisconsin
1913	National Casket Co.	Albany, New York
1916	United States Casket Co.	Scottsdale, Pennsylvania
1918	Atlantic Coffin & Casket Co.	Rose Hill, North Carolina
1922	Des Moines Casket Co.	Des Moines, Iowa
1927	Bristol Manufacturing Co.	Bristol, Vermont
1930	National Casket Co.	Albany, New York
1934	John Marsellus Casket Co.	Syracuse, New York
1936	Boyertown Burial Casket Co.	Boyertown, Pennsylvania
1952	Boyertown Burial Casket Co.	Boyertown, Pennsylvania

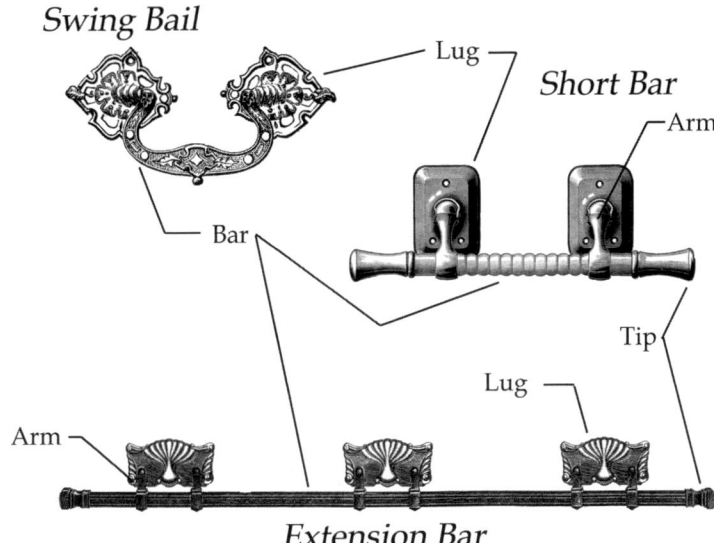

FIGURE 1. Handle types from 15 coffin hardware catalogs, dating from 1875 to 1952.

popular until about 1920. These results are shown graphically as a more conventional seriation in Figure 2B.

Although these data can certainly be refined, we believe that they offer important general information to a broad range of researchers who simply do not have the collections or time to conduct more exhaustive research. Of course, wholesale availability does not necessarily translate into popular acceptance, especially in areas where there may be considerable conservativism. This potential divergence between catalog repertoire and consumer choice may be illustrated by the three McClung samples from 1891, ca. 1905,

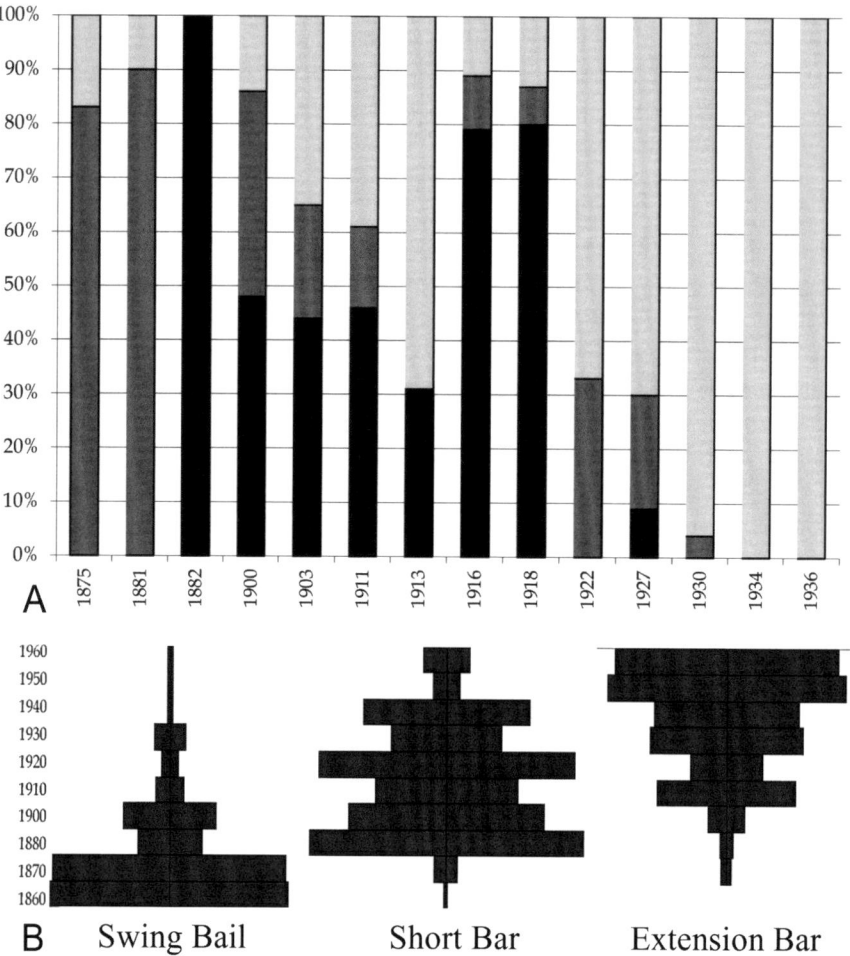

FIGURE 2. (A) Periods of commercial availability of handle types and periods of popularity of no coffin handles; black = short bar, mid-gray = no handles, pale gray = extension bar. (B) Seriation of coffin handles.

and ca. 1912. In each case the catalog illustrates styles that, judging by other catalogs, have already waned in popularity. What is not clear, of course, is why these styles were being offered by McClung and whether they were actually being purchased and used by the public.

Another way of examining the data is to look at widely available coffin catalogs to determine the hardware styles used by the manufacturers. Of course, it is important to realize that many coffins were being offered to undertakers without any trimmings, allowing the shell to be purchased separately, and these are frequently illustrated in the catalogs. Moreover, although it seems reasonable that manufacturers would illustrate their wares with the most modern trimmings, this fashionability was perhaps tempered by their equal desire to provide the public with what was popular, regardless of how recently introduced the item might be.

In spite of a substantial collection of coffin catalogs many could not be used since they lacked reliable dating (being identified only as a number or letter), leaving a very small sample of only 15 that we could incorporate in this study. These suggest that during the nineteenth century coffin manufacturers tended to offer their wares without hardware, allowing the local undertaker or furniture dealer to trim the coffin directly. With just a couple of anomalies, by the twentieth century coffin manufacturers began to at least illustrate their wares with "tasteful" trimmings (some casket manufacturers even began producing their own hardware). And again, excepting two catalogs, the prevalence of extension bar handles rises dramatically; by the 1930s they are almost the only style being illustrated.

Thus, although the hardware catalogs continued to offer the short bar (and even swing bails) into the last half of the twentieth century, the coffin manufacturers themselves were rapidly focusing on the new and improved hardware to sell their products.

Funeral Home Records

Another source of data is funeral home records. Davidson was very fortunate to have a variety of detailed records at his disposal in Dallas. Most of us are not so fortunate, and these records are incredibly scarce. For South Carolina we have been able to identify only three sets—those of the J. M. Connelley Funeral Home in Charleston, South Carolina, spanning 1889–1897; those of the McDougald Funeral Home in Anderson, South Carolina, spanning 1934–1952; and those of the J. W. McCormick Funeral Home in Columbia, South Carolina, spanning 1906–1915 (Trinkley and Hacker, 2004). Unfortunately, the Connelley and McDougald records were transcribed only for their genealogical information and contain no data on burial costs or items purchased. The McCormick records are more fully transcribed and the 10-year period includes 2,101 individuals once those from the South Carolina Penitentiary and South Carolina State Hospital for the Insane are both removed. Only 44 (just 2%) of these are identified as African Americans, so we will discount these as well. That leaves 1,829 burials with costs. Of these, only seven have any details concerning handle hardware, and they are entirely descriptive. None provide style numbers, and only two provide pricing. The only other hardware mentioned is a single plate, with engraving, priced at $1.00.

Thus, the South Carolina data do not offer nearly the precision that Davidson had at the Freedman's Cemetery in Dallas. Nevertheless, we can gain some insights. For example, the average coffin cost was $64.23 (equivalent to $1,578 in 2017, and the mode was $70.00 ($1,720 in 2017), with a range from $4.00 to $600.00 ($98 to $14,745 in 2017). These prices take on greater meaning when we realize that the average family income in 1914 was only about $627 ($15,409 in 2017). The distribution of coffin purchases by price provides a bell curve suggesting a demand curve in simple microeconomics, but with many intervening prices that do not cleanly fit (Figure 3A), although a different graphic presentation is more revealing, helping to identify McCormick Funeral Home's four seemingly well-defined price points, each corresponding to relatively high demand (Figure 3B). Of the coffins priced at $20 or under (332 in all), 29 were for stillborns, with coffins ranging from $5.00 to $15.00 (average was $8.29, and the modal price was $8.00). An additional 94 were for children (on the basis of sizes under 5/0 and/or other features). Thus, of the 332 coffins in the least expensive range, 221 (67%) were for infants and children, accounting for the inexpensive price points. Only 50 (15%) can definitively be considered adult (on the basis of size).

The proportion of children's coffins displayed by price range reveals that more than $45 was rarely spent on a child's coffin and that there are two clearly defined price point ranges: $20 or less and $31–$35 (Figure 4A). Mortality rates for South Carolina children during this time period are difficult to find, but we do know that 37% of the deaths in

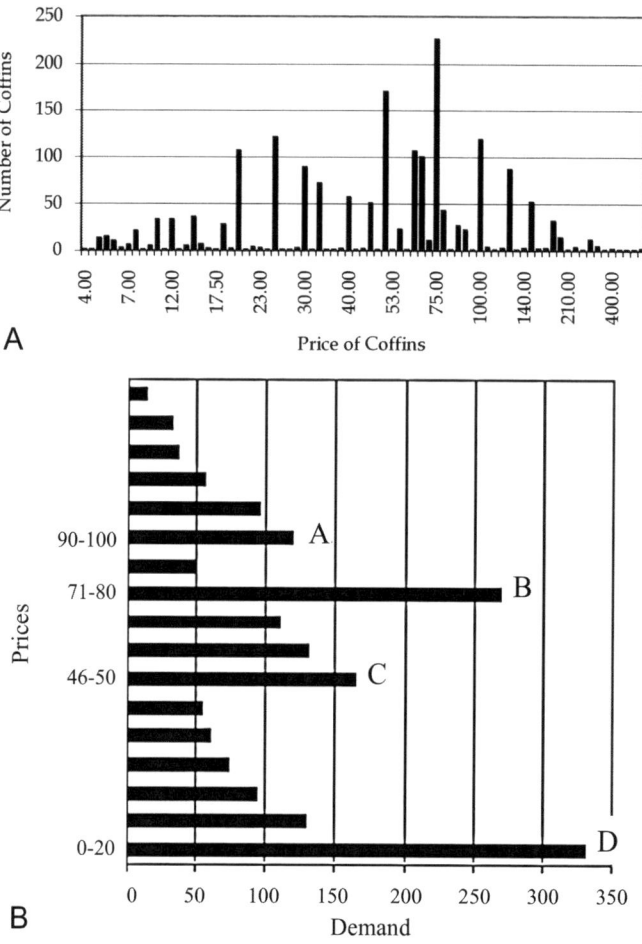

FIGURE 3. Coffin costs based on catalog data. (A) Frequency of coffin choices at various prices. (B) Demand for coffins indicating the four price points (A–D) defined by the McCormick Funeral Home.

Charleston (the only reporting city in South Carolina) were of children under the age of 15. The high child mortality rate (estimated at a rate of about 110; Haines, 1998) may have been reason enough to limit the cost of children's coffins. The costs were also limited by size, construction, and materials used.

Although the McCormick data allow us to sample socioeconomic issues only among whites, we note that the average cost of coffins for males (using a random sample of 50) is $88, compared to $70 for females. This is not a dramatic difference; moreover, the standard deviation for the coffin prices for males is $73, whereas for females it is only $44, perhaps suggestive of much greater status variation among Columbia area males than females. Differences in coffin styles are far less noticeable. Black coffins were used only for men, and white coffins were not quite twice as common among females. Silver or silver-gray coffins were used nearly equally for both males and females. And although pink was used only for females, plushette was found to be used only for males.

The McCormick records provide a few other details. For example, of the 1,829 itemized coffins, 1,520 (83%) included boxes, suggesting that, at least in this market, archaeologists can expect to find evidence of boxes in the burials. In contrast, only 158 (3%) were

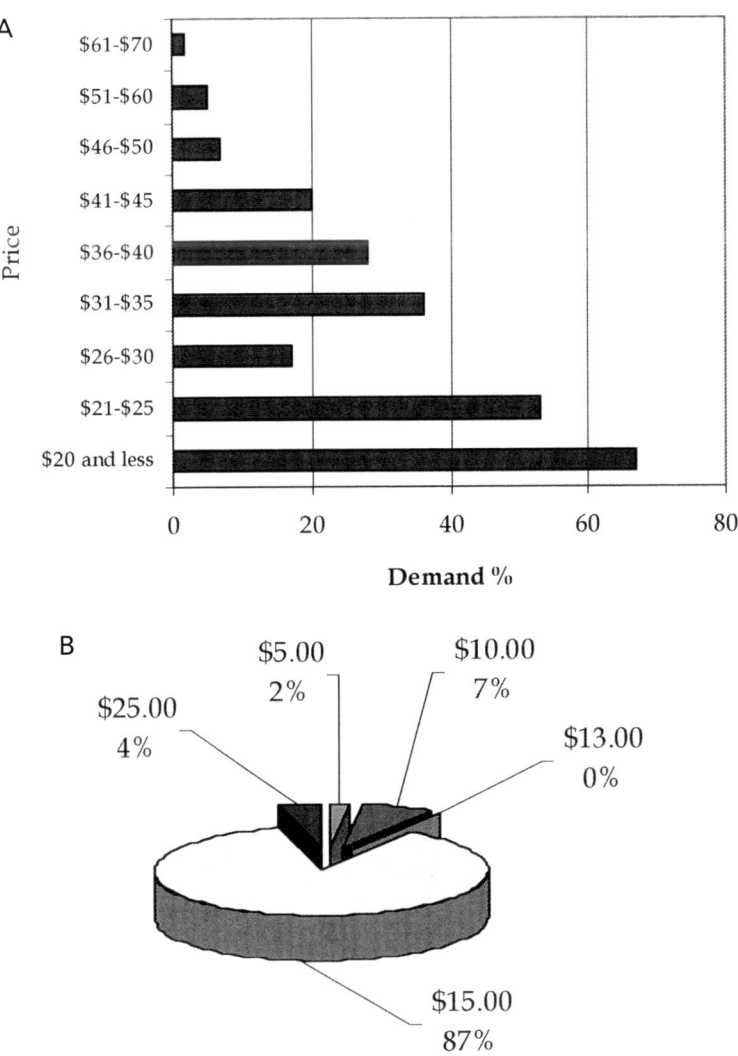

FIGURE 4. McCormick Funeral Home price data. (A) Proportion of children's coffins by price range. (B) Body "preparation" costs.

sold with vaults. Of those sold with vaults, only nine (6%) were also sold with a box. This difference suggests that boxes were seen as a substitute, albeit a poor one, for a vault. This is borne out by coffin costs. The average cost with vaults was $138.28, compared to an average cost of only $57.27 without a vault.

Where the vault material was identified, it was consistently slate, ranging in price from $30 to $50 (although $50 was the norm). Where the material was not identified, costs ranged from $5 to $50. Vaults in the $30 to $50 range may also have been slate and, if so, only two (costing $5 and $10) are left. These prices are so low that they may refer only to "lined graves"—graves that had boards placed in them to hold back the soil and create a temporary vault. There are several brick vaults mentioned but never with a burial where the coffin cost was identified. Where they occur, costs range from $25 to $40 and likely represent laid brick linings. These prices seem to be generally in keeping with the few cemetery publications where such work is listed.

One last observation is worth making before leaving the McCormick Funeral Home data. During this period only 729 of the bodies with identified coffin prices were "preserved" or embalmed (about 40%). The conventional wisdom (see, for example, Laderman, 2003:6) is that acceptance of embalming spread rapidly—a view that is certainly not supported by the McCormick data. Although dating at least to the Civil War, five decades later just two-fifths of McCormick's clientele were selecting this service. It may be that some of this resistance (if there was resistance, as opposed to simple poverty that precluded widespread acceptance) was founded on the Protestant belief that embalming mutilated the body and rendered it adulterated, potentially affecting its ultimate resurrection (Habenstein and Lamers, 1955:336; Laderman, 1996:53–54). Regardless, the highest embalming cost was $25, paid for 30 individuals (five of whom were being shipped). With an average cost of $14.87, the vast majority of the 729 bodies received "preparation" costing only $15 (Figure 4B). Where embalming was paid for, the average coffin cost was $91.03, nearly 1.5 times the overall average coffin cost. Moreover, 102 of the 158 (64%) vaults are found with embalmed remains, suggesting a strong correlation.

These data may be compared to very similar records we have identified from Pennsylvania, dating between 1910 and 1918. Although the sample consists of only 81 burials with priced coffins, the average coffin price was $59.92, with a modal value of $65 and a range from $5 to $165. These figures are very similar to McCormick's data, although we do not have the high-end coffins. Of the 81 coffins, 24 were also sold with boxes (30%), far less than for McCormick.

Nineteen of the coffins were sold with vaults. Seven (37%) were clearly identified as planks or lining, with costs of $1 to $10. Eight were slate, ranging in price from $26 to $36. One, for only $40, was steel. One was brick ($3.75), and one was stone. As with McCormick, the vaults are found with more expensive coffins (the average coffin price with a vault was $81.53; without was $53.75).

Embalming was performed on 57 of the bodies (70% of the total), presenting starkly different data than Columbia. In addition, the cost varied from $2 to $10, with a mean of $5.64, reflecting only a third the cost of McCormick. Embalming, however, was still associated with higher prices paid for coffins (average of $70.97 with embalming but only $37.81 without).

These differences suggest that we may see significant regional variation. Of course, this was observed by Quincy Dowd in his 1921 examination of the funeral industry. Speaking of arterial injection, he noted, "in the South it is little practiced as yet, not at all with colored people" (Dowd, 1921:52).

Coffin Hardware Costs

Turning briefly to the issue of hardware costs, Davidson has been able, with enough catalogs and adequate time, to identify specific hardware and assign specific wholesale costs, allowing very accurate costs to be determined for individual burials. It seems regrettably unlikely that this approach will be widely adapted, especially for small, marginally funded projects. But is there an alternative? We have examined hardware costs for swing bail, short bar, and extension handles, using both period costs and costs standardized to 2005 dollars.

The period costs for swing bail and short bar handles increase only modestly over the nearly 100-year period (Figure 5), and if the period costs are converted to 2005 dollars, the trend is almost stagnant. Of course, there are differences between manufacturers

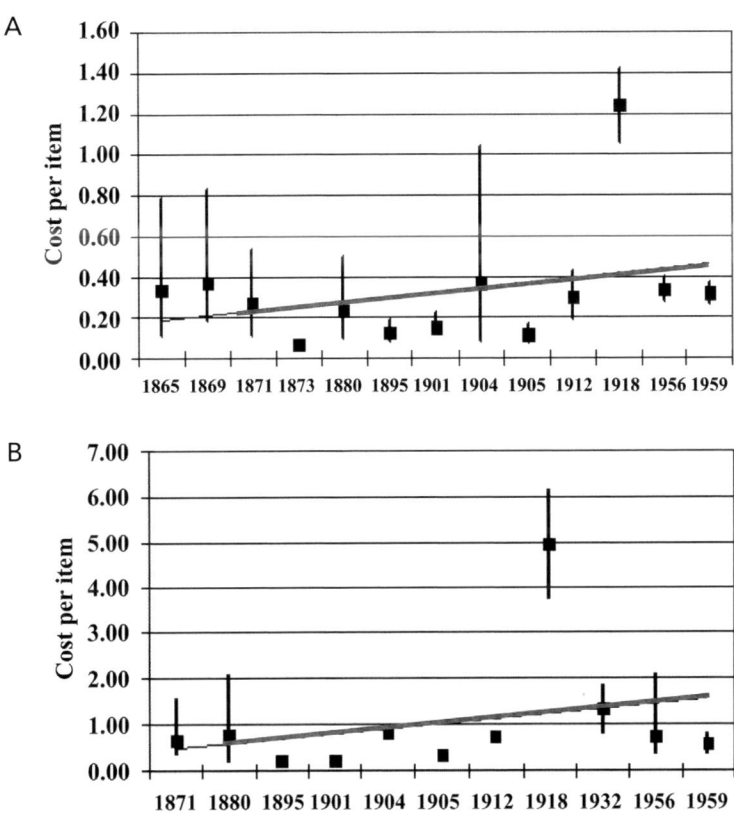

FIGURE 5. Coffin hardware prices, 1865–1959, based on catalogs. (A) Swing bail handle. (B) Short bar handle.

and wholesalers. For example, for whatever reason the 1918 prices by Simmons appear significantly out of line, although we have no close comparisons, and this may reflect the 18% inflation rate caused by World War I. If the catalog was issued late in the year (post-September, perhaps), then the death rate from the influenza pandemic may also have played a role. In addition, many of the distributors offered a wide range in styles and finishes, resulting in the ability to distinguish individual coffins through the use of more expensive hardware, significantly above the overall cost average. This opportunity to elaborate, at least for swing bails, appears to decline into the twentieth century.

Extension bar costs suggest a very different pricing mechanism. Using period costs, the trend prices appear clearly stagnant, whereas the 2005 prices reveal that the costs actually declined as the new style became more firmly entrenched. There remained throughout, however, considerable price variation that allowed families to upgrade the hardware. Curiously, coffin plates exhibit the most noticeable increase in price, whether period or standardized 2005 prices are examined. In addition, plates offered the greatest opportunity for either savings or display by families (Figure 6).

These data, although preliminary and clearly needing larger samples, suggest several conclusions and support the observations of Bryan's 1917 handbook for funeral directors in which he outlines how to match the value of hardware to that of the casket. Arguing that the funeral director is "justly entitled to liberal compensation" and a "legitimate profit," he provided a series of tables that sought to outline the appropriate value of hardware

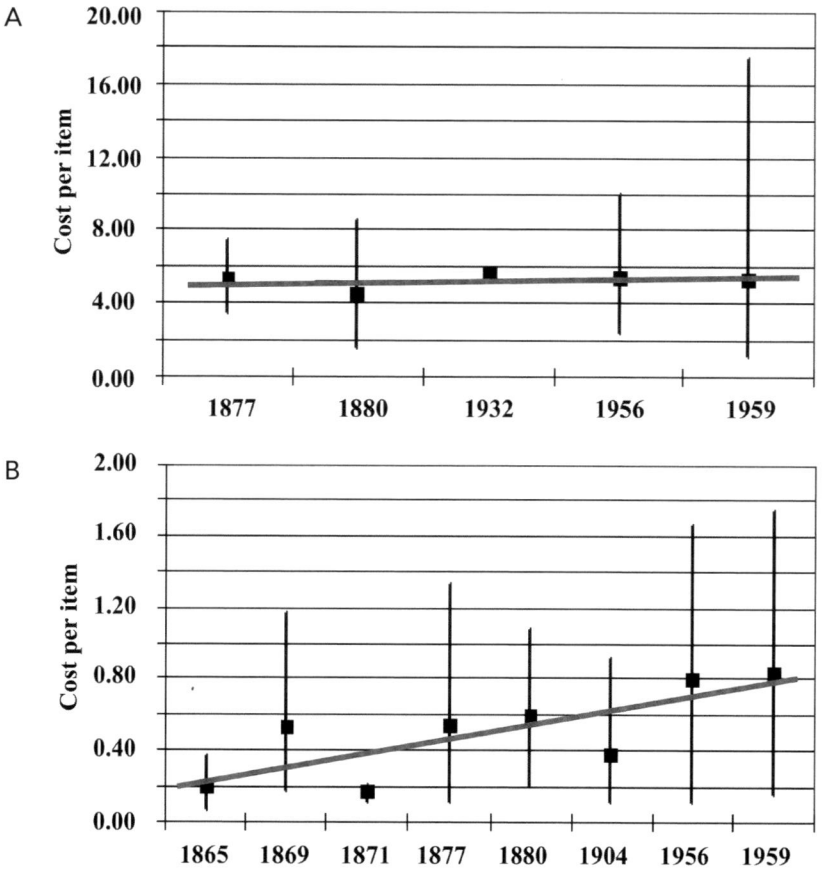

FIGURE 6. Coffin hardware prices, 1865–1959, based on catalogs. (A) Extension bar. (B) Coffin plates.

associated with each coffin. He also offered a series of pithy adages, such as "cheap handles to carry a heavy body is poor economy," "your customer will be better pleased to have paid more and had the casket well-trimmed," "proper trimming is more essential for appropriateness than the casket," and "many of the wealthiest class want the least pretentious yet want the Best" (Bryan, 1917). Clearly, the hardware manufacturers were heeding this advice and providing undertakers with a wide variety and cost. This variability in product and price suggests that the level of detail in analysis espoused by Davidson is virtually essential. Very simple analyses will offer only the most basic information. For example, swing bails are typically less costly than short bars, and short bars in turn are less costly than extension handles. Further, a casket with four handles will likely have less hardware costs than a casket with six similar handles. Thus, very simple economic observations may be possible, but they may offer relatively little assistance. Of course, even Davidson's careful attention to design motifs may not provide assistance to determine if the handle tips were silver chased or gold tipped, if bars were crystallized or oxidized, or if they were nontarnish copper-brass or had a top plated finish, all of which could result in a substantial difference in wholesale cost.

These data suggest that coffin plates may be among the most cost sensitive items, although, again, variation is considerable and analysis must go beyond simple pattern identification. What is interesting to us is how—or perhaps why—these plates not only lasted so long but also had such variability. Even Bryan (1917) observed that "to inform your patrons that the price (on a high-grade casket) includes a solid silver plate stamps value on the entire outfit." Perhaps we are seeing the height of luxury?

Throughout all of these discussions it is important to remember that we—like Davidson—are using wholesale costs, which may have little resemblance to the price actually paid by the consumer. Dowd notes that retail prices on caskets could be 5–10 times the wholesale cost (Dowd, 1921:15). In addition, he observes that a large proportion of the undertakers carried little or no stock, virtually eliminating their overhead costs. Certainly, both coffin and hardware wholesalers promoted this approach through liberal terms and quick shipments. Our own examination of the McCormick Funeral Home records reveals markups beginning at 150% on the wholesale cost. Stillborn coffins that manufacturers sold for 75¢ to 90¢, McCormick was selling for $7 to $10. Coffins being sold for $3.75 to $5.25, McCormick was retailing for $20 to $25. Even considering freight, these prices represent a very hefty profit margin on death.

Thus, when we examine coffin hardware from a burial, wholesale costs may provide a standardized approach, but they fail to truly represent the cost to the consumer or the family's public display to the community.

Conclusions

Our retrospective reveals the value and potential of the research. Although not prepared to dismiss the potential for this research to provide significant insight into status and economic display, we are also more cautious in the mechanics and approach. We hope that there will be a renewed interest in—at the very least—more carefully documenting the coffins and hardware resulting from relocation projects.

References

Bell, E. L. 1987. The Historical Archaeology of Mortuary Behavior at a Nineteenth-Century Almshouse Burial Ground. M.A. thesis, Boston University, Boston.

Bell, E. L. 1990. The Historical Archaeology of Mortuary Behavior: Coffin Hardware from Uxbridge, Massachusetts. *Historical Archaeology*, 24(3):54–78.

Bryan, H. C. 1917. *The Funeral Director's Guide*. Pittsburg: McMillen Printing.

Davidson, J. M. 1999a. Freeman's Cemetery (1869–1907): A Chronological Reconstruction of an Excavated African-American Burial Ground, Dallas, Texas. M.A. diss., University of Arkansas, Fayetteville.

Davidson, J. M. 1999b. Freeman's Cemetery (1869–1907): Establishing a Chronology for Exhumed Burials from an African-American Burial Ground, Dallas, Texas. *African Diaspora Archaeology Newsletter*, 6(4): Article 5. http://scholarworks.umass.edu/adan/vol6/iss4/5 (accessed 28 November 2017).

Davidson, J. M. 2004. Mediating Race and Class through the Death Experience: Power Relations and Resistance Strategies of an African-American Community, Dallas, Texas (1869–1907). Ph.D. diss., University of Texas at Austin, Austin.

Dowd, Q. L. 1921. *Funeral Management and Costs: A World-Survey of Burial and Cremation*. Chicago: University of Chicago Press.

Garrow, P. 1987. "A Preliminary Seriation of Coffin Hardware Forms in Late Nineteenth and Early Twentieth Century Georgia." Paper presented at the Annual Meeting of the Eastern States Archaeological Federation, Charleston, S.C.

Habenstein, R. W., and W. M. Lamers. 1955. *The History of American Funeral Directing*. Milwaukee, Wis.: Bulfin Printers.

Hacker-Norton, D., and M. Trinkley. 1984. *Remember Man Thou Art Dust: Coffin Hardware of the Early Twentieth Century*. Research Series 2. Columbia, S.C.: Chicora Foundation.

Haines, M. R. 1998. "The Relationship between Infant and Child Mortality and Fertility: Some Historical and Contemporary Evidence for the United States." In *From Death to Birth: Mortality Decline and Reproductive Change*, ed. M. R. Montgomery and B. Cohen, pp. 227–253. Washington, D.C.: National Academy Press.

Laderman, G. 1996. *The Sacred Remains: American Attitudes toward Death, 1799–1883*. New Haven: Yale University Press.

Laderman, G. 2003. *Rest in Peace: A Cultural History of Death and the Funeral Home in Twentieth Century America*. New York: Oxford University Press.

Little, B. J., K. M. Lamphear, and D. W. Owsley. 1990. Mortuary Display and Status in a Nineteenth-Century Anglo-American Cemetery in Manassas, Virginia. *American Antiquity*, 57:397–418.

Trinkley, M., and D. Hacker. 2004. *McCormick Funeral Records, Vols. 2–8, April 1906 through June 1915*. Research Contribution 395. Columbia, S.C.: Chicora Foundation.

CHAPTER 7

A Preliminary Seriation of Coffin Hardware in Nineteenth- and Twentieth-Century Georgia: Thirty Years Later

Patrick H. Garrow

Thirty years ago I proposed a preliminary seriation of coffin hardware types found in historic cemeteries in Georgia (Garrow, 1987). That seriation was based on archaeological investigations and observations from two cemeteries, one from the metropolitan Atlanta area (Garrow et al., 1985) and the other from a rural cemetery in Talbot County, Georgia (Garrow and Symes, 1987). Both cemeteries were studied by what was then Garrow & Associates. I subsequently studied two large cemeteries and use them in this paper to update the 1987 seriation.

The Study Cemeteries

Hopewell Baptist Church was investigated from 1988 to 1991. That cemetery was located in an Atlanta suburb, where 220 graves were moved as the result of civil litigation. An overview of the investigations was presented at the 1992 Society for Historical Archaeology in Jamaica (Garrow, 1992), but detailed grave data were available only in the unpublished field forms prior to the current paper. The Edwards-Attaway cemetery was investigated in 1994, and data from the 63 graves moved from that cemetery have been reported in a limited-distribution contract report (Garrow and Jones, 1996).

The metropolitan Atlanta cemetery was a portion of the Nancy Creek Primitive Baptist Church Cemetery that faced adverse impacts from construction of a proposed Metropolitan Atlanta Rapid Transit Authority rail line. Fifty-six graves were investigated under that project, of which 16 could be identified by individual on the basis of inscribed headstones or other data. The graves of all of the identified individuals were fully removed by a burial removal company, with no archaeological or forensic study. Scaled drawings of selected hardware from those graves were prepared, however, and notes were taken concerning the contents of the graves. Nine of the remaining 40 graves were removed through archaeological excavation and were fully recorded, whereas limited study was allowed on the 31 graves not included in the archaeological sample (Garrow et al., 1985:1). The grave removal protocols employed at the Nancy Creek Cemetery were certainly less than ideal but were dictated by the project memorandum of agreement (MOA) and the research design prepared to address the MOA (Symes and Garrow, 1984).

The rural Talbot County cemetery was excavated as a result of emergency discovery during construction of a state park. That cemetery contained six surviving graves that had been almost completely graded away. Only the coffin chambers remained of the graves when excavation began. Two of the six graves had been almost completely removed prior to arrival of the excavation team, and one of those was too badly damaged to include in the seriation study sample. The graves were thoroughly excavated and recorded, and the physical remains and artifacts were returned to the laboratory for study (Garrow and Symes, 1987).

Dating Coffin Hardware Forms: 1987

Seven of the graves from the Nancy Creek cemetery could not be used in the seriation study. One of the dated graves contained a sealed concrete vault that could not be opened. One grave yielded a human bone, but no coffin outline was visible, and there was no associated hardware. Another grave was largely destroyed by the backhoe before it was identified, and four other graves could not even be positively identified as graves. The remaining 49 graves from Nancy Creek and the 5 useable graves from Talbot County spanned a time range from the 1850s to 1979. The 15 graves identified by individual at Nancy Creek where the coffins and hardware could be viewed provided crucial dating keys for the coffin forms and hardware those graves contained (Garrow et al., 1985).

Little published information was available about coffin hardware at the time of the Nancy Creek and Talbot County cemetery studies. Fortunately, the excellent studies by Hacker-Norton and Trinkley (1984) and Trinkley and Hacker-Norton (1984) were available and provided the terminology for the coffin hardware forms discussed in the 1987 seriation article.

The seriation scheme proposed in the 1987 article was based primarily on changes in coffin handle shapes over time. Three basic handle types were described, and date ranges were proposed for each. The three described handle types, in the order of their historic appearance, were bail, short bar, and extended bar types.

Bail handles (Figure 1), originally defined by Hacker-Norton and Trinkley (1984:9), were described as "composed of two lugs connected by bail swing arms and a bar" (Garrow, 1987:29). The bail handles included in the study sample were made of white metal and in some instances had been silver plated.

The second type of handle defined in the 1987 seriation was termed the "short bar" type (Figure 2). That type, also originally defined by Hacker-Norton and Trinkley (1984:9), was composed of "two lugs, each with a swing or fixed arm, connected by a bar that contains metal tips added at each end" (Garrow, 1987:29). The most common form of short bar handle had white-metal lugs, swing arms, and finials, with a bar made of wood clad with rolled sheet zinc and finished with a fabric such as velvet. Short bar handles made entirely of white metal were found, but those appear to have been much less common than those with the zinc-clad wood and fabric bars. Short bar handles referred to as white-metal short bars in this paper refer to the early types made entirely of white metal or made with white-metal lugs, swing arms, and finials.

The third coffin handle type defined in the 1987 article was the extended bar type (Figure 3). This type of handle was made of iron in the single case from Nancy Creek.

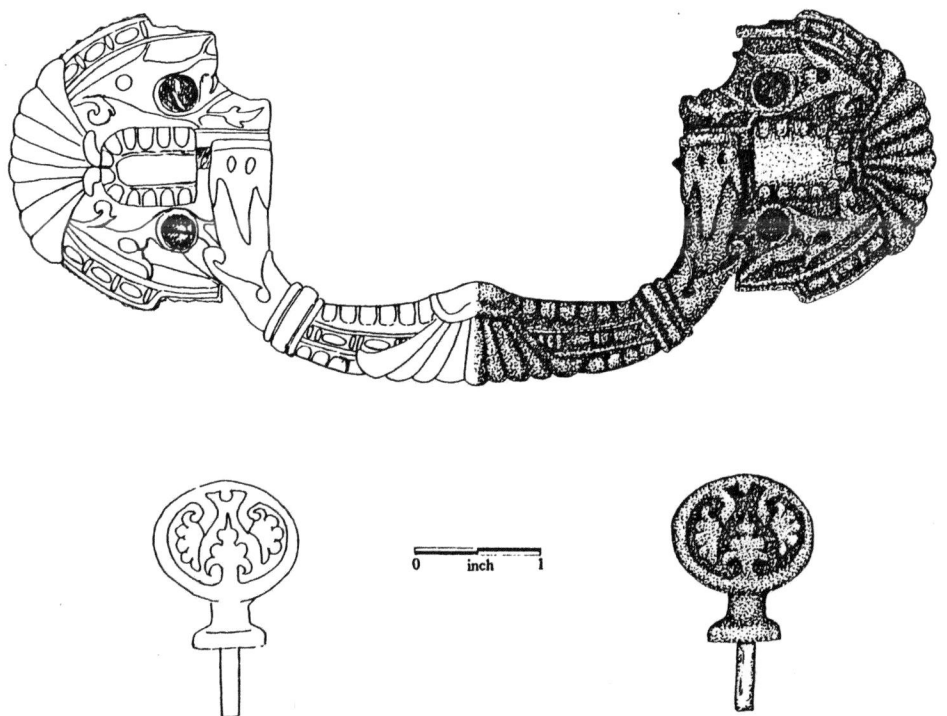

FIGURE 1. Bail handle and thumbscrews, Talbot County cemetery (Garrow and Symes, 1987).

FIGURE 2. Short bar handle. Author's collection.

Extended bar handles, as originally defined by Hacker-Norton and Trinkley (1984:7), were "similar to the short bar handle, but . . . can be long enough to extend the full length of the coffin" (Garrow, 1987:34).

The burials that contained coffin handles from both Nancy Creek and Talbot County were dated using headstone dates, nail types used to make the coffins, patent dates from hardware, and dates assigned to associated artifacts. Those date ranges were then used to construct date ranges when the different coffin handle types were most commonly used. Table 1 illustrates the date ranges assigned for the graves with coffin handles from the study collection.

FIGURE 3. Coffin with long bar handles, Edwards-Attaway cemetery. Photo by author.

Garrow (1987:34) assigned date ranges to the bail handle types of "the 1870s to shortly after 1900," and "short bar handles appear to begin replacing bail types within the Nancy Creek cemetery around 1900." The short bar handles recovered from burial 229 were made of plated iron, whereas those from 212 were made of white metal and zinc-clad wood. A date range of ca. 1900 to ca. 1920 has been used by Garrow (1990), Garrow et al.

Table 1. Chronological distribution of coffin handles by type (Garrow 1987:35). An X indicates a particular handle type was present; a dash (—) indicates it was absent.

Burial date	Burial No.	Bail	Short bar	Extended bar
1850–1900	235	X	—	—
1860–1900	206	X	—	—
1879	228	X	—	—
1875–1884	102	X	—	—
1870s–1884	169	X	—	—
1884	167	X	—	—
1893	224	X	—	—
1892–1903	109	X[b]	—	—
1902	199	X[b]	—	—
ca. 1900	TC5[a]	X	—	—
ca. 1900–ca. 1906	200	X	—	—
1900–1910	TC6[a]	X	—	—
1900–1909	226	—	X	—
1900–1918	209	—	X	—
1903–1920	207	—	X	—
1907–1915	210	—	X	—
1915	211	—	X	—
1918	212	—	X	—
ca. 1921	229	—	X	—
1943	223	—	—	X
1979	203	—	X	—

[a]TC numbers are graves from the Talbot County cemetery.
[b]These bail handles share characteristics with short bar types and may be transitional.

(1994), Jones et al. (1995), and Garrow and Jones (1996), among others, to date short bar handles with white-metal lugs, arms, and finials with zinc-clad wooden bars, although that date range is not explicitly stated in the 1987 article.

Extended bar handles made of stamped and painted iron or aluminum appear to replace short bar types using white metal after 1920. The only extended bar type included in the 1987 artifact seriation dated to 1943. It is significant to note that the short bar handles found in the 1979 grave at Nancy Creek cemetery were made of aluminum (Garrow et al., 1985:29).

Additional coffin hardware types discussed by Garrow (1987) included coffin tacks or screws with white-metal heads, thumbscrews and escutcheons, glass viewing ports, upholstery items, coffin plates, caplifters, and ornamental metal objects. Coffin closures or fasteners made of iron were recovered from five graves. Tacks and screws with white-metal heads were thought to generally predate thumbscrews and escutcheons and were believed to be lid closure items. Thumbscrews and escutcheons were found with both bail and short bar handles, but not with the extended bar or the late (1979) short bar types (Garrow, 1987:35–41).

Garrow (1987) noted that the size and shape of glass viewing ports may have chronological value. He noted that the earlier ports "were oval and covered the face and parts of the upper torso. As time passed, the viewing ports appeared to get larger to the point they covered the upper half of the body." Glass viewing ports appear to have been used to the point that embalming became common, which would have been the early 1920s in the Atlanta area. It is important to note that the single grave that contained embalming fluid bottles dated to ca. 1921 and lacked a glass viewing port.

Garrow (1987:27) further noted that it was possible to assign very rough date ranges to graves on the basis of coffin shape. Blakely and Beck (1982:188) assigned a date of 1850 for the introduction of rectangular coffins. That date is probably far too early, however, as all of the rectangular coffins found at Nancy Creek and Talbot County appear to postdate the Civil War. Garrow assigned a transition date of the 1870s for hexagonal to rectangular coffins.

The Hopewell Baptist Church Cemetery

Hopewell Baptist Church is located in Norcross, which is a suburb of Atlanta. The church is reportedly the oldest African American church in Gwinnett County and, according to church oral history, was founded immediately after the Civil War. It is believed that the founding date was ca. 1870, although no solid historical data support that assumption. Hopewell Baptist Church was the only black church in the county that accepted African Americans for burial until 20 to 30 years ago. The church grew from a membership of no more than 200–300 in the early 1980s to a congregation of almost 3,000 by the early 1990s. The minister responsible for the rapid growth of the congregation was from outside of Georgia, and few of the new members had ties to the old church or Norcross (Garrow, 1992:1).

The rapid growth of Hopewell soon required that the church's facilities be expanded, and plans for a new sanctuary building were prepared. The site chosen for the new building was the oldest part of the church cemetery. The church leadership claimed that 169 graves were moved from the cemetery to an adjacent tract called the "Memorial Garden" before construction began (Garrow, 1992:1). An injunction was filed to stop construction after a portion of the cemetery had been leveled and prepared for construction (Garrow, 1992:1). I was hired by an attorney who represented a woman whose husband was allegedly buried in the disturbed cemetery. I was appointed the court's expert as legal action proceeded and undertook investigations in the disturbed cemetery at the order of the Superior Court judge in charge of the case (Garrow, 1992:1).

Legal action in the Hopewell Baptist cemetery case extended from November 1988 to March 1991. It became clear early during that period that few graves had actually been moved, and most of the graves were intact beneath the construction site. Parts of nine individuals were found strewn around the surface of the construction site, and an additional 220 graves were moved from the construction site during February and March 1990 by a team that included the same burial removal firm that moved the Nancy Creek graves and archaeologists from Garrow & Associates. The methods used to move the graves were dictated by the Superior Court judge and were far from ideal for recovery of archaeological data. The remains, coffin hardware, and wood were shoveled out of the graves and into reinterment boxes by the burial removal firm. The Garrow & Associates archaeologists monitored the move and inventoried the contents of each grave to ensure each had been fully moved. Standard forms were used to capture as much physical data and information on the coffins and coffin hardware as possible before the remains were sealed in their reburial boxes. All remains were reburied the same day they were removed. The remains of the plaintiff's husband were found and positively identified during those investigations (Garrow, 1992:7–10).

The Edwards-Attataway Cemetery

The Edwards-Attaway cemetery was located near Kennesaw, a suburb of Atlanta located north of the city. The cemetery was located in what had been rural Cobb County at the time of the interments and contained members of the Edwards, Attaway, and Kendrick families. Sixty-three graves were identified and moved from this cemetery, and each was excavated and recorded using archaeological methods. Bone preservation was generally quite poor, but physical data were collected as possible (Garrow and Jones, 1996).

The initial attempt to move the Edwards-Attaway cemetery to make way for a car dealership in October 1989 was terminated following a public protest. Litigation over the planned move followed between the developer and Cobb County, and the law under which the initial permit had been granted to move the cemetery was declared unconstitutional. The Abandoned Cemeteries and Burial Grounds Act (sections 36–72) was passed by the Georgia legislature to replace the old law in 1991, and the Edwards-Attaway move was the first relocation to be permitted under the new law. The developer filed suit questioning the constitutionality of the new law, and a group that believed they had relatives buried in the cemetery filed suit in an attempt to overturn approval of the disinterment/reinterment permit. The separate legal actions were settled by the spring of 1994. The graves were moved in October 1994 (Garrow and Jones, 1996:1–3). The disinterment/reinterment plan approved for the cemetery required that the grave contents be placed in their reburial boxes as soon as the graves were recorded; no off-site study of the artifacts or physical remains was allowed. The remains were kept in a secure warehouse until the last grave was removed, and all of the reinterments were made at a nearby cemetery (Garrow and Jones, 1996:5).

The graves excavated at the Edwards-Attaway cemetery spanned the period from ca. 1840 to 1948. Nine of the graves were marked with inscribed headstones that contained death dates. One other grave could be directly associated with Civil War battles in the immediate area and could be tightly dated. The tightly dateable graves thus ranged in age from 1864 to 1948 (Garrow and Jones, 1996).

Dating Coffin Hardware Forms: 2007

Data recovered from both Hopewell Baptist Church and the Edwards-Attaway cemetery indicate that coffin shape is, indeed, an important dating key. Table 2 summarizes the data from hexagonal coffin forms at those cemeteries, as well as from Nancy Creek and Talbot County.

In addition to the hardware listed in Table 2, one hexagonal coffin from Edwards-Attaway decorated with handles, thumbscrews, and a glass viewing port also contained a caplifter. A second hexagonal coffin from the same cemetery that was otherwise unadorned contained 18 brass upholstery tacks. One set of slotted screws from Edwards-Attaway was made of brass, but all other slotted screws or tacks were made of white metal. The handles from both Hopewell and Edwards-Attaway were bail types.

The earliest date that could be confirmed for hexagonal coffins from the four cemeteries was 1855 from a dated grave at Nancy Creek (Garrow, 1897:28). All eight hexagonal

Table 2. Coffin hardware found on hexagonal coffins from all four cemeteries (Garrow, 1987:28; Garrow and Jones, 1996).

Cemetery[a]	None	Slotted	Handles	Escutcheon	Thumbscrew	Plate	Port Glass
Nancy Creek (9)	6	3	0	0	0	0	0
Talbot County (3)	3	0	0	0	0	0	0
Hopewell (13)	8	1	2	2	2	1	1
Edwards-Attaway (27)	20	4	3	2	3	0	3

[a]Numbers in parentheses indicate the number of graves studied.

coffins at Hopewell should date to 1870 or later (Garrow, 1992). One of the Edwards-Attaway hexagonal coffins contained what was believed to be the remains of a Civil War soldier since the cemetery was in what had been a battlefield during the Battle of Kennesaw Mountain, and the grave contained a double amputee and his surgically removed limbs. His amputated limbs were buried next to him in a rectangular box. Patent dates were found on escutcheons that had adorned two of the Edwards-Attaway hexagonal coffins, and those dates were 1878 and 1884. It is clear that the hexagonal shape lasted at least to 1884 at the Edwards-Attaway cemetery, and use of that coffin type overlapped with and was replaced by the rectangular forms (Garrow and Jones, 1996).

The balance of the coffins from all four cemeteries were, with a single exception, rectangular. The exception was a tapered form with a rounded end at the head found at Edwards-Attaway that contained an adult male who died on 18 May 1894 (Garrow and Jones, 1996:30). That coffin has been included with the rectangular forms for purposes of these analyses. The rectangular coffins, when adorned with hardware, often contained an array of items such as thumbscrews and escutcheons, caplifters, ornamental items of white metal or brass, glass viewing ports, and brass upholstery tacks. Slotted screws with white-metal heads were found on four rectangular coffins at Nancy Creek, four at Edwards-Attaway, and two at Hopewell. No other types of coffin hardware co-occurred with the white-metal-headed fasteners in any instance.

The number of handles used on a coffin varied by adult and infant/child graves, with children's coffins more often having just four handles. Coffins that contained handles appear to have contained four or six, with two or three to a side. Using only bail examples made of white metal or silver-plated white metal, one adult grave at Nancy Creek had four handles, whereas eight contained six. Five Hopewell graves had four white-metal or silver-plated bail handles versus 30 with six, and Edwards-Attaway had five of each. It is doubtful that the number of handles on a coffin, beyond simple presence or absence, means much in socioeconomic terms.

The coffin handle types observed on the rectangular coffins from all four cemeteries are summarized in Table 3. Two of the 21 (9.5%) rectangular coffins without handles at Nancy Creek contained adults, whereas 7 of the 19 (36.8%) rectangular coffins without handles contained adults at Edwards-Attaway. The highest relative percentage of adult burials in rectangular coffins without handles was at Hopewell, where 33 of the 80 (41.3%) graves without handles contained adults.

The age ranges reflected by the handle types on rectangular coffins from the four cemeteries is clarified by considering the material of manufacture of the handles. Table 4

Table 3. Handle types on rectangular coffins by cemetery (Garrow, 1987:28; Garrow and Jones, 1996).

Cemetery[a]	None	Bail	Short Bar	Extended
Nancy Creek (39)	21	10	7	1
Talbot County (2)	0	2	0	0
Hopewell (184)[b]	80	79	40	7
Edwards-Attaway (36)	19	12	4	1

[a]Numbers in parentheses indicate the number of graves studied.
[b]Some graves contained more than one handle type.

Table 4. Handle types and material of manufacture by cemetery (Garrow, 1987:28; Garrow and Jones, 1996).

Type/Material[a]	Nancy Creek	Talbot County	Hopewell	Edwards-Attaway
Bail/WM	10	2	51	9
Bail/SP WM	0	0	10	3
Bail/iron	0	0	18	0
Short bar/WM	7	0	25	4
Short bar/WM SP	0	0	5	0
Short bar/iron	0	0	4	0
Short bar/iron and tin	0	0	1	0
Short bar/Alum	1	0	1	0
Short bar/tin and iron	0	0	2	0
Extend bar/tin	0	0	3	0
Extend bar/Alum	0	0	1	0
Extend bar/iron	1	0	1	0
Extend bar/tin and WM	0	0	1	0

[a]WM = white metal, SP = silver plated, Alum = aluminum.

presents those data. It should be noted that some graves at Hopewell contained more than one handle type. Nancy Creek yielded two graves that clearly postdated 1921, one from 1943 and the other from 1976. The extended bar handle came from the 1943 burial, whereas the aluminum short bar type came from the 1976 interment. The Talbot County interments dated to the early 1900s and earlier. The latest interment at Edwards-Attaway cemetery was placed there in 1948. There was a considerable gap between that interment and the next youngest marked grave (1915), and it is doubtful that there were interments during the intervening time period.

The Hopewell Baptist Church cemetery appears to have been continuously used from ca. 1870 to the late 1980s. One grave that was moved and then encroached upon by construction had been buried no more than a year or so before construction began. Another factor encountered at Hopewell is that there were seven instances in which iron bail handles were found along with short bar handles with white-metal elements on the same rectangular coffin. The iron bail handles in those instance probably were functional handles fitted on shipping boxes, whereas the short bar handles were coffin adornments.

The iron bail handles that were not used on shipping boxes, as well as the short bars made of iron, tin, or aluminum, probably postdate 1920 and represent a shift from cast white-metal forms to stamped iron or tin elements.

Glass viewing ports were found on coffins decorated with iron handles at Hopewell, which may indicate that embalming was a later introduction at Hopewell than at Edwards-Attaway or Nancy Creek. That observation is not surprising given the probable social and economic positions of those who used the Hopewell cemetery versus those who buried their dead at Nancy Creek and Edwards-Attaway.

The remaining coffin hardware found on coffins from the four cemeteries appears to have minimal value for close dating. Thumbscrews and escutcheons begin to replace slotted white-metal-head screws as coffin closures after the Civil War and disappear with the rise of professionally made coffins with closure mechanisms used to secure the lid. That replacement probably becomes general after ca. 1920. Caplifters are common elements on coffins that have glass viewing ports and are used to raise a cover that was placed over the glass viewing port. That element also largely disappears by ca. 1920. Coffin plates were common on pre-1920s coffins and expressed sentiments such as "At Rest," "Our Darling," "Rest in Peace," or the like. Coffin plates appear to have been cast in white metal prior to ca. 1920 and made of iron or even silver or silver plate after that time.

Social Dimensions of Relative Grave Sizes

Prior to managed cemeteries and the excavation of graves with heavy equipment, graves were normally hand dug in two stages. The first stage consisted of the main shaft, which was excavated to the depth at which the gravedigger(s) wanted to place the top of the coffin. A coffin chamber the exact size and shape of the coffin was then excavated, which helped protect the coffin from the lateral movement of soils and collapse during backfilling. This method of excavation allows the exact size and shape of a coffin to be determined even after all of the coffin wood is gone (Garrow, 1989:19–21).

The manner in which most of the graves were removed at Nancy Creek and Hopewell made it difficult to record absolute grave sizes, and the grave shafts had been removed to the coffin chamber at Talbot County before excavation began. That said, field observations at Hopewell indicated that the grave shafts were only slightly larger than the coffin chambers. The shaft and coffin chamber sizes were recorded at Edwards-Attaway, and it was noted that most of the shafts were much larger than the coffin chambers. One extreme example, burial 52, had a shaft that measured 6.75 feet long by 2.75 feet wide and contained a coffin chamber that measured only 3.95 feet long by a maximum of 1.05 feet wide (Garrow and Jones, 1996:37). The relative differences in the grave shaft sizes between Edwards-Attaway and Hopewell can be attributed to the manner in which the graves were dug. The smaller entry shafts observed at Hopewell were probably the work of single paid gravediggers. The larger shafts at Edwards-Attaway suggest that more than one person worked on the grave at a time, which probably reflects those graves being dug by the family and friends of the deceased. The Hopewell cemetery was attached to a church, which could have dictated the way the graves were dug. Alternatively, the manner in which the graves were dug at Hopewell and Edwards-Attaway may reflect differential practices among African Americans and whites in the area around Atlanta prior to the rise of professionally managed burials by funeral homes. More research is obviously needed to address this question.

The 2017 Seriation of Coffin Hardware Types

Research conducted at the Hopewell and Edwards Attaway cemeteries generally supports the preliminary seriation of coffin hardware forms posed in 1987. Data from those cemeteries do allow some dating refinements. Slotted white-metal-headed screws and tacks (Figure 4) should have been more clearly included in the 1987 seriation, because they are early hardware forms. Bell (1990:64) indicated that screws and tacks with white-metal heads can be dated through manufacturer's catalogs from 1853 to "at least 1877." That date range fits the archaeological evidence from Nancy Creek, Hopewell, and Edwards-Attaway, and that coffin hardware form has been added to the 1987 seriation with that date range.

The use dates of specific coffin hardware forms appear to be dependent on two factors. The first factor is the manufacturing date range. This equates to the date range during which a specific type of hardware was produced. The ability to mass produce specific hardware forms such as bail handles and distribute those items to markets throughout the country is a basic determinate of the date range during which that form will be used.

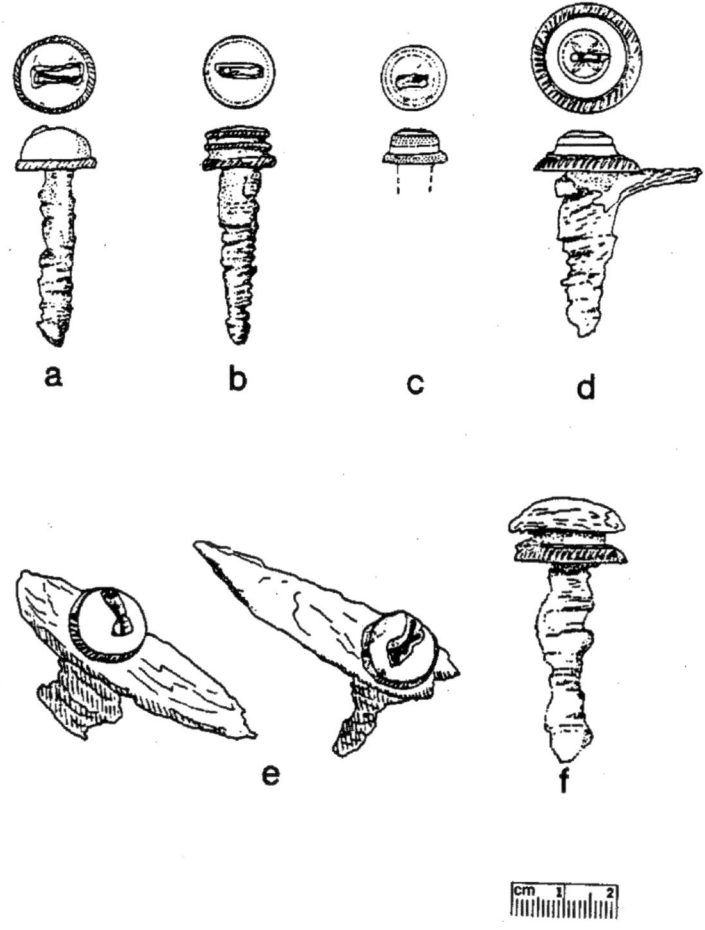

FIGURE 4. Slotted white-metal screws, Uxbridge, Massachusetts.

Coffin hardware cast from white metal and mass produced in molds provided an inexpensive way to adorn coffins for rich and poor alike (Bell, 1990:55).

The second factor that influenced the use-life of specific coffin hardware types was popularity. I have used the concept of popularity date ranges to explain decorative changes in ceramics from the mid-nineteenth through the first quarter of the twentieth century on a number of research projects (Henry and Garrow, 1982; Garrow, 1995; Garrow et al., 1996). It has been observed that broad decorative ceramic types become popular and maintain their popularity for about a generation, when that type is, in turn, phased out in favor of decorative types from the previous generation. In simple terms, popularity waves in ceramics appear to stem from children rejecting the decorative types embraced by their parents in favor of versions of decorative types used by their grandparents. It should be noted that popularity date ranges are not designed to capture the absolute earliest or latest potential use of an item but instead to gauge the most likely time span during which an item was used.

The popularity dating of ceramics may or may not be a close fit for the changes in popular acceptance of coffin hardware forms, but the use of white-metal-headed screws and tacks, followed by bail handles, followed by short bar handles to extended handles appears to have a time span of about a generation for each type. Bail and short bar handles never completely disappear but are, in time, expressed in other materials such as stamped iron, tin, or cast aluminum.

The basic seriation of Georgia coffin hardware forms now stands as follows. The oldest coffin hardware forms found, excluding hinges, are white-metal-headed screws and tacks. Those items have a popularity use range from the 1850s to 1870s, when they are replaced by thumbscrews that typically have escutcheons. Bail handles appear by the 1870s in Georgia and were common in white metal or silver-plated white metal until around 1900. Short bar handles with white-metal lugs, arms, and finials with wooden bars clad with zinc and covered with cloth were common from the 1890s to about 1920. Extended bar handles appear by about 1920 and are still used today. It should be noted that coffin elements such as glass ports, caplifters, and thumbscrews appear to disappear by the 1920s.

Coffin forms and the choice of adornments on coffins appear to be the purview of funeral homes and funeral directors by the 1920s in Georgia. Locally made coffins appear to give way to commercially produced coffins by that time, and coffin forms largely become standardized by the funeral industry. It is still possible to buy a hexagonal coffin with bail handles, but today, it is necessary to acquire coffins like that from specialty manufacturers (Trappist Caskets, 2016). The design and supply of coffins were tightly controlled by the funeral industry in this country until the last decade. It is now possible to buy coffins in traditional stores not associated with funeral homes and online (americancasketstore.com, 2016; funeraldepot.com, 2016; tributedirect.com, 2016), which should mean that market factors such as popularity could once again affect design and supply of coffins and coffin adornments.

Conclusions

The basic seriation of coffin hardware forms as suggested in the 1987 article appears to have held up fairly well over the past 30 years. The only major addition to the scheme is that white-metal-headed screws and tacks need to be added as a coffin hardware form that predates and overlaps with bail handles. The screws and tacks were used from the 1850s to the 1870s. Coffins after ca. 1920 are much less heavily adorned than those used earlier, and items such as thumbscrews and escutcheons, glass viewing ports, and caplifters appear to have been phased out by that point. The use of white metal for handles seems to have largely been dropped at around the same time and replaced by stamped iron or tin, with the later addition of cast aluminum.

It now appears that hexagonal coffin forms survived in reduced numbers until at least 1884, as dated from a patent date on an escutcheon mounted on a hexagonal coffin at the Edwards-Attaway cemetery. Rectangular coffins appear to have been in wide scale use by the 1870s, and examples of rectangular coffins with white-metal-headed screws and tacks were found at Nancy Creek, Hopewell, and Edwards-Attaway. None of the coffins that contained white-metal-headed screws or tacks had any other type of coffin hardware, with the exception of a hexagonal form with a hinge at Nancy Creek.

Few differences noted at Hopewell versus the other cemeteries could be attributed to the low socioeconomic position or race of those at Hopewell. The highest percentage of rectangular coffins that had contained adults and lacked handles was at Hopewell with 41.3% (33 of 80), but Edwards-Attaway was close behind with 36.8% (7 of 19). Only 9.5% (2 of 21) of the rectangular coffins that had contained adults at Nancy Creek lacked handles, which may mean that those buried at Nancy Creek had enjoyed a higher economic and perhaps social status than those at both Hopewell and Edwards-Attaway.

One possible factor that requires additional research is the perceived difference in the way graves were dug at Hopewell versus Edwards-Attaway. Field observations that are not supported by consistent field measurements indicate that the grave shafts at Hopewell were only slightly larger than the coffin chambers. The grave shafts at Edwards-Attaway were measured and were much larger than the coffin chambers. The difference in relative grave shaft sizes at Hopewell and Edwards-Attaway probably reflects the use of a professional gravedigger at Hopewell versus graves being dug by friends and relatives at Edwards-Attaway.

References

americancasketstore.com. 2016. http://www.americancasketstore.com/ (accessed 4 August 2016).

Bell, E. L. 1990. The Historical Archaeology of Mortuary Behavior: Coffin Hardware from Uxbridge, Massachusetts. *Historical Archaeology*, 24(3):54–78.

Blakely, R. L., and L. A. Beck. 1982. "Bioarchaeology in the Urban Context." In *Archaeology of Urban America*, ed. R. S. Dickens Jr., pp. 175–208. New York: Academic Press.

funeraldepot.com. 2016. http://ww2.funeraldepot.com/ (accessed 4 August 2016).

Garrow, P. H. 1987. A Preliminary Seriation of Coffin Hardware Forms in Nineteenth and Twentieth Century Georgia. *Early Georgia*, 15(1–2):19–45.

Garrow, P. H. 1990. Archaeological Investigations of the Sandy Creek Cemetery, Lot 31, Block "B", Sandy Creek Estates, Clarke County, Georgia. Submitted to the Superior Court of Clarke County, Athens, Georgia. Atlanta: Garrow & Associates.

Garrow, P. H. 1992. "At Rest in the Arms of Hopewell." Paper Presented at the Annual Meeting of the Society for Historical Archaeology, Kingston, Jamaica.

Garrow, P. H. 1995. Ballast Point Ceramic Analysis: Study of Two Centuries of Occupation along San Diego Bay, San Diego, California. Submitted to Naval Command, Control, and Surveillance Center, San Diego. Atlanta: Garrow & Associates.

Garrow, P. H., J. L. Holland, L. Pietak, and L. Kennedy. 1996. Knoxville Courthouse Block: Archaeological Data Recovery on Site 40KN145, Knoxville, Tennessee. Submitted to Barber & McMurray, Knoxville, Tenn. Atlanta: Garrow & Associates.

Garrow, P. H., and D. H. Jones. 1996. Archaeological Investigations of the Edwards-Attaway Cemetery, Cobb County, Georgia. Submitted to The Nally Companies, Atlanta. Atlanta: Garrow & Associates.

Garrow, P. H., D. H. Jones, and J. L. Holland. 1994. An Archaeological, Genealogical, and Forensic Study of the Martin Cemetery, Douglas County, Georgia. Submitted to IDI, Sewanee, Ga. Atlanta: Garrow & Associates.

Garrow, P. H., and S. A. Symes. 1987. The Big Lazer Creek Unmarked Cemetery: A Multidisciplinary Investigation. Submitted to the Fisheries Management Section, Game and Fish Division, Georgia Department of Natural Resources, Atlanta. Atlanta: Garrow & Associates.

Garrow, P. H., S. A. Symes, and H. W. Case. 1985. Physical Anthropology and Archaeological Investigations of the Nancy Creek Primitive Baptist Church Cemetery, Chamblee, Georgia. Submitted to Parsons, Brinckerhoff, Quade & Douglas/Tudor Engineering Company, Atlanta. Atlanta: Garrow & Associates.

Hacker-Norton, D., and M. Trinkley. 1984. *Remember Man Thou Art Dust: Coffin Hardware of the Early Twentieth Century*. Research Series 2. Columbia, S.C.: Chicora Foundation.

Henry, S. L., and P. H. Garrow, eds. 1982. Archaeological Data Recovery on Blocks 1 and 2 of the Original Phoenix Townsite, AZ T:12:42 (ASM), Phoenix, Arizona. Volume 1: The Historic Component. Submitted to the City of Phoenix, Central Phoenix Redevelopment Agency, Phoenix. Phoenix: Professional Service Industries.

Jones, D. C., P. H. Garrow, and J. L. Holland. 1995. Archaeological Disinterment of the Morrow Cemetery, Gwinnett County, Georgia. Submitted to Pope and Land, Lawrenceville, Ga. Atlanta: Garrow & Associates.

Symes, S. A., and P. H. Garrow. 1984. Research Design Physical Anthropology Studies Cemetery Relocation, MARTA North Line, N760 Contract EX3-1. Submitted to the Metropolitan Atlanta Rapid Transit Authority, Atlanta. Atlanta: Garrow & Associates.

Trappist Caskets. 2016. From the Monks of New Melleray Abbey Trappist Caskets. http://trappistcaskets.com/ (accessed 4 August 2016).

tributedirect.com. 2016. http://ww1.tributedirect.com/ (accessed 4 August 2016).

Trinkley, M., and D. Hacker-Norton. 1984. *Analysis of Coffin Hardware from 38CH778, Charleston County, South Carolina*. Research Series 3. Columbia, S.C.: Chicora Foundation.

CHAPTER 8

The Need for Greater Precision in Mortuary Hardware Terminology

†Roderick Sprague

Recent efforts to encourage greater detail and precision in the description of burials and associated features (Sprague, 2005) were the third and major effort by me toward this objective. Rather than stopping with this objective, we should be looking for greater precision and detail in minor areas of mortuary practices. Efforts such as that of Litten (1985:53) to make sense of coffin furniture (hardware) through time is admirable but need more chronology and detailed drawings to be useful as a dating device.

Some artifacts, such as nails, used in coffin manufacture are readily categorized through previous studies. The literature on nail dating is fairly extensive but, until recently (Wells, 1998), has not been especially concise. On the other hand, LeeDecker et al. (1995:53–58) and Riordan (2000:4–3) have shown how to accurately draw the configuration of nails in a coffin, a factor that may prove to be more useful than the actual nail chronologies for dating.

One class of coffin hardware that might prove useful in making the point above is the coffin hinge. In earlier periods most locally made coffins were not fitted with hinges, and when they were, the hinges were probably what was easily manufactured by a local blacksmith, what was on hand in stock, or what was quickly available to the builder from mass-produced hinge suppliers. Hinges became important when undertakers started preparing bodies for viewing, especially in cloth-lined or upholstered coffins.

Signal or alarm coffins were designed to alert the living when someone was buried alive and revived, a virtually impossible situation but still a fear before the use of embalming fluid. The earliest model of such a device required a hinge and, according to Habenstein and Lamers (1962:288–289), was patented in 1843. Habenstein and Lamers (1962:291) doubt that any models were sold, and apparently, none have been found archaeologically. An earlier and equally rare use of hinges on coffins was the parish coffin or slip coffin, which had a hinged false bottom permitting the recovery of the coffin for reuse (Litten, 1991:98; Iserson, 1994:472, 603). Such coffins, largely English in use, logically should not be in the ground but could be retired in a grave; however, none have been reported archaeologically.

Terminology

The archaeological cemetery descriptions found in the literature *may* mention that hinges are present but usually with no more useful description. As with nails, there may be some possible dating of coffin hinges based on the general hardware literature, but we must have better description in order to make use of such data.

Presented below is a sample of the terminology pertaining to hinges as found in period catalogs as well as from the standard archaeological worked on hinges (Priess, 1978, 2000; Suckling, 1983). Any study should include both the modern contemporary terms as well as the terms contemporaneous with the suspected date of the coffin or site. The most recent work by Peter Priess (2000) is the current standard in archaeology for terminology of building hardware and is recommended for application to coffin and casket hinges whenever possible.

Only as an example of the diverse terminology and in no way a complete glossary, the following is offered (always followed by the word hinge): aesthetic, ball bearing butt, bar pintle strap, bolt and nut pintle, box, butt, butterfly, capped butt, cock's head, continuous (piano), corrugated, crossed garnet, double-action butt, double-action spring butt, dove tail, double strap, face, fast joint, floor, friction, H, half-mortise butt, halved joint strap, HL, hospital, knuckle, leaf, long chest, loose joint butt, loose pin butt, mortise butt, olive knuckle butt, pin, pintle, plate, rattail, prison, screen door, screw hook pintle and strap, shutter butt, spike pintle, spiral spring butt, spring, surface, strap, T, V double-leaf strap, V pintle strap, and wood screw pintle.

Added to such a list would be the complete terminology of parts and special features. Just the hinge pin—consisting of the shaft and tip—can be loose or fixed, whereas the tip of the pin can be flat, oval, button, ball acorn, steeple, hospital, spun, prison, or Baldwin's "patent secret joint." Loose joint butts can be left- or right-handed, and a leaf can be female or male. But hinges and some varieties can be swaged or not swaged, with swaging typical of the more expensive hinges.

The first major division in hinge description beyond the shape terminology should be the type of metal and how it was worked. Any hinge prior to mass production but in the historic period would most likely be made of cast or wrought iron or cast brass. "During the nineteenth century, however, manufacture shifted to machine or mass-produced methods, initially using wrought iron and later steel" (Priess, 2000:51), a factor of more concern below for dating.

Selection and Use

Prior to the mass production of coffins and in the West, where transportation was still not well established, the types of hinges used would most likely have been loose-pin, external hinges (Priess, 2000) similar to shutter hinges. This type of hinge would be easy to attach by one not trained in carpentry and would have permitted the removal of the lid with little effort. Craftsmen with more ability and/or pride in their work would probably have favored a butt hinge that could be mortised and thus would not have been visible when the box was closed.

Not only was the "on-hand" supply of mass-produced hinges a factor in choice, but the logic of the situation, as erroneous as it may be, is also an important factor. For example, coffins are long and thin in overall shape, as is also a piano or continuous hinge, yet such a hinge is not suited to the task. The most likely hinge selection from stock would have been the square butt hinge. Priess's (2000:60) comments of a door-hanging process speak to the use of the butt hinge on a coffin thus: "Hinges attached to the edge of a door [lid] and to the inside surface of the door [coffin] frame are referred to as 'butt' hinges. They are generally symmetrical and relatively narrow to accommodate the thinness of the door [coffin side]." Priess (2000:61) suggests that cast-iron and brass butt hinges were available by the last quarter of the eighteenth century but "mechanized production" in wrought iron and, later, steel did not begin until the second quarter of the nineteenth century.

What would be found on a coffin or modern casket from the last century would be largely a matter of expertise of the maker, the cost (especially today), the material used for the container, and the need for viewing with an open casket. Modern casket hinges tend to be grouped at either end of the cost scale, largely dependent on the material used in the manufacture of the actual box. Although some wooden containers are made of expensive wood with equally expensive finishing, most wooden caskets today are inexpensive and hinged with very crude and simple hinges of rough cast iron. The hinges have a minimum of finishing and are well below that of any hardware store hinge today. The leaf arrangement is one roughly cut square leaf between two leaves with no more combined surface than the center leaf. The screw holes are countersunk, so the use of flathead screws permits a reasonably tight, but not especially precise, closure of the lid. The rough-finished hinges on these modern wooden caskets are hidden from view by the upholstery.

In contrast to the wooden casket hinges the modern metal casket usually has very elaborate and expensive hinges to permit a tight seal of a rubber gasket. The hinges are integral to the lid and serve, along with latches in the front of the cover or lid, to force the whole top to seal uniformly and around the periphery. In some expensive models, a threaded rod is turned with a wrench from the outside in a mechanism that forces a tight seal. A threaded cap is used to seal the wrench access hole. This type of hinge probably will be dated in the future more by patent records than by typological changes through time.

Dating

The earliest date for a mass-produced hinge is perhaps the patent date of 1775 for the Baldwin "Secret Joint Hinge" (Hommel, 1944). This hinge is still subject to speculation concerning whether it was truly mass produced and if the 1775 patent describes the hinges imprinted with "Baldwin." Priess (2000:58), in a more precise date than he gives above, states that the "technology for machine production of hinges was probably introduced by the 1840s." Blacksmith production of butterfly-type shutter hinges is briefly described by Romaine (1976) and is used mostly to show the variation possible in these hinges and in blacksmith work. The H- and HL-type hinges are illustrated in only one of more than two dozen catalogs in my collection, which leads to the conclusion that at the beginning of mass production they fell out of popularity and thus explains the lack of small examples of this simple hinge of coffins.

Even more important for dating is the variation noted by Bell (1990:63) in the placement of the hinges. He notes three different configurations for hinges that are transverse and located at the widest point or farthest toward the head (Figure 1 A–1C) and are in contrast to the later and modern pattern of the hinged portion being lateral and at the back and away from the viewer (Figure 1D). Bell (1990:63) describes the three transverse hinge locations with one form of lid opening up and folding forward toward the feet, another

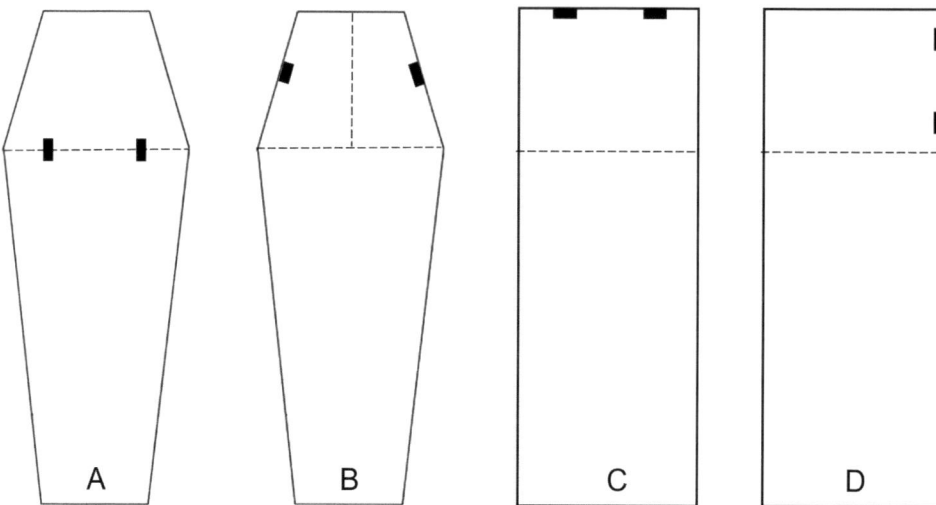

FIGURE 1. Configuration of hinges on coffins. (A) Opening folds over rest of coffin lid. (B) Two sections open to the coffin sides. (C) Opening folds from the coffin end. (D) Lid folds from the coffin side away from viewer.

opening like window shutters to the sides of the coffin, and the third opening up and folding down the head end. These designs were "probably used between 1831 and 1872" at Uxbridge (Bell, 1990:63).

Trinkley and Hacker-Norton (1984:12) date the Mount Pleasant cemetery, South Carolina (38CH778), a site with no hinges, as mid-nineteenth century through early twentieth century. They also state in another source (Hacker-Norton and Trinkley, 1984:11) that caplifters "now are obsolete as casket lids are hinged and balanced for easy lifting." Caplifters were small handles much like a drawer pull used to remove the coffin lid. They note that the last catalog they observed as listing caplifters was ca. 1925.

Hinges, dated to the middle of the nineteenth century by Bell (1990:63–64), in the Uxbridge site in Massachusetts were mass-produced cabinet hinges very similar to butterfly hinges. According to Priess (2000:56) both types fall into the double-strap hinge class. If small cabinet-size hinges are considered then Priess (2000:56–57) is in error in stating that "butterfly hinges do not seem to have persisted beyond the hand-forging era."

Hacker-Norton and Trinkley (1984:46) list four hardware catalogs dating from 1856 (two), 1871, and 1877, all of which list coffin hinges; however, another three catalogs from the same time period do not list hinges, nor do any contemporary trade journals. Thus, from the sites and the catalog evidence it is difficult to determine which are better for dating: (1) the distinctive shape of the "coffin hinges," (2) the unusual arrangement of the hinged lids, or (3) the presence of or complete absence of hinges. In any event, there is no clear indication of hinges as a precise dating device for coffins in the mid-nineteenth century in the eastern United States. Other factors such a local economies or local cultural practices as well as widespread samples must be collected to aid in future dating studies.

Conclusions

This brief summary of the use of hinges on coffins and caskets is not intended to present a chronology for dating or in any way to be even a progress report; it is simply an effort to show the range of detail that can be found in the study of any of the various hardware, or "furniture," items of burial containers. A first step in this kind of study would be a complete review of the hardware and archaeological burial literature of the specific hardware type. Second, we need to reproduce as many catalogs of coffin and mortuary devices as is possible to find. With this basic collection in hand, we can then begin to seriously work on mortuary hardware.

References

Bell, E. L. 1990. The Historical Archaeology of Mortuary Behavior: Coffin Hardware from Uxbridge, Massachusetts. *Historical Archaeology*, 24(3):55–78.

Habenstein, R. W., and W. N. Lamers. 1962. *The History of American Funeral Directing*. Rev. ed. Milwaukee, Wis.: Bulfin Press.

Hacker-Norton, D., and M. Trinkley. 1984. *Remember Man Thou Art Dust: Coffin Hardware of the Early Twentieth Century*. Research Series 2. Columbia, S.C.: Chicora Foundation.

Hommel, R. 1944. The Secret Joint Hinge. *Chronicle of the Early American Industries Association*, 3(1):3–4. Reprint, South Burlington, Vt.: Early American Industries Association, 1976.

Iserson, K.V. 1994. *Death to Dust: What Happens to Dead Bodies*. Tucson, Ariz.: Galen Press.

LeeDecker, C. H., J. Bloom, I. Wuebber, and M.-L. Pipes. 1995. *Final Archaeological Excavations at a Late 18th-Century Family Cemetery for the U.S. Route 113 Dualization, Milford to Georgetown, Sussex County, Delaware*. With K. R. Rosenberg. DelDOT Archaeology Series 134. Dover: Delaware Department of Transportation.

Litten, J. W. S. 1985. Post-Medieval Burial Vaults: Their Construction and Contents. *Bulletin of the Council for British Archaeology Churches Committee*, 23:9–17.

Litten, J. W. S. 1991. *The English Way of Death: The Common Funeral Since 1450*. London: Robert Hale.

Priess, P. J. 1978. *An Annotated Bibliography for the Study of Building Hardware*. History and Archaeology 21. Ottawa: Parks Canada.

Priess, P. J. 2000. "Historic Door Hardware." In *Studies in Material Culture Research*, ed. K. Karklins, pp. 46–95. Tucson, AZ: Society for Historical Archaeology.

Riordan, T. B. 2000. *Dig a Grave Both Wide and Deep*. St. Mary's City, Md.: Historic St. Mary's City Commission.

Romaine, L. B. 1976. Butterfly Hinges. *Chronicle of the Early American Industries Association* 1(19):7. First published South Burlington, Vt.: Early American Industries Association, 1936.

Sprague, R. 2005. *Burial Terminology: A Guide for Researchers*. Lanham, Md.: AltaMira Press.

Suckling, M. D. 1978. "A Preliminary Report on the Hinges Excavated from English Camp (45-SJ-24) San Juan Island, Washington." In *Miscellaneous San Juan Island Reports 1976–1977*, by C. Johnson and Mark D. Suckling, pp. 55–114. University of Idaho Anthropological Research Manuscript 46. Moscow: Laboratory of Anthropology, University of Idaho.

Suckling, M. D. 1983. "The Comparison of Hinges from American Camp and English Camp." In *San Juan Island Archaeology*, ed. R. Sprague, pp. 735–757. Moscow: Laboratory of Anthropology, University of Idaho.

Trinkley, M., and D. Hacker-Norton. 1984. *Analysis of Coffin Hardware from 38CH778, Charleston County, South Carolina*. Research Series 3. Columbia, S.C.: Chicora Foundation

Wells, T. 1998. Nail Chronology: The Use of Technologically Derived Features. *Historical Archaeology*, 32(2):78–99.

CHAPTER 9

Eighteenth- and Nineteenth-Century Coffin Furniture from St. George's Crypt, Bloomsbury, and the Churchyard and Crypt of St. Luke's, Islington

Louise Loe and Ceridwen Boston

Eighteenth- and nineteenth-century coffin furniture provides a wealth of information about Georgian and Victorian England (Litten, 1991), but it still continues to be an underexploited resource. Reeve and Adams (1993) first highlighted this when publishing the corpus of coffin fittings from the crypts at Christ Church, Spitalfields, London, and establishing a chronological sequence for eighteenth- and nineteenth-century burials. The classification of coffin fittings at Spitalfields has become the standard against which all new finds are compared, although some of the forms could not be dated on the evidence from that site and more designs have subsequently been discovered. The Spitalfields publications and also some of the background archival data used to create the classification are now widely available online through the Archaeology Data Service, which allows anyone in Britain or across the world to consult it.

Background to the Sites

Since the early 1990s, the number of archaeological recording projects on coffin furniture assemblages has been increasing markedly, but only a limited number of these reach publication (for example, see Hancox, 2006; Bashford and Sibun, 2007; Miles et al., 2008). Work undertaken throughout England by Oxford Archaeology since the early 1990s has identified many new coffin fitting styles, which, in comparison with the Spitalfields data, has made it possible to refine their dating and to identify many hitherto unrecognized designs. Two assemblages, both from London, are presented here: from St. Luke's, Islington, and St. Georges, Bloomsbury, each comprising over 700 furnished coffins in variable states of preservation and completeness. The frequency and range of the different types of fittings are explored, and their date ranges are refined beyond that possible at Spitalfields. Some of the main trends in styles, symbolism, and metal used are also discussed in relation to status and chronology. This chapter therefore provides an important adjunct to the Spitalfields research and outlines the current range of designs across the whole range of coffin fittings used in the eighteenth and nineteenth centuries in London.

St. Luke's Crypt and Churchyard, Old Street, Islington, London

St. Luke's Church, Old Street, is a Grade I listed eighteenth-century church that was designed by Hawksmoor as part of the Commission for Building Fifty New Churches (Cherry and Pevsner, 1998), which was set up in 1711, to alleviate the lack of places of worship caused by the Great Fire and exacerbated by rapid population growth at the time. Consecrated in 1733, it was built over a brick semi-subterranean crypt, with a number of vaults or bays. This space was originally prohibited from use for burial, but that did not remain the case for long; the vestry minutes list burial fees in 1740 (St. Luke's, Islington, 1740).

By 1810 the vaults were being described as large and commodious but dark, damp, neglected, and highly offensive. Sufficient ventilation had not been secured, and wooden coffins rather than lead had been admitted. The committee recommended that funerals of opulent individuals should be promoted in the vaults and churchyards and that the fees for interment in the vaults and churchyards should not be enhanced. They also wished that no corpse be permitted to be placed in the vaults except in leaden or metal coffins and that 3-foot-diameter apertures be made in the walls at the east and west ends of the church to ventilate the vaults. In 1853 the vestry minutes record that a petition to Prime Minister Viscount Palmerston for an extension of time before closing burial grounds and vaults was turned down: burials (including those in the vaults) were to be discontinued at the end of the year and the vaults sealed (St. Luke's, Islington, 1853).

An archaeological recording program was undertaken at the church in 2000 in advance of construction and refurbishment works to provide new educational and rehearsal facilities for the London Symphony Orchestra (Boyle et al., 2005). This program included the recording and removing of all the burials in the crypt and in the southern and northern sides of the churchyard; 1,053 burials were recorded and removed.

St. George's Crypt, Bloomsbury, London

The Grade I listed church of St. George, Bloomsbury, was designed by the architect Nicholas Hawksmoor and completed in 1732 (Downes et al., 2008). Like St. Luke's, it was constructed as part of the Commission for Building Fifty New Churches. For its first 90 years, the vaults were not used, until in 1803 when the vestry met to consider "adopting measures for depositing dead bodies in the vaults under the church as they foresaw the burial ground would otherwise be full within 30 years." It was resolved that "an opening be made in the floor of the church and an apparatus constructed from thence into the vaults" (St. George's, Bloomsbury, 1803). The fee for the privilege of intramural burial was 10 guineas if buried under the church nave and 14 guineas under the chancel. It was a condition that all bodies be encased within lead coffins.

Clearly the expense both of the interment and the cost of a lead shell precluded all but the affluent of the parish—a factor that has considerable ramifications when interpreting the funerary material culture from the crypt. Despite the prescribed lead lining to all coffins interred within the crypt, by 1844 many coffins were in such a decayed and "offensive" state that the vestry decided they should be placed in a side vault and bricked up. In 1856 the vestry finally resolved "hermetically to seal the entrance to the vaults." It was made clear that "parties whose connections lie in the vaults take the necessary steps for the removal of the remains of their connections" (St. George's, Bloomsbury, 1856). It is unclear to what extent this directive was followed, but one memorial in the church records the removal of the remains of Sophia (surname illegible) to the family vault in the newly fashionable cemetery of Kensal Green.

The crypt was closed for burial in 1856, a directive that was both due to the poor state of the coffins within the crypt and overcrowding of the burial ground and also in accordance with the Burial Act of 1852, which prohibited further burial within crypts and churchyards in London in favor of the new garden cemeteries such as Kensal Green and Highgate (Curl, 2002; Friar, 2003:69).

In advance of major refurbishment of the church, Oxford Archaeology was appointed to record and remove all of the burials from within the crypt (Boston et al., 2009). These totaled 781 coffined burials within seven vaults, dating between 1800 and 1856.

Background to British Coffin Furniture in the Eighteenth and Nineteenth Centuries

The period spanning the late eighteenth and late nineteenth centuries saw a marked change in the style and use of coffin furniture (Litten, 1991). The introduction of the power-assisted stamping method in 1769 allowed a wider range of coffin furniture to be produced more cost effectively than had been possible on hand-operated machines. This development coincided with popular sentiment that placed great emphasis on providing a decent burial, even among the poor, with significant financial investment in the funeral. Throughout the course of the eighteenth century, coffin decoration became increasingly elaborate, the latter part seeing coffins that were furnished with a suite of metal fittings, often lavishly decorated with motifs that were heavily imbued with symbolism. By the late nineteenth century such effusive displays of mourning were regarded as excessive and undesirable, and coffin furniture became much simpler in terms of both its design and the number of fittings used (Mytum, 2004).

During the eighteenth century London was at the center of coffin furniture production, but by the early nineteenth century the focus had shifted to Birmingham. The principal types of coffin furniture used in the eighteenth and nineteenth centuries are referred to by the trade catalogs of the day as "grips," "grip plates," "breast plates" or "depositum plates," "motifs," "nails," and "escutcheons" or "drops" (side decorations; Litten, 1991:107). Grips were the handles that were mounted onto grip plates, which themselves were attached to the outside of the coffin. Depositum plates were plaques that bore biographical details of the deceased and were attached to the front (breastplates), foot end (foot plates), and head end (head plates) of the coffin. Motifs and escutcheons were decorative metal plates that were attached to the front and sides of the coffin, respectively. The outer coffin was usually upholstered, in either velvet or baize, and fixed with studwork or upholstery pins ("nails"). Also used, but less frequently, was coffin lace, a metal strip alternative to upholstery nails, coronets, and decorative hinges.

Methods

All coffin fittings were recorded on pro forma sheets, and fittings were classified with reference to the published catalog of coffin fitting styles from Christ Church, Spitalfields (Reeve and Adams, 1993). Those that matched were assigned the style code as it is given in the catalog (a number prefixed with the code CCS). Individual types that could not be paralleled were drawn and/or photographed and assigned a new style code: a number prefixed by OLR (for St. Luke's) or BBM (for St. George's). The fittings from St. George's were recorded at a later date than those from St. Luke's, and therefore, any styles not observed at Christ Church were also compared with new styles from St. Luke's. If a match was made, fittings were classified under the OLR code.

No agreed standards exist for identifying new styles of coffin fitting in Britain. Thus, the extent to which two fittings need to differ before they are classified as two different types has not been established. For the present study, if three or more differences were observed between types, they were classified as being different. The coffin fittings have been analyzed by the following categories: depositum plates, grips and grip plates, lid motifs and escutcheons, and upholstery studwork.

Depositum Plates

The inner breastplate and foot and head plates were generally far less decorative than the outer breastplate. Many were completely plain, bearing nothing but the inscription, but a number were bordered with simple lines of punched circles or stylized leaf or flower motifs. Only outer breastplate styles are considered here.

St. Luke's

A total of 188 breastplates survived in good enough condition to observe their styles, although none are illustrated here (Table A1). There were 62 different designs in total. Sixteen of these matched those from the Spitalfields (CCS) taxonomy, being present on 101 breastplates. In addition, 46 new styles (OLR 1–46) were identified on 87 breastplates. The most common styles were all rectangular in shape and largely comprised variations on floral motifs, often with a small shield at the top of the plate. Cherubs featured occasionally. These most popular styles accounted for 43% (81/188) of the total number of breastplates observed, or 18% (11/62) of the different designs observed (Table 1).

Less popular styles (i.e., those occurring only once or twice) accounted for 79% of the designs (49/62), or 30.8% of all breastplates (58/188). These findings show that a wide range of styles was used at St. Luke's, but each tended to be limited to only one or two coffins.

St. George's

At St. George's 226 breastplates were observed (Table A1). Fifty-five different styles were identified, 29 of which were matched to Spitalfields (192 breastplates); 7 matched St. Luke's (13 breastplates), and 19 were identified as new styles and prefixed with the code

Table 1. Breastplate styles observed at St. Luke's having three or more occurrences (in order of the most frequent). A dash (—) indicates that a particular style is not known from multiple sites. Comparator sites are: Christ Church, Spitalfields; St Luke's Islington; St George's, Bloomsbury; St Bartholomew's Penn, Wolverhampton.

Type	Number found/ Total (%)	Shape and predominant motifs	Date range based on comparator sites	Date range observed at St. Luke's
CCS 21	27/188 (14.4)	Tapered, foliage, flowers and shield	1812–1850; early/mid-nineteenth century	1828–1850
CCS 20	18/188 (9.6)	Tapered, plain	1790–1853; late eighteenth to mid-nineteenth centuries	1790–1853
CCS 82	17/188 (9.0)	Rectangular, flowers (roses), foliage, shield	1800–1848; early eighteenth century	1800–1830
OLR 29	14/188 (7.4)	Rectangular, flowers and foliage, shield	—	1835–1844
CCS 6	10/188 (5.3)	Rectangular, cherubs, angels	1783–1852; late eighteenth to mid-nineteenth centuries	1802–1822
CCS 8	9/188 (4.8)	Rectangular, flowers and foliage	1767–1880	1785–1880
OLR 26	8/188 (4.3)	Rectangular, shield, flowers and foliage	—	1820–1844
CCS 9	7/188 (3.7)	Rectangular, angel, cherub, urn, flowers and foliage	1773–1834	1773–1814
OLR 4	5/188 (2.7)	Rectangular, flowers and foliage	—	1797–1824
OLR 22	4/188 (2.1)	Rectangular, flowers and foliage, shield	—	1844–1853
OLR 28	4/188 (2.1)	Rectangular, flowers and foliage, shield	—	1841–1849
CCS 84	4/188 (2.1)	Tapered, flowers and foliage, shield	1828–1835	1828–1842
OLR 27	3/188 (1.6)	Rectangular, flowers and foliage, shield	—	1846–1850

BBM (21 breastplates). As at St. Luke's, the most frequent styles were already known forms, CCS 82, CCS 21, and CCS 20, comprising flowers, foliage, and shields, with cherubs featuring occasionally. Rectangular, tapered, and lozenge-shaped breastplates were among the most common shapes observed. Again, as at St. Luke's, the use of a wide range of designs is reflected by the fact that 78% of the styles (43/55) occurred in only one or two cases, but a lower percentage, 23% (53/226), of the total number of breastplates observed was of these less popular types.

Grips and Grip Plates

Usually, eight grips were fitted to the sides of adult coffins, and four were fitted to the coffins of children. Grip plates are backings for the grips and are often decorative.

St. Luke's

Grip plates from 142 coffins were recovered, many very poorly preserved and consisting of small fragments corroded onto the reverse of the more robust grips, but 73 coffins had grip plates that were well enough preserved for identification (Table A2). There were 17 different styles, including 11 (59 coffins) that matched the Spitalfields taxonomy and 6 new styles (OLR 1–6) on 14 coffins (Figure 1).

The most common style was an elaborate oval plate with foliage, winged cherubs, and fans (CCS 3), which was found on 30 coffins (30/73; 41.0%; Figure 2). A rectangular, plain

OLR 3, Grip plate, coffin 909

OLR 4, Grip plate, coffin 1089

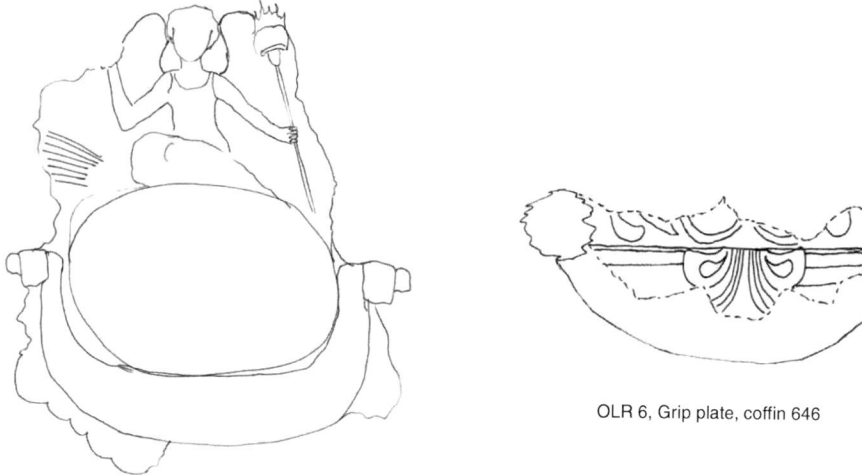

OLR 5, Grip plate, OLR 9 grip, coffin 254

OLR 6, Grip plate, coffin 646

FIGURE 1. Selection of newly identified grip plate styles OLR 3–OLR 6 from St. Luke's, Islington.

FIGURE 2. Grip plate CCS 3 and grip CCS 4, common forms first identified at Christ Church, Spitalfields.

plate (OLR 1) was the next most frequent, observed on 8 coffins (8/73; 11%), followed by CCS 6, a simple oval plate with a winged cherub, found on 7 coffins (9.6%; 7/73). Less popular were a simple, plain rectangular plate with linear borders, CCS 5, on 6 coffins (8.2%; 6/73); CCS 4, a simple V-shaped plate with a winged cherub, on 5 coffins (6.8%; 5/73); and CCS 31, an elaborate oval plate with winged cherubs and foliage on 3 coffins (4.1%; 3/73). As with depositum plates, a high prevalence of designs (11 in total, or 65% of all 17) were seen in only one or two instances, reflecting the overall tendency toward individuality.

Coffin grips were recovered from 243 coffins; predominantly of iron, many had suffered considerable corrosion, and the style of decoration could be identified for only 171. Among these were 18 different designs, with 135 grips (79%; 135/171) matching 9 types from Spitalfields. In addition, nine new styles (OLR 1–9) were identified (Figure 3), of which one (OLR 7) was also seen at St. George's, Bloomsbury (BBM 2).

The most common grip types were CCS 3b (28.7%), CCS 2a (17%), and OLR 4 (16.4%) (Table A3). These are detailed in Table 2, which presents the prevalence of all grip styles that occurred three or more times. Nine other grip types occurred only once (50% of

Table 2. Incidence of common grip types at St. Luke's for which three or more examples were identified.

Type	Number found	Percentage of total
CCS 3b	49	28.7
CCS 2a	29	17.0
OLR 4	28	16.4
CCS 1	12	7.0
CCS 4	12	7.0
CCS 3a	11	6.4
CCS 6	10	5.8
CCS 5	8	4.7
CCS 3	3	1.8

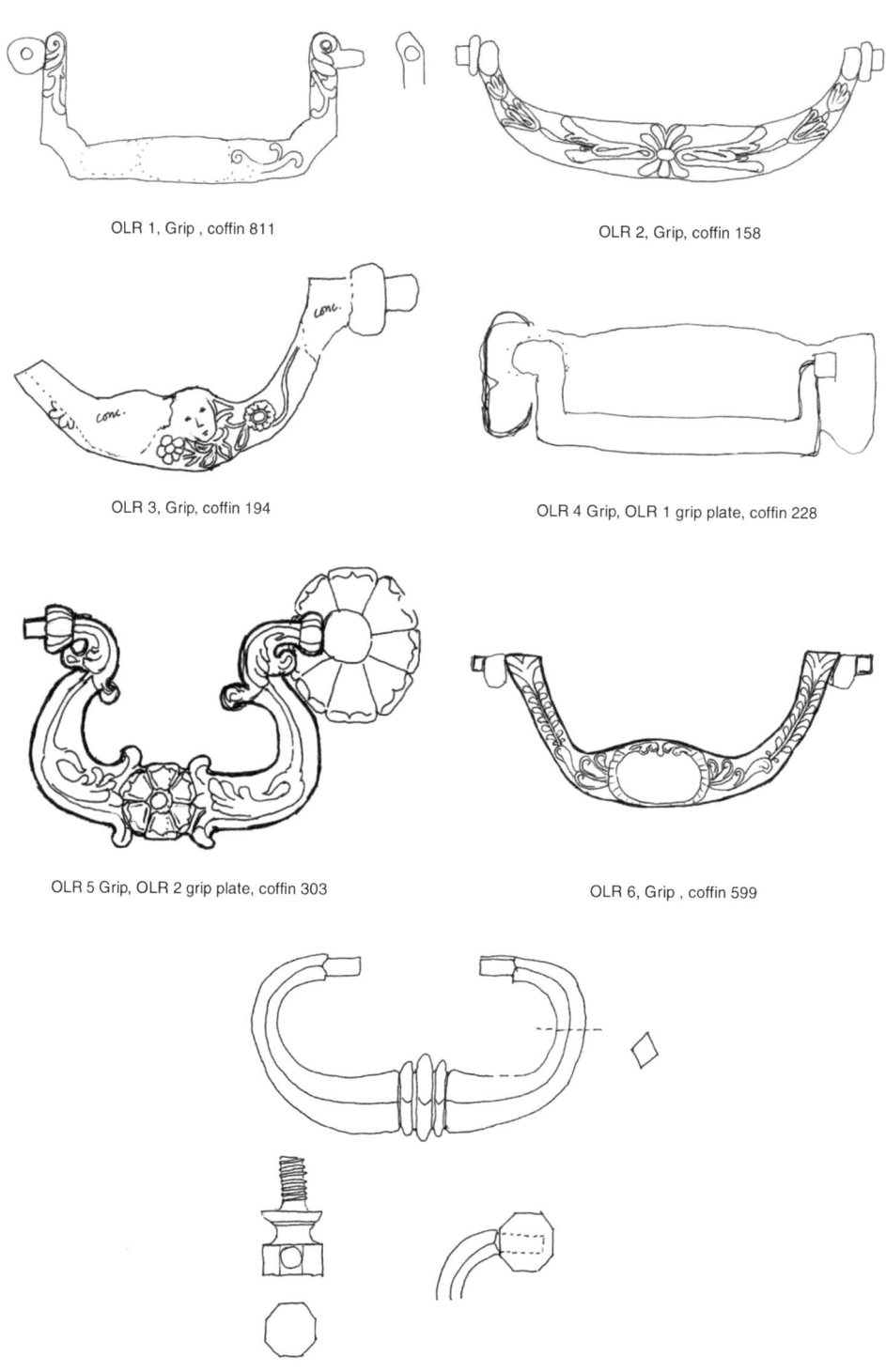

FIGURE 3. Additional grip styles OLR 1–OLR 7, recovered from St. Luke's, Islington.

the total number of designs identified). Frequently, but certainly not in all cases, grip plate CCS 3 and grip CCS 4 were found together as a set (Figure 2).

St. George's

Eleven grip plate styles were recorded on 61 coffins, 7 with new types noted. By far the most common design was CCS 3 (Figure 2), which accounted for 54% (33/61) of all coffins (Table A2). The next most common types were CCS 31 (6/61; 10%) and CCS 14 (4/61; 7%). Three previously unrecorded grip plate types (BBM 1–3) were identified (Figures 4, 5), and they include stylized foliage (BBM 1), a geometric design (BBM 2), and a cartouche with foliage and cherubs (BBM 3). Frequently, but certainly not in all cases, grip plate CCS 3 and grip CCS 4 were found together as a set.

In total 13 different grip styles were observed, including 8 that matched the Spitalfields typology (90 coffins) and 1 that matched a type seen at St. Luke's (1 coffin, OLR 7). Four newly identified designs, BBM 1–BBM 4, were recognized, found on 6 coffins (Figure 5). The most common grips were, in order of frequency, CCS 4 (71/97; 73%), CCS 5 (7/97; 7%), CCS 6 (5/97 coffins; 5%), and CCS 3 (3/97; 3%; Table A3).

Lid Motifs and Escutcheons

Lid motifs and escutcheons are stamped pieces of metal decorating the upholstery of the outer wooden case. Lid motifs are larger than escutcheons and tend to be located centrally in the chest and knee areas of the coffin lid. Escutcheons are most commonly found in the corners and along the margin of the upholstery studwork panels of the coffin lid and side panels of the outer wooden case.

FIGURE 4. Newly identified grip plate styles BBM 2 and BBM 3 from St. George's, Bloomsbury, and escutcheon OLR 1 from St. Luke's, Islington.

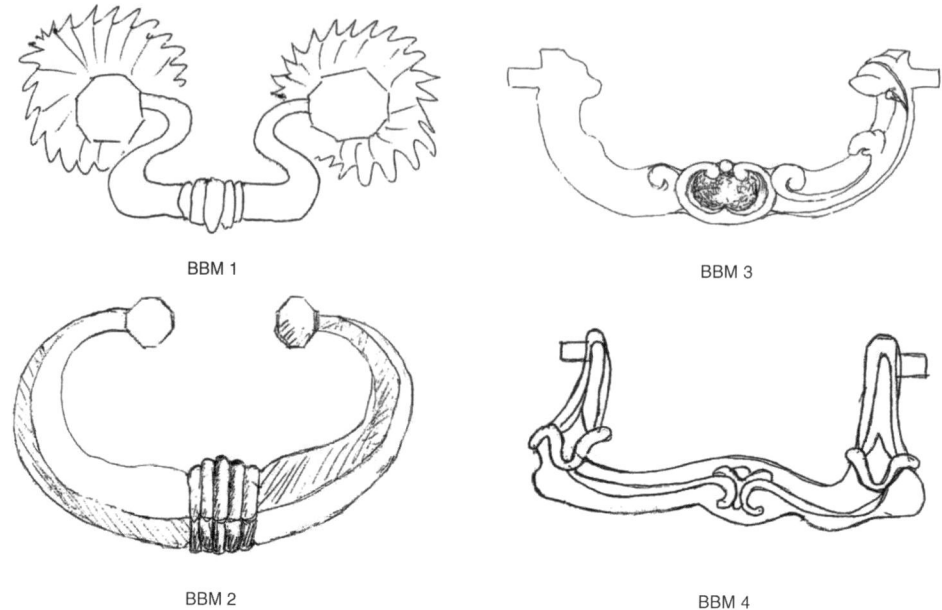

FIGURE 5. Additional grip styles BBM 1–BBM 4 recovered from St. George's, Bloomsbury. Illustration of grip BBM 1 also includes additional grip plate BBM 1.

St. Luke's

Nineteen lid motifs, representing 13 different styles, could be classified (Table A4), with 13 (8 different styles) matched at Spitalfields. They include three motifs (CCS 4, CCS 14, and CCS 19) that could not be dated at Spitalfields owing to poor preservation, but the dated coffins at St. Luke's has made this possible. This places them in the early to mid-nineteenth century. Five newly discovered designs (OLR 1–5) were identified on six coffins. These included three flaming urns and one *resurgam* motif (Figure 6). The most common lid motif was CCS 4 (3/19; 16%), with a snake eating its tail forming a circle, with a downward-pointing torch. Other common types comprised urns (CCS 2 and OLR 3, both 2/19; 11%), angels with a coronet and cherubs (CCS 6, 2/19; 11%), and winged cherubs (CCS 14, 2/19; 11%).

Twenty-one escutcheons were recovered from 15 coffins (Table A5), and all but one can be paralleled at Spitalfields in 9 different styles, the most common of which was CCS 1 (5/21; 23.8%), an oval motif with a leaf border and plain center. Other common styles were CCS 12 (4/21; 19%), a slightly more elaborate variation of CCS 1; CCS 4 (3/21; 14.3%), the same as CCS 1 but with an angel at the top of the leaf border; and CCS 6 (3/21; 14.3%), a stylized flower design. One newly discovered style, OLR 1, an oval stylized leaf design comparatively less elaborate than the former (Figure 4), was identified.

St. George's

Lid motifs from 83 coffins were sufficiently preserved to observe their styles (Table A4); 67 (10 different styles) matched Spitalfields, and 16 were in new styles (13 different designs). The most popular motif was CCS 6 (19/83; 22.9%), two angels holding aloft a

FIGURE 6. Newly identified lid motifs from St. Luke's, Islington, including flaming urns and resurgam motif.

crown, followed by CCS 14 (17/83; 20.5%), essentially the same design as grip plate CCS 3, a design of a cartouche encircled by scrolls and foliage and surmounted by two cherubim. It was possible to assign date ranges to four previously undated Spitalfields styles (CCS 12, 13, 14, and 25).

The new lid motif types that were identified (BBM 1–13; Figure 7) included four that were composite motifs, composed of between three and five separate pieces of decorative molded metal placed together (BBM 6, 7, 9 and 10). Some of the smaller elements were used elsewhere singly as escutcheons. For example, BBM 9 is composed of four corner escutcheons placed together to form a star, and BB7 was made of escutcheon BBM 5 (a flower motif) and a stylized foliage motif. BBM 10 is composed of four escutcheons: two BBM 4 and two CCS 9. The other lid motifs were single pieces of lead, tin, or copper. They depict a crown, a bible, an angel, the crucifixion of a very Herculean Christ, tombs, and flaming urns. Lid motif BBM 11 was the same style as grip plate CCS 16 but was found attached to the coffin lid in the position of a lid motif and hence has been included here as a new type. A single match was found between lid motifs from St. George's and St. Luke's, Islington: BBM 9, a circular ray (dated 1830), which very closely resembles OLR 5.

Escutcheons from 80 coffins could be recorded in detail (Table A5), with 72 (12 different styles) matched with types from Spitalfields (Table 3) and 8 (all different designs) classified as new types (BBM 1–8; Figure 8). The most common style was CCS 1 (a cartouche motif surrounded by swirling foliage), accounting for 33.8% (27/80) of the total assemblage. This was followed by CCS 6, a stylized flower motif (14/80; 17.5%). Of the new types, three depicted stars in different stylistic forms (BBM 1, 2, and 6; Figure 8); one depicted an angel (BBM 3), one depicted a flower (BBM 5), and three were abstract designs of foliage of classical inspiration (BBM 4, 7, and 8). All were made of brass, except for BBM 7, which was of black painted tin, matching the other fittings on coffin 2007.

Upholstery Studwork

St. Luke's

The preservation of upholstery fabric was very poor, with only 33 coffins retaining vestiges of recognizable textile on the outer wooden coffin. Of these, 28 were of baize, and 2 were of velvet. On 3 coffins a loosely woven, coarse fabric was identified. It was probably shoddy, a rough cloth made of woolen yarn often used as a backing for velvet upholstery that had presumably since decayed. Traditionally, the color of coffin upholstery was black, but colored cloth began to be used in the early nineteenth century (Litten, 1991); coffin 158 was covered with yellow fabric, and coffin 188 was covered with green fabric.

Because of the poor preservation of the outer wooden coffins little of the decorative arrangement of the studs could be identified. Indeed, in the vast majority of cases only single loose studs or short rows of 3–10 studs were recovered from the grave backfill. Only two coffins' upholstery stud designs could be matched to those from Christ Church, Spitalfields: CCS 3 (coffin 479) and CCS 36b (coffin 1089).

St. George's

Although the charcoal that had overlaid the coffin stacks had blackened many of the coffins' upholstery, colored velvets were observed in the adult and child coffins. Black

FIGURE 7. Additional lid motif types from St. George's, Bloomsbury.

Table 3. Types of metals used for coffin fittings at St. Luke's, Islington (total = 750).

Fitting type	Number found	Iron	Lead	Silvered tin	Brass	Tin pewter
Depositum plates	204	19 (9.4%)	153 (75.4%)	16 (7.9%)	15 (7.4%)	1 (0.5%)
Coffin grips	243	241 (99.2%)	0	0	2 (0.8%)	0
Grip plates	142	122 (85.9%)	6 (4.2%)	2 (1.4%)	0	12 (8.5%)
Lid motifs	23	17 (73.9%)	2 (8.7%)	0	0	4 (17.4%)
Escutcheons	15	8 (53.3%)	0	1 (6.7%)	2 (13.3%)	4 (26.7%)
Upholstery studs	123	82 (66.7%)	0	0	41 (33.3%)	0

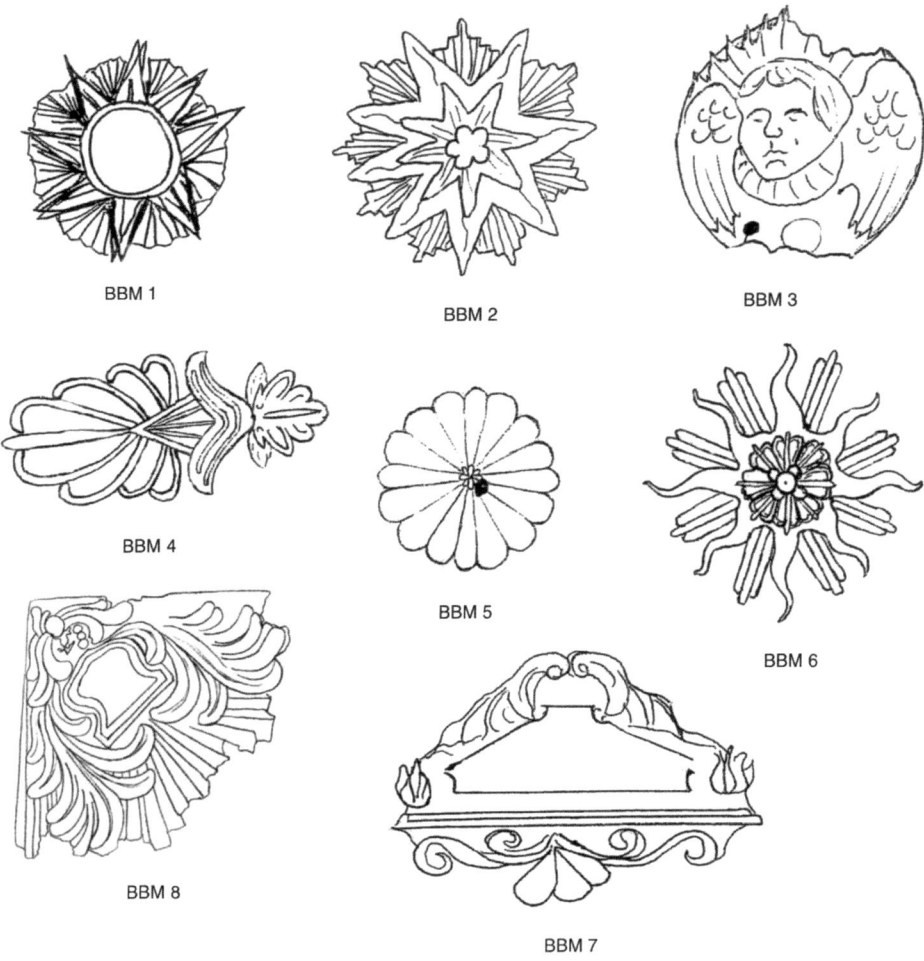

FIGURE 8. Newly identified escutcheon types from St. George's, Bloomsbury.

was overwhelmingly the most common, but mustard yellow, dark blue, dark green, red, and brown were also observed. Several infant coffins were upholstered in turquoise, a color particularly popular for baby burials in the early nineteenth century (Litten, 1991). Because of vertical crushing of many of the lower coffins, few of the side panels of the outer wooden cases were preserved. The lids fared better, with large numbers being preserved sufficiently well to identify the upholstery stud decoration (Table A6). In addition to the 47 matches made with Spitalfields, 29 new upholstery stud styles were identified, in most cases from the lid pattern alone.

Metals Used in Coffin Fittings

St. Luke's

Two hundred and four *depositum* plates were recorded (Table 3), the majority (153) made of lead (75.37%). Other metals used for plates in the assemblage were iron (9.36%), silvered tin (7.88%), brass (7.38%), and tin pewter (0.49%). Iron was overwhelmingly popular for grips, constituting 99.18% of the total assemblage, the remainder being of brass. Iron was also the most popular metal for grip plates (85.92%), followed by tin pewter (8.45%), lead (4.23%), and silvered tin (1.41%).

Only 23 lid motifs were recovered, probably because of poor preservation rather than a genuine absence from the original assemblage. The vast majority comprised very thin sheets of stamped iron, and many more had probably rusted away altogether. The surviving lid motifs were made of iron (74%), tin pewter (17%), and lead (9%). Eight coffins had escutcheons made from iron (53.33%), four from tin pewter (26.67%), two from brass (13.33%), and one from silvered tin (6.67%).

Upholstery studs were exclusively brass or iron. Of the 123 coffins with extant studs, 82 used iron, and 41 used brass. In a number of cases these were painted black, and in one case the brass studs had been gilded.

St. George's

Most outer breastplates (403) were made of lead or brass, the former being heavily decorated with a stamped central motif and borders. Of the assemblage of known material (9 were unrecorded), 62% (244) were lead, 32% (125) were brass, 3% (11) were iron, 2% (8) were silvered tin, and 1.5% (6) were tin pewter. Lead breastplates were occasionally enameled or painted black, with brass ones more plain, although four bore inscribed coats of arms. These were difficult to discern because of the fineness of the inscription and the oxidation of the brass.

Other depositum plates (i.e., inner breastplates, head plates, and foot plates) were almost exclusively of lead (Table 4). Of the 427 inner breastplates recovered from St. George's Church, only 3 were not of lead (0.7%). These were composed of iron. The material for the end plates (176), likewise, was overwhelmingly of lead (98%). Three exceptions were composed of iron.

One hundred and eight of the 134 coffins with grips of recognized metal (81%) were of iron. Of the remainder, 25 were of brass (19%), and 1 was of ormolu (0.746%). Of the 67 coffins with grip plates of known material, 43% were of brass, 31.34% were of iron, 12% were of silvered tin, 9% were of tin pewter, and 4% were of lead.

Table 4. Summary of known metals used for coffin fittings from St. Luke's and St. George's (total = 1,623).

Fitting type	Number found	Iron	Lead	Brass	Silvered tin	Tin pewter	Ormolu
Outer breastplate	394	11 (2.79%)	244 (61.93 %)	125 (31.73%)	8 (2.03%)	6 (1.52%)	0
Inner breastplate	427	3 (0.70%)	424 (99.30%)	0	0	0	0
End plate	176	3 (1.71%)	173 (98.30%)	0	0	0	0
Coffin grips	134	108 (80.60%)	0	25 (18.66 %)	0	0	1 (0.74 %)
Grip plates	67	21 (31.34%)	3 (4.47%)	30 (44.78%)	8 (11.94%)	5 (7.46%)	0
Lid motifs	49	19 (38.78%)	4 (8.16%)	21 (42.86%)	2 (4.08%)	3 (6.12%)	0
Escutcheons	53	16 (30.19%)	4 (7.55%)	32 (60.37%)	0	1 (1.89%)	0
Upholstery studs	323	152 (47.06%)	0	173 (53.56%)	0	0	0

Two hundred and twenty-one lid motifs were recovered at St. George's Church. Being composed of thin stamped sheets of metal, lid motifs are more prone to corrosion than thicker, more robust coffin fittings. The worst-preserved lid motifs were those made of iron, the details of the decoration often being indiscernible because of rusting. The metal composition of 49 lid motifs was recorded, with brass being the most popular material (60%), followed by iron (30%), lead (8.16%), tin pewter (6%), and silvered tin (4%).

At St. George's Church, upholstery studs were made exclusively of brass or of iron (Table 4). Of the 395 coffins with extant studwork, recordings of the metals used were made on 325 coffins (82%). Copper alloy was the more popular metal, recovered from 173 coffins (54%), and iron was recovered from 152 coffins (47%). Of the latter, 5 had been painted or enameled black, and 2 had been dipped in tin to create a silvered effect.

Discussion

Data collected on coffin furniture from St. Luke's and St. George's have been analyzed with the primary aim of expanding the corpus of published styles and expanding and refining date ranges. Through this analysis, it is possible to be more confident in exploring the frequency and range of styles. The evidence clearly demonstrates that for all categories of fittings, simple designs were uncommon. Most styles tend to be elaborate but also very varied, with many examples of just one style being identified. More variation was seen at St. Luke's than at St. George's. Many designs were found to match those at Christ Church, Spitalfields, but date ranges have been identified or extended, and the tables will now provide an important checklist for future researchers against which to compare new discoveries.

Some Limitations of the Data

The present analysis has focused on only broad patterns in the incidence of fitting styles. With a few exceptions, it has not attempted to explore this in relation to different variables, such as age, sex, intramural versus extramural burials, and different occupations. These analyses would afford far greater insight into the prevalence and distribution of fitting styles in the late eighteenth and early nineteenth centuries, as has been demonstrated by Hancox (2006), who compared fitting materials found in two contemporaneous vaults from St. Martin's-in-the-Bullring, Birmingham.

Between them, St. Luke's and St. George's comprise one of the largest assemblages of coffin fittings to have been examined to date. Unfortunately, despite this size, the number of actual fittings that could be examined was reduced (sometimes drastically) as a result of poor preservation. Although X-radiography probably would have increased sample size in some cases, this facility was not available at the time of analysis. In particular, the poor preservation of the outer wooden coffins at St. Luke's and vertical crushing of many of the lower stacked coffins at St. George's meant that little of the decorative arrangement of the upholstery studs could be identified. Indeed, in the vast majority of cases, only single loose studs or short rows of 3–10 studs were recovered from the grave backfill. The absence of identified patterns therefore should not be taken to imply that upholstery studs were not used to create elaborate patterns on these coffins, but rather only that the designs could not be recognized. Fittings composed of thin stamped sheets of metal, such as lid motifs, also suffered particularly badly, being more prone to corrosion and rust (especially those composed of iron) than thicker, more robust coffin fittings. Thus, the original prevalence of different fitting styles was probably significantly higher than that presented here.

Comparisons between styles seen at St. George's and St. Luke's have been limited to that of the Spitalfields corpus. No doubt many more matches with fittings from other sites would further refine dating, as well as expand taxonomies. Similarly, no comparison with the trade catalogs held at the Victoria and Albert Museum has been made and would, no doubt, signal further significant trends.

Incidence of Coffin Fitting Styles

The vast majority of styles identified at St. Luke's and St. George's matched those that were seen among the crypt burials at Christ Church, Spitalfields. All of the types observed at St. Luke's and St. George's, including new types, are tabulated with their assigned date ranges in the Appendix.

Some of the most popular motifs included the winged cherub, seen on grip plates OLR 3 (Figure 1) and BBM 3 (Figure 4). This motif is very common in post-medieval graveyards (see Mytum, "Explaining Stylistic Change in Mortuary Material Culture," this volume) and is associated with all social classes (Boore, 1998:73). This motif dates to the period 1740–1850, but at the churchyard of St. Martin's, Birmingham, it makes an appearance only in the first third of the nineteenth century. Oval grip plates with a repoussé design of winged cherub's heads and stamped iron depositum plates with a concave oval cartouche encircled by a garland of flowers design first appear at the end of the seventeenth century (Litten, 1991). The urn motif is popular at St. Martin's, Birmingham. The greater variation of styles that was seen at St. Luke's may be a result of a burial population that comprised a broader cross section of society, being composed of crypt and churchyard burials, rather than just crypt burials, as was observed from St. George's and, indeed, Spitalfields. However, St. Luke's was also used for a slightly longer period of time, and therefore, the greater variation may be a result of this.

The styles seen at both sites are consistent with the expected range for the late eighteenth and early nineteenth centuries, as reflected in the trade catalogs from this period. Using the trade catalogs, Hancox (2006:159–160) has summarized chronological trends in coffin furniture, further explored by Mytum (2016; "Explaining Stylistic Change in Mortuary Material Culture," this volume). In the late eighteenth century fittings were elaborate, with the urn and flower design and angels and cherubs being popular motifs. Coffin lace was not used, and upholstery studs were employed only in simple decorations, either in single or double rows around the edges of the coffin. By the early nineteenth century there were more varied designs, with new motifs appearing, such as the rose and thistle and Masonic eye (but cherubs, angels, and urn and flower designs also remained popular). Upholstery studs were employed in more elaborate designs, including diamonds and triple rows, and coffin lace was used. By the late nineteenth century, angel, cherub, and flower motifs had disappeared, and simpler designs were being selected.

The predominance of rectangular or tapered plates is paralleled in other London assemblages (for example, Christ Church, Spitalfields, and St. Marylebone Church) but is in contrast to the lower-status assemblage from St. Martin's, Birmingham, where the majority of plates were shields (Hancox, 2006).

Table 5. St. George's lozenge- and shield-shaped breastplates by age, sex, and marital status (includes only those that were legible).

Shape	Type	Number of coffins	Sex	Age
Lozenge	CCS 30	3	Female	66 years
			Female	16 years
			Female	78 years
Lozenge	CCS 32	1	Female	15 years
Lozenge	CCS 46	7	Female	16 months, 7 days
			Female	5 years, 6 months
			Female	13 years, 9 months
			Female	No age
			Female	No age
			Female	No age
			Female	No age
Shield	CCS 47	2	Male	No age
			Male	No age

Other breastplate shapes observed include the lozenge and shield. Where it was possible to observe relevant details, at St. George's all lozenge shapes were associated with females, both children and adults (Table 5). The titles of the females were all "Miss," indicating that they were unmarried. The two shield breastplates that could be associated with sexed individuals were, in contrast, associated with adult males. Although admittedly these samples are small, these observations are consistent with heraldic convention in which the shape of depositum plates referred to the sex and marital status of the deceased. Thus, lozenge shapes were reserved for young girls and spinsters; shields were reserved for boys and young men (Litten, 1993:109).

Only two examples of lozenge-shaped breastplates and one example of a shield-shaped breastplate were found at St. Luke's. The extent to which the dictates of heraldry prevailed at St. George's and St. Luke's requires further analysis. From the beginning of the eighteenth century heraldic convention started to fall out of popularity, with the result being that by the nineteenth century coffin fitters were unfamiliar with this convention, even though the shapes continued to be used (Litten, 1993). It is therefore noteworthy that the use of lozenge and shield shapes at St. George's reflects a familiarity with heraldic convention by undertakers and possibly also their clients. In contrast, this familiarity was not seen at Christ Church, Spitalfields, and St. Martin's, Birmingham (Hancox, 2006). Other claimed conventions were rectangles with a central cartouche and rectangles with central squares, which were associated with married women or widows and married men or widowers, respectively, but these have not yet been tested against archaeological assemblages.

Throughout the eighteenth and nineteenth centuries grips tended to be of a plain, rounded style with no embellishments (Miles et al., 2008). At St. Luke's and Bloomsbury, this plainness was not the case, with the majority of grips having some form of decoration, including the form with two winged cherubs at the center above a central flower with floral and leaf motifs (Figure 4), which is a very common design from the late eighteenth and nineteenth centuries (Miles et al., 2008:64) and is similar to CCS 4.

Symbolism

Winged cherubs, angels, flowers, foliage, and urns were all popular motifs on the fittings from both St. Luke's and St. George's and are typical of the period (see Mytum, "Explaining Stylistic Change in Mortuary Material Culture," this volume). The urn, an ancient Greek symbol of mourning, was especially popular, used well into the 1850s, but it was not very prevalent at St. Luke's or St. George's. Cherubim were favored for the coffins of infants and children but at both St. Luke's and St. George's were associated with adults and children alike. Most often, they were depicted as just a head without a body, a symbol of the soul. Angels refer to heaven and the afterlife and, when shown blowing trumpets (as some were at St. Luke's and St. George's), represent God's glory and victory over death or, alternatively, the day of judgment.

Flowers and foliage were very frequent among the coffin fittings from both sites, in particular on breastplates and grip plates. Many represented stylized and generic plants that could not be identified to species, but roses, chrysanthemums, and oak leaves were identified and frequent. Lilies and chrysanthemums have long been associated with death. Lilies, seen to represent purity, resurrection, and restoration of innocence of the soul at death, are particularly associated with the Virgin Mary. They were most commonly associated with the burial of women. Roses represent beauty, hope, and unfailing love. Depending on the stage of their opening, roses may represent the age of the person at the time of death: a bud denotes a child, a partial bloom indicates a teenager, and a rose in full bloom denotes an adult, but sample sizes are too small to see if this symbolism was actually the motive for choices on coffin fittings. Oak leaves are associated with stability, strength, honor, eternity, the cross of Jesus, and liberty.

Socioeconomic Status

The predominance of elaborate coffin fittings from both churches is consistent with the high status held by those who were buried there. Lawyers, doctors, members of Parliament, imperial administrators, and librarians of the nearby British Museum are all listed in the burial registers. Individuals from less elevated professions were also present, however. For example, a carpenter, servant, and butcher are recorded in burial registers. Unfortunately, none of these individuals could be identified from their coffin fittings.

St. Luke's vestry minutes indicate that the wealthy were also buried in the southern and northern churchyards, as well as within the crypt. Indeed, the vestry minutes record that on 12 October 1810, the committee recommended that funerals of opulent inhabitants should be promoted in the vaults and churchyards, with the pest ground reserved for poor inhabitants, which implies this had not always been the case up to that point. Further, the cost of burial was most expensive in the crypt, followed by the southern part of the churchyard (a more visible location because the entrance to the church was on that side), then the northern part of the churchyard, with the pest ground being the cheapest burial location. A cursory analysis of the distribution of coffin materials in the crypt, southern churchyard, and northern churchyard reflects this hierarchy of burial practice. Unlike St. George's, very little information on the occupations held by individuals who were recovered from St. Luke's survives. In fact, only two occupations, both ecclesiastical (one a rector, the other listed as just "church"), are listed (Boston and Scott, 2009).

Metal Used in Coffin Fittings

Relatively little analysis has been undertaken on the metals used for coffin fittings within Britain, although it was developments in the manufacturing and finishing processes that were so important in creating this form of funerary display. The range of materials found includes lead, pewter, tin, brass, and stamped iron.

It is not surprising to find that many of the breastplates from St. Luke's and St. George's consisted of stamped lead plates (Tables 1, 5). These continued to be common in vaults in the late eighteenth and early nineteenth centuries as a more expensive alternative to the tin-dipped stamped iron furniture that could not be engraved (Litten, 1991:108–109). Pure tin was rare because of its expense, but by the end of the eighteenth century pewter and pure tin—natural or silvered—were being used for breastplates, grip plates, and lid motifs, although the nobility and others appear to have remained loyal to brass as more convenient for the engraver to work, especially if a coat of arms was to be included.

The stamped iron furniture, shiny and bright if tinned or made black through a variety of processes, formed the majority of fittings from the later eighteenth century onward, notably for breastplates, lid motifs, escutcheons, and grip plates. Needing to be robust, the metals used for grips were restricted to iron and brass, and most grips were made of iron.

Conclusions

The excavation of assemblages from London has increased the range of identified coffin fitting designs and has refined the dating of those already classified from Christ Church, Spitalfields. The assemblages provide a complex set of data that will allow further analysis according to social and religious categories. The analysis of fittings by materials on a large scale for the first time indicates that material choice was among the options available for the bereaved and demonstrates further the complexity of choice in the production and distribution of coffin furniture. As more assemblages are recovered, the chronology of forms will become clearer, and the chronological gap between largely later eighteenth and early to mid-nineteenth century archaeological examples, and the data largely derived from the later nineteenth century trade catalogs, will be closed.

Appendix

Tables A1–A6 present the frequency and date ranges assigned to all of the Christ Church, Spitalfields, types by site, including St. Luke's, Islington, and St. George's, Bloomsbury. Data from St. Bartholomew's, Penn, available at the time of data entry are also included.

Table A1. Breastplates. A dash (—) indicates a particular type was not identified at a particular location.

Type	Christ Church, Spitalfields		St. Luke's, Islington		St. George's, Bloomsbury		St. Bartholomew's, Penn, Wolverhampton		Overall date range from the four sites	Total	Percentage (total = 667)
	Date range	Number found	Date range	Number found	Date range	Number found	Date range	Number found			
CCS 1	1729–1807	15	1775	1	1848	1	1811–1855	40	1729–1855	57	8.5
CCS 2	1839–1845	2	1814	1	1830	1	Undated	1	1814–1845	5	0.7
CCS 3	1810–1821	11	—	—	—	—	—	—	1810–1821	11	1.6
CCS 4	1783–1822	5	Undated	1	1819	1	—	—	1783–1822	7	1.0
CCS 5	1827–1847	3	—	—	—	—	—	—	1827–1847	3	0.4
CCS 6	1783–1852	25	1802–1822	10	1805–1824	16	—	—	1783–1852	51	7.6
CCS 7	1779–1794	2	—	—	1827	1	Undated	2	1779–1827	5	0.7
CCS 8	1767–1825	34	1785–1880	9	1805–1832	18	—	—	1767–1880	61	9.1
CCS 9	1773–1797	12	1773–1814	7	1825–1834	4	—	—	1773–1834	23	3.4
CCS 10	Undated	1	—	—	—	—	—	—	Undated	1	0.1
CCS 11	Undated	1	—	—	—	—	—	—	Undated	1	0.1
CCS 12	Undated	2	—	—	—	—	—	—	Undated	2	0.3
CCS 13	1799	1	—	—	—	—	—	—	1799	1	0.1
CCS 14	1743–1818	4	—	—	1818	1	—	—	1743–1818	5	0.7
CCS 15	1824	2	—	—	—	—	—	—	1824	2	0.3
CCS 16	1835	1	—	—	—	—	—	—	1835	1	0.1
CCS 17	1828	1	—	—	—	—	—	—	1828	1	0.1
CCS 18	1765	10	—	—	—	—	—	—	1765	10	1.5
CCS 19	1761	1	—	—	—	—	—	—	1761	1	0.1
CCS 20	1813–1847	3	1790–1853	18	1814–1852	19	—	—	1790–1853	40	5.9
CCS 21	1824–1847	21	1828–1850	27	1812–1846	29	—	—	1812–1850	77	11.5

ID	Date	n	Date	n	Date	n	Date	n	Date	n	%
CCS 22	1821	1	—	—	—	—	1818–1819	2	1818–1821	3	0.4
CCS 23	1831	1	—	—	—	—	1830–1843	2	1830–1843	3	0.4
CCS 24	1782–1819	4	—	—	—	—	1809–1826	3	1782–1826	7	1.0
CCS 25	1832	1	—	—	—	—	1845	1	1832–1845	2	0.3
CCS 26	1832–1849	3	—	—	—	—	1835	1	1832–1849	4	0.6
CCS 27	1788–1839	3	—	—	Undated	2	1814	1	1788–1839	6	0.9
CCS 28	1829–1842	4	1844	1	—	—	1822–1823	2	1822–1844	7	1.0
CCS 29	Undated	2	—	—	—	—	—	—	Undated	2	0.3
CCS 30	1809–1832	3	—	—	—	—	1819–1826	3	1809–1832	6	0.9
CCS 31	1759–1821	3	—	—	—	—	—	—	1759–1821	3	0.4
CCS 32	1830	1	—	—	—	—	1833	1	1830–1833	2	0.3
CCS 33	1802	1	—	—	—	—	—	—	1802	1	0.1
CCS 34	1820	1	—	—	—	—	—	—	1820	1	0.1
CCS 35	1806–1825	6	—	—	—	—	—	—	1806–1825	6	0.9
CCS 36	1821	1	—	—	—	—	—	—	1821	1	0.1
CCS 37	1796	1	1795	1	—	—	—	—	1795–1796	2	0.3
CCS 38	1779–1825	6	—	—	—	—	—	—	1779–1825	6	0.9
CCS 39	1794	2	—	—	—	—	—	—	1794	2	0.3
CCS 40	1788	1	—	—	—	—	—	—	1788	1	0.1
CCS 41	1764–1767	3	—	—	—	—	—	—	1764–1767	3	0.4
CCS 42	1777	1	—	—	—	—	—	—	1777	1	0.1
CCS 43	1793–1797	2	—	—	—	—	—	—	1793–1797	2	0.3
CCS 44	1828–1829	2	—	—	—	—	—	—	1828–1829	2	0.3
CCS 45	Undated	1	—	—	—	—	—	—	Undated	1	0.1
CCS 46	1771–1821	6	—	—	1806–1846	7	—	—	1771–1846	13	1.9
CCS 47	Undated	1	—	—	1810–1840	2	—	—	1810–1840	3	0.4
CCS 48	1835	1	—	—	—	—	—	—	1835	1	0.1
CCS 49	Undated	1	—	—	Undated	2	—	—	Undated	3	0.4

Table A1. (Continued)

Type	Christ Church, Spitalfields		St. Luke's, Islington		St. George's, Bloomsbury		St. Bartholomew's, Penn, Wolverhampton		Overall date range from the four sites	Total	Percentage (total = 667)
	Date range	Number found	Date range	Number found	Date range	Number found	Date range	Number found			
CCS 50	1780–1821	6	—	—	—	—	—	—	1780–1821	6	0.9
CCS 51	1795	1	—	—	—	—	—	—	1795	1	0.1
CCS 52	1778–1794	4	—	—	—	—	—	—	1778–1794	4	0.6
CCS 53	1834	1	—	—	1825–1833	2	—	—	1825–1833	3	0.4
CCS 54	1827	1	—	—	—	—	—	—	1827	1	0.1
CCS 55	1820–1826	3	—	—	—	—	—	—	1820–1826	3	0.4
CCS 56	1825	2	—	—	—	—	—	—	1825	2	0.3
CCS 57	1812–1824	2	—	—	—	—	—	—	1812–1824	2	0.3
CCS 58	1823	1	—	—	—	—	—	—	1823	1	0.1
CCS 59	1793	1	—	—	—	—	—	—	1793	1	0.1
CCS 60	Undated	1	—	—	—	—	—	—	Undated	1	0.1
CCS 61	1765–1786	3	1808	1	1811	1	—	—	1765–1811	5	0.7
CCS 62	1811	1	—	—	—	—	—	—	1811	1	0.1
CCS 63	1775	1	—	—	—	—	—	—	1775	1	0.1
CCS 64	1777–1794	4	1783	1	—	—	—	—	1777–1794	5	0.7
CCS 65	1778	1	—	—	—	—	—	—	1778	1	0.1
CCS 66	1761–1770	6	—	—	—	—	—	—	1761–1770	6	0.9
CCS 67	1769–1777	3	1802	1	1807–1826	8	—	—	1769–1826	12	1.8
CCS 68	1768	1	—	—	—	—	—	—	1768	1	0.1
CCS 69	1765–1803	3	—	—	—	—	—	—	1765–1803	3	0.4
CCS 70	1777–1778	2	—	—	—	—	—	—	1777–1778	2	0.3

ID	Date	Count	Date range	Count	Date range	Count	Date range	Count	Date	Count	Value
CCS 71	1765	1	—	—	—	—	—	—	1765	1	0.1
CCS 72	1765	1	—	—	—	—	—	—	1765	1	0.1
CCS 73	1776	1	—	—	—	—	—	—	1776	1	0.1
CCS 74	1777	1	—	—	—	—	—	—	1777	1	0.1
CCS 75	1782	2	—	—	—	—	—	—	1782	2	0.3
CCS 76	1785–1793	2	—	—	—	—	—	—	1785–1793	2	0.3
CCS 77	1823	1	—	—	—	—	—	—	1823	1	0.1
CCS 78	1827	1	—	—	—	—	—	—	1827	1	0.1
CCS 79	1790	1	—	—	—	—	—	—	1790	1	0.1
CCS 80	1777–1786	2	—	—	—	—	—	—	1777–1786	2	0.3
CCS 81	1836	1	—	—	—	—	—	—	1836	1	0.1
CCS 82	1820–1829	5	1800–1830	17	—	47	1806–1848	—	1800–1848	69	10.3
CCS 83	1747	1	—	—	—	—	—	—	1747	1	0.1
CCS 84	1833–1836	2	1828–1835	4	1810–1842	15	—	—	1828–1842	21	3.1
CCS 85	1835	1	—	—	1810	1	—	—	1810–1835	2	0.3
CCS 86	1795–1811	2	—	—	1805	1	—	—	1795–1811	3	0.4
CCS 87	1827	1	—	—	—	—	—	—	1827	1	0.1
CCS 88	1770	1	—	—	—	—	—	—	1770	1	0.1
CCS 89	1758	2	—	—	—	—	—	—	1758	2	0.3
CCS 90	1827	1	—	—	—	—	—	—	1827	1	0.1
CCS 91	1824	1	1848	1	—	—	—	—	1824	1	0.1
CCS 92	1832	1	—	—	—	—	—	—	1832	2	0.3
CCS 93	1852	1	—	—	—	—	—	—	1852	1	0.1
CCS 94	1829	1	—	—	—	—	—	—	1829	1	0.1
CCS 95	1737–1746	2	—	—	—	—	—	—	1737–1746	2	0.3
CCS 96	1732	1	—	—	—	—	—	—	1732	1	0.1
CCS 97	1793	1	—	—	1823	1	—	—	1793–1823	2	0.3
CCS 98	1776	1	—	—	—	—	—	—	1776	1	0.1

Table A1. *(Continued)*

Type	Christ Church, Spitalfields		St. Luke's, Islington		St. George's, Bloomsbury		St. Bartholomew's, Penn, Wolverhampton		Overall date range from the four sites	Total	Percentage (total = 667)
	Date range	Number found	Date range	Number found	Date range	Number found	Date range	Number found			
CCS 99	1772	1	—	—	—	—	—	—	1772	1	0.1
CCS 100	1775	1	—	—	—	—	—	—	1775	1	0.1
CCS 101	1768	1	—	—	—	—	—	—	1768	1	0.1
CCS 102	1739	1	—	—	—	—	—	—	1739	1	0.1
CCS 103	1806–1809	2	—	—	—	—	—	—	1806–1809	2	0.3
CCS 104	1784–1789	2	—	—	—	—	—	—	1784–1789	2	0.3
CCS 105	1753	1	—	—	—	—	—	—	1753	1	0.1
CCS 106	Undated	1	—	—	—	—	—	—	Undated	1	0.1
CCS 107	1794	1	—	—	—	—	—	—	1749	1	0.1
CCS 108	1806	1	—	—	—	—	—	—	1806	1	0.1
CCS 109	Undated	1	—	—	—	—	—	—	Undated	1	0.1
CCS 110	1827	1	—	—	—	—	—	—	1827	1	0.1
CCS 111	1788	1	—	—	—	—	—	—	1788	1	0.1
CCS 112	1757	2	—	—	—	—	—	—	1757	2	0.3
CCS 113	1811	1	—	—	—	—	—	—	1811	1	0.1
CCS 114	Undated	1	—	—	—	—	—	—	Undated	1	0.1

Table A2. Grip plates. A dash (—) indicates a particular type was not identified at a particular location.

Grip plate type	Christ Church, Spitalfields		St. Luke's, Islington		St. Bartholomew's, Penn		St. George's Bloomsbury			
	Date range	Number found (total = 216)	Date range	Number found (total = 59)	Date range	Number found (total = 10)	Date range	Number found (total = 54)	Overall date range	Overall number found (total = 339)
CCS 1	1812–1825	9	1816–1840	2	—	—	—	—	1812–1840	11
CCS 2	Undated	1	—	—	—	—	1821	1	1821	2
CCS 3	1768–1842	100	1787–1880	30	1837	8	1807–1841	33	1768–1880	171
CCS 4	Undated	2	1807–1850	5	—	—	1827–1843	3	1807–1850	10
CCS 5	1729–1815	15	1807	6	—	—	1829	1	1729–1829	22
CCS 6	Undated	1	1820–1848	7	—	—	—	—	1820–1848	8
CCS 7	1791–1813	5	—	—	—	—	—	—	1791–1813	5
CCS 8	Undated	2	—	—	—	—	—	—	Undated	2
CCS 9	1784–1827	22	—	—	—	—	1826	1	1784–1827	23
CCS 10	Undated	1	—	—	—	—	—	—	Undated	1
CCS 11	1795–1849	2	—	—	—	—	1842	1	1795–1849	3
CCS 12	1761	1	—	—	—	—	—	—	1761	1
CCS 13	1798	1	—	—	—	—	—	—	1798	1
CCS 14	1843–1845	4	1844–1847	2	—	—	1824–1843	4	1824–1847	10
CCS 15	Undated	1	—	—	—	—	—	—	Undated	1
CCS 16	Undated	2	—	—	—	—	1836	1	1836	3
CCS 17	1765–1793	2	1826	1	—	—	1817–1828	2	1765–1828	5
CCS 18	Undated	1	—	—	—	—	—	—	Undated	1
CCS 19	1763	2	—	—	—	—	—	—	1763	2
CCS 20	Undated	4	—	—	—	—	—	—	Undated	4
CCS 21	Undated	1	—	—	—	—	—	—	Undated	1

Table A2. (Continued)

Grip plate type	Christ Church, Spitalfields		St. Luke's, Islington		St. Bartholomew's, Penn		St. George's Bloomsbury			Overall number found (total = 339)
	Date range	Number found (total = 216)	Date range	Number found (total = 59)	Date range	Number found (total = 10)	Date range	Number found (total = 54)	Overall date range	
CCS 22	Undated	1	—	—	—	—	—	—	Undated	1
CCS 23	Undated	1	—	—	—	—	—	—	Undated	1
CCS 24	1794–1806	4	—	—	Undated	1	—	—	1794–1806	5
CCS 25	1833–1847	10	1841	1	Undated	1	1840	1	1833–1847	13
CCS 26	1819	2	—	—	—	—	—	—	1819	2
CCS 27	1779	2	Undated	1	—	—	—	—	1779	3
CCS 28	Undated	1	—	—	—	—	—	—	Undated	1
CCS 29	1776	1	Undated	1	—	—	—	—	1776	2
CCS 30	1747	1	—	—	—	—	—	—	1747	1
CCS 31	1823	3	1810–1830	3	—	—	1810–1846	6	1810–1846	12
CCS 32	Undated	1	—	—	—	—	—	—	Undated	1
CCS 33	1806–1828	8	—	—	—	—	—	—	1806–1828	8
CCS 34	1799	1	—	—	—	—	—	—	1799	1
CCS 35	Undated	1	—	—	—	—	—	—	Undated	1

Table A3. Grips. A dash (—) indicates a particular type was not found at a particular location.

Grip type	Christ Church, Spitalfields Date range	Number found (total = 514)	St. Luke's, Islington Date range	Number found (total = 135)	St. Bartholomew's, Penn Date range	Number found (total = 101)	St. George's, Bloomsbury Date range	Number found (total = 90)	Overall date range	Overall number found (total = 840)
CCS 1	1747–1847	29	1762–1853	12	1811–1849	13	—	—	1747–1853	54
CCS 2	1763–1837	88	—	—	1813	5	1828	1	1763–1837	94
CCS 2a	—	—	1811	29	1830s	33	—	—	1811–1830s	62
CCS 2b	—	—	Undated	1	Undated	5	—	—	Undated	6
CCS 3	1729–1827	121	1820–1850	3	1836–1837	3	1807–1836	3	1729–1850	130
CCS 3a	—	—	1729–1830	11	—	—	—	—	17.9–1830	11
CCS 3b	—	—	1835–1840	49	—	—	—	—	1835–1840	49
CCS 4	1743–1847	176	1761–1880	12	—	40	1805–1847	71	1743–1880	299
CCS 5	1744–1835	72	1796–1822	8	—	—	1809–1830	7	1744–1835	87
CCS 6	1839–1849	19	1777–1844	10	Undated	1	1835–1848	5	1777–1849	35
CCS 7	1821–1849	2	—	—	—	—	1842	1	1821–1849	3
CCS 8	Undated	1	—	—	—	—	1844	1	Undated	2
CCS 9	1770	2	—	—	—	—	—	—	1770–1844	2
CCS 10	1837	2	—	—	Undated	1	1825	1	1825–1837	4
CCS 11	Undated	1	—	—	—	—	—	—	Undated	1
CCS 12	Undated	1	—	—	—	—	—	—	Undated	1

Eighteenth- and Nineteenth-Century Coffin Furniture 157

Table A4. Lid motifs. A dash (—) indicates a particular type was not identified at a particular location.

Lid motif type	Christ Church, Spitalfields		St. Luke's, Islington		St. Bartholomew's, Penn		St. George's, Bloomsbury		Overall	
	Date range	Number found (total =124)	Date range	Number found (total = 13)	Date range	Number found (total = 2)	Date range	Number found (total = 67)	Overall date range	Overall number found (total = 206)
CCS 1	1839	5	1820	1	1829	1	1821–1850	4	1821–1850	11
CCS 2	1795–1847	39	1797–1838	2	—	—	1809–1847	15	1795–1847	56
CCS 3	1821–1824	10	1831	1	—	—	—	—	1821–1831	11
CCS 4	Undated	6	1835–1847	3	—	—	—	—	1835–1847	9
CCS 5	1798	2	—	—	—	—	—	—	1798	2
CCS 6	1779–1847	30	1797–1844	2	Undated	1	1810–1852	19	1779–1852	52
CCS 7	1849	1	—	—	—	—	1842	1	1842–1849	2
CCS 8	1832–1849	3	—	—	—	—	1816	1	1816–1849	4
CCS 9	1849	1	—	—	—	—	1842	1	1842–1849	2
CCS 10	1793–1820	3	Undated	1	—	—	—	—	1793–1820	4
CCS 11	1822–1843	5	—	—	—	—	—	—	1822–1843	5
CCS 12	Undated	1	—	—	—	—	1835	2	1835	3
CCS 13	Undated	3	—	—	—	—	1836–1852	4	1836–1852	7
CCS 14	Undated	1	1822	2	—	—	1813–1841	17	1813–1841	20
CCS 15	Undated	1	—	—	—	—	—	—	Undated	1
CCS 16	1789	1	—	—	—	—	—	—	1789	1
CCS 17	1821–1824	2	—	—	—	—	—	—	1821–1824	2
CCS 18	Undated	1	—	—	—	—	—	—	Undated	1
CCS 19	Undated	1	1840	1	—	—	—	—	1840	2
CCS 20	Undated	1	—	—	—	—	—	—	Undated	1
CCS 21	Undated	1	—	—	—	—	—	—	Undated	1
CCS 22	1794	1	—	—	—	—	—	—	1794	1

CCS 23	Undated	2	—	—	—	—	Undated	2
CCS 24	1798	1	—	—	—	—	1798	1
CCS 25	Undated	1	—	—	1825–1833	3	1825–1833	4
CCS 26	Undated	1	—	—	—	—	Undated	1

Table A5. Escutcheons. A dash (—) indicates a particular type was not identified at a particular location. No escutcheons of the types listed here were found at St. Bartholomew's, Penn.

Escutcheon type	Christ Church, Spitalfields		St. Luke's, Islington		St. George's, Bloomsbury		Overall date range	Overall number found (total = 266)
	Date range	Number found (total = 174)	Date range	Number found (total = 20)	Date range	Number found (total = 72)		
CCS 1	1776–1827	45	1797–1836	5	1804–1847	27	1776–1847	77
CCS 2	1839	2	1822	1	—	—	1822–1839	3
CCS 3	1815	6	1822	1	1837	1	1815–1837	8
CCS 4	1779–1839	24	1787–1831	3	1818–1824	2	1779–1839	29
CCS 5	Undated	3	—	—	1833–1836	2	1833–1836	5
CCS 6	1823–1835	10	1826–1838	3	1806–1846	14	1806–1846	27
CCS 7	Undated	1	—	—	1817	1	1817	2
CCS 8	Undated	1	—	—	—	—	Undated	1
CCS 9	1779	5	—	—	Undated	1	1779	6
CCS 10	1779–1839	17	—	—	1835–1852	3	1779–1852	20
CCS 11	1832–1845	4	1841	1	1835–1852	3	1832–1852	8
CCS 12	1779–1847	30	1799–1807	4	1813–1831	6	1779–1847	40
CCS 13	1833–1835	11	1847	1	1821–1843	11	1821–1847	23
CCS 14	1811–1822	7	—	—	—	—	1811–1822	7
CCS 15	Undated	1	—	—	—	—	Undated	1
CCS 16	1842	2	Undated	1	1829	1	1829–1842	4
CCS 17	Undated	1	—	—	—	—	Undated	1
CCS 18	Undated	1	—	—	—	—	Undated	1
CCS 19	Undated	2	—	—	—	—	Undated	2
CCS 20	Undated	1	—	—	—	—	Undated	1

Table A6. Upholstery studwork. A dash (—) indicates a particular type was not identified at a particular location. No upholstery studwork of the types listed here was recovered from St. Bartholomew's, Penn.

Upholstery studwork type	Christ Church, Spitalfields		St. Luke's, Islington		St. George's, Bloomsbury		Overall	
	Date range	Number found (total = 382)	Date range	Number found (total = 2)	Date range	Number found (total = 47)	Overall date range	Overall number found (total = 430)
CCS 1	1739–1843	104	—	—	1829–1830	2	1739–1843	106
CCS 2	1747–1839	35	—	—	—	—	1747–1839	35
CCS 3	1744–1833	47	1831	1	—	—	1744–1833	48
CCS 4	1743–1821	17	—	—	—	—	1743–1821	17
CCS 5	Undated	2	—	—	—	—	Undated	2
CCS 6	1821	6	—	—	—	—	1821	6
CCS 7	Undated	4	—	—	—	—	Undated	4
CCS 8	1792	3	—	—	—	—	1792	3
CCS 9	1760–1825	23	—	—	1806–1827	4	1760–1827	27
CCS 10	1761–1849	3	—	—	—	—	1761–1849	3
CCS 11	1746–1811	21	—	—	1827	1	1746–1827	22
CCS 12	1781	2	—	—	—	—	1781	2
CCS 13	Undated	1	—	—	—	—	Undated	1
CCS 14	1759–1825	10	—	—	—	—	1759–1825	10
CCS 15	1822	2	—	—	—	—	1822	2
CCS 16	1754	2	—	—	1807	1	1754–1807	3
CCS 17	Undated	1	—	—	—	—	Undated	1
CCS 18	1809	2	—	—	—	—	1809	2
CCS 19	Undated	1	—	—	—	—	Undated	1
CCS 20	1752–1757	2	—	—	—	—	1752–1757	2
CCS 21	Undated	1	—	—	—	—	Undated	1

Eighteenth- and Nineteenth-Century Coffin Furniture

Table A6. (Continued)

Upholstery studwork type	Christ Church, Spitalfields		St. Luke's, Islington		St. George's, Bloomsbury		Overall	
	Date range	Number found (total = 382)	Date range	Number found (total = 2)	Date range	Number found (total = 47)	Overall date range	Overall number found (total = 430)
CCS 22	1808	1	—	—	—	—	1808	1
CCS 23	1813	1	—	—	—	—	1813	1
CCS 24	1812–1852	19	—	—	1826–1856	6	1812–1852	25
CCS 25	1847	5	—	—	—	—	1847	5
CCS 26	1815–1817	2	—	—	—	—	1815–1817	2
CCS 27	1750–1816	2	—	—	—	—	1750–1816	2
CCS 28	Undated	1	—	—	—	—	Undated	1
CCS 29	Undated	1	—	—	—	—	Undated	1
CCS 30	1813	1	—	—	—	—	1813	1
CCS 31	1757	2	—	—	—	—	1757	2
CCS 32	Undated	2	—	—	—	—	Undated	2
CCS 33	Undated	1	—	—	—	—	Undated	1
CCS 34	1823	3	—	—	—	—	1823	3
CCS 35	1825	4	—	—	1826–1836	8	1825–1836	12
CCS 36	1842	4	1847	1	Undated	1	1842–1847	6
CCS 37	1799	1	—	—	—	—	1799	1
CCS 38	1802–1821	2	—	—	—	—	1802–1821	2
CCS 39	Undated	1	—	—	—	—	Undated	1
CCS 40	1825–1839	7	—	—	1828–1845	4	1825–1845	11
CCS 41	Undated	1	—	—	1812–1831	4	1812–1831	5
CCS 42	Undated	1	—	—	—	—	Undated	1
CCS 43	Undated	1	—	—	—	—	Undated	1

CCS 44	1819	2	—	—	—	1819	2
CCS 45	1809–1826	2	—	—	—	1809–1826	2
CCS 46	Undated	2	—	1806–1846	15	1806–1846	17
CCS 47	1820	2	—	—	—	1820	2
CCS 48	1821–1839	2	—	—	—	1821–1839	2
CCS 49	Undated	1	—	—	—	Undated	1
CCS 50	Undated	1	—	1812	—	Undated	1
CCS 51	Undated	1	—	—	1	1812	2
CCS 52	1770–1782	4	—	—	—	1770–1782	4
CCS 53	1794	1	—	—	—	1794	1
CCS 54	Undated	1	—	—	—	Undated	1
CCS 55	Undated	1	—	—	—	Undated	1
CCS 56	Undated	4	—	—	—	Undated	4
CCS 57	Undated	1	—	—	—	Undated	1
CCS 58	Undated	4	—	—	—	Undated	4

References

Bashford, L., and L. Sibun. 2007. Excavations at the Quaker Burial Ground, Kingston-upon-Thames, London. *Post-Medieval Archaeology*, 41(1):100–154.

Boore, E. 1998. Burial Vaults and Coffin Furniture in the West Country. In *Grave Concerns: Death and Burial in England 1700 to 1850*, ed. M. Cox. Council for British Archaeology Research Report, 113

Boston, C., A. Boyle, G. Gill, and A. Witkin. 2009. *Archaeological Recording at St. George's Church, Bloomsbury*. Oxford Archaeology Monograph 8. Oxford: Oxford Archaeology.

Boston, C., and I. Scott. 2009. "The Church, the Parish and Parishioners." In *Archaeological Recording at St. George's Church, Bloomsbury*, by C. Boston A. Boyle, G. Gill, and A. Witkin, pp. 61–94. Oxford Archaeology Monograph 8. Oxford: Oxford Archaeology.

Boyle, A., C. Boston, and A. Witkin. 2005. *The Archaeological Experience at St. Luke's Church, Islington*. Oxford: Oxford Archaeological Unit.

Cherry, B., and N. Pevsner. 1998. *The Buildings of England. London 4. North*. Harmondsworth, UK: Penguin.

Curl, J. S. 2001. *Kensal Green Cemetery: The Origins and Development of the General Cemetery of All Souls, Kensall Green, London, 1824–2001*. Chichester, UK: Phillimore.

Downes, K., C. Amery, and G. Stamp. 2008. *St. George's, Bloomsbury: A Hawksmoor Masterpiece Restored*. London: Scala Books.

Friar, S. 2003. *The Sutton Companion to Churches*. Stroud, UK: Sutton Publishing.

Hancox, H. 2006. "Coffins and Coffin Furniture." In *St. Martin's Uncovered: Investigations in the Churchyard of St. Martin's-in-the-Bull Ring, Birmingham, 2001*, ed. M. Brickley and S. Buteux, pp. 152–160. Oxford: Oxbow Books.

Litten, J. 1991. *The English Way of Death: The Common Funeral Since 1450*. London: Robert Hale.

Miles, A., N. Powers, and R. Wroe-Brown. 2008. *St. Marylebone Church and Burial Ground: Excavations at St. Marylebone School, 1993 and 2004–6*. Museum of London Archaeology Service Monograph 46. London: Museum of London Archaeology Service.

Mytum, H. 2004. *Mortuary Monuments and Burial Grounds of the Historic Period*. New York: Kluwer/Plenum.

Mytum, H. 2016. "The Artefacts of Mortuary Practice: Industrialisation, Choice, and the Individual." In *Nineteenth-Century Material Culture Studies from Britain*, ed. A. Brooks, pp. 274–304. Lincoln: University of Nebraska Press.

Reeve, J., and M. Adams. 1993. *The Spitalfields Project*. Volume 1: *The Archaeology: Across the Styx*. CBA Research Report 85. York: Council for British Archaeology.

St. George's, Bloomsbury. 1803. Vestry Minutes. May. London: St. George's, Bloomsbury.

St. George's, Bloomsbury. 1856. Vestry Minutes X. London: St. George's, Bloomsbury.

St. Luke's, Islington. 1740. Vestry Minutes. 5 December. London: St. Luke's, Islington.

St. Luke's, Islington. 1853. Vestry Minutes. 27 October. London: St. George's Bloomsbury.

CHAPTER 10

Burial at the Edge of the Empire and Beyond: The Divergent Histories of Coffin Furniture and Casket Hardware

Megan E. Springate and Hilda Maclean

Coffin furniture, as it is known in the United Kingdom and parts of the Commonwealth, or casket or coffin hardware, as it is known in North America, consists of handles, hinges, nameplates, and other decorative motifs found on the exterior of burial containers. The rise in the use of coffin furniture coincided with the adoption of the coffin as a burial container for the corpse across all social classes (Litten, 2002:86). Functional elements such as handles and nails became decorative, and purely decorative elements such as lid ornaments emerged. Mass-produced coffin ornamentation has its origins in mid-eighteenth-century England and remains part of contemporary burial practices around the globe. Beginning with an overview of the British origins of coffin furnishings, we will compare the divergent histories of coffin furniture use in Australia, at the edges of the British Commonwealth, and in North America.

Prior to the late eighteenth century, most coffin furniture was made by punching, chasing, and engraving sheet metal using hand-operated die stamping machines. In 1769, John Pickering of London patented a power-assisted stamping process for raising patterns in sheet metal (Church and Smith, 1966:621; Hamilton, 1967:347). This new process led to an 80% decline in the cost of manufacture, making coffin furniture increasingly available to the developing middle class and increasingly profitable to the undertakers (Church and Smith, 1966:622–623; Litten, 2002:106).

By the middle of the nineteenth century, British coffin furniture manufacturers could depend upon their customers to bury several hundred tons of metal every year (Church and Smith, 1966:623). Catalogs of British coffin furniture from the late 1700s through the mid-nineteenth century depict motifs of skulls, crossbones, extinguished torches, and weeping mourners that represent human mortality. Also present are winged cherubs' heads, angels, crowns, and trumpets that represent Christian immortality and the afterlife. On the whole, the mortality symbolism precedes the immortality symbolism (Richmond, 1999:151). These designs were widely copied throughout the coffin furnishings trade, and many remained in circulation into the early twentieth century. For example, the "flowerpot" motif appears in a catalog identified as JB 1783 (located in the Victorian and Albert Museum) and was still available in a Newman Brothers of Birmingham catalog dating from the 1920s (Newman Brothers, 1920s:57).

The Copyright of Designs Act 1839 (2 & 3 Vict c 17) and Ornamental Design Act 1842 (5 & 6 Vict c 100) protected registered designs from being copied and sold by competitors. Coffin furnishings protected by the acts were known as registered coffin furniture and were generally sold in sets; the other furnishings were known as common or general coffin furniture and sold in mix-and-match bulk (*Sydney Morning Herald,* 1851:3). Common furniture was made from the thinnest japanned iron and has often undergone such taphological change that archaeological examples are virtually indistinguishable other than by broad design, and variations that may be associated with individual makers are seldom observed. Registered coffin furniture is often cast rather than pressed and is more likely to retain extensive detail when it is recovered. This differential preservation biases the sample somewhat, as registered furniture is most likely to be found in high-status burials in crypts and vaults.

Although coffin furniture produced in Britain went predominantly to the vast domestic market, a few manufacturers exported some of their wares, supplying undertakers in the British colonies, including India, Australia, Canada, and what was to become the United States (Church and Smith, 1966:622).

Coffin Furniture in Australia

Coffin furniture from England was exported to all of the Australian colonies from the earliest days. The first advertisement for the sale of coffin furniture, recently imported aboard the *Atlas*, appeared in the *Sydney Gazette and New South Wales Advertiser* in April 1803. This, Australia's first newspaper, had commenced publication in the previous month. From that time on, advertisements for the sale of shipments of coffin furniture appeared regularly in the colony's newspapers. The fact that coffin furniture was being imported so early into New South Wales when even currency to pay for it was in short supply indicates that it was highly sought after and a ready market could be found for it. Edward Hunt, cabinet maker and undertaker of Sydney, accepted "wheat and other property taken in part payment" for his services in 1819 (*Sydney Gazette and New South Wales Advertiser,* 1819:4).

Inexpensive to buy in bulk and easy to transport, there were other economic reasons to import rather than manufacture. The small and widespread population of the Australian colonies would have made it uneconomic to import the large powered metal stamping machines as well as the raw materials (lead, copper, tin, and zinc). The first Australian lead was mined in South Australia in 1841, and copper was mined in the same colony a year later (Blainey, 2003:106–108). The first payable quantities of tin were not discovered until the early 1870s with discoveries in Tasmania and New South Wales (Blainey, 2003:130–131). Zinc, alloyed with copper to form brass, was not widely mined until the mid-1870s (Blainey, 2003:254–255). Coffin furniture was imported in bulk by wholesale merchants who dealt in a variety of different imported wares. They then sold the furnishings on to undertakers and general store proprietors. For example, among the unsold stock from the Wong General Store in Fullerton, New South Wales, dating from when the store closed in 1916, is coffin furniture imported from manufacturers Hickman and Clive and Ingall and Parsons, both of Birmingham, England (Powerhouse Museum, 2003).

Data for the discussion of coffin furniture in this section come largely from the North Brisbane Burial Grounds (NBBG), which were active between 1842 and 1875, serving the capital of the colony of Queensland. Seven separate denominational burial grounds made up the total site. Three of these (Episcopalian/general, Presbyterian, and Catholic) were partially excavated between 2000 and 2002 to permit the development of a sporting stadium (Prangnell, 2003). A number of artifacts were recovered from 397 burials, providing a subset of coffin furniture that was actually consumed but not the total range that was available for purchase at the time (Murphy and Rains, 2003). Some examples also come from the Cadia Cemetery in New South Wales, which operated between 1864 and 1927 (Higginbotham, 2002), as well as advertisements, trade catalogs, and other archival sources.

The coffin furniture recovered from the North Brisbane Burial Grounds is consistent with that advertised in British coffin furnishings catalogs and identified in English burial excavations (e.g., Ives and Hogg, 2012). Three burials at North Brisbane had identifiable lid motifs. A common arrangement of these motifs in England is to have one above the nameplate or depositum at head height and another below it. At the City of London Burial Ground at Golden Lane, the most common motifs are an angel or pair of angels at the head and an urn containing flowers at the foot (Connell and Miles, 2010). The urn with flowers was an evolution from the urn containing flames, which tends to be earlier in the English record. Both the flaming urn and flowerpot motifs were recovered from overlapping time periods from the Cadia Cemetery, indicating a time lag in the transmission of style change (Higginbotham, 2002). An urn with a sunflower motif was recovered from the Episcopalian section of the North Brisbane Burial Grounds. The excavation report indicated that there was also a nameplate and motif at head height but that they were too fragmentary to record or recover (Murphy and Rains, 2003:17). Approximately two-thirds of the lid motifs and depositum designs recovered from the North Brisbane Burial Grounds appear in the 1783 catalog, confirming these to be common coffin furniture. One of the two sets positively identified as registered designs is presented below.

A stamped, japanned metal shield-shaped depositum (FS242) was recovered from a grave (F17) in the Episcopalian portion at the North Brisbane Burial Grounds (Murphy and Rains, 2003:18; Figure 1A). It was attached to an adult-sized (190 cm long) hexagonal wooden coffin. The coffin furniture recovered from F17 matches a design registered by Birmingham brass founder and coffin furniture manufacturer John Hands, who was in business by October 1839 (Robson, 1839:50) when he took advantage of the new Copyright of Designs Act (1839) to register and protect his designs for a coffin breastplate and coffin lace (Board of Trade, 1863: 42/1/59 & 60). In October 1863, John Hands registered the design of the breastplate and matching set consisting of a choice of handles, lace, and lid motifs shown in Figure 1B. Coffin handles were more uniform in shape and were interchangeable across a range of handle plates, which, because of the thinness of their construction, usually survive in the archaeological record only as an imprint and are less useful for identification purposes. The poor preservation of grave F17 generally does not allow easy identification of the size of the handles used with the depositum. The only identifiable feature, the palmette pattern, is common to all three handle plate designs (Figure 1B). As the coffin is adult sized, one of the two coffin handle and plate designs on the right-hand side of Figure 1B was most likely to have been used.

Registered design depositum and lid ornaments were purchased in sets with the matching handles available separately because the number required per coffin varied

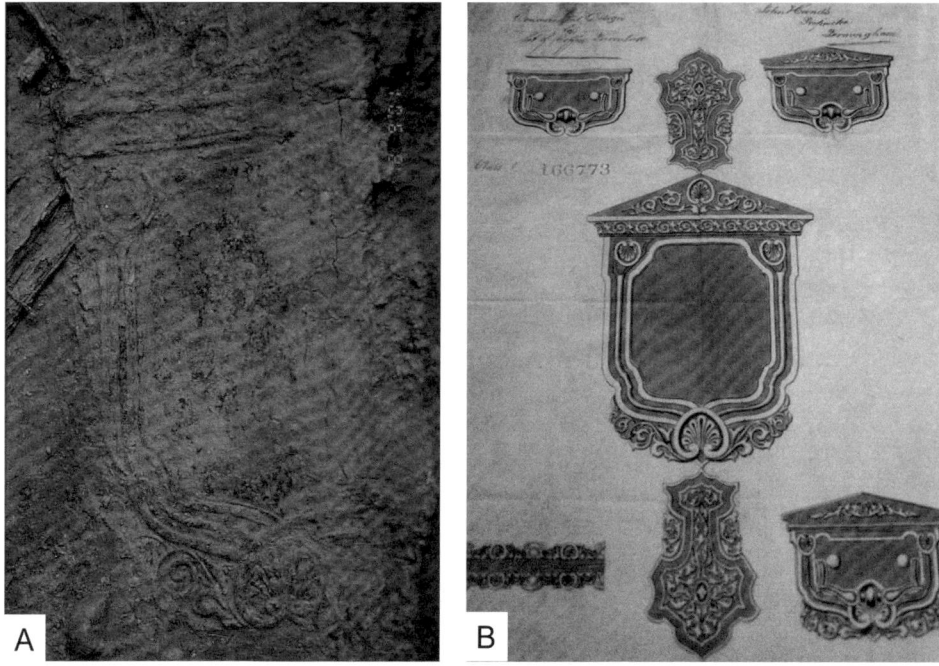

FIGURE 1. Matching excavated evidence with catalogs. (A) Coffin plate (FS242) in situ at the North Brisbane Burial Grounds (UQASU F17_C7-10). (B) Complete set of coffin furniture registered by John Hands in October 1863 (Board of Trade: Patents, Designs and Trade Marks Office, National Archives, Kew 43/15/166773). Photographs H. Maclean.

(Hasluck, [1905] 2010:47). There was no evidence found at excavation that the matching lid decorations and lace were purchased in addition to the depositum and handles. The coffin handle had completely corroded, leaving only an impression in the soil that matched the Hands design (Figure 2).

In 1885, Brisbane undertaker John Smith obtained supplies of coffin furniture by direct importation from a Birmingham manufacturer and through a wholesaler located in Sydney. In May 1885, Smith sent a bank draft of £131 to Oswald Caldicott of Birmingham in reply to a letter received by him from that firm (Smith, 1885:6). Later in the same month Smith sent a check for £20 to Sydney coffin furniture importer and wholesaler James Walford and Co. for "20 sets of No. 9," which he received within the fortnight (Smith, 1885:6). As no coffin furniture catalogs survive in the records of M. K. Smith Undertakers, it is impossible to determine what this coffin furniture looked like, but as it only cost 10 shillings per set, it can be assumed that it was mass-produced pressed-tin furniture of an unregistered design. Smith also sold on some of his excess stock to out-of-town (i.e., not in direct competition) undertakers. He quotes S. W. Whiting of Toowoomba, Queensland, "Silver plate Furniture cost 35/- Adults, 27/6 Youths" (Smith, 1885:13). Undertakers such as John Smith mediated the range of coffin furniture available for purchase by the end client through their ordering practices, which were a combination of their personal taste and their knowledge of what would be most profitable.

Dottridge Brothers advertised directly to Queensland undertakers in 1898, perhaps to cut out the middlemen such as James Walford (Figure 3A). Birmingham manufacturer Gordon and Monro also placed classified advertisements in the Queensland post office directory for the same period but did not go to the expense of a display advertisement

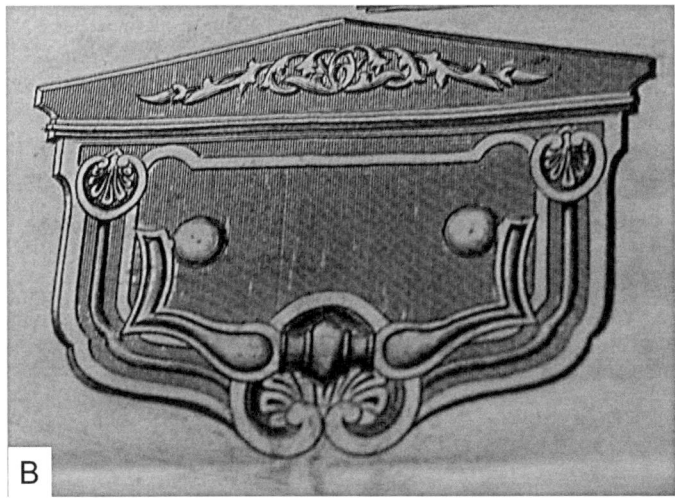

FIGURE 2. Coffin handle plates. (A) Impression of coffin handle plate in situ (grave F17) North Brisbane Burial Grounds (UQASU F17_C7-32). (B) The middle-sized coffin handle and plate from set (Board of Trade: Patents, Designs and Trade Marks Office, National Archives, Kew 43/15/166773). Photographs H. Maclean.

(H. Wise and Co., 1898:xxxv). There was certainly a market for their products as 132 undertakers were listed Queensland-wide the same year (Gordon and Gotch, 1898:483–484).

No evidence that metal coffin furniture was manufactured in the Australian colonies has been uncovered. After federation in 1901, coffin furniture continued to be imported into Australia. For example, Newman Brothers of Birmingham continued to export coffin furniture into the Australian market well into the late 1940s (H. Wise and Co., 1947:iii). Coffin furniture in Australia, then, appears to have closely followed manufacturing trends in the United Kingdom, imported en masse and distributed through the funerary trade.

American Coffin Hardware

In America, however, the trajectory of the mass-produced coffin hardware industry is very different. Data for this section come from archaeological excavations, coffin hardware catalogs, and advertisements. Preceded by locally craft-made hardware, mass-produced

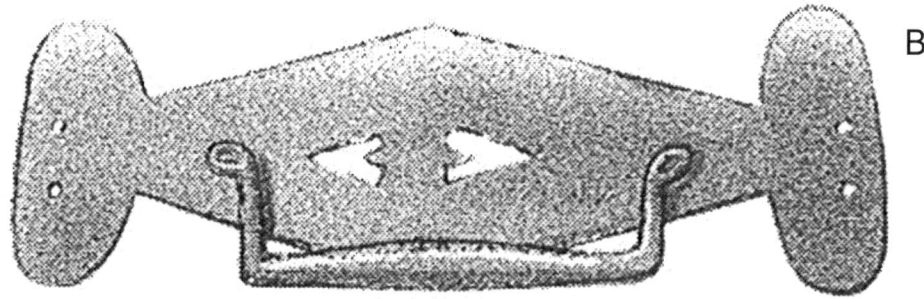

FIGURE 3. (A) Dottridge advertisement in the Queensland Official Directory of 1898–1899 (H. Wise and Co, 1898:9). (B) Composite sketch of iron handles from burials 90 and 176 (ca. 1730 to ca. 1765 or 1776), African Burial Ground, New York City (Perry et al., 2006b, burial 176). Drawing by Cheryl LaRoche and Robert Schultz. Courtesy of the National Park Service.

coffin hardware did not gain a strong foothold in North America until the middle of the 1800s; there are, however, a handful of early examples extending into the eighteenth century, including those from African American contexts (Springate, 2015:52–56). Advertisements by merchants offering coffin handles and other coffin hardware for sale appear as early as 1738 in Philadelphia, well before Pickering's advances in the production of stamped coffin furnishings. Beyond 1748, advertisements of coffin hardware for sale appear nearly every year in Philadelphia until trade was disrupted by the American Revolution (although there is at least one documented example of smuggling; Tharp, 1996, 2003:118). Imported coffin hardware was also advertised in other port cities, including Boston, as early as 1758 (Habenstein and Lamers, 2007:160). Examples of early imported hardware have been recovered archaeologically, including British wrought-iron furniture handles found on coffins buried between circa 1730 and 1776 in the African Burial Ground in Lower Manhattan, New York City (see Figure 3B; Perry et al., 2006a:129, 2006b, burial 101; Springate, 2011). English-made handles, with the large single-lug plate and cherubs, angels, and trumpets as well as the "Glory and Urn" design advertised as early as the 1790s in English pattern books, were recovered from the Tenth Street Cemetery in Philadelphia, Pennsylvania. Associated with the First African Baptist Church, the cemetery was in use from 1810 through 1822 (Crist et al., 1995:242–243).

Unlike in Australia, where coffin furniture was imported throughout the nineteenth century, by the late 1850s and early 1860s, American firms had begun to manufacture

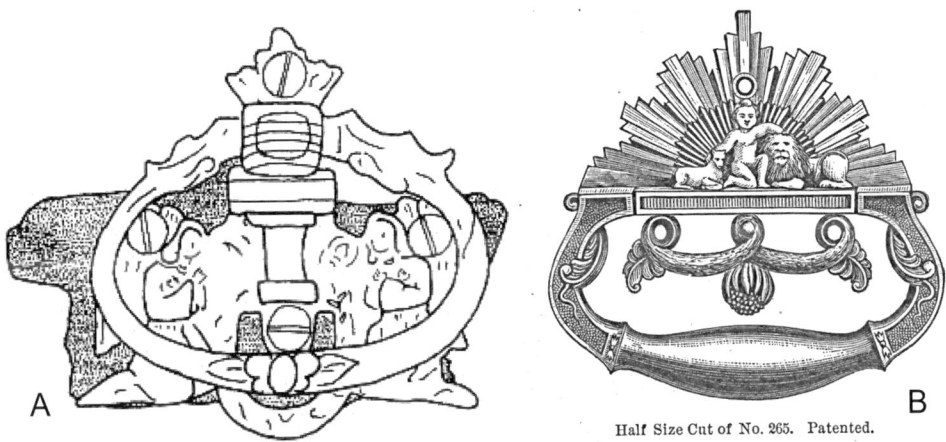

FIGURE 4. (A) Drop handle with praying-angel motif from the 1856 burial of Carter Weir (burial 24), Weir Family Cemetery, Manassas, Virginia (Little et al., 1992:410). Drawing by Carey O'Reilly and courtesy of Barbara J. Little. (B) Children's handle with lamb, lion, and sunburst motif (Sargent & Co., 1874). Courtesy of the Brian Sutton-Smith Library and Archives of Play at The Strong, Rochester, New York.

coffin hardware in the United States. Predating the coffin hardware industry there was the patent metallic burial case business, providing cast-iron burial cases in various forms from the mid-1840s through the late 1850s (Laderman, 1996:46; Springate, 2015:38–39). This American business may be considered a precedent for the domestic manufacture of burial goods.

One of the earliest hardware catalogs of an American manufacturer containing coffin hardware was published in 1859 by the P & F Corbin Company of New Britain, Connecticut. Mass-produced hardware has been recovered archaeologically from burials dating as early as 1854. Of particular note are burials from both the Quaker Burying Ground and the Weir Family Cemetery in Virginia, dating from 1854 and 1856, respectively (Little et al., 1992; Bromberg et al., 2000). Handles recovered from these burials, with their cherubs and tableaux of angels, may well have been imported from England (see Figure 4A). British-identified iconography, including cherubs, angels, and extinguished torches, did appear on early American mass-produced coffin hardware. Coffin handles with cherubs and angels appear in the 1861 J. B. Sargent & Co. and the 1865 Russell & Erwin (Russell & Erwin Manufacturing Company, [1865] 1980) catalogs but are not present in the 1865 Markham and Strong catalog. Although the number of coffin hardware catalogs published expands greatly in the late nineteenth century, angels and cherubs make only fleeting appearances again in single catalogs in 1874 (Sargent & Co.) and 1895 (Kregel Casket Co.) but do not survive into the offerings of future years. This lack of cherubs and angels in the iconography of American coffin hardware is one example of where the American industry diverges significantly from its British roots. Also almost entirely absent from American iconography is the urn or flowerpot of flowers seen in British catalogs from the late eighteenth through the early twentieth centuries, an example of which was excavated from the North Brisbane Burial Grounds.

American coffin hardware is generally less ornate than British coffin furniture. Handle lugs, for example, are smaller, and coffin plates have less ornate borders. Unlike British hardware, which shows remarkable continuity in design and motif over 140 plus years, American hardware designs and forms were always shifting. For example, bail and drop

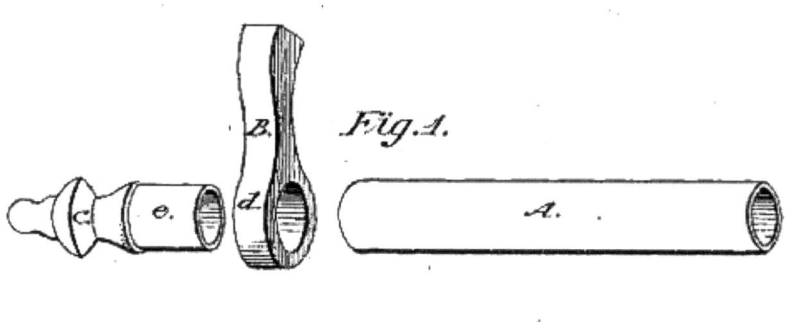

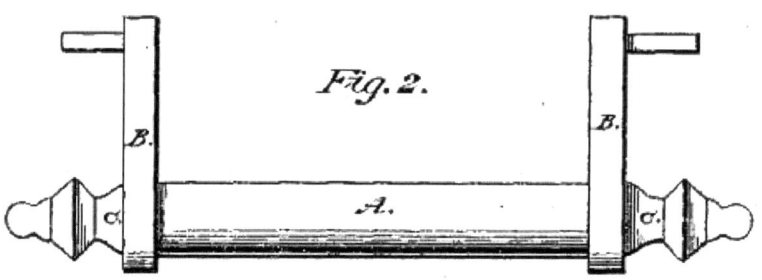

FIGURE 5. Short bar handle showing construction (Strong, 1873).

style handles appeared in the earliest coffin hardware catalogs and were the only styles offered through the mid-1860s (see, for example, Markham and Strong, 1865; Russel and Erwin Manufacturing Company, [1865], 1980). First patented in 1866, short bar handles appeared in catalogs in 1867 (see Figure 5; J. H. Lewis & Co., 1867; Mainfort and Davidson, 2006:124–125). Extended bar handles were also introduced in 1867 (Crane, Breed & Company, 1867). Although each of these styles remained on offer throughout the nineteenth and early twentieth centuries, the trend was toward more and more bar styles and fewer bail and drop handles styles.

Shifts over time in the types of motifs offered and emphasized in catalogs can also be seen. As the nineteenth century progressed, there was less emphasis on designs that incorporate foliage and flowers or scallops and beads in favor of plainer and more geometric designs. Although traditionally associated with changes in ideas about death—following the work of pioneers Deetz and Dethlefsen (Dethlefsen and Deetz, 1966)—recent work finds that many changes in motif can be more appropriately associated with changes in secular design trends (Heinrich, 2013; Springate, 2015:66–67). Uniquely American themes that appear on coffin hardware include American eagles and stars and stripes; symbols of the Independent Order of Oddfellows (who split from their British founders in the 1830s); and the Grand Army of the Republic, an organization of Civil War veterans (Springate, 2015:68). One design, the lamb and sunburst child's handle (see Figure 4B), shows remarkable continuity in both form and presentation (McKillop, 1995). The persistence of this design from the earliest catalogs through the twentieth century reflects continuity in how the death of children was perceived.

Certainly, it was because American industrialists began manufacturing coffin hardware domestically as the common use of hardware was just gaining a foothold that the American trajectory of mass-produced coffin hardware was so different than that in Australia, which relied on British imports. This development allowed American manufacturers to respond directly to American consumers, reflecting uniquely American ideas and ideals shaped, for example, by the developing American middle class; changing ideas about religion, salvation, and death that came out of the Second Great Awakening and the Civil War; the Beautification of Death movement that distanced reminders of death and decay from funerals; architectural design trends; and increasing urbanization and romanticism of nature. Commonly up through the mid-1870s and into the 1880s, coffin hardware was offered for direct purchase to the largely rural public via mail order in general hardware catalogs, as well as marketed to undertakers who worked in urban areas via specialty coffin hardware catalogs. The general public, then, had considerable say regarding styles and types of hardware available during the early years of the industry, voting with their wallets across the country. As the undertaking business professionalized and became more widespread in the 1870s and 1880s, undertakers and funeral directors had more influence as gatekeepers on what coffin hardware would be offered to their clients (Springate, 2015:62–63).

Canada, although sharing a border with the United States, was through much of the nineteenth century still part of the British Empire. Like Australia, it did not develop its own coffin hardware industry, and therefore, one would expect to find imported British hardware in Canadian burials. Although coffin hardware use in Canada appears to have begun later than in the United States, the pattern appears similar to that of its southern neighbor: early use of British imported hardware, followed by a reliance on American manufacturers.

Excavation of an 1855 burial in Ontario, Canada, uncovered a British breastplate like those illustrated in catalogs from the Victoria and Albert Museum in England and those recovered from the North Brisbane Burial Grounds in, Australia; in the same Ontario burial were American-made coffin screws and handles (Woodley, 1992; Murphy and Rains, 2003). Another British breastplate was recovered from an undated context at the same cemetery (Woodley, 1992, figs. 7, 10). Hardware from only American manufacturers is found in Canadian burials from 1861 onward (Woodley, 1991). Not found in Canada are specifically American-themed designs like the stars and stripes. A reason for a Canadian reliance on American product may be proximity to a developed industry—with many of the American manufactories located in the northeastern states, trade to urban Canadian centers like Toronto, Montreal, and Quebec City was often closer and easier than to interior American locations. This trade would have become easier after 1867, with the signing of the British North America Act. With the signing of the act, Canada became the first dominion within the British Empire, gaining autonomy in domestic and foreign affairs and therefore able to negotiate trade and tariffs with its southern neighbor.

This chapter serves as an initial investigation into colonial and postcolonial industrial and consumer experiences, exploring how a common history is and is not reflected materially. Although stemming from the same British source, the histories of mass-produced coffin hardware in Australia and in the United States, as seen in the documentary and archaeological records, are very different. By comparing them side by side, we can see some of the effects that geography, politics, availability of raw materials, economics, globalization, and national histories can have on the development of an industry and how consumers relate to and shape it.

References

Blainey, G. 2003. *The Rush That Never Ended: A History of Australian Mining*. Carlton, Vic.: Melbourne University Press.

Board of Trade. 1863. *Patents, Designs and Trade Marks Office and Predecessor: Ornamental Design Act 1842 Representations*. Volume 15. BT 43. Patents, Designs and Trade Marks Office, The National Archives, Kew.

Bromberg, F. W., S. J. Shephard, B. H. Magid, P. J. Cressey, T. Denee, and B. K. Means. 2000. *"To Find Rest from All Trouble": The Archaeology of the Quaker Burying Ground, Alexandria, Virginia*. Alexandria, Va.: Alexandria Archaeology, Office of Historic Alexandria.

Church, R. A., and B. M. D. Smith. 1966. Competition and Monopoly in the Coffin Furniture Industry, 1870–1915. *Economic History Review*, n.s., 19(3):621–641.

Connell, B., and A. Miles. 2010. *The City Bunhill Burial Ground, Golden Lane, London: Excavations at South Islington Schools, 2006*. London: Museum of London Archaeology.

Crane, Breed & Company. 1867. *Crane, Breed & Co.'s Wholesale Price List of Patent Metallic Burial Cases and Caskets. . . .* Trade Catalogs Collection, microfilm item 671. Winterthur Museum.

Crist, T. A. J., R. H. Pitts, A. Washburn, J. P. McCarthy, and D. G. Roberts. 1995. "A Distinct Church of the Lord Jesus": The History, Archeology, and Physical Anthropology of the Tenth Street First African Baptist Church Cemetery, Philadelphia, Pennsylvania. Report prepared by John Milner Associates, on file at the Pennsylvania Historical and Museum Commission, Harrisburg.

Dethlefsen, E. S., and J. F. Deetz. 1966. Death's Heads, Cherubs, and Willow Trees: Experimental Archaeology in Colonial Cemeteries. *American Antiquity*, 31(4):502–510.

Gordon and Gotch. 1898. *Pugh's Almanac and Queensland Directory for 1898*. Brisbane: Gordon and Gotch.

Habenstein, R. W., and W. M. Lamers. 2007. *The History of American Funeral Directing*. 6th ed. Brookfield, Wis.: National Funeral Directors Association.

Hamilton, H. 1967. *The English Brass and Copper Industries to 1800*. 2nd ed. New York: Augustus M. Kelley, Bookseller.

Hasluck, P. N. (1905) 2010. *Coffin-Making and Undertaking: Special Appliances, Lancashire Coffins, Southern Counties and Other Coffins, Children's Coffins, Adults' Covered Coffins, Polishing Coffins, Inscription Plates, Coffin Furniture, Trimming or Lining, Ornamented and Panelled*. Reprint, Redditch, Worcestershire, England: Read Books Design.

Heinrich, A. R. 2013. Cherubs or Putti? Gravemarkers Demonstrating Conspicuous Consumption and the Rococo Fashion in the Eighteenth Century. *International Journal of Historical Archaeology*, 18(1):37–64.

Higginbotham, E. 2002. *Report on the Excavation of the Cadia Cemetery, Cadia Road, Cadia, NSW 1997–1998*. Volume 5: *Plans, Figures and Photographs*. Report for Cadia Holdings Pty Ltd. Haberfield, NSW: Edward Higginbotham and Associates Pty Ltd.

H. Wise and Co. 1898. *Queensland Official Directory 1898–1899*. Brisbane: H. Wise.

H. Wise and Co. 1947. *Wise's New South Wales Post Office Commercial Directory*. Sydney: H. Wise.

Ives, R., and I. Hogg. 2012. *St. John's School, Peel Grove, Bethnal Green, London Borough of Tower Hamlets: A Post-Excavation Assessment Report*. Twickenham, UK: AOC Archaeology Group.

JB. 1783. *Trade Catalogue*. Southwark, London.

J. B. Sargent & Co. 1861. *J. B. Sargent & Co., New Britain, Conn., Sargent & Co., No. 85 Beekman St., New York, New York*. New York: J. B. Sargent.

J. H. Lewis & Co. 1867. *Wholesale Manufacturers of Coffins and Caskets. . ..* Facsimile edition, American Broadsides and Ephemera Series I, 1760–1900, Readex. American Antiquarian Society, Worcester, Mass.

Kregel Casket Co. 1895. *Illustrated Catalogue.* Brian Sutton-Smith Library and Archives of Play at the Strong, Rochester, N.Y.

Laderman, G. 1996. *The Sacred Remains: American Attitudes Toward Death, 1799–1883.* New Haven, Conn.: Yale University Press.

Litten, J. 2002. *The English Way of Death: The Common Funeral Since 1450.* London: Robert Hale.

Little, B. J., K. M. Lanphear, and D. W. Owsley. 1992. Mortuary Display and Status in a Nineteenth-Century Anglo-American Cemetery in Manassas, Virginia. *American Antiquity,* 57(3):397–418.

Mainfort, R. C., and J. M. Davidson. 2006. *Two Historic Cemeteries in Crawford County, Arkansas.* Arkansas Archeological Survey Research Series 62. Fayetteville: Arkansas Archaeological Survey.

Markham & Strong. 1865. *Revised Price List with Illustrations.* Connecticut Historical Society, Hartford.

McKillop, H. 1995. Recognizing Children's Graves in Nineteenth-Century Cemeteries: Excavations in St. Thomas Anglican Churchyard, Belleville, Ontario, Canada. *Historical Archaeology* 29(2):77–99.

Murphy, A., and K. Rains. 2003. "Material Culture of Burials from the Lang Park Redevelopment Site." In *Suncorp Stadium Archaeological Salvage.* Volume 4: *Skeletal Material and Grave Artefacts*, ed. J. Prangnell, pp. 1–54. University of Queensland Archaeological Services Unit Report 358. St. Lucia: University of Queensland Archaeological Services Unit.

Newman Brothers. 1920s. *Coffin Furniture, Shrouds, Frillings, Side Sheets Etc.* Birmingham: Newman Brothers.

P & F Corbin. 1859. *P. & F. Corbin's Illustrated Catalogue and Price List.* Hugh M. Morris Library, University of Delaware, Newark, Delaware.

Perry, W. R., J. Howson, and B. A. Bianco, eds. 2006a. New York African Burial Ground Archaeology Final Report. Volume 1. Prepared for the U.S. General Services Administration, Northeastern and Caribbean Region. Washington, D.C.: Howard University.

Perry, W. R., J. Howson, and B. A. Bianco, eds. 2006b. New York African Burial Ground Archaeology Final Report. Volume 2: Descriptions of Burials 1 through 200. Prepared for the U.S. General Services Administration, Northeastern and Caribbean Region. Washington, D.C.: Howard University.

Powerhouse Museum. 2003. Coffin Furniture from the Wong Store: Made in England, 1875–1916. Object 2003/35/26. https://collection.maas.museum/object/12070 (accessed 26 November 2017).

Prangnell, J., ed. 2003. *Suncorp Stadium Archaeological Salvage.* Volume 4: *Skeletal Material and Grave Artefacts.* University of Queensland Archaeological Services Unit Report 358. St. Lucia: University of Queensland Archaeological Services Unit.

Richmond, M. 1999. "Archaeologia Victoriana: The Archaeology of the Victorian Funeral." In *The Loved Body's Corruption: Archaeological Contributions to the Study of Human Mortality*, ed. J. Downes and T. Pollard, pp. 145–58. Glasgow: Cruithne Press.

Robson, W. 1839. *Robson's Birmingham & Sheffield Directory.* London: William Robson.

Russell & Erwin Manufacturing Company. (1865) 1980. *Illustrated Catalog of American Hardware of the Russell and Erwin Manufacturing Company.* Reprint, Ottawa: Association for Preservation Technology.

Sargent & Co. 1874. *Price List and Illustrated Catalogue of Hardware.* Brian Sutton-Smith Library and Archives of Play at The Strong, Rochester, N.Y.

Smith, J. 1885. Diary. K. M. Smith Records, OM75-127. John Oxley Library, State Library of Queensland.

Springate, M. E. 2011. Coffin Handles from the African Burial Ground, New York City: Notes on Their Source and Context. *African Diaspora Archaeology Newsletter* 14(2).

Springate, M. E. 2015. *Coffin Hardware in Nineteenth-Century America.* Walnut Creek, CA: Left Coast Press.

Strong, C. 1873. Improvement in Coffin-Handles. United States Patent No. 138,768. Patented May 13, 1873.

Sydney Gazette and New South Wales Advertiser. 1803. Coffin furniture advertisement. 21 April, 3.

Sydney Gazette and New South Wales Advertiser. 1819. Advertisement for Edward Hunt, cabinet maker and undertaker. 30 January, 4.

Sydney Morning Herald. 1851. Coffin furniture advertisement. 25 August, 3.

Tharp, B. W. 1996. "Preserving Their Form and Features:" The Role of Coffins in the American Understanding of Death, 1607–1870. Ph.D. diss., College of William and Mary, Williamsburg, Va.

Tharp, B. W. 2003. "'Preserving Their Form and Features': The Commodification of Coffins in the American Understanding of Death." In *Commodifying Everything: Relationships of the Market*, ed. Susan Strasser, pp. 119–140. New York: Routledge.

Woodley, P. J. 1991. "Coffin Hardware and Artifact Analysis." In *The Links That Bind: The Harvie Family Nineteenth Century Burying Ground*, ed. Shelley Saunders and Richard Lazenby, pp. 41–56. Occasional Papers in Northeastern Archaeology 5. Dundas, ON: Copetown Press.

Woodley, P. J. 1992. The Stirrup Court Cemetery Coffin Hardware. *Ontario Archaeology*, 53:45–64.

CHAPTER 11

"Making a Box Worthy of a Sleeping Beauty": Burial Container Surface Treatments in the United States during the Nineteenth and Early Twentieth Centuries

Jeremy W. Pye

Relatively little has been systematically presented in the published archaeological literature about the types of surface treatments encountered during historic period cemetery or burial excavations. This lack is largely due to the fact that surface treatments are not commonly found preserved in burial contexts. Degree of physical preservation does, indeed, limit the scope of observation, but absence of evidence does not necessarily indicate absence of practice. For example, paint or cloth may not preserve except in association with metal hardware. It is up to the excavators and artifact analysts to piece together enough of the extant information to make accurate, data-informed hypotheses about burial practice and not just assume that no elaboration was present. Not only do researchers need to be observant and document the presence of surface treatments, they also need to document treatments on all surfaces. When surface treatments have been addressed in the previous literature, primacy has been given to the exterior surface treatments. Both exterior and interior surface treatments played a role in the social presentation of the deceased during the funeral, both affected cost of the burial container, and both contribute important information to the archaeological record.

The 1831 price list of the District of Columbia Cabinetmaker's Society illustrates the importance of surface treatment and records costs for various coffins (Garrett, 1975:890), including fees paid for labor involved in the production of certain types and sizes of coffins, as well as the prices paid for extra services, such as finishing (Table 1). The price list attests to the fact that the cost of the burial container could be influenced not only by the selection of different woods and sizes but also by the types of surface treatments chosen. To complicate matters, raw materials with which the craftsman constructed the

Table 1. List of products and services offered by the 1831 Cabinet Makers' price list (Garrett, 1975).

Product or service[a]	Cost
A coffin 2 feet 6 inches long poplar	$1.00
Do. 2 do.—do. mahogany	$1.25
Do. 3 do.—do. poplar	$1.25
Do. 3 do.—do. mahogany	$1.50
Do. 4 do.—do. poplar	$1.50
Do. 4 do.—do. mahogany	$1.75
Do. 5 do.—do. poplar	$2.00
Do. 5 do.—do. mahogany	$2.50
All above 5 feet do. poplar	$2.25
Do. 5 do.—do. mahogany	$3.00
Extra.—If polished with hard wax	$0.50
If top is hinged	$0.50
Putting on breastplate	$0.12
Lining with flannel	$0.31
Covering with cloth	$1.00

[a]The following note accompanied the list: "The above mahogany coffins to be oiled, the poplar to be stained and oiled." Do./do = ditto.

burial container may have required different types of surface treatments. For instance, mahogany coffins mentioned in the price list were to be oiled, whereas the poplar coffins were to be stained and then oiled. The oil acts as a sealant preserving the wood, whereas the stain has no functional purpose. The practice of staining cheaper varieties of wood developed through a process of socially elevating negotiation whereby the lighter-colored wood was transformed into something more reminiscent of an expensive dark hardwood. Although the economic impact of certain practices can be more easily determined, the cultural perception of certain surface treatments tends to be more elusive, and there is little agreement or synthesis about the occurrence or social importance of various surface treatments.

Exterior Surface Treatments

Mainfort and Davidson (2006:113) state that there are generally three methods to finish the exterior of a burial container: (1) staining (including blackening with soot), to which will be added varnishing and waxing; (2) painting; and (3) fabric or cloth covering. Each of these types of surface treatments will be discussed in greater detail below. Other types of exterior embellishments or adornments, such as the addition of decorative hardware (i.e., handles, hinges, coffin screws, coffin tacks, thumbscrews, escutcheons, plaques, caplifters, ornaments, decorative upholstery tacks, etc.) and the addition of wreaths or floral sprays, garland, and wire, can also be considered to be part of the exterior surface treatment of a burial container, but as they are secondary to the actual finishing of the burial container, they are not discussed here (however, see many of the other chapters in this volume).

Staining, Varnishing, and Waxing

Coffins and caskets have historically been constructed from many different types of raw materials, including various qualities of wood. Utilizing light-colored softwoods for the construction of unseen parts of cabinets or furniture tends to be less expensive. In the same way, the bases or bodies of burial containers were sometimes constructed of cheaper materials, whereas more visible parts, such as the lid, were constructed of darker-colored hardwoods. Stains, waxes, and varnishes have been used to create a fine finish on the exterior surface of burial containers, with dark stains being used on light-colored woods (i.e., poplar and pine), most of which are softwoods, to mimic darker hardwoods (i.e., walnut and mahogany), which were more expensive (Coffin, 1976:103; Lang, 1984; LeeDecker et al., 1995; Bastis, 2006:44; Mainfort and Davidson, 2006:114). It has been suggested that this practice of emulating expensive woods is the poor to middle class's attempt to symbolically, or superficially, rise to the socioeconomic appearance of the elite (Bybee, 2007:86–87).

Wood Stain

Wood stain is applied to wood with the intention of transferring pigment into the pores in the substrate of the wood. Stain is composed of three main components: pigment, solvent, and a binding agent. Traditional solvents include turpentine or alcohol, whereas the binding agents used historically ranged from linseed oil to lacquer and resin (Hasluck, 1905; Flexner, 1993). Stain is composed largely of pigment and solvent, designed not to cover the wood like paint but to penetrate and add color to the wood while leaving the grains of the substrate visible (Flexner, 1993).

Varnish

True varnishes, unlike stains, are translucent wood finishes with no pigment added and are designed to create a clear protective coat on the surface of the wood. Varnish is usually composed of two types of binding agents, drying oils and resins, as well as a solvent, such as turpentine. Drying oils include linseed oil, tung oil, and walnut oil, whereas resins include amber, aspaltum, kauri gum, damar (or dammar), copal, rosin, sandarac, balsam, benzoin, shellac, and a wide variety of lacquers. After application, the binding agents in the varnish harden when the solvent has evaporated, leaving the hard protective coating (Flexner, 1993:176). The 1899 Brown-Hutchison Company general hardware catalog provides descriptions and costs for a number of resin varnishes available for purchase in the late nineteenth century (Table 2).

Drying oils, such as linseed oil, have been used historically in England to create a dull finish on the exterior of coffins (Flexner, 1993:50; Plume, n.d.:63–64). Drying oils are single-component varnishes but are not considered true varnishes because the oils cure through an exothermic reaction between the oxygen in the surrounding air and the polyunsaturated fats contained in the oils rather than through the evaporation of a solvent. In contrast to quick-curing resin varnishes, oils remain moist through the curing process, sometimes taking weeks to completely dry (Flexner, 1993:70). Because of this slow drying time and the haste with which most individually tailored coffins were constructed, it is unclear how practical the application of raw oils would have been.

Table 2. Descriptions and costs of varnishes from Brown-Hutchison Company (1899). A dash (—) indicates not applicable.

Description	Cost ($/can)					
	½ pt.	1 pt.	1 qt.	1 gal.	5 gal.	full bbl.
Furniture	0.12	0.18	0.30	0.95	0.85	0.59
Copal No. II	—	—	—	1.10	0.97	0.70
Coach	0.15	0.25	0.40	1.25	1.15	—
No. II coach, extra good	—	—	—	1.40	1.30	0.95
Monarch preservative	—	—	—	1.95	1.85	—
Elastic wood finish	—	—	—	2.25	2.00	—
Monarch outside coach	—	—	—	2.75	2.00	—
Spar varnish	—	—	—	2.90	2.75	—
White demar	—	—	—	1.50	1.40	—
Black aspaltum	—	—	—	0.85	0.65	0.45

Two commonly used resin varnishes are lacquer and shellac. Lacquer refers to a quick-drying, resin varnish that is either clear or can be colored by the addition of iron oxide pigments, which can be used to create various shades of black, red, or yellow (Flexner 1993:162). Lacquer is a resin derived from a tree indigenous to China, known as the varnish tree (*Toxicodendron vernicifluum*), and has been used in the region for thousands of years. Urushiol, the toxic oil present in poison ivy, poison oak, and poison sumac, is the active ingredient in lacquer resin and requires a humid, warm environment for the curing process to be successful (Webb 2000:3–8).

Shellac is a single-component resin varnish derived from the excretions of the female lac bug (*Kerria lacca*), which lives in the forests of India and Thailand. Shellac comes in clear, amber, and even ruby and yellow colors in its refined form. Unlike lacquer, shellac can be dissolved in alcohol. It came into popular usage in the 1800s due to its quick-drying nature and the durability of its protective coating compared with various types of waxes that were previously used for wood finishing (Flexner 1993:144–155).

Waxing

Coffin (1976:103) makes note of the use of beeswax, in particular, which would have been worked into coffin wood using a smoothing iron. Other types of waxes were possibly used in surface treatments of burial containers, but no additional sources noting specific varieties have been located.

Staining, Varnishing, and Waxing in the Archaeological Record

Archaeologically, stains and varnishes are difficult to detect because the exterior surface of the wood is usually in a state of poor preservation when uncovered by archaeologists. Dark varnishes or stains might appear similar to dark-colored paint; however, they would be absorbed into the wood rather than sitting on the surface. Three such cases were identified during burial recovery at the Alameda-Stone Cemetery, Tucson, Arizona, including a black or dark colored lacquer/resin on the burial containers of two infants of unidentified sex, as well as on the burial container of a middle-aged, adult, male (Pye 2010). If varnish or stain is suspected, a cross-section of the wood should indicate only a partial penetration of the dark material in question into the substrate of the wood. Care should be taken in this type of observation since the natural decomposition of the wood may also produce such an appearance. Some researchers have report that varnish and stains can be identified via smells reminiscent of the solvent or oil components of those products (Bybee, personal communication 2007).

Painting

Painting was a very common surface treatment for coffins and caskets historically in the United States. Paints are composed of two elements, the pigment and the vehicle (Lambourne and Strivens, 1999:6). The vehicle consists of components similar to wood stains, including the binder (resin) and the solvent or diluent. The binder effectively seals the surface of the wood after drying, and the liquid solvent dissolves the binder and allows for the application of the coating (pigment). The pigment consists of small particles of minerals or organic compounds that are relatively insoluble in the vehicle, giving coloration to the application through the adhesion of the binder (Zollinger, 2003:1–2). The pigment consists of the following materials: additives, which include catalysts, driers, and flow agents; primary pigments, which are fine particles of organic or inorganic pigment that provide opacity and color and may add anticorrosive properties to primers; and extenders, or coarse particles of organic or inorganic pigments, used to further develop opacity and obliterate undercoat visibility (Lambourne and Strivens, 1999:6).

Many of the period catalogs from the nineteenth and early twentieth centuries sold burial containers with white painted exteriors, known as "gloss white" (Cleveland Burial Case Company, 1882; Hazelton Coffin and Casket Company, 1883; Chappell, Chase, Maxwell & Company, 1884; Paxson, Comfort & Company, 1884, 1898; National Casket Company, 1899; St. Louis Coffin Company, 1901). Mainfort and Davidson (2006:114) posit that this gloss white was likely made of an organic material, possibly a milk-based, or casein-based, paint. Casein is a prominent phosphoprotein in cow's milk and was used commonly as an ingredient in paints in the nineteenth century (J. M. Davidson, University of Florida, personal communication, 2009). It is also possible, however, that this gloss white paint was made with a white mineral pigment, such as zinc white, a popular late nineteenth-century pigment, rather than an organic paint. Whatever the nature of the paint composition, Mainfort and Davidson (2006:114) assert that this white painted coffin was the most common color advertised, especially for children's burial containers; however, it would seem that in the catalogs mentioned above, there were just as many gloss white adult containers as there were child-sized containers.

Other paint colors, such as red, yellow, and blue, have also been noted in the popular funeral literature. Coffin (1976:103–104) noted that some softwood coffins were painted. One "old-timer" in Coffin's discussion is said to have stated,

> The old red paint? Gosh, the kind they put on cheers [sic] and coffins and light stands? That was the plain yellow ochre got out of the ochre pits and roasted or burned into a soft clinker. Same as they get darker ends on the bench bricks 'cause they're

laid nearest the fire, you get red instead of yellow ochre after this extry roasting. Then they ground it up. 'Twas awful cheap so they used it on most everything. I seem to have forgot but I reckon this was the old Venetian Red that folks bought for two cents a pound and mixed with oil or milk. Those that lived down Maine way and was handy to fish, used fish oil to stir it up with, and it kept the powder from flying off. Yes, they was uncommon generous with that old paint.

Yellow ochre was also mentioned by Hasson (2001) in the production of yellow paints. Plume discusses the use of blue pigments in the exterior treatment of children's coffins in England: "it is usual to cover, or colour small coffins with blue . . . pigment, indigo, or ultramarine blue" (Plume, n.d.:39, 41). The 1899 general hardware catalog of the Brown-Hutchison Company shows many different colors of mixed "American" paints that were offered for sale in half-pint to five-gallon cans (Table 3). This resource provides an idea of the types of colors, and therefore the types of pigments, that were available for use in the late nineteenth century. It is the pigments, which give paint color, that will be the focus here.

Paints Commonly Utilized in Exterior Surface Treatments

Linton (1849:412) describes in great detail a number of primary pigments utilized in England in the early nineteenth century, and many of the same pigments would have been used in the production of paints in the United States. Brief discussions are given here for those mineral pigments known to have been, or likely to have been, utilized in the surface treatment of burial containers in the United States on the basis of archaeologically identified paints or those mentioned in period catalogs. These paints include lead white, zinc white, carbon black, Venetian red, cobalt blue, ultramarine, chrome green, emerald green, and yellow ochre.

Whites (Lead White and Zinc White)

Lead occurs naturally in the basic lead (II) carbonate ($PbCO_3$) form in the mineral hydrocerussite (Terry, 1893:183). The pigment lead white is known to have been produced even in ancient Greece (Gettens et al., 1967:126), and it is claimed that it was historically the most important of all white pigments. In fact, it was the only white pigment available in some parts of the world until 1834 when zinc white was introduced as a healthier alternative to lead white (Gettens et al., 1967:127; Casas and de Andrés Llopis, 2002:73). To make lead white, sodium chloride and lead nitrate are combined and heated in a solution to form a white precipitate, lead white. This precipitate, once formed, can be washed, dried, and ground into powder that is ready to be mixed into paint (Lambourne and Strivens, 1999:12). White paints can be tested for both zinc and lead during paint analysis to determine which types of pigments were utilized (Gettens et al., 1967; Casas and de Andrés Llopis, 2002).

Zinc white (zinc oxide, ZnO) was introduced in 1834; however, until the 1850s when domestic production began in the United States, it was always imported and therefore would have been less common in some areas of the country farther from shipping hubs (Casas and de Andrés Llopis, 2002:73). Downs (1976:90) recorded an advertisement for

Table 3. Descriptions of ready mixed "American" paints from Brown-Hutchison Company (1899). Prices: ½ pt. = $0.13; 1 pt. = $0.22; 1 qt. = $0.35; ½ gal. = $0.60; 1 gal. = $1.10; 5 gal. = $5.

Color group	Color description[a]
Browns	Turkey burnt umber
	Turkey raw umber
	Italian burnt siena
	Italian raw siena
	Van Dyke brown
Blacks	Lamp black
	Coach black
	Drop black
	Ivory black
Blues	Prussian blue
	Ultramarine blue
	Chinese blue
	Cobalt blue
Greens	Vernal green, L.M. & D.
	C[h]rome green, L.M. & D.
	3A green, L.M. & D.
	Phoenix green, L.M. & D.
	Bronze green
Reds	English Venetian red
	English Tuscan red
	Imperial Tuscan red
	English Indian red
	Rose pink
	Rose lake
	Aramingo vermilion
	Kensington vermilion
	English Ver[million]., pale and deep
	Flat brick red, L.M. & D.
Yellows	French ochre
	C[h]rome yellow, L.M. & D.
	Dutch pink
	Golden ochre

[a] Meaning of "L.M. & D." not provided in original.

zinc paint in the *Brooklyn Daily Eagle*, dated 14 October 1850, which documents the shift from lead white to zinc white paints:

> ZINC PAINT.—Perhaps the most important of modern discoveries is that of a white material manufactured from zinc, which, when generally known, must entirely supersede the use of white lead. In the manufacturing of this article, there is

nothing deleterious to affect the system of the laborers, while in the process of making white lead, thousands of human beings have been, and still are, yearly sacrificed. The discoverers of the zinc paint are the Messrs. Le Clair & Co., of Paris. We saw, on Saturday, a house that had been painted with it, and it was in every way superior to any specimen of house painting we had previously examined. The paint is of snowy whiteness, and as hard as enamel. For new work it requires about four coats; for old, about three; and afterwards a coat of varnish. Its surface resembles that of a well painted coach panel. In using it there is no risk of taking what is well known to the trade as the "painter's cholic." No dangerous consequences are to be apprehended from the smell of a newly painted house, if painted with the new zinc material. It is cheaper than white lead, and the color stands for any length of time without changing.

After the development of American zinc oxide production in the 1850s, the native product became much more economical than the imported zinc oxide. It quickly surpassed lead white in popularity and spurred the development of the ready mixed paint industry. Zinc white was still widely used through the twentieth century (Downs, 1976:91; Richter and Harlin, 1974:81).

Carbon Black

Carbon black consists of pure elemental carbon and is produced by charring various materials and collecting the black ash or soot produced as the materials break down (Guy, 2004). Lamp black is a type of carbon black formed through the imperfect combustion of oils, fats, resins, etc., on burning oil lamps, whereas ivory black was produced through the charring of ivory or bones (Linton, 1849:412; Terry, 1893:11). Carbon black is one of the simplest of all nineteenth-century pigments and could be used by itself to blacken wood or could be used as an additive into a paint medium for application (Plume, n.d.:63–64).

Blues (Cobalt Blue and Ultramarine)

Ultramarine has been in use in some form since the sixth century in the Near East. Natural ultramarine was made from ground powder of the precious mineral lapis lazuli and was very costly (Terry, 1893:70). This mineral was mixed with wax and kneaded in a solution of diluted lye, thus releasing the color from the minute crystals (Linton, 1849:412; Guy, 2004).

Artificial ultramarine was first discovered in 1787 when blue deposits were observed on the walls of lime kilns. It was not, however, until 1828 that a suitable, inexpensive synthetic ultramarine was produced in France from heating a finely ground mixture of soda ash, china clay, coal, charcoal, silica and sulfur. The resultant compound could then be washed of excess sodium sulfate and ground into fine blue pigment (Guy, 2004).

Cobalt blue is a pigment produced by sintering the stoichiometric mixture of ground CoO and Al_2O_3 at 1200°C to produce cobalt (II) aluminate ($CoAl_2O_4$). It was first produced as a synthetic pigment in 1802, even though cobalt blue has been known since the

Middle Ages in Europe (Guy, 2004). Increased production of cobalt blue did not begin until 1807 in France; it thereafter became a durable substitute for ultramarine in the painting arena (Linton, 1849:412; Terry, 1893:28).

Chrome Green

Chrome green consists of chromium (III) oxide (Cr_2O_3), which occurs naturally in the mineral eskolaite. It is derived from chromite (Cr_2O_4) through a heated reduction with sulfur. Chrome green was a favored pigment of the nineteenth century, being first produced in Europe in 1814 (Richter and Harlin, 1974:79; Guy, 2004).

Emerald Green

Emerald green is produced through a combination of acetate and arsenite of copper. It was commonly used from the early nineteenth century and varied in tint from a dark to a pale green, oftentimes with a bluish cast. Mixed into oil paints without the appropriate balance of components, cobalt blue has the tendency to turn to a greenish tone (Linton, 1849:412; Terry, 1893:28; Guy, 2004). Emerald green is soluble in acids, ammonia, and caustic soda, turning into a blue solution (Terry, 1893:121–124).

Yellow Ochre

Yellow ochre is a natural mineral consisting of silica and clay and is found throughout the world. It is principally a ferric oxide (Fe_2O_3) and has been used to produce pigments ranging in color from yellows to oranges to browns. Yellow ochre is not heat resistant; through the loss of water in the heating process, the yellow ochre becomes calcined and turns into red ochre (Lambourne and Strivens, 1999:74; Guy, 2004).

Venetian Red/Red Ochre

Venetian Red is a pigment derived from pure ferric oxides (Fe_2O_3), also known as red ochre (Terry, 1893:153). The term "Venetian red," according to Linton (1849:412), refers specifically to an inferior quality of red ochre gathered from a mineral source in Italy. The pigment is a dark shade of scarlet. The calcinations of iron oxide produce a range of colors from yellow-toned to blue-toned reds that can easily be dispersed into paint vehicles. Since ferric oxides occur naturally throughout the world, they are one of the cheapest and most durable of pigments available for use historically in the United States (Guy, 2004).

Painting in the Archaeological Record

A number of historic cemetery excavations across the United States and Canada have revealed paints of various colors, including red, green, yellow, orange, pink, blue, gold, and brown, as well as both organic and lead whites (Table 4). The paint that was once present on the coffin or casket does not generally preserve well in most archaeological settings, although it does have a higher probability to be preserved on the underside of hardware or near other metal artifacts. Mainfort and Davidson (2006:114) suggest that what is most often seen archaeologically is the primer layers and not the paint itself. Although this may

Table 4. Sample of archaeological cemetery excavations showing evidence of painting.

Project/Cemetery	Temporal range	Location	Surface treatments	Reference
Becky Wright Cemetery	1870–1900	Arkansas	Red, white	Mainfort and Davidson (2006)
Eddy Cemetery	1870–1900	Arkansas	Red, white	Mainfort and Davidson (2006)
Tucson City Cemetery (Alameda-Stone Cemetery)	1860s–1882	Arizona	Green, white, blue, black, pink, red, gray, green over white, green over yellow, green over black, green over blue, green over blue over yellow, yellow and black, blue and white, pink and red, green and pink and blue	Pye (2010)
Seccombe Lake Cemetery	ca. 1830–1900	California	Red	Marmor et al. (1990, 1991)
Dove Cemetery	1860–1900	California	Blue, yellow, red	Sewell and Stanton (2008)
Madam Felix/Hettick Cemetery	1852–1900	California	Yellow-cream, red, blue, green	Costello (1991)
Bulkeley Tomb	1775–1832	Connecticut	Shellac, red or brown stain, black	Bastis (2006)
Sussex City Cemetery	1752–1799	Delaware	Dark stain	LeeDecker et al. (1995)
Meadowlark Cemetery	1860–1900	Kansas	Yellow ochre over white (lead based) over white-gray primer over black over yellow ochre, yellow ochre over black over red over black over yellow ochre (exterior/interior)	Pye (2007)
15Cp61	1830–1900	Kentucky	White paints and pigments and layered pigments	Bybee (2003b)
15Mm137	1830–1900	Kentucky	Black varnish, white pigments, black paint and layered pigments, white over black over red (int.)	Bybee (2003a)
Old Branham Cemetery	ca. 1825–1900	Kentucky	Light green pigment, white	Bybee (2004)
Las Vegas Gravel Pit Cemetery	1880–1940	New Mexico	Light green pigment, red	Mills (1979)
Seven Rivers Cemetery	1873–1899	New Mexico	Green, white (enamel), red, blue	Ferguson et al. (1993)
African Burial Ground	1627–1800	New York	Red paint?	Perry et al. (2006)
Elmbank Cemetery	1832–1937	Ontario, Canada	Varnish, red, yellow	Lipovitch et al. (2003)

Cemetery	Date	Location	Treatment	Reference
Don Jail Cemetery	1872–1930	Ontario, Canada	Light-colored paint	Crawford et al. (2008)
Voegtly Cemetery	1833–1861	Pennsylvania	Pink or red most common, but also white, green, yellow, orange, blue, and black	Beynon (1989)
First African Baptist Church Cemetery	1823–1842	Pennsylvania	Red paint	Parrington et al. (1989)
Providence Baptist Church Cemetery	1899–1933	Tennessee	White, light blue, red (exterior/interior), gold leaf or gold, red viewing lid, white top	Oster et al. (2005)
Freedman's Cemetery	1869–1907	Texas	Red primer	Peter et al. (2000)
Quantico Corporate Center Tract Burials	1850–1900	Virginia	Paint or varnish, dark	Ezell and Huston (2006b)
Williams Green Cemetery	ca.1800–1880	Virginia	Yellow	Ezell and Huston (2006a)
Quaker Burying Ground	1784–1890s	Virginia	White, off-white/yellowish, varnish or wax	Bromberg et al. (2000)
Burning Springs Branch Cemetery	1795–1818	West Virginia	Light green pigment	Bybee (2003a)
Reynolds Cemetery	1830–1900	West Virginia	White paints and pigments and layered pigments, red over black over white, red over white over black, black over red over black over white over brown	Bybee (2002)
Evans Cemetery	1875–1988	West Virginia	White paint	Bybee (2007)

be true in some cases, some instances of layered pigments clearly represent actual paint layers. For instance, at Meadowlark Cemetery in Manhattan, Kansas, two types of color combinations were notably used as exterior surface treatments (Pye, 2007:134–135). One combination consisted of six layers and the other five. The six-layer variety began near the wood with a whitish-gray, porous, primer layer over which a powdery yellow ochre was applied, followed by a thin, carbonaceous black pigment, a second whitish-gray primer, a white lead-based paint, and, finally, a powdery yellow ochre on the supposed exterior (Pye, 2007:135). The five-layer variety of treatment was observed on both the interior and exterior of several burial containers. Near the surface of the wood lay a yellowish-white pigment possibly consisting of yellow ochre mixed with oil or milk or possibly a beeswax treatment, as mentioned by Coffin (1976:103). Over the yellow lay a carbon black layer, followed by red, a second carbon black, and, finally, a yellow ochre layer (Pye, 2007:134). It is unclear what the final appearance of such a surface treatment would have been or what design elements might have been represented.

In the Alameda-Stone Cemetery, Tucson, Arizona, at least 165 burial containers had been painted on the exterior surfaces (Pye, 2010). Colors encountered, and their frequencies, included green ($n = 114$), blue ($n = 26$), white ($n = 22$), black ($n = 7$), yellow ($n = 4$), pink ($n = 3$), red ($n = 2$), and gray ($n = 1$). In a number of cases, however, multiple colors were noted on the same burial container. Layered pigments included green over white ($n = 2$), green over yellow ($n = 1$), green over black ($n = 1$), green over blue ($n = 9$), and green over blue over yellow ($n = 2$). In other instances, multiple colors occurred, but it was not clear whether they had been layered or applied to different parts of the burial container. These color combinations included one each of yellow and black; blue and white; pink and red; and green, pink, and blue. Instances where only single colors occurred included 98 burial containers that exhibited only green paint, 19 white, 13 blue, 5 black, 1 pink, 1 red, and 1 gray. Yellow pigment appears not to have been used as a stand-alone surface treatment. As suggested by other archaeological cemetery excavations (e.g., Mainfort and Davidson, 2006; Pye, 2007), it is likely that the yellow and gray pigments, and possibly the red pigments, were primer layers rather than true paint coatings.

Decorative paint patterns have also been encountered archaeologically. One burial container at the Alameda-Stone Cemetery seemed to have been painted green and then embellished with yellow swirl patterns, one burial container had a green cross painted on the footboard, and another appeared to have been decorated with green floral and leaf patterns on the top of the lid (Pye, 2010). All of these decorated burial containers contained fetal or infant remains, with the embellishments likely holding some cultural or personal significance to the family or the community.

Although formal chemical paint analyses are rarely undertaken in archaeological studies to date, it is possible to make some general observations and hypotheses about the compositions of paints present in archaeological assemblages. The green and blue paints, although distinct at their extremes, had a great deal of color variation in the blue-green range, possibly a result of the mineral pigments. Some grades of emerald green pigment tended to have a bluish cast, whereas paints produced with cobalt blue pigments had a tendency to turn green under certain conditions. Yellow and red paints were likely produced using some form of ferric oxide. The white paints present in the cemetery were possibly produced using mineral pigments but were more likely formed from organic components such as casein. Pink paints would have been produced using a combination of a base white and an additive such as blood or some other red substance (see Coffin, 1976). The black paints would have been produced using a mineral such as lamp black or some other carbon-based pigment.

It would be wise to follow the advice of Welsh (1982:30), who suggests the use of the Munsell color charts in the identification of paints in order to gain conformity in paint analysis while remaining aware of how certain types of paints might degrade or be stained while buried, thus altering the color and appearance. When only a small fragment of paint remains (e.g., under hardware), the larger decorative elements that might have been on the container might have been obliterated or obscured. For instance, if a small fragment of green paint is recovered, it could mean that the entire burial container had been painted green, but it might also be part of the stem of a flower that was painted on the surface of the burial container.

Merely noting the presence of certain paint colors does not reveal the meaning behind those colors and their importance in the creation of design elements on the surface of burial containers through the application of social traditional knowledge. For example, the Pennsylvania Dutch at Voegtly Cemetery used a wide variety of colors on their coffins and on the furniture produced in the community at large. For them, bright colors represented nature, and the use of such colors was a celebration of God's universe, with death being an integral part of life (Beynon, 1989:108). Future research should focus on the identification of elements of surface treatments with respect to certain culture-specific associations of certain treatments, wood types, and demographics and how these would preserve archaeologically as a comparison to those that are recovered in historic cemetery settings.

Cloth Covering

Cloth coverings evolved out of the pall or mortcloth, which was draped over the burial container or body prior to interment (Mainfort and Davidson, 2006:114). A British guide to coffins and coffin making by Sable Plume was published in the *Undertakers' Journal* and later reprinted in book form, likely sometime in the 1880s, and details the process of covering a coffin with cloth. In this source, a common black (broad)cloth and velvet are mentioned as the most common types of cloth covering. This method of covering was useful because the wood could be of lower quality and left relatively rough (Litten, 1991:103). If the cloth was wide enough to cover both sides, it was divided in such a way as to cover the sides of the coffin. Both pieces would then be tacked at the foot end going in the same direction, the first piece being brought around one side until it reached the head, whereas the second would be folded back over the tacks, hiding them from view, and brought around the opposite side until it met the end of the first piece at the head of the coffin. In this way, only a few tacks at the head would be visible (Plume, n.d.:64). The bottom edges of the material would be folded under and tacked or glued on the bottom of the coffin. In the same way, a piece of material was cut for the lid and folded in to attach to the underside of the lid (Plume, n.d.:65).

One of the earliest recorded cloth-covered coffins was that of Queen Elizabeth I, who died in 1603 (Mainfort and Davidson, 2006:114). The practice was carried over from Europe to the Americas during the colonial period. Coffin (1976:109–110) recorded excerpts from the daybooks of David Evans, a Philadelphia cabinetmaker, from 1774 to 1811. In one entry dated 7 March 1793, Evans states, "Daniel Rundle, making a coffin for his wife Ann Rundle, covered in black cloth, lined with white flannel. Inscription plate, flowerpots, cherubs, handles and full lace, £15" (quoted in Coffin, 1976:109–110).

Mainfort and Davidson (2006:114) state that in the early nineteenth century, people in the United States commonly covered coffins and caskets with broadcloth of various colors.

Table 5. Descriptions of colors of fabrics advertised for cloth covering in National Casket Company (1899). Piqué, crepe, momie cloth, satin jewel, and velvet combinations, as well as sateen combinations, are also listed, but no colors are given.

Material	Color code	Color
Broadcloth	C-5	Silver gray
	P-5	Medium slate
	G-9	Ashes-of-roses
	E-3	Navy blue
	M-17	Silver drab
	G-2	Dark slate
	A-7	Coachman drab
	G-1	Lavender
	H-12	Purple
	P-18	Cream
Silk plushes	H-7	Lavender
	V-2	Purple
	V-2	Cream
	H-6	Baby blue
	Z-12	Peach pink
	V-5	White
	V-6	Black
	S-7	Steel gray
	V-3	Ashes-of-roses
	V-10	Tan drab
	H-8	Coachman drab
	H-5	Rose pink
Embossed plushes	R-7	White
	R-8	Cream
	R-14	Baby blue
	R-25	Purple
	R-26	Lavender
	R-28	Heliotrope
	R-24	Ashes-of-roses
	R-18	Silver gray
	R-10	Dark slate
	R-11	Coachman drab
	R-13	Peach pink

It was not until 1872, however, that a specific line of cloth-covered caskets was patented by Samuel Stein of Stein Manufacturing Company, Rochester, New York (Stein 1872; Habenstein and Lamers, 1955:277; Mainfort and Davidson, 2006:114). Stein specialized in cloth-covered caskets, and later, the National Casket Company, known for its cloth-covered caskets developed out of the Stein cloth-covering department (Habenstein and Lamers, 1985:173–174). Table 5 shows the variety of fabrics and colors one could order from the 1899 National Casket Company's *National Casket Company Complete Price List and*

Telegraph Code Accompanying Pocket Catalogue "D." Included are broadcloths, plushes, piqués, crepe, momie cloth, satin, sateen, and velvet.

Although Stein was the first to have been issued a patent mentioning cloth covering, his specific invention was for improvements in casket design rather than being primarily focused on cloth covering. The practice of cloth covering was already well developed; other coffin and casket manufactures began to advertise cloth-covered caskets at least by the early 1880s and likely even earlier. Hamilton, Lemmon, Arnold & Company produced a line of cloth-covered coffin and caskets as early as 1882. Table 6 indicates the range of cloth-covered caskets available in the 1884 Hamilton, Lemmon, Arnold & Company *Revised Price List of Varnished & Cloth-Covered Burial Cases and Caskets*. Multiple types of fabrics could be chosen, such as broadcloth, brocatelle, piqué, and velvet, in several different colors. Alternatively, combinations of fabrics and trimmings could be ordered.

Archaeologically, it is very difficult to make observations of cloth covering because of the lack of preservation of fabrics in most cases. Unless kept within a protective vault, cloth coverings on coffins or caskets were particularly vulnerable to processes of decomposition because of their immediate contact with the soil. Evidence of cloth coverings may be preserved, however, on certain types of coffin hardware or in special circumstances where preservation is good (Mainfort and Davidson, 2006:114). Therefore, it is important to outline fabrics were commonly used to cover burial containers in order to produce informed archaeological analyses.

Fabrics Commonly Utilized in Exterior Surface Treatments

Brief discussions are provided below for select fabrics known to have been utilized in the exterior surface treatment of burial containers in the United States during the late nineteenth to early twentieth centuries on the basis of period catalogs. These fabrics include broadcloth, brocatelle, crepe, momie cloth, piqué, plush, satin, sateen, and velvet.

Broadcloth

Broadcloth is a densely woven fabric composed originally of wool, but cotton and silk varieties have also been produced. It is a durable and heavy, but also soft and glossy, material used widely for men's clothing, upholstery, insulating fabric, and even the robes of clergymen (Curtis, 1921). Broadcloth is so named because its breadth is usually 60 inches, as it is constructed on an extra wide loom with the warp (lengthwise/longitudinal threads/yarns, also known as "ends") and weft (transverse threads/yarns drawn through the warp, also known as "picks") tightly woven in a twilled or a plain-weave pattern (Cole, 1892; Curtis, 1921). After weaving, the cloth is dipped in water, causing the wool to shrink before being put through a fulling or felting process, which entangles the wool fibers of the weft and the warp, producing the soft, glossy, and durable quality of the cloth (Cole, 1892).

Brocatelle

Brocatelle is a coarse, brocaded fabric, which is constructed traditionally of cotton, silk, linen, or wool. The silk or wool forms the face of the fabric, whereas the cotton or linen forms the back. Brocatelle fabrics are commonly used for tapestries and upholstery and are classed as a double-cloth fabric with two interwoven warps and fillings. As the face and back are

Table 6. Descriptions and costs of cloth-covered burial cases and caskets advertised in Hamilton, Lemmon, Arnold & Company (1884a). A dash (—) indicates not applicable.

		Cost ($)			
Item No.	Description	2'0" to 2'9"	3'0" to 3'9"	4'0" to 4'9"	5'0" to 6'3"
25	Best black broadcloth, combination velvet or all cloth, sliding glass, covered on red cedar, black walnut, or cypress, with cloth or velvet molding	—	—	—	22.00
26	Best black broadcloth, combination velvet or all cloth, hinged full length, covered on red cedar, black walnut, or cypress, with cloth or velvet molding	—	—	—	26.00
27	Child's casket, covered with white broadcloth, with glass	8.00	10.00	12.00	—
29	Children's caskets, covered with fine white broadcloth, elliptic ends, hinged lid	9.50	12.00	15.00	—
30	Black or white broadcloth, combination velvet, or all cloth casket, hinged full length, rayed, covered on chestnut with cloth or velvet moldings	—	—	—	22.00
41	Best black or white broadcloth draped casket, combination velvet or all cloth, hinged full length, or sliding glass, covered on red cedar, black walnut or cypress	—	—	—	42.50
42	Fine black or white broadcloth casket, combination velvet or all cloth covered on chestnut with cloth or velvet molding, sliding glass, elliptic ends	—	—	—	18.00
42.5	Black broadcloth casket, all cloth or velvet combination, cloth or velvet molding, sliding glass, elliptic ends	—	—	—	15.00
43	Black broadcloth casket, combination velvet or all cloth; silver, frosted, ebony, cloth or velvet moldings	—	—	—	12.00
45	Covered on white wood with white embossed velvet	—	—	—	16.00
46	Ornamental puffed corners, octagon ends, sliding glass	—	—	—	15.00
46	Brocatelle cloth, octagon caskets, sliding glass	—	—	—	9.50
47	Child's white brocade, or piqué covered casket, hinged full length, rayed	6.00	8.00	12.00	14.00
47.5	Child's white embossed velvet caskets, hinged full length, rayed	6.50	8.50	12.75	—

48	Child's white brocade cloth or piqué covered caskets, with glass	5.00	7.50	10.50	12.50
48.5	Child's white embossed velvet caskets, with glass	5.50	8.00	11.25	—
51	Drape casket, black broadcloth, all cloth or combination velvet, sliding glass, elliptic	—	—	—	20.00
52	Octagon end, black cloth casket, combination velvet or all cloth, hinged lid, rayed	—	—	—	16.00
53	The paragon casket, covered with fine black broadcloth, on walnut, red cedar or cypress, with fancy black saw bead and tufting, sliding glass, etched	—	—	—	35.00
54	Extra fine black or white broadcloth casket with heavy drapery, extra fine silk and chenille fringe, tassels and cord, hinged lid, rayed	—	—	—	53.00
55	Extra fine black broadcloth casket, elliptic ends, fancy satin molding, panels ornamented with satin tufting, covered on red cedar or walnut, etched glass	—	—	—	55.00

constructed of different materials, the weave is constructed in such a way that the face warp threads do not show on the back of the fabric but the face filling threads do and vice versa. Brocatelle fabrics have a satin or twill weave pattern on a plain-weave backing (Cole, 1892).

Elaborate brocatelles were originally woven with figuring threads of silver and gold but are now commonly woven with threads of harmonious colors often forming intricate floral designs (Curtis, 1921). The fabric itself requires no finishing as the colors are dyed on the silk, wool, or cotton yarns. Colors include light slate, olive brown, light brown, olive green, green, black, violet, scarlet, salmon, rose, and lavender for wool yarns. Silk yarns can be dyed salmon, light lavender, olive green, rose, navy blue, red, light green, and light yellow. Cotton yarns can be dyed blue, light brown, olive brown, tan, green, navy blue, olive, and red. Finished, brocatelle fabrics with silk faces can have approximately 200 ends per inch (epi), with the filling having about 116 picks per inch (ppi; Frank P. Bennett & Company, 1914:528–532; hereafter referred to as Bennett & Co.).

Crepe

Crepe (also crêpe or crape) is a thin, semitransparent material made from silk or cotton. It is characteristically crinkled in either irregular or long parallel ridges, and it comes in white, black, or colored varieties (Cole, 1892; Curtis, 1921). Black crepes were traditionally used in nineteenth-century funeral settings (Cole, 1892; Coffin, 1976). These so-called mourning crepes are produced from hand-spun yarns and crimped by being passed through heavy steel rollers with irregular surfaces. The irregular wavy appearance of the fabric is not purely a product of the crinkling process but also a result of some of the weft threads being constructed with a reverse twisted pattern. Four left-twisted weft threads are then fed into the weave from one side while four right-twisted weft threads are fed from the other side. The fabrics are removed from the loom and boiled for shrinking before being dried, dyed, and/or printed. During the boiling process, the weft loses its twist and gives the fabric its characteristic appearance (Cole, 1892; Curtis, 1921).

Momie Cloth

Momie, the French word for mummy, refers to the linen material that was used to wrap human bodies during the mummification process in ancient Egypt. The original mummy cloth was in the form of bandages wrapped around the bodies and had a rough and irregular weave with a fine warp thread intersecting a heavy weft at irregular intervals. The term "momie" now refers to this type of weave rather than the materials from which the fabric is composed. Linen, cotton, and wool varieties have all been made in various regions and time periods (Cole, 1892).

Piqué

Piqué refers to a quilted weave applied to cotton fabrics and is also known as marcella, or, more appropriately, Marseilles. It has a double-cloth construction characterized by parallel cords or fine ribbing, with the face being moderately close, plain weave and the back being a more open, plain weave. The two sides of the cloth are then stitched together with stuffing or wadding, forming an intermediate layer. In order to give it its characteristic embossed effect, it is necessary to use considerably more tension on the back warp than on the face, requiring cotton yarns that can withstand greater tension. Analysis of the fabric yields 64 warp threads per inch on the face and only 32 on the back. Piqué is a stiffer fabric often used for ties and shirt collars (Bennett & Co., 1914:336–337).

Plush

Plush is a fabric composed of the pile and the back. The pile has been made of various materials such as mohair, worsted yarn, or silk. It has a distinctive soft, cut nap, with its manufacturing process being nearly identical to that of velvet; however, the pile of plush is generally ⅛ inch thick or more, in contrast to velvet, which has a low-profile pile. Traditionally, plush has been used for upholstering furniture but has also been used in the making of stuffed animals. Embossed plush is most commonly used as a cloth covering for burial containers. The embossing process for the manufacture involves the application of an embossing agent and often a coloring agent, working these agents to the base of the pile. The fabric is then heated through a calendaring process with decorated rollers that effectively burn the design into the fabric (Cole, 1892).

Satin

Satin is a warp-dominated, silken fabric with both a glossy side and a dull side. The glossy side has a high luster produced because of the high number of floats and low frequency of interlacing used in its construction. The term "float" refers to the placement of the warp thread over the top of the weft thread, or vice versa, without interlacing. The warp passes under the weft at irregular intervals, such as every eighth, tenth, twelfth, or even sixteenth thread. This weaving technique allows light to reflect from the arrangement of fine silk warp threads visible on the face, thus producing the glossy appearance on one side of the fabric. The glossy surface is enhanced by rolling the fabric through a calendaring process. The threads of satin are often dyed prior to construction of the fabric because the open, floating character of the fabric may become frayed in the dyeing process. Satin has been used primarily in garments and is often used as a backing for wool and velvet fabrics. It has also been used for fine slippers and pillows (Cole, 1892).

Sateen

Sateen, or satine, is a cotton fabric with a smooth, lustrous surface, made to resemble satin fabrics. Sateens are produced using long-fibered cottons that have been mercerized—the cotton fibers have been soaked in a pool of sodium hydroxide, thus strengthening the fibers and producing a surface luster. The yarns are often dyed prior to construction of the fabric. Colors used include pink, heliotrope, navy blue, gray, light slate, peacock blue, red, slate, royal blue, tan brown, sky blue, brown, wine, and scarlet. A satin-weave construction technique is then used to make sateens, which means that they are formed by the same number of ends as picks, with each end and each pick interlacing twice in each repeat. Sateens are sheared and then calendered with hot steam rollers to further enhance the luster of the fabric. Characteristics of sateens differ depending on the quality of the material and its intended use; for example, a warp sateen striped cloth used for upholstery may have 96 ends and 52 picks per inch, whereas a finer-quality warp sateen may have 152 ends and 80 picks per inch (Bennett & Co., 1914:535–536).

Velvet

Velvet is a densely woven fabric with a low-cut pile less than ⅛ inch long. It has a soft texture and other fine qualities that, historically, set this fabric apart for royalty and other special individuals or events. The origin of this fabric is somewhat ambiguous, but the most expensive varieties of velvet have been produced in Genoa, Florence, and Venice. The first velvet mill was established in the United States 1865 but was short-lived, so the majority of velvet sold in the United States in the nineteenth and early twentieth centuries was imported. The dominant colors of velvet on the market prior to the early nineteenth century were black and scarlet. During the early nineteenth century, midnight-blue, holly-green, and turquoise varieties appeared. Additionally, combination velvets were produced with black and scarlet being the main colors with blue or green forming borders (Litten, 1991:112–113).

Velvet is produced by inserting short pieces of silk thread (known as pile thread) under the weft threads so that the ends of the silk stand upright. These threads are so densely packed that the foundation of the fabric is entirely concealed. The pile threads are inserted into the loom running parallel to the regular warp threads, so that they may be taken up together and passed over the weft threads. Long brass wires are laid across the width of the fabric, and the weaving commences with the pile threads forming a loop over these wires, which are secured by the subsequent weaving of the next weft thread. When the wires are removed, the loop is cut, forming the dense pile characteristic of velvet. Fine qualities of velvet contain 40 to 50 pile loops to an inch of fabric, resulting in 80 to 100 silk fibers per inch when cutting. After weaving, the fabric is brushed and trimmed. It can be stamped or embossed. The stamping is effected through the application of stamping irons on the face of the fabric, whereas the embossing process takes the fabric through hot steam rollers (Cole, 1892).

Cloth Covering in the Archaeological Record

Preservation of exterior cloth covering is poor in most archaeological contexts, although there are some situations in which the cloth covering, or large portions of fabric, might be preserved, such as within crypts, mausoleums, or sealed/intact burial vaults. Smaller portions of fabric might also be preserved in association with metal hardware or other adornments on the exterior of the burial container. Evidence of cloth covering in most archaeological contexts, however, is typically less overt than the above examples and is often overlooked by researchers conducting burial relocations. Two of the most common indicators of exterior cloth covering are the presence of fabric impressions on the surface of metal hardware that would have been in contact with cloth covering and the specific types of hardware designed for, or used in association with, cloth covering or specifically designed for use in association with cloth covering.

Fabric impressions can be left on the heads of nails used in the construction of the burial container, on the heads of tacks used to secure folds of the cloth covering, or on the backs of decorative hardware. A fabric impression can be defined as the transference of a fabric's construction pattern to the surface of another material. In the case of iron nails and tacks, the development of ferrous corrosion on the head of the hardware forms around the threads of the cloth forming the fabric's structure. Upon deterioration of the actual fabric, the impression remains.

Lining tacks (Figure 1) are typically used to affix cloth lining within a burial container but may also be employed on the exterior perimeter of the burial container. The presence of

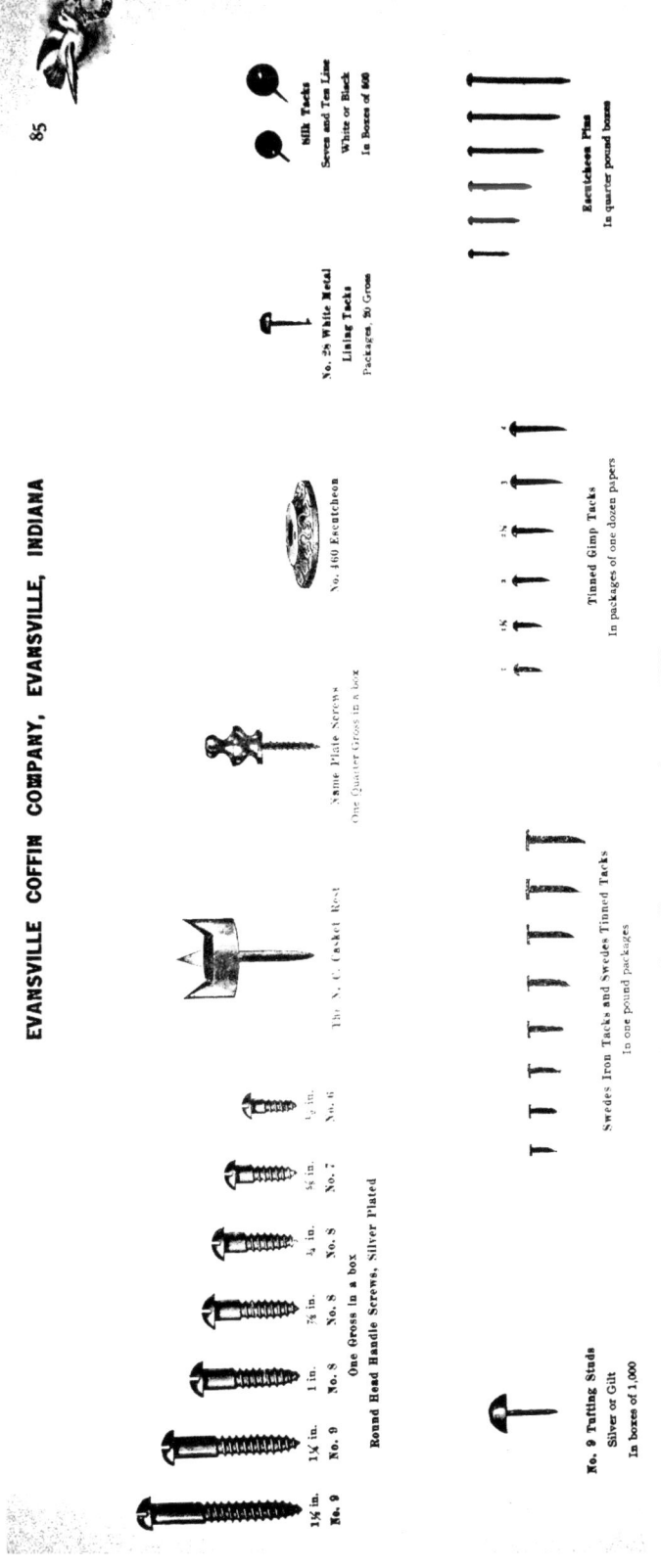

FIGURE 1. Iron cut lining tacks and gimp tacks illustrated in the Evansville Coffin Company catalog, circa 1909.

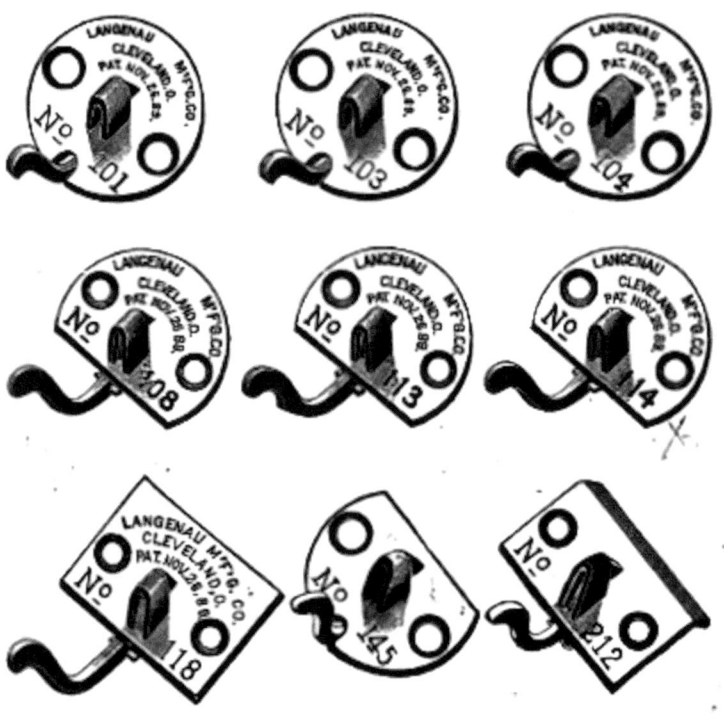

FIGURE 2. Catches used for cloth work as advertised for sale in a Langenau Manufacturing Company catalog, circa 1920s–1930s.

exterior lining tacks or upholstery tacks is also a good indicator of cloth covering; however, because of collapse of the burial container and/or disturbance of the burial feature, the context of exterior tacks is often mingled with tacks used originally to affix interior linings. The heads of tacks should be inspected for fabric impressions, but as some types of tacks were cloth headed, fabric impressions on the heads of tacks should be taken as evidence of the presence of a cloth head rather than an impression of burial container cloth covering. Other types of hardware that specifically indicate the use of cloth covering are certain types of catches designed specifically to be used in conjunction with cloth work (Figure 2).

A note of caution is warranted, however. One should not be too quick to assume the presence of cloth covering on the basis of the mere identification of exterior "lining" tacks or other types of tacks without consideration of the archaeological context. Small tacks were also used to secure other decorative elements such as tassels or cordage on the exterior of a burial container. Beynon (1989) reports the presence of serpentine, copper wire rickrack tacked around the outside perimeter of some cloth-covered coffins present at the Voegtly Cemetery in Pennsylvania. As evidenced by excavations from earlier cemeteries, such as the New York African Burial Ground (Perry et al., 2006), in New York, and the Bulkeley Tomb, in Colchester, Connecticut (Bastis, 2006), tacks could also be used by themselves to decorate the exterior of the burial container. Small tacks were often placed on the lids of coffins in order to give information such as death dates or names, or merely as aesthetic elements (Lang, 1984:23; Rauschenburg, 1990:41; Bromberg et al., 2000:162).

Little attention has been given to fabric analysis in recent cemetery projects, so no synthesis is yet possible, although fabric impressions found on the heads of nails in a number of burial containers recovered from the Meadowlark Cemetery in Manhattan, Kansas (Pye, 2007), indicate the potential. A more detailed analysis of fabrics used as cloth coverings on burial containers was possible during the study of materials from the Alameda-Stone Cemetery in Tucson, Arizona. At least 219 burial containers in the Alameda-Stone Cemetery showed clear evidence of having been covered with some sort of cloth (Pye, 2010). This evidence most often took the form of fabric impressions on the heads of nails or on the surfaces of other metal hardware. Small pieces of preserved fabric were present in some instances, however, and were represented by black velvet, scarlet velvet, floral embossed plush, and white cotton plain-weave fabrics with thread structures preserved to the extent that the epi and ppi of the material could be reasonably estimated. Judging by the exhibited characteristics of the plain-weave fabrics, it is possible that these fabrics represented muslins and piqués. Other fabrics or fabric impressions noted during excavations were not as easily identified because of limited preservation. Colors noted in this category were cream, tan, brown, black, and green. Approximately 26 burial containers appeared to have been covered with a plain or balance-weave fabric. The texture of such fabrics ranged from very fine (possibly silk or satin) varieties to fine, medium-coarse, and coarse varieties. A larger sample would be needed for a definitive identification (Pye, 2010).

Combination Treatments

Although many exterior surface treatments would have been uniform and exclusive on a single burial container, sometimes combination treatments were applied. Combination treatment refers to the occurrence of more than one type of surface treatment. Although it would have been unusual for a painted surface to then be varnished and vice versa, it was not unheard of for a cloth-covered burial container to also be painted. Painted cloth covering was reported in 60 graves investigated at the Alameda-Stone Cemetery in Tucson, Arizona. Green was the most common paint color associated with fabric, with 39 occurrences. There were also four blues, five whites, two blacks, five blue and green combinations, one green and yellow combination, one green, pink, and blue combination, and two green, blue, and yellow combinations. In all of these instances, it appeared that the paint was applied to the outer surface of the fabric. It is possible that the paint and fabric were applied to different portions of the exterior of some burial containers. For example, one grave held a burial container that exhibited green and black paint on the exterior surface of the lid, whereas fabric impressions were located on nails on the sides of the container. This combination could suggest that only the body of the container had been cloth covered, while the lid had been painted (Pye, 2010).

Interior Surface Treatments

The interior of a burial container sometimes would have been left bare for various reasons, but more often than not, the interior surface also received some form of treatment.

For the local craftsmen, cabinetmakers, undertakers, and commercial coffin and casket manufacturers, just as much time, energy, and money were devoted to treating the interior of burial containers as the exterior. The most common interior treatment would have been simple cloth lining, although occasionally the interior surfaces were painted (see the exterior treatment section on painting).

Just like the exterior treatment, the interior treatments of coffins and caskets reflected cultural traditions and beliefs and carried certain social meanings. Coffin (1976:102) states,

> Traditionally, old-time carpenters brushed together all of the sawdust and shavings accumulated from making a coffin and placed these scraps inside it. Superstition taught that if these bits of leftover wood were tracked into a house or carelessly shaken from clothing, they would endanger whomever they touched, and that person might become death's next victim.

These wood shavings, although having a social reason for inclusion in the coffin, also served a functional purpose. After construction of the burial container, the cracks were filled with pitch as a sealant, and the sawdust acted as extra padding to prevent shifting of the body but primarily was used to absorb the fluids resulting from primary decomposition (Litten, 1991:92, 1998:11; Janaway, 1998:23; Stock, 1998:148). In some cases, newspapers, bran, straw, or cotton waste was also used to make linings appear fuller, more textured, and more luxuriant (Hasson, 2001; Plume, n.d.:21).

In the late nineteenth century, the development of the professional funeral industry and the perception of the burial container as a bed-like vessel prompted further elaboration of coffin and casket linings. Mattresses developed out of the layer of sawdust, or other absorbent material, upon which the linings were placed. Mattresses covered the entire bottom of the burial container and consisted of plain woven covers or cloth embellished with frills or rosettes (Janaway, 1998:22). Pillows were also often included in the burial container. Sets of linings could often be purchased from period catalogs that sometimes included both mattresses and pillows of the same decorative style (Janaway, 1998:22). In the following text, burial container liners will be discussed in greater detail. Lining tacks and pillows will also be discussed, as they played important parts in the lining of the burial container.

Burial Container Linings

Davidson (2004:417) asserts, "except in the cheapest of burials, all coffins were once upholstered and then lined in cloth." In fact, one of the more substantial portions of the total cost of a funeral, or at least of a burial container, would have been the lining. The National Casket Company (1899) listed the prices associated with lining a coffin with materials such as muslin, satin, merino, and canton flannel (Table 7). This price list shows that prices could vary considerably for different materials and for lining burial containers of different dimensions.

Plume (n.d.:21–23) details the process of lining a coffin (for a description of lining a casket, see also Hohenschuh, 1900:126–132). At the very least, coffins required only a simple inside lining or heading (Figure 3, top). This lining could be a single piece of fabric depending on the width of the material or could be composed of side wall pieces and a bottom piece. After placing the pitch around the inside of the coffin to seal the container, a

Table 7. Prices for lining coffins and caskets as advertised in National Casket Company (1899). A dash (—) indicates not applicable. Length given as feet (') and inches (").

Description	Length range	Unit of cost	Cost ($/unit)
Lining with muslin	2'0"to 4'0"	Each	0.50
	4'3"to 4'9"	Each	0.75
	5'0"to 6'3"	Each	1.00
Lining with canton flannel	2'0"to 4'0"	Each	0.75
	4'3"to 4'9"	Each	1.15
	5'0"to 6'3"	Each	1.50
Satin mattress for bottom	—	Per yard	1.00
Merino mattress for bottom	—	Per yard	0.75
Cashmere mattress for bottom	—	Per yard	0.65
Bottoms lined with Spanish satin	—	—	0.25 extra
Bottoms line with satin	—	—	1.50 extra
Full satin plaited adult caskets	—	—	From 9.00 to 15.00 according to quality
Full satin plaited children's caskets	—	—	From 4.00 to 10.00 according to size and quality

layer of sawdust, or excelsior, was used to stabilize the body. Over this sawdust was placed a piece of cloth cut to the shape of the bottom. This bottom piece of fabric would later earn the title of a "mattress." The side pieces were cut from a cloth long enough that the pieces might reach along one side, across the head, and 4 inches over, matching the shape of the side of the coffin. Either the lining could be tacked near the top edge of the coffin, thus allowing the wood to show, or the fabric could be pulled over the edge and tacked down from the top, covering the wood.

To this most basic level of coffin lining it is possible to add several varieties of trimming, including a top, fringe, gimp, lace, tassels, and cords. The development of the hinged half lid on the coffin, and later the fully or half-hinged lid of the casket, prompted the introduction of the skirt and the overskirt. A glance through the price lists of burial robes and linings of the Hamilton, Lemmon, Arnold & Company (1882, 1884a, 1884b, 1886a, 1886b; Table A1) reveals that almost 200 types of linings were offered for sale, with a variety of trimmings in different combinations and colors. Lining and trimming materials were also sold individually as piece dry goods. The descriptions and costs of such items as they were advertised in Hamilton, Lemmon, Arnold & Company's revised price list (1884b) are also a valuable resource (Table A2). Analysis of these price lists suggests that buying the full range of materials needed to line a coffin or casket piecemeal would incur a greater total cost than purchasing combination sets of linings.

Fabrics Commonly Utilized in Interior Burial Container Treatments

Several of the fabrics utilized as cloth coverings for burial containers were also used as interior linings. Specifically, broadcloth, momie cloth, piqué, sateen, and velvet were

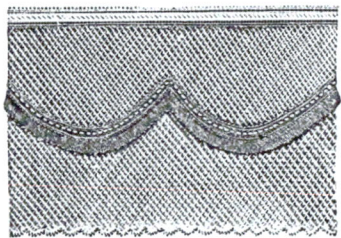
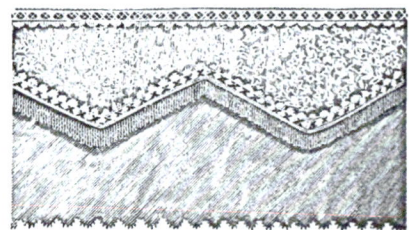

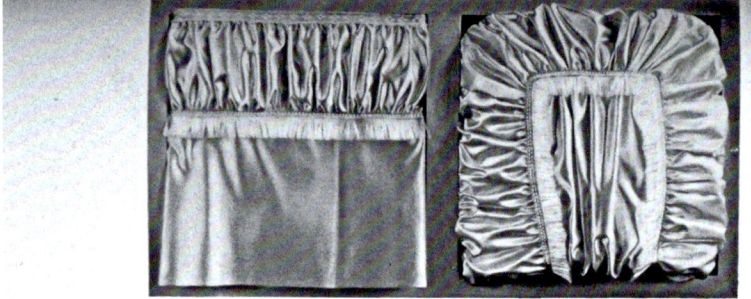

LINING SET No. 200.

Pillow shown is Style A. Style AR. is same with a 6-inch ruffle.

	Lining	Pillow Style A	Pillow Style AR	Set A Pillow	Set AR Pillow		Lining	Pillow	Set A Pillow
No. 200—First Grade Satin	$1.20	$3.00	$3.80	$9.30	$10.30	No. 515—Fig. Jap Silk heading; Coburg Skirt	$0.56	$2.20	$5.10
No. 140—Second "	.86	2.50	3.20	7.00	7.70	No. 611—Bosco Silk	.90	2.70	7.40
No. 615—Third "	.70	2.40	3.00	6.10	6.70	No. 647—Bosco Silk heading; mercerized Sateen Skirt	.60	2.30	5.50
No. 28—Fourth "	.58	2.30	2.80	5.30	5.80	No. 675—Embossed Sateen.	.32	.....	
No. 505—Bosco heading, Satin Skirt	.70	2.30	2.80	6.00	6.60				

FIGURE 3. Coffin linings. (top) Linings in the F. H. Hill catalog, 1881. (bottom) Lining set and pillow, Crane, Breed & Company catalog, 1910.

utilized for various parts of linings or trimmings on the basis of product offerings in period catalogs. These fabrics have been previously discussed and will not be discussed below; however, brief descriptions of some of the other fabrics used as interior cloth linings are provided below and include brocade, cambric, canton flannel, cashmere, China gauffer, coburg, Henrietta cloth, Italian cloth, lawn, merino, muslin, serge, and silk.

Brocade

Brocade fabrics are shuttle-woven fabrics made with a variety of silks mixed with cotton yarns and/or metallic threads. Brocade has, historically, been used for upholstering furniture as well as making tapestries and drapes. It is created using a standard weft and a supplemental weft, which produces a final product showing patterns similar to embroidery. It is stated that these fabrics were expensive to produce at their finest quality and represented some of the most expensive fabrics in the domestic market. Black was the most common base color for brocades, which would exhibit gold interlacings. Brocades average 50 epi and 60 ppi, but the thread counts could vary depending on quality of the weave (Bennett & Co., 1914:307–309; Hunter, 1918).

Cambric

Cambric was a fine linen fabric, also known as batiste, produced by the weaver Baptiste of Chambray in southern France. Cambric now more commonly refers to a finely woven cotton fabric made of hard, twisted cotton yarns, more closely resembling muslin. Cambric has a plain weave and a glazed, smooth surface appearance. This glossy effect is obtained in the finishing process when the fabric is passed through the calendar and heated with steam rollers, tightening the fibers and bringing them into alignment. Prior to being sent through the calendar, the fabric is dyed. Colors commonly used for cambric include black, sulfur black, bottle green, pea green, navy blue, dark slate, brown, light brown, old gold, slate, maroon, green, blue, wine, pink, sky blue, and heliotrope. Although various types and qualities of cambric exist, analysis of the finished fabrics reveals an average of 70 epi and 54 ppi (Bennett & Co., 1914:544–547).

Canton Flannel

Canton flannel is an all-cotton fabric showing a twill effect on one side and a soft nap on the other, constructed from one warp layer and one filling layer. The warp is produced from regular cotton yarns woven in the twill weave with characteristic diagonal ribs or twill lines, and the filling is made with a slack twist to facilitate finer napping. Regular quality canton flannel typically has 68 epi and 48 ppi when finished. It can be dyed in various colors, such as light blue, light brown, pink, red, heliotrope, green, scarlet, olive, orange, blue, slate, and maroon (Bennett & Co., 1914:395–398).

Cashmere

Cashmere is a woolen fabric made from the fur of the Kashmir goat (*Capra hircus laniger*), which originated in the Kashmir region of the Himalayas, along the border of India and Pakistan. The goats have also been raised in China, Tibet, Mongolia, Afghanistan, and Iran. Cashmere fabric has a silken texture and is relatively light weight. The fur of the goat is harvested by combing during molting, or it is shorn. The fibers are then woven, spun, or worsted before being used in the manufacture of fabric. Cashmere naturally comes in whites, grays, and browns, although it can be dyed easily into darker colors (Frank, 2001:136–140).

China Gauffer

China gauffer refers to a type of ornamental fringe made of silk. As the name implies, this particular trim is primarily made in China (Frank, 2001). No further information could be gathered about the specific qualities of this particular item; however, it was listed for sale in the 1884 price list of Hamilton, Lemmon, Arnold & Company (see Table A2).

Coburg

Coburg is a thin fabric made from all cotton, cotton and worsted wool, or cotton and silk. Coburg fabric derives its name from the city in Germany where it was first manufactured. Coburg fabric is commonly used for dress goods, including wrappers, shirtwaists, and suits. Coburg is produced using an uneven-sided twill weave with twice as many epi as ppi. In the analysis of some coburg fabrics, one will find 120 epi and 54 ppi. The weave repeats after three ends and two intersections.

Coburg fabrics are woven with gray yarns. After weaving, they are finished through either dyeing, printing, or bleaching, followed by printing. All-cotton coburgs are commonly dyed black, wine, light blue, navy blue, brown, green, scarlet, slate, red, olive, peacock blue, sky blue, or mauve (Bennett & Co., 1914:650–653).

Henrietta Cloth

Henrietta cloth is a light-weight, woolen fabric often used for women's wear. The cheaper varieties are made with cotton and worsted wool, with more expensive varieties of worsted yarn and silk. The fabric is generally constructed using a twill weave with a one-up, two-down pattern with the weave repeating on three ends and three picks. The twill weave produces a pattern of parallel, diagonal ribs. Approximately one-third of the warp is visible on the face, whereas two-thirds of the filling is visible. The twill weave and the fact that the coarser of the yarns is used for the warp give the face a finer feel than the back of the material. Good-quality Henrietta cloth has approximately 76 epi finished fabric with a filling of 66 ppi.

The cloth is dyed after it is woven. It is dipped once using the worsted dyeing process for which the cotton yarns are specially prepared; otherwise, two dyeing processes would be necessary. Colors represented in the historical literature include union black, light brown, navy blue, red, light tan, slate, purple, scarlet, pea green, royal blue, dark green, and ruby (Bennett & Co., 1914:541–544).

Italian Cloth

Italian cloth is made of cotton and worsted, cotton and wool, or cotton and mohair but can also be an all-cotton variety. It is characterized by a light, glossy appearance and is commonly said to be reminiscent of satin fabric, with some varieties being known as "farmer's satin" or "Spanish satin." It was used as linings for garments, such as ladies' dresses, as well as for undergarments. It is constructed of gray yarns in a satin foundation weave, meaning that the intersections of the warp and weft are arranged as evenly as possible across the surface of the fabric. After construction, the fabric is boiled, bleached, and then dyed in various colors, such as pink, salmon, light buff, light slate, light gray, light brown, red, sky blue, pearl, black, navy blue, and light green. The final step in the finishing process is to run the fabric through a calendar with heated rollers, which gives the fabric a glossy face. The finished fabric yields 102 epi and ppi if the threads are evenly distributed (Bennet & Co., 1914:483–487).

Lawn

Lawn is a light-weight, sheer, single-cloth, all-cotton fabric that uses a plain-weave pattern. It is produced in various quality grades of cotton yard but is always made of simple gray yarns. Any design elements present on the fabric are printed rather than woven. Lawns have a very smooth surface when finished through a process of brushing and light starching. After bleaching, lawns are often tinted light shades of blue, pink, cream, ecru, pearl, or green, using dyes added directly to the starch. The finished product usually contains 64 epi and 62 ppi (Bennett & Co., 1914:447–448).

Merino

Merino is the name of a wool-bearing sheep bred originally in Spain. The term now refers to a wide variety of wools from this species of sheep raised throughout the world. The climate of different regions where the sheep are bred greatly affects the quality of the wool produced, however. The fabric constructed from the merino fleece is a thin, light-weight material with an identical back and face. This characteristic is produced through a double-twilled weaving technique (Cole, 1892; Frank, 2001).

Muslin

Muslin is a soft cotton fabric used for a variety of purposes, such as garments and sheeting. It is called by a number of different names typically alluding to the location of its manufacture or its intended function (i.e., butcher's muslin). Often, the functions of certain types of muslin are reflected by the quality of their production. A fair grade of butcher's muslin may have around 52 epi and 38 ppi. Butcher's muslin is a plain-weave fabric that can be purchased either in an unbleached form, which means no finishing is required, or in a finished form. The finished form must be boiled and then subjected to bleaching chemicals after being removed from the loom (Bennett & Co., 1914:539–540).

Serge

Serge is a type of twill weave fabric that has wool, silk, and cotton varieties. The cotton variety itself is very similar to fine satin aside from the fact that serge is constructed with a twill weave. Cotton serge was used regularly in dressmaking but had many different applications. Wool serge has been primarily used for uniforms and suits, whereas the more fragile silk serge is used for fine inner linings of garments. Historically, in Europe, serge was expensive to produce because of the amount of labor that was necessary to process the raw materials and to weave the fabric. Because of the fine quality of the yarns required, the weave in this cloth has a high thread count, with as many as 100 epi and 172 ppi (Bennett & Co., 1914:273–275).

Silk

Raw silk thread was too fine to be woven and therefore was subjected to a "throwing" process in which several threads were twisted together, forming more substantial yarns for fabric manufacture. The yarns could be dyed prior to weaving or knitting, or the fabric could be piece dyed using a variety of dye colors (Cole, 1892). In order for the dye to adhere to the silk fibers or fabric, the natural sericin in the silk fibers must be removed through a degumming or boiling process, thus producing the fine, soft quality of silk fabric.

Silks are constructed in a number of different ways. Frank (2001:30) discusses four main families of silk weaves: tabby (or plain weave), serge, satin, and crepes. Crepe, serge, and satin have been discussed previously and will not be further detailed here. The plain-weave tabby silk is constructed through a weaving process whereby one warp thread is passed over one weft thread and then under the next weft thread (Frank, 2001:31).

Secondary Components and Trimmings of the Burial Container Linings

The primary burial container liners were composed of the mattress and the head lining, but a number of secondary lining components were introduced over the course of the nineteenth century, including the top, skirt, overskirt, and pillow (Figure 3). In addition, interiors of burial containers were often accentuated by a variety of decorative elements known as trimmings. Common types of liner trimmings available for sale in period catalogs included fringe, gimp, lace, tassels, and cords. Each of these secondary components are discussed briefly below.

Top

The top refers to the piece of fabric affixed to the underside of the coffin lid or that which is inserted into or tacked onto the lid of a casket. The top is cut to the shape of the lid, with the edges turned under and tacked down to fit just inside the top edge of the coffin.

Skirt

In modern terminology the skirt refers to the piece of fabric that hangs down from the closed, lower portion of the lid, which reaches the deceased near the midsection and hides the interior foot of the container from view. This item would not have been popularly used with hexagonal coffins but was primarily a product seen with rectangular, hinged caskets. During the earlier period, the skirt possibly could have referred to the extralarge fringe that could be unfolded to drape over the side of the burial container when the lid was open.

Overskirt

The term "overskirt" is somewhat esoteric and is not known to have modern usage. It could have referred to a couple of modern components of the casket lining: the apron/throw or the extendover. The apron, or throw, is the fabric piece that lies across the foot panel, the skirt of which hangs into the casket as mentioned above. The extendover is the piece of fabric that attaches to the inside of the casket and hangs down around the exterior to the level of the handle lugs. Overskirts, whatever their function and placement, much like skirts, were used primarily for caskets rather than for coffins.

Fringe

The fringe, also known as frilling, is an ornamental border at the top of the head lining (Plume, n.d.:23). It could consist of an assortment of loose threads or yarns of various lengths joined together via stitching onto a solid border. Fringes may also consist of frayed, textured, or otherwise ornamented fabrics (Cole, 1892). A number of such fringes are depicted in the undated (but probably pre-1878) *Illustrated Catalogue of Undertakers' Supplies*, published by Paxson, Comfort & Company.

Fringes could be attached in a couple of different ways according to Plume (n.d.:23). The first way involved creating a fold in the fringe fabric leaving a narrow and a long portion. The fabric fold could then be tacked to the upper inside edge of the burial container, allowing the long part of the fringe to drape inside the coffin while the narrow edge would fold up and inward, creating a fabric lip at the edge of the coffin. This first method was used when the top of the coffin wood was left visible. The second method was to tack the fringe down in such a way that it is on top of the coffin edge and completely covering the wood. In this case, Plume suggests using brass gimp tacks to secure the fringe; these tacks would be visible and so should be attractive. The fringe should be started at the head of the coffin, and the corners should be folded rather than cut (Plume, n.d.:23).

Gimp

Gimp is the term for a flat trimming made from twisted silk, worsted wool, or cotton yarns. The term originally referred to the stiff metallic wire or coarse cord that runs through the center and acts as a foundation for the braids, beads, or spangles characteristic of certain types of gimp (Cole, 1892). Several different varieties of cotton gimps are depicted in the undated (but probably pre-1878) *Illustrated Catalogue of Undertakers' Supplies*, published by Paxson, Comfort & Company. Gimps usually range from a quarter of an inch to an inch wide and are tacked to the top of the fringe using gimp tacks, either on the upper inner margin of the coffin or along the top of the coffin walls.

Lace

Lace is a very old type of ornamental fringe; originally meaning a braid or a tie, it evolved into the current form by interweaving fine linen laces with other fine threads on a parchment pattern. Designs and ornamentation are incorporated into the lace either through the weaving process or through needlework and embroidery, the latter type known as point lace. The lace was often applied to the interior of the coffin in place of a fringe or frill to cover the corners of the interior lining or as a border for the top. It could also be used to decorate the exterior of the coffin (although it should not be confused with metal lace, which may have imitated the cloth form; see Figure 3 (bottom). Plume (n.d.:40) describes using lace to cover the seam of cloth coverings by bringing the seam near one corner of the coffin and then folding lace around each corner. Different types of lace could be considered to be in the gimp and fringe categories, but it is not known what type of lace was used in burial container ornamentation.

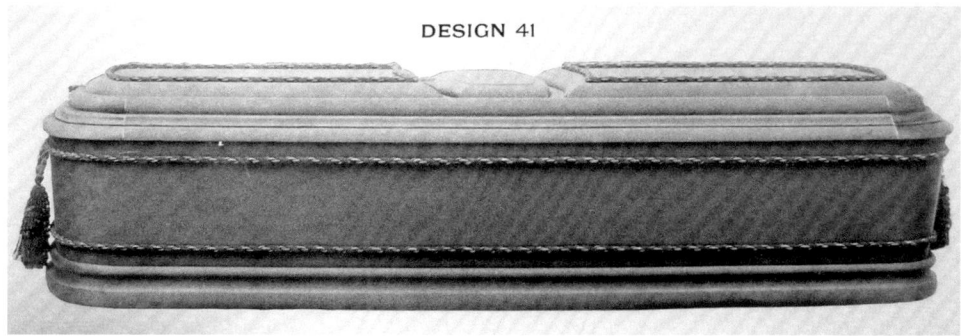

FIGURE 4. Tassels and cords on casket, Paxson, Comfort & Company catalog, 1898.

Tassels

Tassels, often made of silk or other fine fibers, were often used to augment the aesthetic quality of the fringe on the interior of the coffin. If a scalloped fringe was used, then the tassels would be placed in the depression between two adjacent scallops. The 1895 *Illustrated Catalogue of Hearses and Trimmings*, published by Crane, Breed & Company, depicted several types of such tassels. Tassels came in various sizes and designs and were also commonly used with decorative cords to wrap around the exterior of coffins, caskets (Figure 4), and even hearses (Paxson, Comfort & Company, 1898).

Cords

Cords are braided or twisted decorative ropes made from various fibers, yarns, or threads, such as cotton, silk, or metallic wire. Such cords are generally one-quarter to a half inch thick and would be used as border material across the top inner edge of the burial container. They were also often used with tassels and wrapped around the exterior of the coffin or casket, as in casket design 41 from the 1898 Paxson, Comfort & Company catalog (Figure 4).

Pillows

One other aspect of interior coffin treatment yet to be discussed is the presence of a pillow or some object upon which the head of the deceased is laid. During the late nineteenth century's Beautification of Death Movement (Bell, 1990, 1994), the deceased was often characterized as sleeping, a conception that acted to normalize the view of the coffin or casket as a bed. Pillows were often formed initially from the bottom lining by adding extra stuffing in the head region (Janaway, 1998:23). Alternatively, separate pillows could be included in the burial container (Litten, 1991:103). Pillows appeared in period catalogs once mortuary supply companies expanded production beyond hardware.

A review of period mortuary merchandise catalogs indicates that pillows could be made from a variety of materials and came in many different styles. The Paxson, Comfort & Company ([ca. 1890]:161) catalog *Wholesale Pricelist of Burial Robes, Wrappers, Dresses, Suits, Habits* advertises "very fine artistic hand-embroidered pillows made from coburg, sateen, cashmere, wool merino, silk and satin." Those fabrics could be produced in colors such as

Table 8. Satin pillows listed for sale in Stein Manufacturing Company (1887).

No.	Description	Cost
1	White or cream satin, bonanz embroidered spray, edged with fine fringes, 3 inches deep	$3.50
2	White or cream satin, bonanz embroidery, and words "At Rest," edged with fine silk fringes, 3 inches deep	$4.00
3	White satin pillow, made plain, with medium satin	$3.00
4	Finest satin, any color; princess puffing on top, edged with rose satin trimming, made for either octagon, elliptical, or round end caskets	$10.00
5	Satin pillow similar to No. 4, made for 3 foot, 6 inch child's casket (other sizes to order)	$5.00
6	Finest ribbon-embroidered satin pillow, similar in design to one placed in the "Grant State Casket"	$20.00
7	Medium satin, double row of puffing	$1.80
	No. 7, unfilled, in dozen lots	$18.00
8	Reverse plaited satin top of extra fine quality, tulip trimmed	$8.50
9	Princess satin plaited top, tulip trimming, medium quality	$7.00
10	Duchess satin puffed top, tulip trimmed	$6.00
11	Circle end, box plaited top, trimmed with lace	$4.00
12	Circle end, princess top, finished with lace ribbon	$5.00

white, cream, drab, steel gray, pink, blue, and black to match the style and color of associated Paxson, Comfort & Company coffin and casket linings. Several styles mentioned include puffed, plaited, and honeycomb, although it is mentioned that other popular designs could be ordered for a cost ranging between $0.25 and $25.00.

Satin was by far the most popular material for manufacturing pillows, as evident in the available catalogs. Hamilton, Lemmon, Arnold & Company's price list of 1 November 1886 (1886b) lists six types of satin pillows for adult-sized caskets with three different levels of product quality ranging in price from $2.00 to $6.00 and three types of satin pillows for children's caskets ranging in price from $0.80 to $1.75. Unfortunately, no illustrated catalogs were available for comparison matches to be made with the Hamilton, Lemmon, Arnold & Company price lists. The most complete description of a series of pillows for sale comes from the 1 June 1887 Stein Manufacturing Company *Revised Price List and Telegraph Key*. They list 12 types of satin pillows ranging in price from $0.80 to $20.00 (Table 8).

Burial Container Linings in the Archaeological Record

Preservation of interior cloth linings is typically poor in most archaeological contexts, although when preservation is favorable, the linings tend to survive better than exterior cloth coverings. Smaller portions of fabric might also be preserved in association with metal hardware or even jewelry or other items placed within the burial container. As was the case with the exterior cloth covering, when preservation is not ideal, evidence of cloth linings may be limited to the presence of lining tacks, complex internal hardware designed for use with cloth, or, less commonly, fabric impressions on the heads of tacks located under folds of the lining fabric. All of these situations have been discussed above in regard to external cloth covering.

Davidson (1999, 2004:417) suggested that any number of small tacks recovered from a burial probably served as lining tacks. Lining tacks include ferrous or cuprous flat-headed cut tacks, ferrous or cuprous domed-headed gimp tacks (see Figure 1), and 7-line to 14-line silk-headed lining tacks. Davidson (2004:417) reported that the most common type of tack found in excavations at Freedman's Cemetery in Dallas, Texas, was composed of two parts: a short iron shank and a plain, domed lead head. Furthermore, the presence of these supposed lining tacks could act as a proxy indicator for the presence of lining materials in cases of poor preservation of organic materials. Evidence of coffin lining is most commonly found on the underside of tack heads or in association with other metal coffin elements or metallic personal items such as cuprous medallions or crosses. It is often very difficult, if not impossible, to distinguish between coffin lining material and articles of clothing, but the presence or absence of coffin or casket lining is an important economic observation. The recovery and accurate analysis of lining tacks serves to give greater assurance to the presence of coffin lining (Davidson, 2004:418).

Table 9 reveals the listings of lining tacks present in the 1884 Hamilton, Lemmon, Arnold & Company (1884a) price list. As the names of the tacks sometimes imply, certain types of tacks were designed to be used in specific contexts or for specific purposes. The

Table 9. Descriptions of tacks listed in Hamilton, Lemmon, Arnold & Company (1884a). A dash (—) indicates not applicable. "Per M" probably indicates "per 1,000 items."

Description	Weight (oz.)	Unit of cost	Cost ($/unit)
Blue tacks	1.5	Per pound	0.70
	1.5	Per paper	0.04
	2	Per pound	0.70
	2	Per paper	0.05
	12	Per paper	0.10
	2.5	Per pound	0.60
	2.5	Per paper	0.05
	4	Per paper	0.06
Gimp tacks, round head	2	Per paper	0.06
	3	Per paper	0.07
	4	Per paper	0.08
Gimp or lace, flat head	2	Per paper	0.06
	2.5	Per paper	0.06
Bright lining tacks, oval head	2.5	Per paper	0.09
Bright tufting tacks, oval head	12	Per paper	0.09
Silver cast head	—	Per box of 144	0.10
Small silk head lining tack, 7 lines	—	Per M	2.40
Large silk head lining tack, 10 lines	—	Per M	2.50
Silver silk head lining tack	—	Per M	2.50
Gold silk head lining tack	—	Per M	2.50
French nails	—	Per M	1.00
Large silk head lining tacks, 14 lines	—	Per M	3.50

gimp tack, for instance, would tack down the gimp around the upper margin of the burial container perimeter, whereas the lace tack and tufting tack fixed those textiles. Although certain types of tacks were commonly used as lining tacks, other varieties could also be used, including upholstery tacks, or French nails. Indeed, any simple steel, iron, or brass tack and even small brads or nails could be utilized to tack down interior linings or exterior cloth covering.

Little attention has been given to fabric analysis in recent cemetery projects, so no synthesis of interior cloth linings in the archaeological literature is yet possible. A detailed analysis of burial container fabrics was possible on the Alameda-Stone Cemetery project, however, and it indicates the potential. Approximately 500 burial containers in the Tucson cemetery appeared to have been lined with some sort of fabric, suggested either by the presence of interior lining tacks or by remnants of lining fabric. Because it is difficult to distinguish between remnants of clothing and lining fabric, interior lining tacks are a better indicator of burial container linings. Five types of tacks were present: silk head lining tacks, which appeared in 28 burials; domed-head ferrous tacks, found in 21 burials; flat-head ferrous tacks, recovered in 456 burials; flat-head brass tacks, included in 7 burials; and decorative French nails/upholstery tacks found in only 1 burial. All flat- and domed-head brass and ferrous tacks were cut with sheared, pointed tips. The silk head tacks and upholstery tacks appeared to have rounded, pointed shafts (Pye, 2010).

In those situations where fabric was preserved, a range of colors and materials was indicated: brown, yellow/brown, white/cream, white, green, black, and pink/green. All fabrics were somewhat degraded, and colors may not represent the originals. Types of fabrics included finely woven silks, fine cottons, pleated cottons, medium-coarse woven fabrics, coarse grass fiber matting, coarse twilled fabric, possible felts, and velvet. Because of poor organic preservation, little can be said of the grand demographic pattern of burial container linings, although some observations can be made. Velvets, or possible velvets or felts, occurred with at least two adult males and one subadult. Satin, silk, or other finely woven fabrics seemed to occur with the burials of infants and adult females. A preserved segment of gimp in one burial of an adult of unknown sex or cultural affiliation consisted of dark green and yellow/white yarns interwoven so that the dark green strands formed distinct vertical bands while the white threads were visible on the face, forming X patterns horizontally across the gimp. This material had been tacked to the upper margin of the interior of the burial container (Pye, 2010).

The presence of pillows within burial containers is also rarely discernable because of lack of preservation, although three individuals in the Alameda-Stone Cemetery were buried with their heads resting on some type of object, including an adobe brick, a degraded satin-covered pillow filled with a sawdust material, and a possible pillow stuffed with cotton or wool and covered with a degraded wool fabric (Pye, 2010). Even though fabric pillows were identifiable in these two cases, a much higher degree of physical preservation would be necessary to be able to match the style of the pillow to period merchandise catalogs.

Painting

Painting was a widely used exterior surface treatment on nineteenth- and early twentieth-century burial containers, but the interior could also be painted. A wide range of colors were applied to the interiors of 72 burial containers recovered during the Alameda-Stone Cemetery project in Tucson, Arizona. Colors included green, blue, white, brown, black, pink, and red; in most cases the paint was preserved only in small patches on wood or associated with metal hardware. Because the evidence of paint was scant, it is difficult or impossible to say whether the entire interior surface had been painted or only certain portions. In one burial container, two types of paint were identified: green paint was found on the bottom of the container, and a dark gray paint was applied to the underside of the lid. This observation allows for the possibility of multiple paints within the same burial container in other burials in the cemetery. There were also two cases where blue and green paints were layered (Pye, 2010).

Combination Treatments

The presence of paint on the interior of a burial container does not preclude the presence of a lining. In 26 cases in the Alameda-Stone Cemetery both paint and fabric were present. In most cases, as with the paint-fabric combinations on the exterior surfaces, the paint was applied to the outer surface of the fabric. It is unknown to what extent the paint and fabric were applied together or applied to different portions of the interior, such as paint on the underside of the lid and fabric on the bottom and side walls. No burial containers suggested that paint and fabric were used for separate portions of the interior surface, but it is a possibility (Pye, 2010), one that can be extended to other cemeteries throughout the country.

Conclusion

Period mortuary merchandise catalogs and price lists from the nineteenth to early twentieth centuries attest that burial container surface treatment could be quite varied, with both the exterior and interior surfaces being means of expression and elaboration. Relatively little has been systematically presented in the published archaeological literature about the types of surface treatments encountered during historic period cemetery or burial excavations, largely because of limited preservation. This may restrict the scope of observation, but through careful scrutiny of the archaeological record such as in corrosion products of coffin hardware and an appreciation for the valuable information present in the period mortuary and general supply catalogs, it is possible to develop a fuller understanding of the socioeconomic role a burial container might have played during the funeral.

Appendix

Tables A1 and A2 present the descriptions and costs of items listed in price lists published by Hamilton, Lemmon, Arnold & Company.

Table A1. Descriptions and costs of coffin and casket linings combined from partial listings in Hamilton, Lemmon, Arnold & Company (1882, 1884a, 1884b, 1886a, and 1886b).

Lining No.	Catalog date	Width (inches)	Description	Cost ($/yard)
0	1884	5.0	Best Spanish satin skirt and overskirt, cotton heading	0.06
X	1884	6.0	Best flowered satin lining, no overskirt, cotton heading	0.04
1	1884	11.0	Best Spanish satin pinked overskirt, Spanish satin skirt, cotton heading	0.10
2	1882	6.5	Satin top embroidered cashmere skirt	0.50
3	1884	10.0	Cashmere lining, with silk fringe to imitate pointed overskirt, silk heading	0.25
4	1884	10.0	Same as No. 3, only the fringe and heading is black and white	0.25
5	1884	10.0	Shirred satin top cashmere skirt, silk fringe and heading	0.40
6	1882	10.0	Cashmere skirt, silk fringe, gimp, and tassels	0.35
7	1884	6.0	Fluted top, best Spanish satin skirt, cotton heading	0.10
8	1882	10.0	Cashmere, black and white silk fringe, gimp, and tassels	0.35
9	1882	10.0	Puffed top, best stamped satin skirt, silk fringe and gimp	0.35
10	1882	8.0	Puffed satin top, watered satin skirt, silk fringe and gimp	0.40
12	1882	7.0	Cashmere, silk fringe and gimp	0.33
13	1884	11.0	Best Spanish satin skirt, flowered satin overskirt, cotton heading	0.13
16	1884	5.5	Shirred satin with lace edge overskirt, cashmere skirt, silk heading	0.25
17	1882	12.0	Plain white satin, with overskirt, silk fringe, gimp, cord, and tassels	1.70
18	1882	8.5	Plain white satin, with overskirt, silk fringe, gimp, cord, and tassels	1.45
19	1884	6.0	Satin lining with fringe and tassels to imitate pointed overskirt, silk heading	0.55
20	1882	6.0	Embroidered satin top, cashmere skirt	0.45
21	1884	11.0	Fluted top best Spanish satin skirt, cotton heading	0.15
22	1882	8.0	Puffed satin top, satin skirt, silk fringe and gimp	0.70
24	1882	12.0	Watered satin, with overskirt, silk fringe, gimp, cord, and tassels	1.00
27	1884	8.0	Satin box plaited and fringe for overskirt, plain satin skirt, silk heading	1.00
28	1884	12.0	Satin box plaited and fringe for overskirt, plain satin skirt, silk heading	1.20
29	1884	6.5	Flowered satin overskirt, plain sateen skirt, silk heading	0.22

Table A1. (*Continued*)

Lining No.	Catalog date	Width (inches)	Description	Cost ($/yard)
30	1884	10.0	Flowered sateen overskirt, plain sateen skirt, silk heading	0.30
31	1882	10.5	Fancy top, flowered skirt	0.20
32	1882	6.5	Fancy top, flowered skirt	0.15
35	1882	6.5	Embroidered Italian cloth, top and skirt	0.35
36	1882	10.5	Embroidered Italian cloth, top and skirt	1.50
37	1882	7.5	Embroidered satin cloth	1.60
38	1884	10.0	Sateen box plaited and fringe for overskirt, sateen box plaited skirt, silk heading	0.50
39	1882	12.0	Cashmere, honeycomb	0.85
41	1884	10.0	White brocade cloth and fringe, tassels, pointed, for overskirt, brocade cloth skirt, silk heading	0.50
42	1884	8.0	White brocade cloth and fringe, tassels, pointed, for overskirt, brocade cloth skirt, silk heading	0.40
43	1884	10.0	Italian cloth, fringe, ribbon, and buttons, festooned for overskirt, Italian cloth plain for skirt, silk heading	0.70
44	1882	10.0	Stamped silk, skirt and overskirt, silk fringe	0.45
45	1884	5.0	Flowered sateen overskirt, Spanish satin skirt, cotton heading	0.10
46	1884	6.3	Flowered sateen overskirt, Spanish satin skirt, cotton heading	0.12
47	1882	8.0	Stamped silk overskirt, Spanish satin skirt	0.08
48	1882	10.5	Stamped silk overskirt, Spanish satin skirt	0.12
50	1884	11.0	Sateen embroidered and Spanish satin overskirt, fluted skirt, cotton heading	0.22
54	1884	10.0	Fine white satin quilted and embroidered, silk heading	1.75
55	1884	10.0	Fine white satin quilted and embroidered, "At Rest," silk heading	1.50
56	1884	12.0	Double row of puffed cashmere and fringe for top cashmere skirt, silk heading	0.35
59	1884	10.0	Fluted satin and fringe for top cashmere skirt, silk heading	0.45
61	1884	10.0	Scalloped satin embroidered top, satin de chine embossed for skirt, silk heading	1.00
62	1884	10.5	Fine cashmere quilted and embroidered, "I.O.O.F.," silk heading	1.00
63	1884	10.5	Fine cashmere quilted and embroidered, "F.&A.M.," silk heading	1.00
64	1884	10.0	Satin shirred cross ways with fringe, making very puffy overskirt, plain sateen skirt, silk heading	0.65
65	1884	11.0	Cashmere, wadded and quilted	0.35

Table A1. (*Continued*)

Lining No.	Catalog date	Width (inches)	Description	Cost ($/yard)
74	1884	10.5	Scalloped satin embroidered cross and fringe for overskirt, plain cashmere skirt, silk heading	0.75
76	1884	10.0	Overskirt fancy crimpled cashmere, flowered cashmere skirt, silk heading	0.50
77	1884	10.0	Fancy Spanish satin overskirt, Spanish satin skirt, cotton heading	0.09
80	1884	10.0	Fancy Spanish satin overskirt, Spanish satin skirt	0.10
82	1884	10.0	Fancy crimped and fluted overskirt, with fancy skirt	0.35
85	1884	10.5	Scalloped satin embroidered ornament and fringe for overskirt, plain cashmere skirt, silk heading	0.75
87	1882	10.5	Embroidered and quilted satin	0.75
93	1884	10.0	Figured cambric, embroidered to imitate pointed overskirt, cotton heading	0.10
94	1884	10.0	Figured cambric, embroidered to imitate pointed overskirt, cotton heading, black and white	0.10
97	1884	6.0	Blue fluting edged with fringe for top, figured cambric skirt, silk heading	0.15
98	1884	11.0	Brown fluting edged with fringe for top, figured cambric skirt, cotton heading	0.15
100	1884	10.0	Satin puffed and scalloped, lace and fringe for overskirt, plain cotton heading	1.10
104	1884	8.0	Satin puffed and scalloped, fringe and gimp for overskirt, plain cashmere skirt, silk heading	0.55
108	1884	12.0	Cashmere puffed and quilted, with fringe for overskirt, plain cashmere skirt, silk heading	0.50
110	1884	10.0	____ [Cashmere] trimming with lace edge for top, plain cashmere skirt, silk heading	0.85
113	1884	10.0	Cashmere embroidered in white and pinked for top, plain cashmere skirt	0.20
114	1884	10.0	Cashmere embroidered in blue and pinked for top, plain cashmere skirt	0.20
117	1884	11.0	Satin scalloped, fringe and cord for overskirt, plain cashmere skirt, silk heading	0.35
118	1884	10.0	Serge puffing, Spanish satin scallops pinked, and fringe for overskirt, piqué skirt, cotton heading	0.25
120	1884	10.0	Satin box plaited and fringe for overskirt, plain cashmere skirt, silk heading	0.50
122	1884	10.0	Figured velvet overskirt, piqué skirt	0.30
124	1884	10.0	Shirred satin with wide lace edge for overskirt, plain cashmere skirt, silk heading	0.70
125	1884	7.5	Lining flowered overskirt, fancy sateen skirt	0.15
126	1884	10.5	Lining flowered overskirt, fancy sateen skirt	0.18
127	1884	10.5	Lining flowered sateen overskirt and skirt	0.18

Table A1. (*Continued*)

Lining No.	Catalog date	Width (inches)	Description	Cost ($/yard)
134	1886	11.0	Embroidered coburg, cotton heading	0.25
135	1886	11.0	Embroidered cashmere lining, silk heading	0.35
136	1886	12.0	Satin, box plaited, extra heavy silk fringe top	1.00
137	1886	12.0	All merino, silk fringe and heading	0.85
138	1886	13.0	Fine satin Africane, silk fringe and heading	0.90
139	1886	6.5	Coburg silk, lace overskirt, lace heading	0.45
140	1886	6.5	Brocade satin, box plaited silk heading	0.60
141	1886	7.5	Momie cloth skirt, embroidered top, silk fringe and heading	0.35
142	1886	7.5	Momie cloth skirt, blue embroidered overskirt, silk fringe and heading	0.35
143	1886	9.0	Striped satin skirt and double shirred top, shell trimming, silk fringe and heading	0.65
144	1886	12.0	Brocade satin skirt and overskirt, silk fringe and heading	0.30
145	1886	11.0	Cashmere skirt, brocaded satin top, silk fringe and gimp	0.40
146	1886	12.0	Satin skirt, satin top, fan tail trimming, silk heading and fringe	1.00
147	1886	12.0	Cashmere skirt, satin overskirt, silk fringe and heading	0.80
148	1886	12.0	Satin skirt, revered finger plaited satin top, silk fringe and heading	1.00
149	1886	12.0	Cashmere skirt, revered plaited satin top, silk fringe and heading	0.90
150	1886	12.5	Satin skirt and overskirt, silk fringe and heading	0.60
151	1886	8.0	Cashmere skirt, shirred satin top, silk fringe and heading	0.40
152	1886	13.0	Cashmere skirt, satin top, silk fringe and heading	1.00
153	1886	11.5	Polka dot skirt, satin top, silk fringe and heading	0.60
154	1884	10.0	Satin quilted and embroidered, silk heading	1.00
155	1884	10.0	Fine white cashmere, quilted and embroidered "At Rest," silk heading	1.00
156	1886	8.0	Cashmere skirt, satin top, silk fringe and heading	0.50
157	1886	11.0	Shirred satin, silk heading	0.80
158	1886	10.5	Brocade Spanish satin, imitation crepe top, embroidered satin edging, silk heading	0.35
159	1886	12.0	Spanish satin skirt, top lawn fluting and shirring, cotton lace and heading	0.22
160	1886	11.0	Brocade Spanish satin, imitation overskirt with frilling, cotton heading	0.11
161	1886	11.0	Cashmere skirt, satin top, silk fringe and heading	0.50
162	1886	6.5	Embossed Spanish satin, no heading	0.08

Table A1. (*Continued*)

Lining No.	Catalog date	Width (inches)	Description	Cost ($/yard)
163	1886	12.0	Spanish satin skirt, top lawn fluting, cotton fringe and heading	0.22
166	1886	7.5	All cashmere, bonanz work, silk fringe and heading	0.50
167	1886	8.5	All satin, silk fringe and heading	0.55
174	1884	10.5	Scalloped satin embroidered cross and fringe for overskirt, plain cashmere skirt, silk heading	0.50
185	1884	10.5	Scalloped satin embroidered ornament and fringe for overskirt, plain cashmere skirt, silk heading	0.50
1690	1886	11.0	Brocade Spanish satin skirt, piqué scallops, sateen reverse plaited top, cotton fringe and heading	0.16

Table A2. Descriptions and costs of piece dry goods listed in Hamilton, Lemmon, Arnold & Company (1884a). A dash (—) indicates not applicable.

Material	Item No.	Width (inches)	Description	Cost
Broadcloth	1	52	Black	$1.50/yard
	2	54	Black	$2.20/yard
	3	54	Black	$2.50/yard
	4	54	Black	$2.80/yard
	5	54	White	$2.00/yard
	6	54	White	$2.80/yard
Velvet	1	22	Black	$0.50/yard
	2	22	Black	$0.62/yard
	3	22	Black	$0.85/yard
	4	22	Black	$3.25/yard
	5	22	White	$0.62/yard
	6	22	Purple	$0.77/yard
Merino	1	40	White or cream	$0.90/yard
	2	40	Black	$0.95/yard
	3	40	Brown	$0.95/yard
Cashmere, first quality	1	40	White or cream	$0.45/yard
	2	40	Black	$0.50/yard
	3	40	Brown	$0.50/yard
Cashmere, second quality	1	40	White or cream	$0.25/yard
	2	40	Black	$0.27/yard
	3	40	Brown	$0.27/yard
Satins	C	24	White	$0.55/yard
	M	20	White	$0.78/yard
	G	24	White	$1.00/yard
	B	22	White	$1.25/yard

Table A2. (*Continued*)

Material	Item No.	Width (inches)	Description	Cost
	A	24	Black	$0.67/yard
	A	—	Black, with embossed flower	$1.00/yard
	P	—	Black, with embossed stripe	$1.00/yard
	L	20	Pale blue	$0.85/yard
	D	20	Navy blue	$1.00/yard
	W	19	Light brown	$1.15/yard
	H	19	Black	$1.20/yard
	F	—	White, with embossed flower	$0.80/yard
	S	—	White, with embossed stripe	$0.80/yard
Muslins	1	36	"Rival" muslin	$0.07/yard
	2	42	"Cabot" muslin	$0.11/yard
	—	36	White cambric muslin	$0.06/yard
Lawns	1	40	White	$0.15/yard
	2	40	Black	$0.16/yard
	3	40	Brown	$0.16/yard
Corded serge	—	40	Black	$0.35/yard
Satin de Chine	1	27	White	$0.50/yard
	2	32	White	$0.60/yard
	3	32	White	$0.70/yard
	4	32	White	$0.80/yard
Striped Italian cloth	—	32	Cream	$0.65/yard
Brocade cloth	—	27	White (same as 41 lining)	$0.30/yard
Watered sateens	—	40	White (same as 38 lining)	$0.40/yard
China gauffer	—	25	White	$0.40/yard
Spanish satins	1	20	Black	$0.08/yard
	2	20	Black	$0.08/yard
	3	20	White	$0.08/yard
	4	20	White	$0.08/yard
	5	20	White	$0.08/yard
	6	20	Brown	$0.08/yard
	7	20	Brown	$0.08/yard
	8	—	White, extra heavy to order	$0.10/yard
Corded silk	—	24	White	$1.12/yard
Piqué	—	27	White	$0.30/yard
Cotton gimp[a]	1	Narrow	White	$0.20/bolt
	2	Medium	White	$0.25/bolt
	2.5	Medium	White	$0.25/bolt
	3	Wide	Black and white	$0.50/bolt

Table A2. (Continued)

Material	Item No.	Width (inches)	Description	Cost
Silk gimp[b]	3.5	Wide	Black and white	$0.50/bolt
	4	Narrow	White	$0.90/piece
	4.5	Medium	Black and white	$1.40/piece
	5	Medium	White	$1.40/piece
	5.5	Medium	Black and white	$1.40/piece
	6	Wide	White	$1.40/piece
	6.5	Narrow	Black and white	$0.90/piece
	7	Wide	White	$2.00/piece
	7.5	Wide	Black and white	$2.00/piece
	8	Wide	White	$4.00/piece
	216	—	—	$2.30/piece
	999	—	—	$2.75/piece
	1013	—	—	$0.80/piece
	1013	—	Brown	$1.00/piece
	1018	—	Brown	$1.25/piece
	1018	—	——	$1.25/piece
	1021	—	——	$1.50/piece
	1021	—	Black	$1.50/piece
	1021	—	Brown	$1.50/piece
	1033	—	—	$1.60/piece
	1043	—	—	$1.55/piece
Silk cord[c]	10	—	White chenille	$1.00/piece
	20	—	White	$0.60/piece
	20	—	Brown	$0.70/piece
	30	—	Brown	$0.80/piece
	30	—	White	$0.75/piece
	30	—	Black	$0.75/piece
	40	—	Black	$0.90/piece
	40	—	White	$0.90/piece
	60	—	Black	$1.15/piece
Silk tassels	1	—	Black (for draped caskets)	$5.60/dozen
	2	—	Black (for draped caskets)	$8.50/dozen
	3	—	White (for draped caskets)	$6.30/dozen
	4	—	White, or black, for lining	$0.20/dozen
	6	—	White, or black, for lining	$0.30/dozen
Silk and cotton fringe[a]	—	0.5	White silk	$1.00/bolt
	—	1	White silk	$1.60/bolt
	—	1.5	White silk	$2.00/bolt
	—	2	White silk	$3.00/bolt
	—	1	Black and white silk	$1.60/bolt
	—	1.5	Black and white silk	$2.00/bolt
	—	1	Black and white cotton	$0.40/bolt
	—	1	White cotton	$0.40/bolt

Table A2. (*Continued*)

Material	Item No.	Width (inches)	Description	Cost
Lace	1	1	White	$1.00/dozen yards
	2	1.5	White	$1.50/dozen yards
	3	1.5	White	$2.00/dozen yards
	4	2.5	White	$3.40/dozen yards
	5	3	White	$5.00/dozen yards
	6	1	Black	$1.00/dozen yards
	7	1.25	Black	$1.50/dozen yards
	8	2.5	Black	$3.40/dozen yards

[a] A bolt is 24 yards.
[b] A piece is 24 yards.
[c] A piece is 18 yards.

References

Bastis, K. 2006. Health, Wealth, and Available Material: The Bioarchaeology of the Bulkeley Tomb in Colchester, Connecticut. Master's thesis, University of Connecticut, Storrs.

Bell, E. L. 1990. The Historical Archaeology of Mortuary Behavior: Coffin Hardware from Uxbridge, Massachusetts. *Historical Archaeology*, 24(3):54–78.

Bell, E. L. 1994. *Vestiges of Mortality and Remembrance: A Bibliography on the Historical Archaeology of Cemeteries*. Metuchen, N.J.: Scarecrow Press.

Beynon, D. E. 1989. *Remember Me as You Pass By: Excavation of the Voegtly Cemetery. A Nineteenth Century German-American Churchyard in Pittsburgh, Pennsylvania*. 3 vols. Report to the Pennsylvania Department of Transportation. Monroeville, Pa.: GAI Consultants.

Bromberg, F. W., S. J. Shepard, B. H. Magid, P. J. Cressey, T. Dennée, and B. K. Means. 2000. *"To Find Rest from All Trouble": The Archaeology of the Quaker Burying Ground, Alexandria, Virginia*. Alexandria, Va.: Alexandria Archaeology, Office of Historic Alexandria.

Brown-Hutchison Company. 1899. *Illustrated Catalog and Cash Price List No. 3 [September 21, 1899]*. Pittsburgh: Brown-Hutchison.

Bybee, A. D. 2002. Bioanthropological Investigations of the Reynolds Cemetery (46Ka349) in Kanawha County, West Virginia. Prepared for Dr. Robert F. Maslowski, Huntington District Corp of Engineers, Huntington, W.Va. Hurricane, W.Va.: Cultural Resource Analysts.

Bybee, A. D. 2003a. Bioanthropological Investigations of the Burning Spring Branch Cemetery (46Ka142) in Kanawha County, West Virginia. Prepared for Dr. Robert F. Maslowski, Huntington District Corps of Engineers, Huntington, W.Va. Hurricane, W.Va.: Cultural Resource Analysts.

Bybee, A. D. 2003b. Bioarchaeological Investigations of Unmarked Graves at the Samuel Robinson and Upper Prater Cemeteries (15PI190 and 15PI191), Pike County, Kentucky (Item No. 12-263.00). Prepared for Mr. Doug Lambert, Palmer Engineering, Winchester, Ky. Lexington, Ky.: Cultural Resource Analysts.

Bybee, A. D. 2004. Old Branham (15Fd94): Bioarchaeological Investigations of an Historic Cemetery, Floyd County, Kentucky (Item No. 12-301.00). Prepared for Mr. David Waldner, P. E., Director, Kentucky Transportation Cabinet, Division of Environmental Analysis, Frankfort, Ky. Lexington, Ky.: Cultural Resource Analysts.

Bybee, A. D. 2007. Bioarchaeological Investigations of the Evans Cemetery (46MD62), McDowell County, West Virginia. Contract Publication Series WV07-03. Prepared for Mr. Timothy B. Sedosky, Potesta & Associates, Inc., Charleston, W.Va. Hurricane, W.Va.: Cultural Resource Analysts.

Casas, A. P., and J. de Andrés Llopis. 2002. A Spot Test for Zinc White. *Studies in Conservation*, 47(4):273–276

Chappell, Chase, Maxwell & Company. 1884. *Illustrated Catalogue: Cloth, Velvet-Covered, and Wood Finished Burial Caskets.* Oneida, N.Y.: Chappell, Chase, Maxwell.

Cleveland Burial Case Company. 1882. *Illustrated Catalogue of Wood, Cloth Covered, and Metallic Caskets.* Cleveland: Cleveland Burial Case.

Coffin, M. M. 1976. *Death in Early America.* Nashville: Thomas Nelson.

Cole, G. S. 1892. *A Complete Dictionary of Dry Goods, and History of Silk, Cotton, Linen, Wool and Other Fibrous Substances Including a Full Explanation of the Modern Processes of Spinning, Dyeing and Weaving, with an Appendix Containing a Treatise on Window Trimming, German Words and Phrases, with Their English Pronunciation and Significance, Together with Various Useful Tables.* Chicago: W. B. Conkey.

Costello, J. G. 1991. Excavation of Burials from the Madam Felix/Hettick Cemetery, CA-CAL-1122H. Prepared for Meridan Gold Company, Copperpolis, Calif. Mokelumne Hill, Calif.: Foothill Resource Associates.

Crane, Breed & Company. 1895. *Illustrated Catalogue of Hearses and Trimmings.* Cincinnati: Crane, Breed.

Crane, Breed & Company. 1910. *Catalogue "D" Burial Garments, Robes, Casket Linings, Pillow and Lining Sets, Door Crapes.* Cincinnati: Crane & Breed.

Crawford, K., A. Hutcheson, E. MacDonald, B. Nahri, D. Robertson, and R. Williamson. 2008. Ontario Cemeteries Act Site Investigation, the Old Don Jail Burial Area. Proposed Draft Plan of Subdivision, Part of Lot 15, Concession 1. From the Bay, Geographic Township of York and Part of Block U, Don Improvement Plan, City of Toronto Archaeological Services, Inc., Toronto, Ontario, Canada. Prepared for Bridgepoint Health and Cemeteries Regulation Unit, Ministry of Small Business and Consumer Services, Toronto, Ontario, Canada.

Curtis, H. P. 1921. *Glossary of Textile Terms.* Manchester, U.K.: Marsden.

Davidson, J. M. 1999. Freedman's Cemetery (1869–1907): A Chronological Reconstruction of an Excavated African-American Burial Ground, Dallas, Texas. Master's thesis, University of Arkansas, Fayetteville.

Davidson, J. M. 2004. Mediating Race and Class through the Death Experience: Power Relations and Resistance Strategies of an African-American Community, Dallas, Texas (1869–1907). Ph.D. diss., University of Texas at Austin. University Microfilm International, Ann Arbor, Mich.

Downs, A. C., Jr. 1976. Zinc for Paint and Architectural Use in the Nineteenth Century. *Bulletin of the Association for Preservation Technology,* 8(4):80–99.

Evansville Coffin Company. [ca. 1909]. *Catalogue.* Evansville, Ind.: Evansville Coffin.

Ezell, R., and C. A. Huston. 2006a. Archaeological Removal of Historic Burials at the Williams-Green Cemetery (44CU134) on the Continental 181 Fund, LLC Tract in Culpeper County,

Virginia. Prepared for Ms. Sara Schrank, Continental Properties Company, Inc., Continental 181 Fund, LLC, Menomonee Falls, Wis. Fredericksburg, Va.: ECS Mid-Atlantic.

Ezell, R., and C. A. Huston. 2006b. Archaeological Removal of Five Historic Burials from Site 44ST00613 at the Quantico Corporate Center Tract, Stafford County, Virginia. Prepared for Mr. Samer Shalaby, Development Consulting Services, PLC, Fredericksburg, Va. Fredericksburg, Va.: ECS Mid-Atlantic.

Ferguson, B. H., S. K. Ireland, G. A. Agogino, and R. Holloway. 1993. *"And They Laid Them to Rest in the Little Plot Beside the Pecos": Final Report on the Relocation of the Old Seven Rivers Cemetery, Eddy County, New Mexico*. Denver: Denver Office, Bureau of Reclamation.

F. H. Hill & Company. 1881. *Illustrated Catalogue of Burial Cases and Caskets, and Undertakers' Supplies*. Chicago: F. H. Hill.

Flexner, B. 1993. *Understanding Wood Finishing: How to Select and Apply the Right Finish*. Emmaus, Pa.: Rodale Press.

Frank, R. R., ed. 2001. *Silk, Mohair, Cashmere and Other Luxury Fibres*. Boca Raton, Fla.: CRC Press.

Frank P. Bennett & Company. 1914. *A Cottons Fabrics Glossary*. Boston: Frank P. Bennett.

Garrett, W. 1975. The Price Book of the District of Columbia Cabinetmakers, 1831. *Antiques*, 107(5):888–897.

Gettens, R. J., H. Kuhn, and W. T. Chase. 1967. Lead White. *Studies in Conservation*, 12(4):125–139.

Guy, A. 2004. "Coatings Components beyond Binders." In *The Chemistry and Physics of Coatings*, 2nd ed., ed. A. Marrion, pp. 267–316. London: Royal Society of Chemistry.

Habenstein, R. W., and W. M. Lamers. 1955. *The History of American Funeral Directing*. Milwaukee, Wis.: Bulfin Printers. Originally published 1955

Habenstein, R. W., and W. M. Lamers. 1985. *The History of American Funeral Directing*. Milwaukee, Wis.: National Funeral Directors' Association.

Hamilton, Lemmon, Arnold & Company. 1882. *Excelsior Coffin and Casket Works: Price Lists of Hardware, Robes, Linings, Trimmings, etc. Manufactured by Hamilton, Lemmon, Arnold & Company*. Pittsburgh: Hamilton, Lemmon, Arnold.

Hamilton, Lemmon, Arnold & Company. 1884a. *Excelsior Coffin & Casket Works Price List of Hardware, Robes, Linings, Trimmings, &c. Manufactured by Hamilton, Lemmon, Arnold & Company*. Pittsburgh: Hamilton, Lemmon, Arnold.

Hamilton, Lemmon, Arnold & Company. 1884b. *Revised Price List of Varnished & Cloth-Covered Burial Cases and Caskets Manufactured by Hamilton, Lemmon, Arnold & Company, Excelsior Coffin & Casket Works*. Pittsburgh: Hamilton, Lemmon, Arnold.

Hamilton, Lemmon, Arnold & Company. 1886a. *Excelsior Coffin & Casket Works: Revised Price List of Coffin & Casket Hardware, Manufactured by Hamilton, Lemmon, Arnold & Company*. Pittsburgh: Hamilton, Lemmon, Arnold.

Hamilton, Lemmon, Arnold & Company. 1886b. *Excelsior Coffin and Casket Works: Price List of Wrappers, Robes, Linings, Trimmings, &c. Manufactured by Hamilton, Lemmon, Arnold & Company*. Pittsburgh: Hamilton, Lemmon, Arnold.

Hasluck, P. N., ed. 1905. *Coffin Making and Undertaking*. Mechanics' Manuals. London: Cassell.

Hasson, J. S. 2001. *Widows, Weepers & Wakes: Mourning in Middle Tennessee*. Nashville: Parris Printing.

Hazelton Coffin & Casket Company. 1883. *Illustrated Catalogue of Wood and Cloth Covered Burial Cases and Caskets*. Hazelton, Pa.: Hazelton Coffin & Casket.

Hohenschuh, W. P. 1900. *The Modern Funeral: Its Management—A Treatise on the Management of Funeral, with Suggestions for the Guidance of Funeral Directors*. Chicago: Trade Periodicals.

Hunter, G. L. 1918. *Decorative Textiles: An Illustrated Book on Coverings for Furniture, Walls and Floors, Including Damasks, Brocades and Velvets, Laces, Embroideries, Chintzes, Cretons, Drapery and Furniture Trimmings, Wall Papers, Carpets and Rugs, Tooled and Illuminated Leathers.* Philadelphia: J. B. Lippincott.

Janaway, R. 1998. "An Introductory Guide to Textiles from 18th and 19th Century Burials." In *Grave Concerns: Death and Burial in England, 1700 to 1850*, ed. M. Cox, pp. 17-32. CBA Research Report 113. York: Council for British Archaeology.

Lambourne, R., and T. A. Strivens. 1999. *Paint and Surface Coatings: Theory and Practice.* 2nd ed. Cambridge: Woodhead Publishing.

Lang, K. A. 1984. Coffins and Caskets: Their Contribution to the Archaeological Record. Master's thesis, University of Idaho, Moscow.

Langenau Manufacturing Company n.d. [ca. 1920s–1930s]. Hardware Specialities. Cleveland, OH: Langenau Manufacturing Company.

LeeDecker, C. H., J. Bloom, I. Wuebber, and M.-L. Pipes. 1995. *Final Archaeological Excavations at a Late 18th-Century Family Cemetery for the U.S. Route 113 Dualization, Milford to Georgetown, Sussex County, Delaware.* With K. R. Rosenberg. DelDOT Archaeology Series 134. With Karen R. Rosenberg. Dover: Delaware Department of Transportation.

Linton, W. 1849. A List of the Principal Colours Used in Painting, with Notices of Their Chemical and Artistical Properties. *Builder,* 7(1 September):412.

Lipovitch, D., E. MacDonald, I. Miklavcic, D. Robertson, and R. Williamson. 2003. Archaeological Investigations of the Elmbank Church and Cemetery, Former Lot 8, Concession 5, Toronto Township, Peel County, Ontario. Prepared for Greater Toronto Airports Authority, Lester B. Pearson International Airport, Toronto AMF, ON, Canada. Toronto: Archaeological Services.

Litten, J. 1991. *The English Way of Death: The Common Funeral Since 1450.* London: Robert Hale.

Litten, J. 1998. "The English Funeral 1700–1850." In *Grave Concerns: Death and Burial in England, 1700 to 1850*, ed. M. Cox, pp. 3–16. CBA Research Report 113. York: Council for British Archaeology.

Mainfort, R. C., Jr., and J. M. Davidson, eds. 2006. *Two Historic Cemeteries in Crawford County, Arkansas.* Arkansas Archeological Survey Research Series 62. Fayetteville: Arkansas Archeological Survey.

Marmor, J., S. Crownover, and W. Breece. 1990. The Location and Preliminary Description of Eleven Historic Burials Located in Seccombe Lake Park, San Bernardino, California. Prepared for City of San Bernardino, Parks, Recreation, and Community Services Department, San Bernardino, Calif.

Marmor, J., P. L. Walker, and C. Lippo. 1991. Phase II Archaeological Investigations and Removal of Human Burials from an Historic Cemetery in Seccombe Lake Park, San Bernardino, California. Prepared for City of San Bernardino, Parks, Recreation, and Community Services Department, San Bernardino, Calif. Irvine, Calif.: LSA Associates.

Mills, E. S. 1979. Graves in the Gravel: The Unmarked Cemetery of Las Vegas, New Mexico. Master's thesis, New Mexico Highlands University, Las Vegas.

National Casket Company. 1899. *National Casket Company Complete Price List and Telegraph Code Accompanying Pocket Catalogue "D."* New York: National Casket.

Oster, W. J., G. G. Weaver, J. P. Richardson, and J. M. Wyatt. 2005. Archaeological and Osteological Investigations of the Providence Baptist Church Cemetery (40SY619), Memphis-Shelby County Airport, Memphis, Shelby County, Tennessee. Submitted to Memphis-Shelby County Airport Authority, Memphis, Tenn., and Allen & Hoshall, Memphis, Tenn. Memphis, Tenn.: Weaver & Associates.

Parrington, M., D. G. Roberts, S. A. Pinter, and J. C. Wideman. 1989. The First African American Baptist Church Cemetery: Bioarchaeology, Demography, and Acculturation of Early Nineteenth Century Blacks. 3 vols. Report submitted to the Redevelopment Authority of the City of Philadelphia. West Chester, Pa.: John Milner Associates.

Paxson, Comfort & Company. n.d. *Illustrated Catalogue of Undertakers' Supplies*. Philadelphia: Paxson, Comfort.

Paxson, Comfort & Company. 1884. *Illustrated and Descriptive Catalogue of Wood, Metallic, and Cloth Covered Burial Caskets*. Philadelphia: Paxson, Comfort.

Paxson, Comfort & Company. [ca. 1890]. *Wholesale Pricelist of Burial Robes, Wrappers, Dresses, Suits, Habits, &c, &c.* Manufactured by Paxson, Comfort & Co. Philadelphia: Paxson, Comfort.

Paxson, Comfort & Company. 1898. *Illustrated and Descriptive Catalogue of Wood, Cloth-covered and Metallic Burial Caskets and Coffins for Sale to the Trade Only by Paxson, Comfort & Co.*. Philadelphia: Paxson, Comfort.

Perry, W. R., J. Howson, and B. A. Bianco, eds. 2006. New York African Burial Ground, Archaeology Final Report. 4 vols. Prepared for the U.S. General Services Administration, Northeastern and Caribbean Region. Washington, D.C.: Howard University.

Peter, D. E., M. Prior, M. M. Green, and V. G. Clow, eds. 2000. *Freedman's Cemetery: A Legacy of a Pioneer Black Community in Dallas, Texas*. 2 vols. Geo-Marine, Inc., Special Publication 6. Texas Department of Transportation, Environmental Affairs Division, Archaeology Studies Program, Report 21. Plano, Tex.: Geo-Marine.

Plume, S. n.d. *Coffins and Coffin Making*. London: Undertakers' Journal.

Pye, J. W. 2007. *A Look through the Viewing Glass: Social Status and Grave Analysis in a Nineteenth Century Kansas Cemetery*. M.A. thesis, University of Arkansas, Fayetteville.

Pye, J. W. 2010. Analysis of Burial Container Construction and Elaboration at the Tucson City Cemetery, Tucson, Arizona. Prepared for Statistical Research Inc., Tucson, and Pima County Cultural Resources and Historic Preservation Office, Tucson.

Rauschenburg, B. L. 1990. Coffin Making and Undertaking in Charleston and Its Environs, 1705–1820. *Journal of Early Southern Decorative Arts*, 16(1):19–63.

Richter, E. L., and H. Harlin. 1974. A Nineteenth-Century Collection of Pigments and Painting Materials. *Studies in Conservation*, 19(2):76–82.

Sewell, K., and P. Stanton. 2008. Dove Cemetery: Reflections on Cultural Identity at the Edge of Western Expansion—The Excavation and Interpretation of Dove Cemetery, CA-SLO-1892H, San Luis Obispo County, California. Technical Report 06-55. Prepared for Grant Robbins, Centex Homes, Central Coast Division, San Luis Obispo, Calif. Redlands, Calif.: Statistical Research.

Stein, S. 1872. Improvements in Burial-Caskets U.S. Letters Patent 132,605, issued 29 October 1872.

Stein Manufacturing Company. 1887. *Revised Price List and Telegraph Key for Stein Mfg. Company Producer of Fine Funeral Supplies and Textile Covered Caskets (June 1, 1887)*. Rochester, N.Y.: Stein Manufacturing.

St. Louis Coffin Company. 1911. *Catalog No. 22 (Coffins, Caskets, Vaults, Hearses)*. St. Louis, Mo.: St. Louis Coffin.

Stock, G. 1998. "The 18th and 19th Century Quaker Burial Ground at Bathford, Bath and North-East Somerset." In *Grave Concerns: Death and Burial in England, 1700 to 1850*, ed. M. Cox, pp. 129–143. CBA Research Report 113. York: Council for British Archaeology.

Sunnyside (New York). 1892. Cincinnati Coffin Company advertisement. 1 July.

Terry, G. 1893. *Pigments, Paint and Painting: A Practical Book for Practical Men*. London: E. & F. N. Spon.

Webb, M. 2000. *Lacquer: Technology and Conservation*. Oxford: Butterworth-Heinemann.

Welsh, F. S. 1982. Paint Analysis. *Bulletin of the Association for Preservation Technology*, 14(4):29–30.

Zollinger, H. 2003. *Color Chemistry: Syntheses, Properties, and Applications of Organic Dyes and Pigments*. 3rd ed. Weinheim: Wiley-VCH.

Protecting the Body

CHAPTER 12

Body Snatchers and Mortsafes: An Archaeology of Fear

Harold Mytum and Katie Webb

During the eighteenth century in Britain it was normal for the middle classes to commission coffins elaborately decorated with cloth covering, panel pins, and tin plate fittings, and even those from the workhouse were interred in wooden coffins, albeit simple (Mytum, 2004). Gradually, the relevance of the reusable parish coffin diminished (Houlbrooke, 1998:341), and bodies were not placed in the ground wrapped only in a shroud. During the same century an increasing number of burials were made within family vaults or brick-lined shafts or church crypts or were at least marked by a permanent stone marker, often proclaiming ownership of the plot or "here lies" the deceased (Mytum, 2004).

The important changes in mortuary behavior regarding body and grave protection can be explained in part by the increasing overcrowding in burial grounds and the desire to protect the recently deceased from disturbance, and this form of insurance is seen in its most dramatic physical form through mortsafes and other types of protection offered to fresh interments. These were created not to prevent the disarticulation of the skeleton by gravediggers preparing the ground for subsequent interments but the illicit removal of the corpse soon after the funeral by body snatchers, often called resurrection men or resurrectionists, who would obtain cadavers for sale to students of medical schools for dissection. Although there has been a long archaeological and historical interest in mortsafes and other protective strategies (Ritchie, 1912, 1921; Gorman, 2010; Holder, 2010), there has previously been no classification, analysis, or placement of these material remains in the context of the documentary sources derived from newspapers and mortsafe and watching society records. The main focus of this chapter is on the relatively plentiful Scottish data, with reference to the smaller amounts of English and Irish material. The conclusions also consider why body protection against body snatching was little considered in North America.

Increased interest in medical knowledge during the Enlightenment meant that anatomy schools, both attached to hospitals and privately run, were founded during the eighteenth century in London, Edinburgh, Glasgow, St. Andrews, Aberdeen, Dublin, and New England (Waite, 1945). In the nineteenth century, for surgeons to have a working knowledge of the human body, dissection was used to understand the way body systems worked. In 1800, the Royal College of Surgeons was founded by royal charter (Bailey, 1896:23), and by the 1820s, it was believed that 800 corpses were dissected by the London anatomy students alone (Brooks, 1989:6). Although a few bodies—those of executed murderers—were provided by the state (this being the case for Britain, Ireland, and North America), they were not sufficient for the number of students studying anatomy. Many of the Scottish universities did not provide bodies, and therefore, the students were left to obtain bodies for their own use. The Aberdeen Medico-Chirurgical Society, founded in 1789, was essentially a body-snatching organization for the medical students (Fido, 1988:19), but by 1795 there were professional body snatchers operating in and around cities to supply the medical schools (Richardson, 1987:57). Adult bodies could cost between 3 and 20 guineas, whereas children cost about 6 shillings for the first foot and 7 pence per inch thereafter (Richardson, 1987:57; Wise, 2005:30). Body snatching was a lucrative business, and therefore an attractive one, since it was possible to earn £600 per year—five times more than most unskilled laborers (Roach, 2003:44). From 1800 to 1831, there was a fivefold increase in enrollment in British medical schools, so the demand for bodies also quintupled (Fido, 1988:33). A similar pattern of behavior could be found in Ireland (Fleetwood, 1959, 1988, 1993) and in North America (Sappol, 2002).

In some instances, bodies were illegally acquired before interment. Those who had died at workhouses or hospitals but had yet to be claimed by their families could be obtained, or undertakers or sextons could be bribed to hand over the bodies from any source before they were buried. Gravediggers were also known to sell bodies to earn extra money (Bailey, 1896:55). There is archaeological evidence of bodies being replaced with rocks to simulate the correct weight. These methods, however, did not produce a sufficient supply of cadavers, so obtaining recently interred remains was also necessary.

The method used by body snatchers to extract a buried body varied depending on the circumstances and might involve removal of all the recent grave backfill, a method particularly desirable if there were several paupers who had been buried together at the same time (Shultz, 1992:33). For a single corpse it was sometimes possible to excavate down to the head of the coffin to then break open the lid and tie a rope either around the neck or under the arms so that the body could be pulled from the grave (Bailey, 1896:61). Resurrectionists would be sure to remove all clothing and jewelry from the body and leave these behind as they were legally considered property, so taking them would be theft. The removed body, however, was not considered property, so it could not be stolen; the greatest threat from the law would seem to have been an offense against public mores (Bailey, 1896:98; Richardson, 1987:58–59). It was against these activities, with legal threats of little more than fines, that communities developed patterns of observation and physical impediments to prevent this activity; some still surviving early in the twentieth century were recorded in Scotland (Ritchie, 1912, 1921), and some remain to this day. Following the passing of the Anatomy Act of 1832 in Britain and Ireland, which allowed for unclaimed cadavers from workhouses and hospitals to be used for dissection, and greater regulation of the sources of human remains for medical purposes, the threat of body snatching disappeared. After the passage of the Anatomy Act, 57,000 bodies were used between 1832 and 1932. Of these bodies, 99.5% were from institutions for the poor (Marshall, 1995:32). From 1832 the equipment and structures to prevent body snatching were either abandoned or reused, but they can still reveal considerable information about the process of body snatching, the ingenuity of those concerned with preventing it, and the emotions engendered by the fear of the resurrectionists. Although at one level they are explained by the threats from this gruesome trade, they also reflect changing attitudes to the body.

In North America, the fear of body snatching led to riots in New York, New Haven, and Baltimore during the eighteenth and very early nineteenth centuries (Waite, 1945;

Frank, 1976). As in Britain, the use of those whose bodies were not claimed—usually the poor from workhouses, hospitals, and asylums—was made legal through state legislation (Nystrom, 2017). Massachusetts was the first to pass such laws in the 1830s, but even states such as New York did not do so until the 1850s, and many western and southern states brought in such legislation only in the late nineteenth or early twentieth century (Humphrey, 1973; Davidson, 2007). Demands grew particularly after the 1820s when dissection practiced by students, rather than only observed, became a necessary part of many medical training programs, requiring thousands of illicitly obtained bodies each year (Humphrey, 1973:822). These were taken mainly from burial grounds of the poor and during the winter when they were required for practical classes (Highet, 2005:420; Crist et al., 2017). There is clear evidence that African American bodies were often taken, and indeed, before emancipation sick but live slaves could be sold to medical schools (Halperin, 2007:492). The relative powerlessness of African Americans meant that it was relatively easy to acquire their bodies, sometimes with the connivance of cemetery officials, as at Lebanon Cemetery, Philadelphia (Kaufman and Hanawalt, 1971).

The Archaeological Evidence for Body Snatching

Archaeological evidence has shown that autopsy and dissection were occurring before 1832, although the evidence is very scattered and merely examples are given here. Only where preservation has been very good and later grave digging has not destroyed the evidence will the absence of a body in a coffin be easily identifiable. For example, the Cross Bones Burial Ground in Southwark was a site that seems to have been a target for body snatchers, but the density of burial and frequency or disturbance of interments with the insertion of later burials were such that no such evidence could be identified (Brickley et al., 1999). Nevertheless, other excavations have also shown that empty coffins occur in several eighteenth- and nineteenth-century churchyards and vaults.

During the clearance of the vault at Christ Church, Spitalfields, a coffin was found filled with building rubble. Traces of bones were not found within the coffin, so either a coffin was placed in the vault empty and later filled with rubble or a weighted coffin was placed in the vault because the body had been removed. A number of the Spitalfields coffins were reinforced with iron bands, which would have impeded any attempt to break them open; 3 rectangular and 27 single-break coffins were so reinforced, one also having an iron chain also wrapped around it. (Reeve and Adams, 1993:81–82). A further sign that the threat of robbing was justified is demonstrated by the fact that the most protected coffin in the Spitalfields crypt was that for William Horne, an undertaker, who was likely to be more aware than most of the risks. He had commissioned a layered coffin, reinforced with iron bars on the inner and outer coffins (Cox, 1996:107–108). An iron coffin that could be locked survives from St. Bride's church crypt, Fleet Street, London (Fowler and Powers, 2012:146). At Dunfermline Abbey (Robertson et al., 1981), several interments were protected by mortsafes that had been left in place; these are discussed within the mortsafe classification outlined below.

Other forms of illegal examination of cadavers can also be recognized archaeologically. At the Newcastle Infirmary burial ground, 10% of the 600 individuals show craniotomies. Several of these individuals have bones sawn in such a way as to show structure or demonstrate pathology (Chamberlain, 2012). Although these marks on the bone may have been a result of an autopsy, hospital doctors would have used the opportunity to teach students. One skeleton was found incomplete below the fourth vertebrae. In order to disguise that a dissection had taken place, the coffin was buried with a stone slab to substitute for the weight of the lower half of the body (Chamberlain, 2012). Doctors at hospitals had the opportunity to perform postmortem examinations on those patients without relatives to claim them or those too poor to cover the cost of their burial (Marshall, 1995:138). Dissected human and animal remains were also discovered in London buried on an anatomist's property (Chamberlain, 2012), in London Hospital's burial ground (Fowler and Powers, 2012:151–200), and in Trinity College Dublin's Herb Garden (Murphy, 2011).

In North America, the most dramatic evidence of illicit body snatching was that recovered from beneath the cellar floor of the Medical College of Georgia, Augusta (Blakely and Harrington, 1997). In this case, 80% of the remains could be identified as African American. The Freedman's Cemetery, Dallas, revealed some additional evidence from grave 558, with two bodies showing signs of use as medical cadavers placed within one simple wooden coffin (Davidson, 2007). The presence of two individuals, an adolescent and an infant, with craniometries from Spring Street Presbyterian Church burial vaults may have been subject to illegal dissection (Novak and Willoughby, 2010). A number of excavations have now produced evidence for dissection and anatomical teaching, although most are within a legal context even if the ethics of cadaver supply and disposal often now seems hardly ethical (Nystrom, 2017).

Reactions to the Threat

Once the fear of body snatching became prevalent, many parishes would collect money to add security measures to the churchyard. The height of walls was frequently increased to make it more difficult for the body snatchers to climb over. At St. Cuthbert's churchyard in Edinburgh, the walls were raised to a height of 8 feet in 1738 to help prevent body snatching (Willsher, 1985:10).

One method was for the family to keep watch over the grave or hire watchmen until the body would no longer be useful to the anatomists (Bailey, 1896:72). Frequently, protection societies were founded within cities to take turns watching over the graves of the recently buried (Cole, 1964:97). One watching society has extant records, and others are mentioned in passing, but they are not discussed further here. Watching societies often constructed small buildings in churchyards to house the watchers in some comfort (Ritchie, 1912, 1921; Willsher, 1985:10). Watchhouses could be a dwelling house close by with a view of the churchyard, or they could be small buildings placed within the churchyard, such as at Dunbog, Fife, which has the inscription "ERECTED for protection of the dead." Watchtowers were often more substantial structures, where the first floor could be used to store tools and the second floor provided a more complete view of the burial ground (Ritchie, 1912:292). A large number of watchhouses are known from Scotland, with others in Ireland and a few in England (Gorman, 2010), but as yet there has been no academic study of these as a category, and they are beyond the scope of this chapter to analyze in detail. These visible buildings were meant to deter the body snatchers from frequenting these churchyards, but it was not difficult to ply the watchmen with drink, distracting them while other resurrection men went to work.

Alternatives to watching arrangements involved direct physical protection of the corpse, and three methods are discussed here: morthouses or deadhouses, in which bodies were stored for a period before interment; mortstones that covered the grave and impeded exhumation; and mortsafes, which were more elaborate items of equipment or structures that protected the coffin and could be either temporary or permanent. The forms that these took are discussed below, after consideration of the societies that were formed beyond the existing parish committees to manage these deterrents.

Mortsafe and Watching Societies

Mortsafe and watching societies were developed in some areas of Scotland by parishioners who that felt the corpses of the area were under threat from the body snatchers. Watching society members were required to keep watch over the graves of the recently deceased until a sufficient period had passed to make the remains unusable for the anatomists, whereas mortsafe society members pledged money for the purchase of mortsafes that would be used for a designated period to protect the coffin from being disturbed by resurrection men. The mortsafes employed by these societies were typically iron shells that were placed around the coffin, then buried for a period of time, although their designs varied greatly (see below). These mortsafes were heavy objects that would require a great deal of time to remove from the grave in order to reach the corpse. It was hoped that the effort required to move the mortsafe and to open it would deter the body snatchers from stealing the body. The wealthy had a permanent cast-iron cage constructed around the grave, with precautions to prevent tunneling from the side.

Four mortsafe societies were created in the early nineteenth century that have surviving records, at Auchtertool, Newburn, and Anstruther in Fife and Newbattle (Rae, letters to Lord Ancram) in Midlothian. Unfortunately, no documentation is known for the sites where mortsafes survive, although a much-damaged janker stone survives at Auchtertool and some other societies are mentioned in passing and some mortsafes may have been commissioned by individuals or families. For example, the Anstruther Mortsafe Society is known only from an item in the *Glasgow Herald* when in 1874 the society was dissolved after about 45 years of activity and its equipment, described as iron safes, was sold for scrap; the Linlithgow Mortsafe Society was founded in 1819, but little else is known about its operation.

The ways the societies allocated use of the mortsafes, the amount of time that the recently deceased were placed within them, and the cost of membership can be obtained from kirk records containing mortsafe society minutes. Mortsafe society cashbooks also make it possible to determine the amount of money required to maintain membership in the society, which would give one the ability to use the mortsafe upon death.

The Auchtertool Mortsafe Association was established 12 April 1830 when "a number of the inhabitants of this [Auchtertool] area and neighbouring parishes met and formed themselves into an association for the purposes of protection the corpses of the deceased" (Auchtertool Accounts, 12 April 1830). The first order of business for the society was to obtain mortsafes, so bids were accepted to create a mortsafe "the same as those adopted by the Aberdour Association, with this exception; that they should have each three bars, 3 inches broad and $1\frac{1}{2}$ thick, plate of iron not joined" (Auchtertool Accounts, 21 April 1830). The mention of the Aberdour Mortsafe Association indicates that the mortsafe society founded in Auchtertool was not alone in its fear of resurrection men.

Many mortsafe societies did not keep records in the same detail as those at Auchtertool or even Newburn, perhaps only using a cashbook to record when the members had paid their subscriptions. For example, a cashbook for the mortsafe society at Inchinnan provides very basic information about the society and does not explain the exact reasons the parish decided to create a mortsafe society in the first place, but it is likely that their reasons were similar to those of the parishioners of Auchtertool and Newburn.

By 1824, body snatching was occurring with regularity in Scotland, so in that year the parish of Newburn founded its mortsafe society, and the parish at Traquair established its watching society. It was not until the murderers Burke and Hare began selling bodies to surgeons in Edinburgh in 1827 and 1828 that a large-scale panic spread through the country. Auchtertool did not found their mortsafe society until 1830, which was after the Burke and Hare murders and the activities of the resurrection men were becoming even better known within Scotland. At Inchinnan, the cashbook begins in 1834 and runs through to 1843. Throughout the 1830s and 1840s, all of the societies continued to gain members, even though the Anatomy Act had been passed. Although the cashbook from the mortsafe society at Inchinnan shows only subscriptions until 1843, the cashbook was taken into evidence in a murder trial (Gilmour Evidence, 1844), so if the society had continued, another cashbook would have been recalled. The other groups remained intact through to the latter half of the nineteenth century, well beyond the passage of the Anatomy Act in 1832, which would have made it unnecessary for body snatchers to take bodies from churchyards. The Traquair watching society had to fold in 1858 because there were only 15 members in the watching society, which was not sufficient to keep watch properly for six weeks. The mortsafe societies of Auchtertool and Newburn were dissolved in 1863 and 1877, respectively. The long life of these societies, and presumably the use of mortsafes and watching procedures for decades after the end of body snatching, indicates a level of fear about desecration of the body that was not linked to a reasoned calculation of risk. It reveals attitudes to the body and the necessity of its integrity.

To protect the recently deceased from the resurrection men, the parishioners had to keep the body safe until it was unusable by the anatomists. At both Newburn and Traquair, this time of protection is specified as six weeks. The records from Auchtertool do not give a specified time, but the records indicate that mortsafes remained on the coffins for several weeks before being removed. In order for the societies to work properly, each member had to make a contribution. At Traquair, every member of the watching society was required to do their part, unless they were unable. Each member had to keep watch or was required to find a substitute. Failing that, the person was fined 5 shillings. Two members of the society were to be on watch one and a half hours after sunset until one and a half hours before dawn in winter or until 4 am in summer (Traquair Watching Society, 7 January 1824). At Newburn and Auchtertool, each member of the mortsafe society was required to pay a subscription to purchase and maintain the mortsafe and the janker mechanism for moving the mortsafes. The price of initial subscription at Newburn is 3 shillings, and 6 pence was also required at the time of interment (Newburn Mortsafe, April 1824). To avoid the physical effort of working the janker (a long pole with wheels used to maneuver the mortsafe), a payment of 15 shillings could be made. If anyone wanted to use the mortsafe for someone who had not been a member of the society, the cost was 1 guinea. At Auchtertool, the subscription was 3 shillings and 6 pence. Frequently, those seeking use of the mortsafes were required to pay an additional sum, often to pay the janker men for their work (Auchtertool Accounts, 3 October 1836). Occasionally, paupers or members of the society who had made significant contributions were able to use the mortsafes without paying fees at the time of interment (Auchtertool Accounts, 22 June 1831 and 30 September 1835).

The average cost of the adult mortsafes was just about £4. At Auchtertool, the society paid £6 3s. 0d. for a large mortsafe and a small mortsafe and £7 0s. 7½d. for two large mortsafes, one of which was slightly enlarged (Auchtertool Accounts, 26 June 1830 and 7 February 1832). At Newburn, the price of three large mortsafes and one small one was £19 12s. 0d. (Newburn Mortsafe, April 1824). Since these mortsafes were constructed by local craftsmen, no standard price existed for such items, and costs would also have varied according to the design.

Money collected from the societies was commonly used for general upkeep of equipment, as well as for the purchase of new mortsafes. At Auchtertool, a set of wheels were purchased in order to move the mortsafe from the janker house, the shed where the janker and spare mortsafe were stored, to the grave (Auchtertool Accounts, 21 January 1833). Repairs of the mortsafes were also required, such as a coating of lead tar to slow the rusting; the janker also had to be repaired and painted (Auchtertool Accounts, 16 August 1833). The Kilninver watching society agreed to subscribe money for half of the price of a watchhouse if the heritors agreed to provide the other half of the cost. The watchhouse was used to accommodate the watch and also to keep the wheels and shovels dry (Campbell Family Papers, 15 May 1856).

The subscriptions to the societies provided additional benefits beyond the protection of the recently deceased. In 1835, the Auchtertool mortsafe society decided to pay 5 shillings to the Beadle, on behalf of the deceased, for the digging of the grave (Auchtertool Accounts, 15 August 1835). In 1836, the society also agreed to provide 3 shillings in order for the family to have a mortcloth for the funeral, although because of a lack of funds, the society was not able provide the mortcloth after 1847 (Auchtertool Accounts, 12 August 1836 and 13 August 1847). The Traquair watching society used the funds received from members to pay to have a fire to be laid for those on watch during the night (Traquair Watching Society, 7 January 1824).

Although the records do not explicitly state the manner in which the mortsafes were recovered from the graves or exactly when this was done, the Auchtertool parish society mentions the janker men. Since the stone used to cover the grave, as an addition to the security provided by the mortsafe, is called a janker stone, it is likely that is was the job of the janker men to remove the stone and the mortsafe after the allotted time of six weeks was over. A wooden mechanism was constructed by a local wright, which would be used in the moving of the mortsafe since it would have been extremely heavy (Auchtertool Accounts, 21 April 1831). Each year the person in charge of organizing the janker men did not wish to continue in his post, so a new person had to be elected (Auchtertool Accounts, 12 November 1830). The reason is possibly because the job of removing the mortsafe from the grave was inconvenient as it had to be done at times when no one in the parish would have to witness the exhumation, which itself was perhaps traumatic and unpleasant, opening a grave six weeks after the deceased was interred and by which time decomposition would have become quite advanced.

Both the mortsafe societies at Auchtertool and Newburn required more than one mortsafe in order to be able to accommodate all of the deaths that occurred within the parish. At Auchtertool, the society began by purchasing three adult mortsafes and one small mortsafe for children (Auchtertool Accounts, 21 April 1830), but only two months later, the members of the Auchtertool mortsafe society decided that another small and another large one were required by the parish (Auchtertool Accounts, 26 June 1830). The number of mortsafes seemed sufficient until 1837, when a wooden mortsafe had to be constructed for James Scott's grave since all of the iron mortsafes were buried (Auchtertool Accounts, 9 January 1837). Only a few weeks later, Mr. Lindsay requested the use of a mortsafe for his wife's body, but no mortsafes were free, and the members decided to create a watch to protect her body until a mortsafe was available (Auchtertool Accounts, 27 January 1837). Newburn also purchased three large mortsafes and one small mortsafe in March 1824 (Newburn Mortsafe, 26 March 1824) yet had to order another mortsafe in 1826 while another mortsafe was being repaired (Newburn Mortsafe, 3 April 1826). Even then, there were not enough safes in 1829 to accommodate all of the recently deceased, so the members decided to remove a mortsafe from a relation of the newly deceased. They then placed the older coffin below, the newer coffin above, and, finally, the mortsafe on top. Although this solved the immediate problem, the society ordered another mortsafe, one that could be dismantled and stored when not in use (Newburn Mortsafe, 12 April 1829). The society also resolved that upon the next occasion when there were not sufficient mortsafes to accommodate all of the deceased, the one that had been in use the longest would be disinterred, and then a watch would be created to protect the body until the end of the six weeks (Newburn Mortsafe, 27 April 1829). The information concerning the Inchinnan mortsafe society indicates only that there were six mortsafes and does not explain what sizes or when they were acquired (Gilmour Evidence, 1844).

Through the later part of the nineteenth century, fewer members joined the mortsafe and watching societies. Society funds were in short supply, and it was difficult for the watching societies to find enough able-bodied individuals to complete the allotted six weeks. Eventually, the mortsafe and watching societies disbanded, well after the fear of body snatching had diminished from the public mind. These mortsafe and watching societies provided a service for the parishes in Scotland during a time when many families were afraid that their recently deceased relations would become the anatomists' "victims." After the passage of the 1832 Anatomy Act, sufficient cadavers were provided to the anatomists for the purpose of teaching and research; in Edinburgh, for example, the relatively steady demand for dissections—between 100 and 150 cadavers per annum—was always supplied by one official means or another, even with church or family resistance (Smith, 2009). This supply meant that body snatching was no longer a lucrative business and that parishioners no longer had to rely on mortsafes to ensure the bodies of their loved ones remained in their grave. It is surprising not that the societies failed in the later nineteenth century but that they continued for so long. East Anstruther closed in 1869 (*Dundee Courier and Argus*, 1869), and Anstruther closed in 1874, over 40 years after the act was passed (*Glasgow Herald*, 1874). This time span suggests that the fear of the resurrection men became so ingrained in the psyche of those alive before the Anatomy Act, even if they were only children, that they continued the protection routines long after the threat had gone.

Morthouses or Deadhouses

The storing of coffins in a temporary structure until decomposition had reached a stage such that the cadavers would no longer be suitable for dissection usually lasted about six weeks (Ritchie, 1912:311). At this point they would be interred in a normal earth grave. This solution required the construction of a secure aboveground or semisubterranean structure, and a number of these survive. They should be differentiated from particular family vaults in which the dead were placed in perpetuity, although they share some similar characteristics, and indeed, some of the structures are simply larger versions of family vaults and were clearly inspired by their design.

Some family vaults were largely sunken, and this design was also chosen for a number of morthouses. Some appear as grassy mounds with a simple passage or opening on a slope, such as at Belhelvie, Aberdeenshire, with rubble masonry walling hidden beneath a grassy mound and rendered internally to create a chamber that could store only a small number of coffins. Perhaps because of its small size, an upstanding morthouse was also built at the site in 1835, with floor dimensions of 20 feet by over 17 feet and two shelves on each side. At morthouses in Fintray and Kemnay in Aberdeenshire, erected in 1830 and 1831, respectively, the problem of damp entering the chamber was alleviated by metal interior lining of the roofs (Ritchie, 1912:312–313).

The upstanding morthouses are generally rectangular, with the door in one of the short sides, and often have two stone shelves running around two or three sides so that coffins could be placed on these and on the floor. Most morthouses also were designed with some form of ventilation through either small apertures in the walls or a flue. They are found in a range of styles, often with a simple gabled roof but sometimes with a more elaborate one, such as that at Crail, Fife, with its crenellations and a date stone with the inscription "ERECTED for securing the DEAD: Ann Dom MDCCCXXVI" over the door (Figure 1A).

Perhaps the most elaborate surviving example is at Udny, Aberdeenshire. An unusual circular public vault was built in Udny Green (Figure 1B). The bodies were placed on a wooden turntable within the vault, and when a new body was placed in the deadhouse, the table would be turned. By the time the first body came around, it could not be used for dissection, and it would be subsequently buried (Cole, 1964:50).

In many cases where the original features survive, the doors are elaborate and are designed to maximize security. At the later Belhelvie morthouse, the outer oak door had a protective bar and two keyholes, and behind that was a second iron door. A similar pattern of double doors was used at Culsalmond, Aberdeenshire, whereas the Udny example has an iron-studded outer door with a protected keyhole, with the iron door sliding up and down in vertical grooves in the door jamb (Ritchie, 1912:321). Where one door was present, it is usually iron, and at Kemnay the lock was hidden behind a thick iron bar that was held in place by a padlocked chain (Ritchie, 1912:313).

Not everyone was protected by a time in the morthouse, and at Culsalmond, Aberdeenshire, the two-floor structure housed a morthouse below that could hold 12 adults and a watchhouse above. As the morthouse was apparently also used by those to be buried in nearby parishes, there may have been times when it was full; this overcrowding certainly occurred elsewhere, where arrangements were made for the oldest body to be interred and a watch to be kept until the full six weeks since death were reached. Clearly, all resources for body protection could be stretched at times of peak mortality.

Willsher (1985:10) suggests that many of the morthouses built in Scotland are the result of the 1828–1829 panic over the Burke and Hare murders, and although some are earlier, those at Duffus, Moray, and Fintray, Aberdeenshire, are dated 1830, with Kemnay being a year later; therefore, these match this period of concern. Others, however, were not erected until after the passing of the Anatomy Act, when all threat of disturbance should have passed. Thus, Udny was commissioned and completed in 1832, with regulations for

FIGURE 1. Morthouses. (A) Walls protected by embanked soil, Kemnay, Aberdeenshire. Photo by authors. (B) Round morthouse at Udny, Aberdeenshire. Photograph by Sagaciousphil, Creative Commons Attribution-ShareAlike 3.0 Unported (CC BY-SA 3.0), https://commons.wikimedia.org/wiki/File:Udny_Mort_House_02.JPG. Photo was made black and white.

its use issued in 1833 (Ritchie, 1912:324–325), and the larger morthouse at Belhelvie was not built until 1835. At Marnoch, Banffshire, a stone built into the structure is incised "Built by Subscription in the year 1832. Addition 1877" (Ritchie, 1921:228). Therefore, this is an original construction that was completed just as the threat receded, but its extension was long after.

Mortstones

Mortstones are large rocks, often roughly the size and space of the grave, that were placed over the recent interment to deter grave robbing. They were normally rectangular, but more roughly shaped and heavier than most ledgers or body stones, such as at Inverurie, Aberdeenshire (Figure 2A), although ledgers in effect served the same purpose and were permanent features of family plots.

FIGURE 2. (A) Body stone, Inverurie, Aberdeenshire. (B) Type 1 mortsafe, Colinton, Aberdeenshire. (C) Type 2 mortsafe, Cluny, Aberdeenshire. All photos by authors.

Mortstones would have been less effective than the morthouses or mortsafes but much cheaper and only needed a simple block and tackle to move into place. They were, however, equally easy to move away, or digging down from beyond the confines of the grave could allow the body to be extracted. Nevertheless, a number of such stones can still be seen in Scottish graveyards, and some, such as those at Gullane, East Lothian, at Kinghorn, Fife, and at Logierait, Perthshire, have two iron rings set in the surface to allow easy lifting. The Prestwick, Argyll, example is unusual in having curved sides reminiscent of but not exactly mirroring a single-break coffin and in having three hooks; two iron straps stretch across the stone and are attached to iron rods that have been inserted into the ground, suggesting that it was more like some of the mortsafes described below.

Mortsafes

Mortsafe is a term that has been used for a variety of physical grave protectors that vary from the mobile and reusable coffin covers through low grave protectors to more substantial aboveground structural features forming cages over the whole plot. All types survive only in a few locations; reusable coffins were often sold off when the mortsafe societies were wound up (*Glasgow Herald*, 1874). Others were reused as water troughs for livestock on farms (Ritchie, 1912:307, 309, 1921:225), and much of the iron was collected, along with many sets of cast-iron railing around curbed plots, as part of the World War II war effort. Nevertheless, the variations in providing both mobile and fixed protection demonstrate that many were local designs, although some foundries clearly found a market in producing products that they probably added to their catalogs of ironwork.

To place the mortsafe into the ground, several members of the parish would be needed, and some form of pulley system was required. One example of this tackle, or janker, survived at Inverurie (Ritchie, 1921:222–223) and was held by the now-closed Carnegie Inverurie Museum (Figure 3B). Some mortsafes show perforations or loops for hooks to be attached to assist with lowering and lifting. An example with cast handles on the side panels comes from Cadder, East Dunbartonshire, whereas the examples from Airth, Falkirk, have two substantial loops extending above the top on each side, and at Banchory-Devenick, Aberdeenshire, there are two perforations on each side panel to allow hooks to be attached. Holes in the stone tops of the mortsafes at Towie, Cluny, Skene, and Old Kinnernie in Aberdeenshire were also probably to allow attachment of lifting gear, although the openwork sides of this form would easily allow chains or ropes to be placed under the slab for lifting purposes.

Mortsafe Types

Mortsafes protected the coffin underground for adequate time for the body to be decomposed sufficiently to be unsuitable for dissection. At this point, the grave would be opened once more, and the mortsafe removed. Some mortsafes were left in place when they were no longer required, but many were removed, even if no one subsequently requested their use. These are mainly the ones that have survived for study, although occasionally a buried example is revealed as old graves are opened for new interments. The mortsafes had to be larger in size than the coffins. From documentary sources and surviving examples, it is possible to ascertain that there were relatively standard adult sizes such as those used at Auchtertool, measuring $6\frac{1}{2}$ feet by $2\frac{1}{4}$ feet, but that a larger adult form

FIGURE 3. (A) Interior of type 1 mortsafe, Durris, Aberdeenshire. Photo by authors. (B) Janker to raise and lower mortsafes, Inverurie, Aberdeenshire. Photograph by Wellcome Images, Wellcome Library, London. Creative Commons Attribution 4.0 International (CC BY 4.0), https://wellcomeimages.org/indexplus/image/L0012145EA.html. No changes made. (C) Adult and child mortsafes with no base formed from a mesh of iron rods, Logierait, Perthshire. Photo by authors.

was ordered by the Auchtertool mortsafe society to measure 7½ feet by 2½ feet, allowing taller individuals to use the mortsafes (Auchtertool Accounts, 9 January 1832). In addition, a record of mortsafes for children exists, although only one from Logierait, Perthshire, survives. Five broad types of coffin-shaped mortsafes are identified here, with varying degrees of disturbance to the coffin once it was time for the mortsafe to be removed and with various forms of construction: the baseless coffin, the stone-topped form, the enclosed iron shell, the iron plate with attachments, and the iron strip form (Figure 3C).

Type 1: Baseless Coffin-Shaped Form

The least disturbance was caused by type 1A, a baseless coffin form. This design could be lowered down into the grave over a coffin that had already been placed there. In some cases it was then bolted onto the coffin beneath. Minimal disturbance to the coffin occurred when the mortsafe was being disinterred as the bolts were simply removed and the entire mortsafe was lifted away from the coffin. The example from Colinton, Edinburgh, is of this type (Figure 2B). The top of the mortsafe had four rectangular openings, one containing an iron plate with a bolt attached. It is likely that all these openings contained similar plates, and they may have been bolted to the top of the coffin. This form of coffin was made of sheet iron soldered together. At Durris, Kincardineshire, the inner surface of the top was further strengthened by iron rods, one placed longitudinally and two across the mortsafe (Figure 3A), and Ritchie (1912:308) notes a similar example at Maryculter. A pair of round holes toward the top of the vertical sides of the mortsafe at Banchory-Devenick, Aberdeenshire, would have allowed hooks to be affixed to allow the raising and lowering of the cover over the coffin. Other arrangements for movement of these heavy items included loops on top at Aberfoyle, Perthshire. Three mortsafes that functioned as coffin covers survive at Logierait, Perthshire, but were not formed from solid iron panels and instead were made from square-section iron rods with iron bands around the sides to form a cage; one of these is a child-sized mortsafe and is a most unusual survival (Figure 3C), although they are often mentioned in the documentary sources.

Type 2: Stone-Topped Mortsafe

The second form of mobile mortsafe combined the concept of the mortstone with that of the iron baseless coffin form, providing some protection against those who would dig down and attempt to tunnel in from the sides with a lattice of iron bands on the sides that would hold the stone above the coffin within the grave. This type did not require complex smithing skills and used locally available stone rather than iron sheets and, indeed, may even have evolved in response to body snatchers digging around body stones. Examples survive at the Aberdeenshire sites of Cluny (Figure 2C), Old Kinnernie, Skene, and Towie (Ritchie, 1912:298–301).

Type 3: Enclosed Coffin-Shaped Form

This design of mortsafe acted as an outer shell to the permanent body container. Multiple layers of coffin were a concept familiar in the funerary industry, and some elaborate coffins could have several shells of wood and lead (Litten, 1991). This shell design fully enclosed the coffin, and there was often a hinged lid, usually in two sections. Several examples from Airth, Falkirk, dated 1831, 1832, and 1837, have the two parts of the lid hinged at the head and foot (Figure 4A). Loops on each lid met and allowed a padlock to seal it securely. Both the coffin and the mortsafe would have to be disinterred after a period of days. The coffin then would have to be unlocked from the mortsafe and returned to the grave.

Type 4: Iron Plate with Bolted Components

A fourth form of mortsafe was a cast-iron plate, hexagonally shaped to be placed within the grave or possibly just to cover it with a cutout pattern of apertures to reduce the weight and make it easier to lower and raise. This plate could be cast as a single piece, such as at Kilmun, Argyll, or could be of two equal portions hinged at what would be about the waist of the deceased. The patterns on the plates vary, so they were not one mass-produced form, and some have rings to attach chains, ropes, or hooks, whereas others must have had these placed through the apertures in the plate. An example at Ayr has "MORT SAFE" in relief at the head of the mortsafe and 1816 in the center of the upper half, indicating its date of production; details of the manufacturer are placed at the foot. Two examples at Alloway, Ayrshire, are of similar design but not identical and are of different dimensions (Figure 4B). The lower portion of the frame contained perforations that allowed iron rods to be placed around the coffin to prevent tunneling from the side, with a top plate that sealed the ends of the rods to prevent them being removed. An example from Bolton, East Lothian, was similar in form but made from a lattice of iron strips and had perforations around the edge that allowed the additional rods to be inserted. In this case there was no cover, but the rods required specific tools to unscrew them from the frame.

Type 5: Iron Strip Frame

This type comes in a wide range of designs, suggesting local smiths created a mortsafe from basic instructions without a specific template to work from. Iron bars or bands run across several points of the width of the coffin, joined together by a longitudinal element that runs down the axis of the coffin, such as at Kincardine (Figure 4C). In some examples the bars ran across the top and down the sides of the coffin, but in others, such as at Dunfermline, they wrapped around the base of the coffin. Another example of this kind was used at Clifton Street Cemetery, Belfast. This type of mortsafe is a relatively low investment version, perhaps designed to be disposable and left in place, which was the case with those fragmentary examples identified during archaeological excavation at Dunfermline Abbey. There, graves 4, 5, and 6 had portions of the iron strip form of mortsafe still in place over the coffins, although corrosion meant that they were incomplete (Robertson et al., 1981). Grave 5 was housed within a lead coffin, with grave 6 being wood with a pattern of brass studs that would originally have held the textile covering in place and created a design on the top and sides of the coffin (see Mytum, "Explaining Stylistic Change in Mortuary Material Culture," this volume); only part of grave 4 was uncovered, but the mortsafe type was similar to the others. Another mortsafe was noted as belonging to a lead coffin below a wooden one containing the remains of Maria Wellwood, who died in 1847. However, safety concerns prevented further investigation of the mortsafe and its associated container. It is notable that even within the church, relatively wealthy families felt it

FIGURE 4. (A) Type 3 mortsafe, Airth, Falkirk. Photograph by Velvet, Creative Commons, Attribution-ShareAlike 3.0 Unported (CC BY-SA 3.0), https://commons.wikimedia.org/wiki/File:Edimbourg_mortsafe.JPG. Photo was made black and white. (B) Type 4 mortsafe, Alloway, Ayrshire. Photograph from the Geograph project collection and copyright owned by Mary and Angus Hogg, Creative Commons Attribution-ShareAlike 2.0 Generic (CC BY-SA 2.0), https://commons.wikimedia.org/wiki/File:Mort-Safe_In_Alloway_Auld_Kirk_-_geograph.org.uk_-_1213375.jpg. Photo was made black and white. (C) Type 5 mortsafe, Kincardine, Kincardineshire. Photograph from the Geograph project collection and copyright owned by Mike Searle, Creative Commons Attribution-ShareAlike 2.0 Generic (CC BY-SA 2.0), http://www.geograph.org.uk/photo/1870295. Photo was made black and white.

necessary to prevent body snatching through investing in mortsafes. The desire to limit disturbance within the building by any form of removal of mortsafes may have encouraged the use of ones that permanently remained over the interments. Two similar mortsafes clearly meant to remain buried were recovered by gravediggers in the early twentieth century, with that from Oyne (Ritchie, 1921:223–224) being very like the Dunfermline examples, whereas that from Tough also had blocks of stone added at the head and foot (Ritchie, 1912:304–305).

Low Protectors

Low, permanent cast-iron structures can be found largely at urban burial grounds, most notably in Edinburgh and Glasgow. An example at Glasgow Cathedral, constructed for the burial of Maria MacAulay in 1849 by W. Fulton and Sons, is a typical example. Four stout legs form the corners of the mortsafe, with a thick iron rail placed around the sides. Each side has a series of iron bars connected to the rail at the top that then extend down into the ground. The top of the plot is covered with an iron lattice. Some examples have hinged covers, usually with two parts that meet in the center that could be locked together. This arrangement allowed maintenance of the plot and also access for further interments. Some designs used cast-iron panels set across the plot to record the details of the deceased. The mortsafe in Edinburgh Greyfriars covering the grave of Elizabeth Jane Lindesay, who died in 1832, has recently been restored (Figure 5A).

Cage Mortsafes

Many of the cage mortsafes are now hard to identify as the stone curbs with sawn-off iron bars are similar to those left by plots with railings. However, a sample still survives intact, with vertical bars to a height of over 2 m and with some form of covering, always designed to cover a double or larger plot. These cages may in some cases be bespoke local productions, but others were cast by foundries who placed their names on their products, such as the case of James Russell in the Ramshorn burial ground, Glasgow, made by Walton & Sons of that city (Figure 5B). The cages all have a hinged door at the foot end of the plot to allow access for grave maintenance, grieving, and further interments. A small number are completely freestanding and contain typical headstones or ledgers, but most are built against a wall at the head end of the grave, and memorials are placed on plaques set into or onto the wall. One example of this form of mortsafe is known to still survive in Ireland, at Drumcondra, County Dublin (Mytum, 2013).

The cage mortsafe is a form that can be linked to a much older Scottish tradition of the enclosed lair, where walls and sometimes a roof created a not only secure but private burial location. With the banishment of burial within churches, the Scottish elite created alternative enclosed forms, and some of these walled plots seem to have continued but with iron rod covers as a protection against body snatching. This mix of traditions can be best seen at Old Calton Cemetery in Edinburgh, where many examples of this form survive, some still with all their ironwork (Figure 5C).

A few grave protectors in America have been interpreted by some as mortsafes, most notably the grave covers at the Old Mount Zion burial ground, Catawissa, Pennsylvania, although these would appear to merely be elaborate covered versions of other forms of grave railings rather than mortsafes, as they are neither large nor substantial. Many

FIGURE 5. Aboveground grave protection. (A) Low protector for Elizabeth Jane Lindesay, Edinburgh Greyfriars. (B) Cage mortsafe for James Russell's plot, Ramshorn burial ground, Glasgow. (C) Walled lair for Daniel Munro's plot with iron gate and cover, Old Calton Cemetery, Edinburgh. All photos by authors.

documentary sources indicate that the middle classes, who would have been able to afford such protection, did not need to concern themselves with threats of the disinterment of their loved ones because the burial grounds of the poor and disadvantaged, notably but not exclusively African Americans, were easily available, sometimes with the connivance of those working at the burial grounds. It is possible that emphasis was placed on the use of metal coffins and burglar-proof vaults as a way of protecting bodies, and these were relatively popular in North America (Springate, 2015:43–50), although rare in Britain. This method may be how undertakers assuaged the fears of the affluent.

Miscellaneous Solutions

Probably many ad hoc designs were tried out by local communities to prevent or at least deter body snatching, although few survive. One solution similar to a mortsafe but not requiring disinterment was provided at Bolton, East Lothian, where a coffin-shaped iron grid known as a graveguard was placed over the grave. Then 28 iron rods were driven into the ground through perforations in the graveguard, and they were secured using three types of nut, each requiring its own bespoke key (Gorman, 2010). A similar solution was provided at Kilmun, Argyle, and Bute, but here the bolts were protected by an additional frame that was locked over the top to cover the bolt heads. This solution was, in effect, a combination of some features of both the low protectors and the coffin-shaped mortsafe and demonstrates how local ingenuity (perhaps informed by observing other forms) could create unique solutions to a widespread problem.

Some coffin protectors were made to be left permanently under the ground, but they are known only if subsequent grave digging reveals them and they are considered worthy of record or preservation. At Tough, Aberdeenshire, an iron cage made heavy by attaching large stones to the head and foot of the coffin was placed within a grave to protect the body (Ritchie, 1912:304). A less substantial iron frame was used at Oyne, Aberdeenshire (Ritchie, 1921:223–224). An even simpler form of body protection was recovered from Kingskettle, Fife, and is now in the National Museum of Scotland, Edinburgh. A simple collar was placed around the neck of the corpse and bolted to the base of the coffin, preventing the body from being dragged out by body snatchers; a similar type was used at St. Andrews.

Conclusions

The documentary and archaeological evidence demonstrates that body snatching was a real threat in the eighteenth and particularly the early nineteenth centuries. In English urban centers it would appear that little beyond heightening graveyard walls and occasionally mounting a guard was done to protect the graves of the poor, often left open as long trenches to be rapidly filled with the bodies of those dying daily in the cramped slums. These bodies were easily obtained by body snatchers, and it may be that the middle classes were largely safe in their burial crypts or suburban graveyards as there was little effort to create the physical protection seen in Scotland. There a range of protective measures can be identified, and many stories of successful and failed attempts at grave robbing are known. This frequency of bodysnatching may be because Scotland had a large number of medical schools, and those at Aberdeen and St. Andrews would have had particularly limited slum churchyards from which to draw, resulting in widespread searching for bodies across the countryside. A plentiful supply of bodies of the poor in cities such as London or Dublin or across North America meant that the scale of investment in body protection was rarely felt to be required.

It may be that the publicity arising from the prosecution of Burke and Hare, although not for grave robbing, led to hysteria and the rapid creation of security measures that with the passing of the 1832 Anatomy Act were no longer necessary. It is clear, however, that some measures were in force decades before, and others were put in place only after the threat had gone. This time span suggests that there was a more widespread and deeper fear of body desecration and that after 1832 it was largely illusory; although there was resistance to bodies going for dissection from both the church and relatives, the evidence suggests supplies were maintained, although the main study has a focus on Edinburgh (Smith, 2009). What is noteworthy is that mortsafe societies were being wound up as late as the 1870s and that investment in buildings such as the Marnoch morthouse extension was as late as 1877. Even the portable mortsafes, such as one of the Airth examples that is cast with the date 1837, were being ordered well after 1832, and stone slabs were buried over a man buried in 1854 at the United Free Church burial ground at Banchory-Devenick, Aberdeenshire (Ritchie, 1912:301–311). Perhaps the propensity for mortality symbols on memorials and the erection of markers at an early date in Scottish burial grounds reflect a certain attitude to the body that was later reinforced by the stories of body snatching and the efforts of those preventing it. The threat may have passed, but there may have been a residual attitude to the body that was much more strongly manifested communally in Scotland and institutionalized in organizations, structures, and equipment that was regularly used in a set of what became ritualized acts of body protection that no longer served a practical function but formed part of the respect offered to the body that those with the resources could demonstrate in their communities.

References

Anstruther Easter Mortsafe Society. Minutebook. 1830–1874. MS 37478. St. Andrews University Library Special Collections.

Auchtertool Accounts. Burials and Minutes. 1830–1863. CH2/25/4. National Archives of Scotland.

Bailey, J. B. 1896. *The Diary of a Resurrectionist: 1811–1812 To Which Are Added an Account of the Resurrection Men in London and Short History of the Passing of the Anatomy Act*. London: Swan Sonnenschein.

Blakely, R. L., and J. M. Harrington, eds. 1997. *Bones in the Basement: Postmortem Racism in Nineteenth-Century Medical Training*. Washington, D.C.: Smithsonian Institution Press.

Brickley, M., A. Miles, and H. Stainer. 1999. *The Cross Bones Burial Ground, Redcross Way, Southwark, London: Archaeological excavations (1991–1998) for the London Underground Limited Jubilee Line Extension Project*. MoLAS Monograph 3. London: Museum of London Archaeology Service.

Brooks, C. 1989. *Mortal Remains: The History and Present State of the Victorian and Edwardian Cemetery*. Exeter: Wheaton Publishers.

Campbell Family, Earls of Breadalbane. Papers. Reports and Inventory. 15 May 1856. GD112/16/3/6. National Archives of Scotland.

Chamberlain, A. T. 2012. "Morbid Osteology: Evidence for Autopsies, Dissection and Surgical Training from the Newcastle Infirmary Burial Ground (1753–1845)." In *Anatomical Dissection in Enlightenment England and Beyond: Autopsy, Pathology and Display*, ed. P. Mitchell, A. Cunningham, and O. P. Grell, pp. 11–22. History of Medicine in Context. London: Routledge.

Cole, H. 1964. *Things for the Surgeon: A History of the Bodysnatchers*. London: Heinemann.

Cox, M. 1996. *Life and Death in Spitalfields: 1700 to 1850*. York: Council for British Archaeology.

Crist, T. A., D. B. Mooney, and K. A. Morrell. 2017. "'The Mangled Remains of What Had Been Humanity': Evidence of Autopsy and Dissection at Philadelphia's Blockley Almshouse, 1835–1895." In *The Bioarchaeology of Dissection and Autopsy in the United States*, ed. K. C. Nystrom, pp. 259–278. New York: Springer.

Davidson, J. M. 2007. "Resurrection Men" in Dallas: The Illegal Use of Black Bodies as Medical Cadavers (1900–1907). *International Journal of Historical Archaeology*, 11(3):193–220.

Dundee Courier and Argus. 1869. 20 May, no. 4927. "Anstruther".

Fido, M. 1988. *Bodysnatchers: A History of the Resurrectionists, 1742–1832*. London: Weidenfeld and Nicolson.

Fleetwood, J. F. 1959. The Irish Resurrectionists. *Irish Journal of Medical Science*, 34(7):304–321.

Fleetwood, J. F. 1988. The Dublin Body Snatchers Part One. *Dublin Historical Record*, 42(2):42–52.

Fleetwood, J. F. 1993. Dublin Private Medical Schools in the Nineteenth Century. *Dublin Historical Record*, 46(1):31–45.

Fowler, L., and N. Powers 2012. *Doctors, Dissection and Resurrection Men: Excavations at the 19th-Century Burial Ground of the London Hospital, 2006*. MOLA Monograph 62. London: Museum of London Archaeology.

Frank, J. B. 1976. Body Snatching: A Grave Medical Problem. *Yale Journal of Biology and Medicine*, 49:399–410.

Gilmour Evidence. 1844. Trial papers relating to Christian or Christina Gilmour for the crime of murder at Inchinnan, Renfrewshire or South or West Grange, Dunlop, Ayrshire. Tried at High Court, Edinburgh. Inchinnan Mortsafe Cashbook. 12 January 1844. JC25/1844/369. National Archives of Scotland.

Glasgow Herald. 1874. 16 November, no. 108851. "Kilmarnock. Anstruther".

Gorman, M. 2010. Echoes of the Resurrection Men. http://www.abdn.ac.uk/bodysnatchers/index.php (accessed 26 November 2017).

Halperin, E. C. 2007. The Poor, the Black, and the Marginalized as the Source of Cadavers in United States Anatomical Education. *Clinical Anatomy*, 20:489–495.

Hamilakis, Y., M. Pluciennik, and S. Tarlow, eds. 2002b. *Thinking through the Body: Archaeologies of Corporeality*. Kluwer: New York.

Highet, M. J. 2005. Body Snatching & Grave Robbing: Bodies for Science. *History and Anthropology*, 16(4):415–440.

Holder, G. 2010. *Scottish Bodysnatchers: A Gazetteer*. Stroud: History Press.

Houlbrooke, R. 1998. *Death, Religion and the Family in England, 1480–1750*. Oxford: Clarendon Press.

Humphrey, D. C. 1973. Dissection and Discrimination: The Social Origins of Cadavers in America, 1760–1915. *Bulletin of the New York Academy of Medicine*, 49(9):819–827.

Kaufman, M., and L. L. Hanawalt. 1971. Body Snatching in the Midwest. *Michigan History*, 55:22–40.

Litten, J. 1991. *The English Way of Death: The Common Funeral Since 1450*. London: Robert Hall.

Marshall, T. 1995. *Murdering to Dissect: Grave-Robbing, Frankenstein and the Anatomy Literature*. Manchester: Manchester University Press.

Murphy, C. 2011. What Can Osteological Investigation Reveal about Medical Education in Eighteenth-Century Dublin? *Archaeology Ireland*, 25(3):30–34.

Mytum, H. C. 2004. *Mortuary Monuments and Burials Grounds of the Historic Period*. London: Kluwer Academic/Plenum Publishers.

Mytum, H. 2013. Combating Dublin Body-Snatchers: The Drumcondra Mortsafe. *Archaeology Ireland*, 27(3):23–25.

Newburn Mortsafe. Newburn Mortsafe Subscribers' Cash Book. 1824–1877. CH2/278/21. National Archives of Scotland.

Novak, S. A., and W. Willoughby. 2014. Resurrectionists' Excursions: Evidence of Postmortem Dissection from the Spring Street Presbyterian Church. *Northeast Historical Archaeology*, 39(1):134–152.

Nystrom, K. C., ed. 2017. *The Bioarchaeology of Dissection and Autopsy in the United States*. New York: Springer.

Rae, J. M., factor at Newbattle. Letters to Lord Ancram, later seventh Marquess of Lothian. 10 April 1826–1 March 1829. GD40/9/295/3. National Archives of Scotland.

Reeve, J., and M. Adams. 1993. *The Spitalfields Project.* Volume 1: *The Archaeology: Across the Styx.* CBA Research Report 85. London: Council for British Archaeology.

Richardson, R. 1987. *Death, Dissection and the Destitute.* London: Routledge and Kegan Paul.

Ritchie, J. 1912. An Account of the Watch-Houses, Mortsafes and Public Vaults in Aberdeenshire Churchyards. *Proceedings of the Society of Antiquaries of Scotland,* 46:285–326.

Ritchie, J. 1921. Relics of the Body-Snatchers: Supplementary Notes on Mortsafe Tackle, Mortsafes, Watch-Houses, and Public Vaults, Mostly in Aberdeenshire. *Proceedings of the Society of Antiquaries of Scotland,* 55:221–229.

Roach, M. 2003. *Stiff: The Curious Lives of Human Cadavers.* London: Viking.

Robertson, T. M., G. H. Williams, G. Haggarty, and N. Reynolds. 1981. Recent Excavations at Dunfermline Abbey, Fife. *Proceedings of the Society of Antiquaries of Scotland,* 111:388–400.

Sappol, M. 2002. *A Traffic of Dead Bodies: Anatomy and Embodied Social Identity in Nineteenth-Century America.* Princeton, N.J.: Princeton University Press.

Schultz, S. M. 1992. *Body Snatching: The Robbing of Graves for the Education of Physicians in Early Nineteenth Century America.* Jefferson, N.C.: McFarland and Company.

Smith, M. 2009. The Church of Scotland and the Funeral Industry in Nineteenth-Century Edinburgh. *Scottish Historical Review,* 88(1):108–133.

Springate, M. E, 2015. *Coffin Hardware in Nineteenth-Century America.* Walnut Creek: Left Coast Press.

Traquair Watching Society. Papers relating to the watchhouse at Traquire churchyard: Minutes and accounts of the Traquair Watching Society. 1821–1879. GD314/114. National Archives of Scotland.

Waite, F. C. 1945. Grave Robbing in New England. *Bulletin of the Medical Library Association,* 33(3):272–294.

Willsher, B. 1985. *How to Record Scottish Graveyards.* Edinburgh: Council for British Archaeology Scotland.

Wise, S. 2005. *The Italian Boy: A Tale of Murder and Body Snatching in 1830s London.* London: Macmillan.

CHAPTER 13

Death, Dogs, and Monuments: Recent Research at Washington's Congressional Cemetery

Laurie Burgess and Douglas W. Owsley

Nineteenth-century brick burial vaults line the main walkways of historic Congressional Cemetery in Washington, D.C., and hold the remains of some of the city's most prominent nineteenth-century families (Figure 1). These semisubterranean structures are showing the effects of time, and as funding becomes available, the cemetery engages historic preservation experts and conservators to repair and restore them. To protect the remains during the restoration, a Smithsonian team excavated each vault and temporarily removed the remains to the National Museum of Natural History, providing an opportunity to study the remains and mortuary material culture of the city's nineteenth-century elite.

The remains and any associated mortuary material culture—coffin hardware, nails, buttons, buckles, and the occasional nameplate—were temporarily transferred to the museum for safekeeping and analysis. While at the museum, the skeletons were aged and sexed by the physical anthropology team, and the associated objects were analyzed to help date the burials. These data were then compared to the excellent records of the cemetery to link names to burials, when possible, and the individuals were reinterred once the restoration was complete. So far, the Smithsonian team has had the opportunity to work in six of the cemetery's high-status burial vaults over the past few years. Four of those six will be discussed here: two brick vaults with sunken, semisubterranean chambers and two subsurface vaults topped by elaborate monuments.

Constructed first in the 1820s, these brick houses of the dead usually contain dozens of coffins to the point where they are often completely filled (Figure 2). The coffins are frequently stacked three deep and have collapsed over time, creating a sort of stratigraphy: coffin base, bones, and coffin lid for each interment, although not always in perfect horizontal alignment since the coffins do not always collapse neatly and elements and coffin hardware sometimes intrude into other interments. Coffin hardware has become a valuable dating tool for burials from the second half of the nineteenth century, and its role in assessing status has also been explored in recent decades.

Status and death go hand in hand in terms of archaeological studies, almost regardless of time period or culture. Archaeologists, long believing in a link between status

FIGURE 1. Brick vaults at the Congressional Cemetery. Photo by Laurie Burgess, courtesy of Smithsonian Institution.

and mortuary practices, attempt to infer social and/or economic position on the basis of material culture associated with an individual's burial. Using data from Congressional Cemetery in Washington, D.C., this chapter explores the degree to which material culture, in this case coffin hardware, can be a reliable indicator of status in historic period burials.

Cemetery History

Congressional Cemetery, originally located at the very fringes of the city in a rural setting overlooking the Anacostia River, now sits well within an urban landscape, near the heart of the city's Capitol Hill neighborhood. The cemetery was founded by private citizens in 1807 and was transferred to the Episcopalian Christ Church in 1812, but most notably, in 1816, 100 of the best sites were allocated for members of Congress who died in office (Sienkewicz, 2005). The allocation of these sites gave the cemetery strong federal ties and gave rise to the name Congressional Cemetery. Although still owned by the Episcopalian church today and leased to the Association for the Preservation of Historic Congressional Cemetery, in 1816 the cemetery's identity began to shift from sacred to secular, an overtone that remains to this day.

These congressional plots and monuments wrought a change upon the landscape, lending gravitas and a strong federal identity to the cemetery, even though most of the monuments are truly cenotaphs, or empty tombs, and bear only the name of the congressman or senator while the body lies elsewhere. The federal overtones embedded in the presence of the cenotaphs still give the perception of ties to the nation's halls of power, a perception that likely resonated even more in the nineteenth century. In addition to the cenotaphs, in the nineteenth century a gravel road ran straight from the cemetery to the

FIGURE 2. Causten vault interior showing the matrix formed by collapsed wooden coffins. Photo by Laurie Burgess, courtesy of Smithsonian Institution.

Capitol, providing a direct physical link to one of Washington's seats of power, and as Sienkewicz (2005:2) wrote of the cemetery, "it began to embody the social structure of the nation's capital." Although archaeologists have been cautioned against using this as a broad assumption, McGuire (1988:451), on the basis of his work with cemeteries in Broome County, New York, has said that for the time period spanning the mid-nineteenth century through the 1920s, "archaeological assumptions concerning a direct relationship between mortuary investment and wealth or power are valid for this time."

This finding holds true for Congressional Cemetery, where the city of the dead did mimic the city of the living during the nineteenth century, with Washington's social structure still very evident in the range of burial vaults and monuments that dot the cemetery's landscape. The wealthy and influential occupy vaults and family plots in the most desirable locations, near the main axes of the cemetery roads and located in predominantly upland areas, and the charitable burials of the poor are physically marginalized and lie in unmarked graves at the cemetery's edges, whereas the burials of the middle class and average citizen cover acres.

It is usually the cemeteries and remains of marginalized people, at least in North America, that have been studied and reported in the literature (Bell, 1994; Nawrocki, 1995; Buikstra, 2000). For the burials studied here, elite status is not to be inferred from a nuanced reading of material culture but is instead writ large in the form of elaborate funerary monuments and in the spatial aspects of social hierarchy that are embedded in the cemetery.

Status is frequently inferred from mortuary practices almost regardless of time period or culture. But the analysis of the materials from the Congressional Cemetery burial vaults, like the findings from other studies, has shown that a direct relationship between the presence and amount of coffin hardware in burials and status cannot necessarily be assumed. Edward Bell's (1990) work at the Uxbridge Almshouse, a nineteenth-century poorhouse, challenged this correlation when he found that 45% of the burials contained coffin hardware. He attributed the high percentage to the Beautification of Death movement, when death was idealized and mortuary material culture became elaborate. He urged archaeologists to consider the effects of popular culture on mortuary practices that influenced even the burials of the poorest members of society (Bell, 1990).

Bromberg and Shephard (2006) also looked at the coffin hardware–status correlation by comparing their research at a Quaker burial ground with the Uxbridge burials and with Little et al.'s (1992) work at the Weir Family Cemetery in Manassas, Virginia. They compared the three assemblages and found that status and coffin hardware were not directly related since the Quakers were of high status but actively chose not to decorate coffins in keeping with their belief system. The higher-status Weir Family Cemetery had 75% of burials with coffin hardware, the Uxbridge Almshouse had 45%, and the Quakers had a low of 33%. The cultural preferences of Quakers appear to have been represented in the low percentage, and the Weirs' inclusion of a much higher percentage of coffin ornamentation clearly reflected another point of view. The active choice inherent in the quantities of hardware variously present in these burials speaks to another aspect of mortuary practices and cemeteries: their role as communication systems.

McGuire (1988:474) has said, "The dead . . . can establish discourse, but not maintain it." As he and others have noted, it is also the living who establish this discourse through the material culture of death, in status displays and social competition, as discussed by Cannon (1989) and others. Little et al. (1992) illustrate this point particularly well at the Weir Family Cemetery; the family had fallen on hard times, yet the amount of mortuary display, in terms of coffin hardware, increased. Little et al. argue that the family wanted to be seen not as they actually were but as they wished to be perceived and link the use of ornamentation to the Beautification of Death movement prevalent at the time. They argue for incorporating "a specific historic context" into any assessments of status using coffin hardware (Little et al., 1992:415).

Status display relates not just to a reflection of status as it is or was but instead represents an idealized display of status, something that is very present in cemeteries (Pearson, 1982). Indeed, it can be argued that an idealized expression of power relations is negotiated through burial rituals (McGuire, 1988), and this negotiation is readily apparent at Congressional Cemetery. Both the idealized display of status and the expression of power relations are especially persistent themes in Washington, then and now.

At Congressional Cemetery, the cenotaphs—the empty tombs of members of Congress—illustrate idealized displays of status in the sphere of death. They show how effective this strategy can be since only about one-third of the cenotaphs actually contain remains, and they make up a tiny percentage of the 67,000 individuals buried at the cemetery, yet for two centuries their presence has conferred status upon the cemetery, in the name it became known by and in the perception of strong links to the uppermost echelons of government and thus to power. The cemetery monuments do function as a communication system: they have carried this and other messages forward into the future and continue to shape the perception of the landscape, whether on the scale of cultural landscape or embodied in individual monuments and vaults.

The vault projects have provided an opportunity to examine the mortuary practices and coffin hardware of high-status families in nineteenth-century Washington, D.C. Two

Table 1. Coffin hardware from Congressional Cemetery, Washington, D.C. An X indicates specific hardware was present, and a dash (—) indicates it was not.

Coffin hardware	Wirt vault, 1830–1885	Coombe vault, 1828–1900s	Causten vault, 1835–1899	Macomb vault, 1842
Coffin handles				
Single lug	X	X	X	—
Double-lug swing bail	X	X	X	—
Short bar	X	X	X	—
Extension	X	—	—	—
Escutcheon plates	X	X	X	—
Thumbscrews	X	X	X	—
Cylindrical	X	—	—	—
Urn shaped	—	—	X	—
Fan shaped	—	—	X	—
Nameplate	X	X	X	X

of the vaults studied are semisubterranean brick vaults: the Coombe vault was in use from the late 1820s to the early twentieth century, and the Causten vault was used from ca. 1835 to 1899. The other two vaults are subsurface, situated beneath elaborate monuments: the Macomb vault, completed in 1842 and apparently used once, and the Wirt vault, constructed in 1853, although two burials dating to the 1830s were moved to the vault. It remained in use until 1885.

The coffin hardware (Table 1) and burial practices of these vaults have been analyzed on multiple scales: on the site-specific level and also within the larger scale of shifting trends of nineteenth-century cemeteries. Since the interments were already known to be those of Washington's wealthy residents, this project provided an opportunity to examine the correlation between coffin hardware and status within known, elite contexts.

The Coombe Vault

Griffith Coombe was one of the founders of the cemetery, and the Coombe vault is located along the main walkway of the cemetery, in the company of the vaults of some of Washington's other leading families. These rather low-roofed brick structures line the walkway that goes from 18th Street SE to the upland area of the cemetery, which progresses to what were sweeping views of the Anacostia River during the nineteenth century.

The Coombe vault interior consists of a vaulted brick burial chamber with an open shaft in the floor to allow for the drainage of groundwater. Because of underlying soil conditions, drainage is a problem in the cemetery. This semisubterranean vault, built in 1828, is much more integrated with the surrounding landscape than many of the later memorials in the cemetery and, in a way, has the appearance of a very large, stylized grave with a small entry door. Although it is substantial, it has a low profile, and it and the other brick vaults of the time period have grass-covered roofs, which tie them directly to the natural landscape. The brick vaults, the earliest in the cemetery, are far less elaborate than the later memorials like the Macomb and Wirt vaults, which were built in the 1840s and

1850s. McGuire (1988) notes that the change in mortuary practices from naturalization (here, low-profile vaults integrated with the surrounding landscape) to denial (in the later creation of parklike settings where the reality of death is minimized or, in the case of Wirt and Macomb, glorified in the abstract) mirrors changes in attitudes about death. With the exception of the Coombe vault and a few others, the brick vaults resemble small houses with ornamented fronts and a small door leading down to the interior floor, sometimes 4 to 5 feet below the surface.

Many of the earlier interments in the Coombe vault, those predating the 1850s, contained no coffin hardware since it was not generally used during that time period. The earlier interments were placed at the far end of the vault, and the more recent ones were closer to the entrance. Many of the coffins had been stacked on top of each other, and the wooden coffins had collapsed over time. In general, in tightly packed vaults a degree of stratigraphy remains after stacked coffins collapse, with the coffin lid and base encapsulating the remains and forming layers. But in the Coombe vault the effects of the collapse were intensified by water damage: a water line was evident on the walls, about 3 feet above the floor, enough to impact all of the coffins. The deteriorated wood, bone, garments, and hardware formed a denser matrix than we encountered in other vaults that were not subject to flooding.

It is noteworthy that both ornate and very plain coffin handles were found in the Coombe vault, reinforcing that the link between coffin hardware and status is context driven, at best. Plain, double-lug swing bail handles were present. If recovered from a different burial context, they would not automatically suggest a high-status burial. This coffin handle variety, according to Hacker-Norton and Trinkley (1984), appears in the 1860s and persists until the early twentieth century. Davidson (2004) points out that single and double lug forms were the predominant type of handles available since the late 1700s and also says that the double lug variety persist until the 1880s, saying that its low cost helped maintain its popularity when the more expensive short bar handles appeared.

The Coombe vault swing bail handles (Figure 3A) were plated with a base metal, probably containing nickel, and this variety of coffin hardware was recovered from multiple interments within the vault. But some of the other hardware does appear to relate to status, like a single-lug coffin handle made from silver-plated cast brass; the presence of sterling silver was verified by using x-ray fluorescence (XRF; Figure 3B). As a side note, XRF was also used on dentures recovered from the Coombe vault on what appeared to be a gold palate, with beautifully rendered porcelain white teeth and pink gums. The gold turned out to be 20 carat. More elaborate short bar coffin handles were also recovered, including handles with crosses and matching cross-shaped thumbscrews.

The appearance of identical coffin hardware types in more than one burial in this vault may indicate several possibilities. It may suggest choice in funerary treatment on the part of the family, or it may represent the hardware stock of the coffin maker. There is also the possibility that some of the smaller hardware elements, like thumbscrews, were intrusive in one or more burials and may have been part of adjacent burials since the collapse and deterioration of many coffins were substantial and subsidence of the burial matrix and some commingling of elements may have occurred over time, especially when the vault flooded. Regardless, the presence of plain and ornate forms within a high-status tomb supports the premise of Bell (1990), Little et al. (1992), and others that a direct correlation between hardware and status cannot be assumed.

FIGURE 3. Coffin handles from Coombe vault. (A) Plain swing bail coffin handle from the Coombe vault. Photo by Chip Clark, courtesy of Smithsonian Institution. (B) Sterling silver–plated brass single-lug coffin handle from the Coombe vault. Photo by Chip Clark, courtesy of Smithsonian Institution.

The Causten Vault

In addition to having a potentially indirect relationship to status, in rare instances coffin hardware could be misleading in terms of establishing dates for elite burials. In another Congressional Cemetery vault, the Causten vault (1835–1899), cemetery records showed that 9 (31%) of the more than 20 interments in the semisubterranean brick vault dated to the first half of the nineteenth century, and 20 (69%) dated to the last half of the century, so we expected that the earlier burials would have little or no coffin hardware and the later burials would potentially contain the typical progression of single-lug handles, swing bail handles, then short bar handles. This particular vault was completely filled with coffins, wall to wall. The cemetery staff told us that the family had had a number of the burials recoffined in the 1870s and produced a receipt showing this (record on file, Historic Congressional Cemetery). The receipt gave totals but did not address any specifics as to which individuals were recoffined.

Of the 29 total interments, 17, or 59%, predated 1870 and so would presumably not contain short bar coffin handles. Seven burials, or 24%, had short bar handles, which would be fairly consistent with the date range of the vault. Although single-lug handles were recovered from three burials, only one swing bail handle was recovered from debris in the SW corner of the vault; it seems likely that it is from one of the recoffined burials. The virtual absence of swing bail handles, commonly used from the 1860s through the 1880s, in any of the excavated interments may be a reflection of the recoffining, but the impact of this activity on the coffin hardware assemblage is difficult to assess. The occurrence of recoffining was an unexpected aspect of elite interments, one we had not previously encountered. Only a high-status family would have had the means to recoffin burials—and potentially alter the material record.

The Wirt Vault

The Wirt vault differs significantly from the Coombe and Causten vaults in that it lies beneath a massive monument that dominates all of the surrounding headstones and memorials (Figure 4). Although the name "Wirt" appears prominently on the front, Wirt's credentials are listed on the side of the vault, "Attorney General of the United States from 1817 to 1820," ensuring that all who pass know who lies within this impressive grave site. The monument and vault date to 1853 and fall well within the time period of the Rural Cemetery and Beautification of Death movements. Here, death and status are clearly linked on a large and public scale.

The monument rests above a subsurface chamber lined with stone slabs with three stone shelves holding the burials. The contents had been vandalized decades ago, but the recent appearance of a skull possibly belonging to William Wirt prompted a forensic anthropological investigation that confirmed this identification (Grabowski et al., 2010). Within the Wirt vault, where dates of death were available for all eight of the interments, the two burials from the first half of the nineteenth century, dating to 1830 and 1834, had no coffin hardware. However, Agnes Wirt (1830) had domed brass tacks decorating her coffin, and William Wirt's lead-lined coffin (1834) had a silver nameplate.

The 1863 burial of Lt. Goldsborough, Wirt's grandson, had very ornate and very large single-lug handles. Davidson (200:104) reports that "larger, more solidly cast" coffin handles cost more than lighter versions and refers to short bar coffin handles in particular,

FIGURE 4. The Wirt monument dominates the surrounding burials. Photo by Laurie Burgess, courtesy of Smithsonian Institution.

FIGURE 5. Massive short bar coffin handles from the Wirt vault. Photo by Chip Clark, courtesy of Smithsonian Institution.

saying that they cost the most. The short bar handles that were recovered from the Wirt vault are massive and ornate (Figure 5). Notably, ornate extension bars were present with the 1877 burial of Rear Admiral Louis Malesherbes Goldsborough, Wirt's son-in-law, and appear to be the earliest documented occurrence of extension bars in the United States. A cast-iron coffin, dating to an 1857 burial, was also present in the vault.

The coffin hardware from the Wirt vault is consistent with the time period of the burials, and some of the more substantial hardware is consistent with higher-cost items. However, as with the Coombe vault, very plain, nickel-plated swing bail handles were also

FIGURE 7. The second funeral for General Alexander Macomb. Photo by Chip Clark, courtesy of Smithsonian Institution.

The next morning, on 17 July 2008, a second funeral was held for General Alexander Macomb at Congressional Cemetery, 166 years after he died (Figure 7). A well-attended service was held in the cemetery's chapel. Family members spoke, and one of them read a poem written by Catherine Macomb, in which Catherine called her husband Sandy, a detail that would otherwise be lost to history, but one that reminded everyone there of the very personal nature of cemetery excavations. The coffin was escorted to the gravesite with War of 1812 reenactors and HPTC team members serving as pallbearers. A second ceremony was held at the now restored monument, and the flag that covered his coffin was folded and presented to the family. The mahogany coffin was lowered out of sight, and General and Catherine Macomb were laid to rest for the second and final time.

The 1842 Macomb vault just predates the period when coffin hardware came into use, but his burial dates to the period when lead liners were being used in high-status interments.

The monument, topped by a Greek warrior's helmet, reflects the neoclassical period of style, when classical Greek and Roman elements were revived and incorporated into architecture—in this case, they were used in mortuary architecture. The Macomb vault, like the Wirt vault, provides an example of displaying status and wealth through means other than coffin hardware. The 7-ton monument memorializes Macomb's military career and evokes a time of ancient warriors and mythic battles. The monument is decorated with symbols, with one side of the base showing a sword clad in oak leaves, evoking war and valor. Another side displays the Greek *ouroboros*, a serpent with its tail in its mouth that is symbolic of cycles and of the eternal return, which is further emphasized by the presence of a butterfly, a symbol of resurrection. A combined design element contains the wings of time, an hourglass, a scythe, and a weeping willow: tempus fugit, death, and mourning. An article in the 29 June 1841 *National Intelligencer* describes Macomb's first funeral, whose list of attendees is perhaps the ultimate mortuary status marker:

> The Funeral of General Macomb, Commander of the Army took place yesterday . . . and was attended by the President, and all the Officers of the Government, both Houses of Congress, the Diplomatic Corps, Military and Naval Officers. . . . The solemn military and civic array which filled the broad avenue through the city presented an imposing spectacle, in keeping with, appropriately closed by, the impressive ceremonies at the tomb.

Conclusion

The material culture of death, including objects and mortuary architecture, and issues of status are clearly related, but the projects in Congressional Cemetery support other studies in finding that the relationship is not always a direct one when it comes to coffin hardware. Very plain and simple hardware occurs in these elite vaults, often alongside burials containing elaborate coffin hardware. As with all things archaeological, context is paramount.

The Coombe and Wirt vaults demonstrate that the connection between coffin hardware and status cannot be assumed. The Causten vault, although it could not provide data to either support or reject the correlation between hardware and status, does provide a valuable lesson about the possibility of rewriting the material record. The Macomb vault reveals an entirely different set of principles for reading status from material culture since it, like the Wirt vault, is topped by a large and imposing monument.

How we bury our dead continues to reflect the social trends of the time period, ranging from the more naturalistic and integrated early vaults of the 1820s to large monuments, some with neoclassical elements, to the pronounced increase in the amount of coffin hardware as the nineteenth century progressed. Underlying all these changes is the deliberately bucolic landscape of the cemetery itself, where the effects of the Rural Cemetery movement can be clearly seen in the pathways, the tree-lined drives, and even the former carriage turn, long gone now, at the most scenic point overlooking the Anacostia River.

In an era when we are kept at arm's length from death, where the care of the dead has moved from the province of home and family to a more detached and commodified state, where the dead are relinquished to the funeral home industry, Congressional Cemetery, unlike other cemeteries, has become a place where the living are a constant part of the landscape of the dead. It is an active cemetery, with plots available and funerals conducted in its chapel and at grave sites. The cemetery's condition and financial support have waned and waxed in the two centuries since it was created, and during a challenging period a number of years ago, the cemetery association engaged the local community in an unconventional way: they created a membership-based dog park.

In the mornings and evenings neighborhood residents walk and visit among the headstones, monuments and vaults while their dogs have the run of over 30 fenced acres. This action revitalized community involvement, helped preserve the grounds and monuments, and reduced vandalism. After spending many days in the cemetery, both above- and belowground, it is hard not to agree with Sienkewicz (2005), who suggests that elements of the Rural Cemetery movement have come into play here once more. As in the nineteenth century, families and friends gather, walk, and socialize in the cemetery, but this time with their canine companions in tow.

References

Bromberg, F. W., and S. J. Shephard. 2006. The Quaker Burial Ground in Alexandria, Virginia: A Study of Burial Practices of the Society of Friends. *Historical Archaeology*, 40(1):57–88.

Buikstra, J. 2000. "Historical Bioarcheology and the Beautification of Death." In *Never Anything So Solemn: An Archeological, Biological and Historical Investigation of the Nineteenth Century Grafton Cemetery*, ed. J. E. Buikstra, J. A. O'Gorman, and C. Sutton, pp. 15–20. Kampsville Studies in Archeology and History 3. Kampsville, Ill.: Center for American Archeology.

Bell, E. 1990. The Historical Archaeology of Mortuary Behavior: Coffin Hardware from Uxbridge, Massachusetts. *Historical Archaeology*, 24(3):54–78.

Bell, E. 1994. *Vestiges of Mortality and Remembrance*. Metuchen, N.J.: Scarecrow Press.

Cannon, A. 1989. The Historical Dimension in Mortuary Expressions of Status and Sentiment. *Current Anthropology*, 30(4):437–458.

Davidson, J. M. 2004. "Material Culture, Chronology and Socioeconomics." In *Two Historic Cemeteries in Crawford County, Arkansas*, ed. R. C. Maintfort Jr. and J. M. Davidson, pp. 73–194. Fayetteville: Arkansas Archeological Survey.

Grabowski, M. W., D. W. Owsley, and K. Bruwelheide. 2010. Cemetery Vandalism: The Strange Case of William Wirt. *Washington History*, Vol. 22:57–68.

Hacker-Norton, D., and M. Trinkley. 1984. *Remember Man Thou Art Dust: Coffin Hardware of the Twentieth Century*. Research Series 2. Columbia, S.C.: Chicora Foundation.

Little, B. J., K. Lamphear, and D. W. Owsley. 1992. Mortuary Display and Status in a Nineteenth Century Anglo-American Cemetery in Manassas, VA. *American Antiquity*, 57(3):397–418.

McGuire, R. H. 1988. "Dialogues with the Dead: Ideology and the Cemetery." In *The Recovery of Meaning*, ed. M. P. Leone and P. B. Potter, pp. 435–480. Washington, D.C.: Smithsonian Institution Press.

National Intelligencer. 1841. The Funeral of General Macomb. 28 June.

National Intelligencer. 1841. Description of the Funeral of General Macomb. 29 June.

Nawrocki, S. P. 1995. "Taphonomic Processes in Historic Cemeteries." In *Bodies of Evidence: Reconstructing History through Skeletal Analysis*, ed. A. L. Grauer, pp. 49–66. New York: Wiley-Liss.

Pearson, M. P. 1982. "Mortuary Practices, Society and Ideology: An Ethnoarchaeological Study in Symbolic and Structural Archaeology." In *Symbolic and Structural Archaeology*, ed. I. Hodder, pp. 99–114. Cambridge: Cambridge University Press.

Sienkewicz, J. A. 2005. *Congressional Cemetery*. Historic American Landscapes Survey HALS DC-1. Washington, D.C.: National Park Service, Department of the Interior.

CHAPTER 14

Lost Governors, Iron Coffins, and Driven Descendants

Charles R. Ewen and Sheri B. Crane

Richard Caswell is one of the most enigmatic men in North Carolina history. His impressive resume includes serving as governor of North Carolina from 1776 to 1780 and again from 1784 to 1787. That alone should have earned a couple volumes, yet a comprehensive work on Caswell was not published until 218 years after his death (Alexander, 2007). Richard Caswell was born in Maryland on 3 August 1729. He moved to Dobbs County (now Lenoir County), North Carolina in 1746 and began a long and controversial career of public service. His political star began to rise during the Revolutionary War. Caswell distinguished himself at the Battle of Moore's Creek Bridge in 1776. Here, the militia force he commanded prevented a large group of Tories from joining an army of British Regulars. His men completely overcame and routed loyalist General MacDonald's forces at the bridge crossing Moore's Creek and thus dampened the Tory uprising in the state (Alexander, 2007:69–70). The accolades accompanying this victory played no small role in winning him the nod as first federal governor of North Carolina then a second term a few years later. He also held the posts of comptroller general, delegate to the Constitutional Convention, and state senator (Alexander, 1946:307–312). Unfortunately, his later life was clouded by fiscal and electoral difficulties. One of the most surprising omissions in our knowledge is the location of his final resting place.

While serving his Senate term in November 1789, Caswell was struck with paralysis (now thought to be a stroke) and, after remaining speechless for several days, died on 10 November, at 60 years of age. A eulogium was pronounced over Caswell's remains, and his body was "conveyed to his family burial-place in Lenoir County, N.C., and there interred," where he was presumed to have been buried in a manner befitting a former grand master of the Masonic Order (Fletcher, n.d.:2).

In the intervening centuries since Caswell's death, the exact location of his grave became lost. Caswell owned two cemeteries at the time of his death. Historical documents that have survived have conflicting information as to which one claims his grave. Even the descendants had lost track of which cemetery houses Caswell's remains. Caswell, himself, confuses the situation by reserving in his will, plots of land for two cemeteries:

> In THE NAME OF GOD AMEN. I, Richard Caswell, of
> Dobbs County in the State of North Carolina, Do this second
> day of July, in the Year of our Lord, one thousand, Seven

hundred and eighty seven, make and declare this to be my last Will and Testament as the one I made on the death of my dearly beloved son, William Caswell, will not suit with my present circumstances. I declare that and all former Wills and Testaments by me made, null and void, holding this and this only for firm and effectual, which is as follows:

First, I reserve for the use of a burying ground for all those of my family and Connections who may choose to bury their Relations and friends there, one half acre of land where the Bones of my dear father and Mother lie, at a place called the Hill, to be laid out East, West, North and South so as to leave those Bones near the center of the said half Acre of Ground, and I also reserve in like manner, one half Acre of Land where the Bones of beloved wife (and) son, William, now lie near the red house, to be laid out in the same manner and for the same purpose as the above half Acre is directed; and these two half Acres to be reserved for the uses afores'd forever. (Quoted in Alexander, 2007:177)

Caswell is traditionally thought to have been buried in the cemetery "near the red house" (Figure 1), now part of the Governor Richard Caswell Memorial/CSS *Neuse* Historic Site on U.S. 70 in Kinston (Alexander, 2007:177). In this cemetery, his grave was said to be marked only by an oak tree. A monument was later placed there in his honor by the

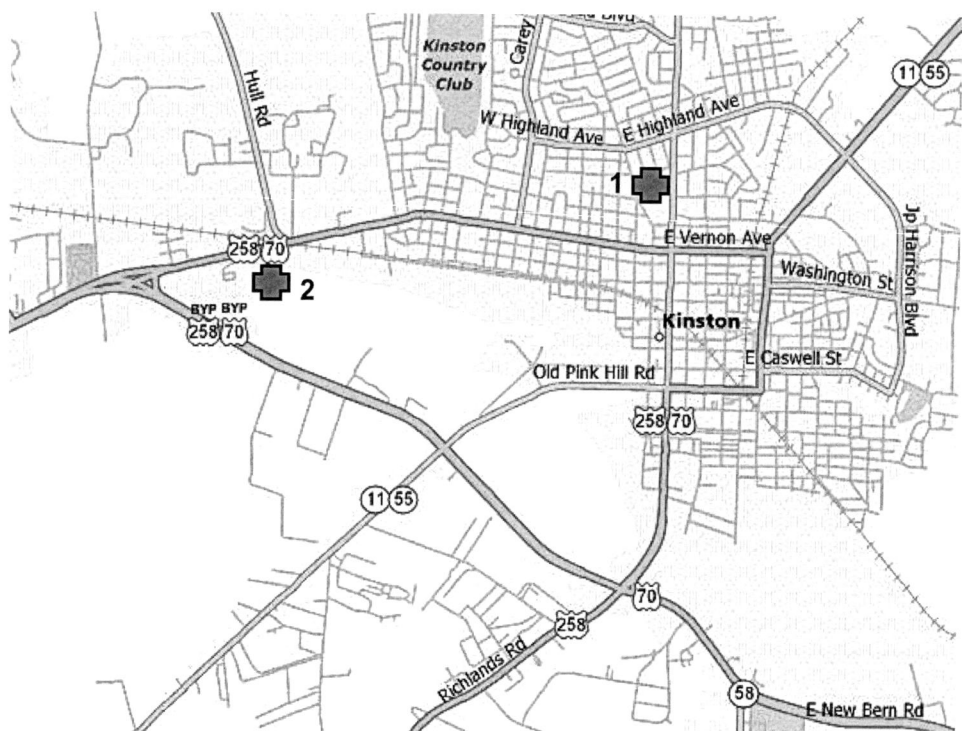

FIGURE 1. Locations of Caswell cemeteries. (1) Vernon Hall, or "the Hill." (2) Governor Richard Caswell Memorial/CSS *Neuse* Historic Site.

Masonic Order since Caswell was a former grand master for North Carolina. However, others hold that Caswell is buried in the cemetery next to Vernon Hall (also referred to as "the Hill"), a house he owned in downtown Kinston. His parents and siblings are also believed be buried there, although their graves are also unmarked.

A series of articles in North Carolina newspapers (e.g., Sampley, 1999) concerning Caswell's resting place jogged the memory of a Kinston resident, who suggested the cemetery at Vernon Hall was, indeed, a likely site. Stephanie Bourdas-Smith, a long-time resident of Kinston, believed she discovered Caswell's vault when she was 10 years old while playing around in the cemetery behind the Kinston Clinic. Four decades after the event, she recounted that a severe storm blew over a large oak. Venturing out after the storm, she and her friends discovered a brick tunnel leading to a wooden coffin and a skeleton. Concerned parents backfilled the "tunnel," but the sight made such an impression that she never forgot it. Her letter to the editor published in the *Kinston Free Press* (Bourdas-Smith, 2000) prompted the dean of the Harriot College of Arts and Sciences at East Carolina University, himself a native Kinstonian, to request that archaeologists from the Department of Anthropology follow up this newly revealed lead.

The Project Phase 1

The undertaking had seemingly little probability of success from the outset. Preliminary research indicated that it was far more likely that Richard Caswell would have been buried in the cemetery west of Kinston, where his wives and children are buried. The authors' experience with alleged tunnels in historic contexts is that they are more properly relegated to the category of urban legend. It also seemed unlikely that Ms. Bourdas-Smith could relocate the exact spot she recalled seeing the tunnel since in the intervening decades the area had become densely overgrown. However, one does not lightly ignore a request from the dean's office, so the undertaking was turned into a class project.

To our amazement, Ms. Bourdas-Smith was able to lead investigators to the location she recalled, which was referenced by a small family cemetery and a large, rotted tree stump. Ewen and student members of his public archaeology course (ANTH 5201) proceeded to formulate a research design and carry out archaeological excavations at the site. It is important to note that our goal was *not* to find the grave of Richard Caswell. That goal had a high probability of failure. The objective was to archaeologically test the hypothesis that Governor Caswell was buried at the Vernon Hall cemetery in the location indicated by Ms. Bourdas-Smith. This subtle difference assured us of an answer to our question, no matter who was or was not found.

Methodology

On Wednesday, 25 October 2000, before excavation began, some preliminary work was done to clear the area of vegetation and to establish a site grid. The entire site was covered by a dense stand of bamboo. Although easily cleared, the extensive root system would make digging difficult. On the following Saturday, 28 October 2000, Richard McCarn and Roy Dail from ProMark, a utilities locating firm, conducted a ground-penetrating radar (GPR) survey of the area surrounding the location that Ms. Bourdas-Smith had indicated. The GPR registered several anomalies, two of which would later be identified as burial crypts. The other anomalies probably denote additional unmarked burials in the

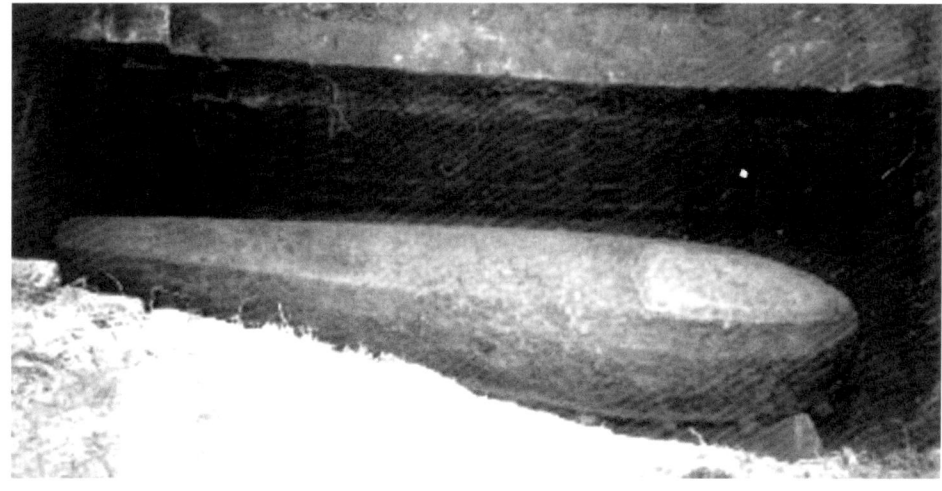

FIGURE 2. First phase of excavations at Vernon Hall. (A) The iron casket within the first brick crypt. (B) The second brick crypt during excavation. Photos by authors.

area but were left unexcavated. On the basis of the GPR data, excavation units were set out, and two graves were almost immediately encountered.

The first grave appeared at about 5 cm below the ground surface when excavators uncovered a brick arch. They removed this layer of bricks, and directly underlying them was a zone of red clay fill approximately 30 cm thick. This, in turn, overlaid another brick arch two courses thick. We determined this feature to be a brick crypt, within which we subsequently found a cast-iron coffin (Figure 2A). Lying on top of the coffin was a scattering of wood, cut nails, and other debris.

The second grave did not have a surface covering of brick. Instead, it was identified by a rectangular stain of dark soil with some disturbance obscuring the northern edge of the feature. After excavating approximately 10 cm into the second feature, a brick arch similar to the upper arch of the first burial was encountered. The brick arch in the second crypt had several missing bricks (Figure 2B), presumably a result of the disturbance caused by a tree falling directly above that location, no doubt the tree Ms. Bourdas-Smith remembered being blown over in the storm. A cast-iron coffin similar to the one found in the first crypt was located within the light-brown loam that filled this crypt. Recovered artifacts include cut nails, wood fragments, and a sample of mortar.

Both of the coffins were tapered from shoulder to foot and from shoulder to head. The head and foot ends were slightly rounded. The coffins consisted of upper and lower halves bolted together with 22 fasteners. Both upper and lower halves were faceted with three sides, giving the cross section a hexagonal shape. Four handles, sporting a winged cherub motif, were located at the head and foot ends on either side of the coffin in line with the seam and closure bolts. Habenstein and Lamers (1962:269) describe a coffin very much like these as a Fisk Model 3 made by Crane, Breed and Company in 1854. They are described as "the 'Plain, or Octagon' pattern, finished in imitation rosewood and polished equal to the finest furniture." These were not inexpensive coffins.

In spite of initial skepticism, the excavators were now confronted with not one but two graves of high status. The two coffins were left in situ until their dates could be determined. The scarcity of published literature led Ewen to consult with several individuals with prior cemetery excavation experience (Pat Garrow, Douglas Owsley, Ed Bell, and James Davidson) concerning the dating of the caskets. All were in agreement that the coffins dated to the mid-nineteenth century, making these burials too recent to be Richard Caswell. Much to the dismay of the legions of onlookers, Ewen had the vaults backfilled with clean sand.

This appeared to be the end of the project. We did not find Governor Caswell, but the project was a resounding success as a class exercise. Ewen's students designed, executed, and reported on an interesting project, and East Carolina University received a lot of good, free publicity. One of the descendants, however, would not let the project die. Susan Burgess Hoffman, a direct descendant of Richard Caswell, relentlessly emailed and called Ewen in hopes of exhuming the coffins and identifying their occupants. Her persistence took its toll.

Ewen agreed to open the coffins only after three criteria had been met: (1) There had to be good candidates as to the occupants of the coffins, and their descendants had to be willing to grant permission for the exhumation. (2) The opening and analysis of the remains needed to fulfill a legitimate research interest. (3) Finally, someone needed to cover the expenses that such excavation and analyses would entail. Confident that these criteria would prove insurmountable, Ewen turned to other projects. However, supporters of the project's continuance redoubled their efforts.

Phase 2: Back to "The Hill"

After research into the sketchy historical records of Lenoir County (the county courthouse burned down twice during the nineteenth century), the descendants, led by Susan Burgess Hoffman, thought they had a handle on who might be buried in the coffins: Lewis Caswell (grandson of governor Richard Caswell) and his wife, Tuscumbia, a Native American. Hoffman, a lineal descendant, was still more than willing to proceed; indeed, she was insistent! So the first criterion for our involvement had been met.

Douglas Owsley, a forensic anthropologist at the Smithsonian's National Museum of Natural History, had examined several other iron coffins (Owsley and Compton, 1997) and was interested in adding two more to his sample. After being informed of our discovery by Hoffman, Owsley contacted Ewen about analyzing the occupants of the caskets.

As in his previous investigations, he would assemble a team of specialists to examine the remains. Thus, the second criterion was satisfied. The dean of the Harriot College of Arts and Sciences, who had compelled Ewen to undertake the original project, agreed to cover the expenses of exhumation and transportation of the coffins, Ewen, and two students to Washington, D.C. Thus ensnared in a trap of his own devising, Ewen undertook the second phase of the project.

On 28 July 2005, within an hour the excavation area was cleared, and the graves were relocated. Unlike the previous project, where we had been forced to hack through a dense root mat, digging through the layer of clean sand with which we had backfilled the graves was easy. The first coffin (NC-2) was extracted using three sets of rope looped beneath the casket and raised by four men on each side. The coffin, although extraordinarily heavy, was removed and secured to a 2-foot by 8-foot sheet of plywood with straps and set on a waiting wheelbarrow. The wheelbarrow was then maneuvered to the parking lot, and the secured coffin was placed in the bed of the lab pickup truck. It should be noted that although heavier than expected, the coffin appeared intact. There were no visible breaches in the exterior and no evidence of leakage.

The second coffin (NC-1) was more deeply buried and in a narrower crypt. Scraps of wood were encountered in the fill, which in 2000 were interpreted as part of the form for building the crypt. However, the wood consisted of relatively thin strips of what appeared to be cedar, probably the remains of the faux rosewood box referred to by Habenstein and Lamers (1962:269) that may have originally encased the casket. The coffin was initially lying partially on its side, and it was much heavier than the first coffin. It had to be tilted further on its side to extract it from the narrow opening but was secured next to the other coffin in the back of the pickup by early afternoon.

Both coffins, although heavy, appeared to be in excellent shape. The 22 bolts securing the coffin halves and the iron plate covering the glass faceplate all appeared intact. Comparison with pictures taken when they were originally exposed in October 2000 showed little deterioration since their first exposure. No fluid was leaking from either of the coffins. Both coffins and their pallets were lashed to the back of the pickup for transport to the Smithsonian.

At the Smithsonian

The coffins were unloaded and weighed at the museum's loading dock. The second coffin reexcavated (NC-1) weighed 517 lbs., much more than would be expected with only a body inside. Although the casket appeared to be intact, a hole was drilled in the bottom half to drain any water that might be present, and it was completely filled with water. After draining, the bolts were drilled out, and the sprue was then ground off with a grinder/cutting blade. The halves were carefully separated with a series of wedges, then removed.

When the coffin was opened, it was discovered that the bones in the coffin had been jumbled around over time. The skull was located at the foot end, and the pelvis was at the head end. Curiously, the faceplate was not broken, and close examination of the inside of the top half of the coffin suggested that the gasket around the faceplate had pulled away from the glass. It appears that the brick crypts had, rather than protecting the coffins, acted as cisterns that retained water that eventually seeped into them.

Decomposition of the soft tissue was nearly complete, although the skeleton was well preserved. A surprising discovery was that a large quantity of hair was present as well as the fingernails of the deceased. These remains are composed primarily of protein and resist decay. The hair had been elaborately styled and held in place with various combs and pins. The bones exhibited evidence of abrasion, probably due to their movement over time in the casket. The abrasions were not fresh and did not appear to be a consequence of transporting the coffins.

Owsley and another forensic anthropologist, Kari Bruwelheide, had assembled an impressive team to examine the remains. Skeletal analysis would be undertaken by Owsley and Bruwelheide with physical anthropologist David Hunt consulting. The soft tissue, had there been any, was to be analyzed by Arthur and Mary Auferderheide and pathologist Larry Cartmell. Tom Goulick was standing by to extract DNA if necessary or possible. Shelly Foote and Beth Eubanks were on hand to examine the burial clothing. Laurie Burgess and Ewen provided archaeological expertise. Rounding out the analytical team were two East Carolina University students, Mattie Rasberry and Tracy Gurnsey, and the chair of the Department of Anthropology, Linda Wolfe. The students were assigned the task of straining the sediment and fluids from the coffins to recover even the smallest remains.

Analysis indicated that the skeleton was that of a woman aged between 35 and 42 with robust limbs, indicating that she was very active and probably right-handed. She appeared to have given birth to at least one child (Owsley et al., 2006:3–7). She had extensive and expensive dental work; several teeth had gold fillings, and a porcelain crown was recovered. Although bones and hair were present, no soft tissue was visible, except for some extremely degraded brain tissue. The hair was dark, wound in a chignon, and held in place with a snood. Artifacts (Figure 3) included hairpins, tortoiseshell hair comb fragments, hairpins, a wedding ring (18-karat gold), and two Prosser-type white buttons, with a terminus post quem of 1840 (Sprague, 2002). The buttons indicated that the woman had been buried only in a nightgown, which had been fastened at the neck.

The coffin was completely emptied, and the dark, fine sediment at the bottom was scooped out and sieved through a fine mesh in an effort to collect everything of interest. It should be noted that none of the sand fill that was used to rebury the coffins was found inside the coffins. Its absence indicated that water had infiltrated the coffins prior to our original investigation in October 2000.

The other coffin (NC-2) was somewhat smaller and weighed only 341 lbs. The experience with the first coffin caused Owsley to order a CT scan, which showed the casket to be half full of water and the bones similarly jumbled. The coffin's midline seal appears to have failed, and water had leaked where the two halves were joined. When opened, the second skeleton was in a condition similar to the first one. The bones were concentrated at the head and foot ends, although the skull was at the head end this time. Again, there was evidence of extensive dental work (i.e., gold fillings) similar to the teeth in the first coffin. Hair was present but not as elaborately styled, and there were no other hair ornaments.

The occupant of the second coffin was determined to be another woman (age 40–49) who was also right-handed. Two large gallstones were recovered, which may have contributed to her death. She also had a herniated disk in her spine. The only artifacts recovered were two white porcelain buttons. Interestingly, rosemary leaves were also present. Rosemary is considered the herb of remembrance and affection (Owsley et al., 2006:7–13).

After completion of the analyses, the skeletons were replaced into the coffin, and the halves were rebolted. They were returned to their crypts and reburied in a ceremony conducted by Reverend A. Michael Singer of St. Mary's Episcopal Church in Kinston.

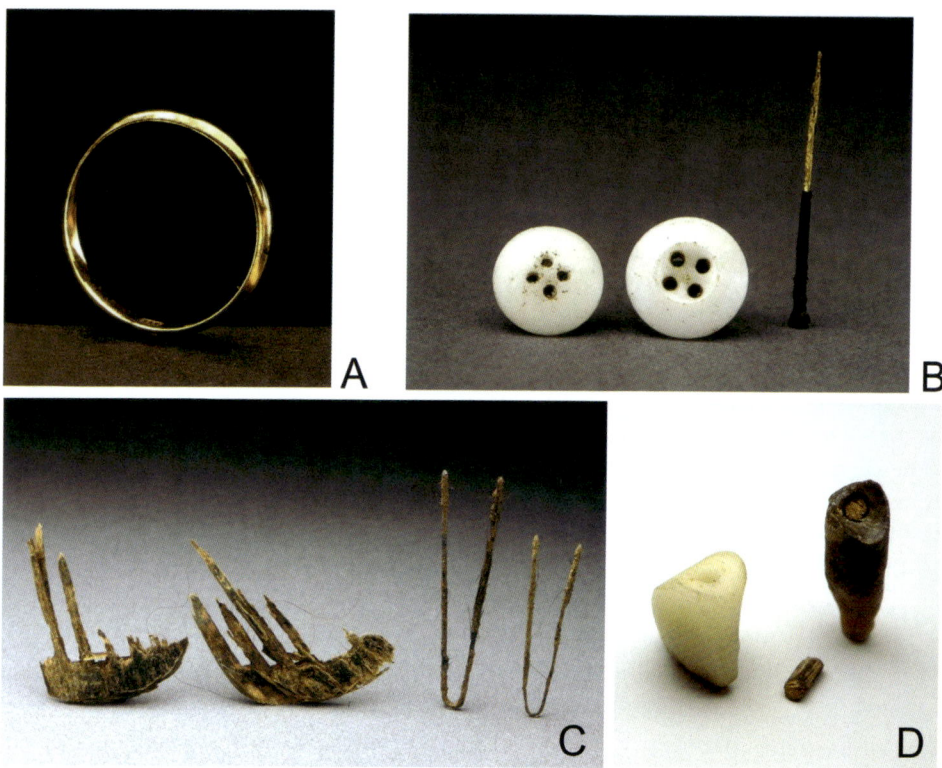

FIGURE 3. Artifacts from the first casket. (A) Gold wedding band. (B) Prosser buttons and straight pin. (C) Hair combs and pins. (D) Porcelain crowns. Photos by authors.

Clearly, Lewis Caswell was not in either of the coffins, but who were the ladies? After extensive genealogical research by local genealogist Martha Marble (personal communication, 2006), who was involved with the project from the outset, the following identifications were proffered. The first burial was a 36 year-old married woman who died shortly after childbirth, tentatively identified as Mrs. Louisa Hernandez Washington, wife of George Washington of Kinston. Born in St. Augustine, Florida, she died on the 12 May 1859. The second burial was a woman in her mid-forties, who may have died of gallstones (identification still pending), but remains unidentified. Both women were wealthy but probably not related, at least by birth. Both died between 1854 and 1864. The project did not end with the reburial of the coffins. New information concerning the location of Richard Caswell's grave surfaced early in 2007. An investigation of the documentation associated with the Caswell cemetery west of Kinston suggests that this was, indeed, the governor's final resting place.

Phase III: The Red House Cemetery

The third phase of the Caswell grave project began with a black-and-white photograph of the Red House cemetery taken by Erastus A. Parker sometime between 1900 and 1914 and currently housed in the North Carolina Museum of History (Alexander, 2007). At that time the graves appear to be on the edge of a partially cleared wooded lot. Written across the bottom of the photograph from left to right are the numbers 1 through 4, which

FIGURE 4. Photograph of the Red House cemetery in Kinston, North Carolina, taken 1900–1914.

correspond to an attached note explaining the numbers (Figure 4). It is believed that a local Kinston historian and genealogist, Sybil Hyatt, wrote the inscription since she donated the photograph to the North Carolina Museum of History (Alexander, 2007).

Number 1, written below an overgrown pile of bricks, marks the grave of Caswell's first wife, Mary Mackilwean Caswell. Richard Caswell's grave is denoted with a number 2, written below a large tree, which according to oral history was the aforementioned oak tree marking his grave. The grave of Caswell's second wife, Sarah Herritage Caswell, is indicated with the number 3 upon the ground. Last, the number 4 is directly below the headstone of Susan Caswell Gatlin, Caswell's daughter. Susan's headstone, although slightly damaged, is still standing at the Red House cemetery (Figure 5A).

Additional historical documents include later historical newspaper accounts, mainly from the mid- to late 1800s, which describe visits to Caswell's grave at the Red House cemetery (*American Advocate*, 1859a, 1859b; *Fayetteville Observer*, 1863; North Carolina Collection Clipping File, n.d.). For example, there is reference to Caswell's burial between his first and second wives, both of whom are presumed to be buried at the Red House cemetery (*American Advocate*, 1859a, 1859b; *Fayetteville Observer*, 1863; Alexander, 2007).

In addition to the similar narratives about the grave's location, the articles exhibit other parallels. For instance, all authors express their distress at finding nothing marking his grave apart from an oak tree that one article explained was "growing from an acorn, accidentally dropped directly at the head of the grave of the first governor" (North Carolina Collection Clipping File, n.d.:802). The belief that Caswell's grave was marked by an oak tree continued into the twentieth and twenty-first centuries, with the 1900–1914 black-and-white photograph of the Red House cemetery showing an oak tree growing over what is marked as Caswell's grave (Alexander, 2007).

Further evidence supporting the Red House cemetery as Caswell's final resting place is found in an 1862 Confederate map, a 1929 land deed, newspaper articles from the

FIGURE 5. Surviving memorials at Vernon Hall. (A) Susan Gatlin's headstone. (B) Base of the current Caswell memorial. Photos by authors.

mid-1950s, a 1954 petition, and a 1955 proposed bill. The Confederate map, depicting the route the troops were to take to Goldsborough, North Carolina, places Caswell's grave near the Atlantic and North Carolina Railroad and the Neuse River in Kinston (O'Reilly et al., 1987).

On 19 June 1929, Rachel L. Brown Watford and her husband, John R. Watford, donated the Red House cemetery to the Moseley-Bright Chapter of the Daughters of the American Revolution. The deed in trust states the land included an oak tree marking the grave of Governor Caswell (Lenoir County Register of Deeds, 1929, book 105:164). Rachel Watford's reason for donating the cemetery was "for patriotic reasons in a desire to share the hallowed ground with the public and to insure its restoration and perpetual care'" (North Carolina Society Daughters of the American Revolution, 1998:191). In the early spring of 2008 at the CSS *Neuse*/Richard Caswell Memorial site in Kinston, North Carolina, the cemetery was spatially oriented with a total station for the subsequent GPR survey. Both the cemetery and the land immediately to the west and south of the cemetery fence line were surveyed in two overlapping grids, one 60 feet by 135 feet and the other 24 feet by 85 feet. Each survey began in the southwest corner of the grid and collected data along a unidirectional south-to-north transect every 3 feet. Because the surviving headstones and footstones indicate an east–west burial pattern, surveying in a north–south direction greatly increased the probability of consistently locating unmarked graves.

All GPR data were analyzed for the detection of anomalies in plan, profile, and slice views with RADAN software. Additionally, the total station and GPR data were combined to gain a fuller understanding of the data and to discern any patterns of anomalies. Typically, historic burial GPR anomalies assume the shape of diffraction hyperbolas (Bevan, 1991; Mellett, 1992; Moore, 2007), and analysis indicated a number of anomalies in the area of interest. Combined with the historical documents, the 1910–1914 photograph, and oral history, the anomalies led researchers to believe there was sufficient evidence for further testing of the area through excavation.

On 18 April 2008, one north–south excavation trench was laid out on the east side of the current Caswell memorial. After topsoil was mechanically stripped and the area was cleaned with hand trowels, three closely aligned grave shafts and one brick grave surface feature aligned east to west appeared (Figure 6A). Taking into account the historical evidence, the second northernmost shaft, believed to be Richard Caswell's, was partially excavated to a depth of approximately 5 feet until water was encountered. A small test pit, approximately 6 inches square and 1 foot deep, was dug into the wet sediments of the grave shaft until we encountered a solid wood plank. A small white rectangular cut stone was located within the fill near the west end of the grave shaft approximately 2 feet below the ground surface.

The small test pit was expanded to further confirm the preservation status of the wood and any human remains, to obtain photographs, and to design a strategy for the future excavation of the entire grave shaft. Two degraded nails and a few rust stains were discovered at the transition between a lighter sandy soil and a darker sandy soil underneath. The darker soil continued within the grave shaft until it met the very well preserved wooden planks approximately 6 feet below the ground surface.

In retrospect, the dark sandy soil and nails appeared to represent the remnants of the top of the coffin, which had decayed beyond preservation. The dark soil may be indicative of decomposed organic matter, such as human remains. The wooden planks were the bottom of the coffin. Given the limited nature of the testing, however, the researchers were prepared for a situation in which the wooden planks were the top of the coffin. If this were the case, any human remains and associated artifacts would have been submerged under the water table and potentially extremely well preserved. A number of conservators were standing by to assist when the remaining grave shaft was excavated.

The final phase of fieldwork occurred over two days, 13 and 14 May 2008. A backhoe removed the soil from the foot of the grave shaft to create a north–south sump trench. A second small white rectangular cut stone was discovered approximately 2.5 feet below the current ground surface while digging the trench at the other end of the shaft. Its location could have indicated either the foot of Caswell's grave or the head of an adjoining grave that was located to the east of Caswell's grave.

Continued excavation yielded a transition between the lighter sandy soil of the grave shaft and the darker sandy soil of the coffin fill and yielded what may have been the wooden coffin lid. The dark sandy soil continued within the grave shaft, taking on the shape of a hexagonal coffin. Directly beneath this dark sandy soil were two wooden planks cut into a six-sided hexagonal coffin (Figure 6B). The coffin was constructed out of two southern yellow pine planks supported by two long rectangular wooden blocks, one at each end of the coffin. The base of the coffin, measuring 6 feet, 3 inches in length, 1 foot, 9 inches in width, and 1 inch in thickness was also accompanied by a long, thin strip of wood on the southern edge, the remainder of one of the sides of the coffin. In total, eight highly degraded nails were discovered both near the edge of the coffin and within the screened soil from the coffin fill. Additionally, a small, cupped iron concretion was discovered within the fill. No human remains were recovered from the grave. All artifacts with the exception of the coffin bottom, which was reburied, were transported to the Department of Anthropology at East Carolina University for further analysis in the Phelps Archaeology Lab.

FIGURE 6. Later phases of excavations at Vernon Hall. (A) Grave shafts after removal of topsoil in April 2008: Susan Caswell Gatlin, Sarah Herritage, Richard Caswell (possible), and Mary Mackilwean Caswell. (B): Planks of coffin bottom revealed in May 2008. Photos by authors.

Although initially discouraging, the lack of skeletal remains did not necessarily preclude the possibility that this was Caswell's grave. The examination of eighteenth-century funeral customs that can directly be related to Caswell's funeral, burial taphonomy, and organic chemistry soil analyses suggested not only that the excavated grave belonged to Richard Caswell but that his body decomposed within the grave.

Caswell was thought to have attended the early Episcopal Christ Church in New Bern, North Carolina, and Caswell's childhood and teenage years were spent in Harford

County, Maryland, a large Quaker area (Alexander, 2007), but details of his beliefs at death are unknown. Deaths frequently occurred within the individual's home, or in Caswell's case a tavern, and it was in the home that the corpse was prepared for burial and subsequent funeral (Geddes, 1981; Larkin, 1988; Sloane, 1991). Preparation of the body by the women of the household or a town or village midwife or nurse included washing, straightening of the limbs, "laying out" or shrouding, and situating the body within a made-to-order coffin (Geddes, 1981; Sloane, 1991). Shrouds, prefabricated from linen or cerecloth, a wax-impregnated unbleached linen, had the appearance of a long dress or shirt and were bound at the head and feet with strips of cloth (Geddes, 1981; Litten, 1991; LeeDecker et al., 1995). Impoverished individuals were often clothed in a winding sheet, a solitary lengthy piece of sheeting fabric (Larkin, 1988).

It was customary in colonial times to utilize the shroud as the sole means of dressing the corpse with no additional clothing (Bybee, 2003; LeeDecker, 2001). However, in seventeenth-century England and in some parts of the New World, the individual may also have worn a shirt, cap, and chin cloth underneath the shroud (Litten, 1991). One of the only documents to refer to a shroud and cap for Caswell is a letter dated 22 November 1789, written by William Blount to William White, a close Caswell family friend. The letter reads in part

> Arants charges £3 for shaving, washing and laying out the Corps. Boyakin £3 for making the Shroud and dressing. Mr McAustin's Bill for Linen for scarfs and Bands, for Ribband to tie the scarfs & Bands and for Cambrick for the Cap of the Shroud and other little Articles must be between £36 and £40. The Price of the Coffin will be from £6 to £8 and the Doctors Bill can't be over £10 that is Cutler's, Ingram and Maclaine attended him as Friends. (Keith, 1952, vol. 1:517–518).

The most common eighteenth-century coffin style found in historic cemeteries across the colonies is the hexagonal flat-lidded coffin that continued to be utilized until the mid- to late nineteenth century (Larkin, 1988; Riordan, 2000, 2009; LeeDecker, 2001; Bromberg and Shephard, 2006). The selection of wood was determined by local availability, preference, and financial standing of the deceased's family members. It has been suggested that pine was preferred for its easy working qualities (Larkin, 1988). Members of higher socio-economic classes could afford burial in lead or metal-clad wood coffins, whereas those at the other end of the financial spectrum commonly used pine for their unadorned coffins (Parrington et al., 1989; Bromberg et al., 2000; LeeDecker, 2001; McKeown and Owsley, 2002). The coffin bottom that was discovered during excavation corresponds well to eighteenth-century customs in that it was hexagonal in shape, but that form was also the norm through most of the nineteenth century. Also, if the coffin did, in fact, belong to Caswell, who died destitute, it is not surprising it was constructed out of pine. In addition to examining eighteenth-century mortuary behavior in an attempt to determine if the excavated grave belong to Richard Caswell we also utilized burial taphonomy and organic chemistry soil analyses to establish if a body decomposed within the grave (Haglund and Sorg, 1997; Connor, 2007). In this case, this type of soil analysis can be used to explain why a skeleton can decompose completely, leaving no observable trace except for a soil silhouette.

One of the primary threats to the preservation of historic period inhumations is water from precipitation, melting snow or ice, or the groundwater table (Henderson, 1987;

Nawrocki, 1995). In all cases of exposure, water hydrolyzes bone collagen proteins into smaller polypeptides. In turn, this causes a breakdown of the mineral-protein bonds, the relationship that is crucial to the integrity of the bone structure, thereby causing deterioration of the skeletal remains. Because of the intermittent nature of rainfall, the amount of damage to the bones it causes is much less than the degradation caused by the water table. Extremely wet burial surroundings, such as the groundwater table, can accelerate skeletal decay, resulting in poor preservation, and can cause total destruction within a few years (Rodriguez, 1997; Forbes, 2008).

Fluctuation of the water table level, causing some or all of the human remains to become waterlogged then dried out, and then waterlogged again can also be skeletally destructive (Bromberg et al., 2000). The fluctuating rise and fall of the water table causes chemical and/or microorganism activity to occur on a more repeated basis, leading to what one researcher has deemed "catastrophic" skeletal disintegration (Hugh Matternes, mortuary archaeologist, New South Associates Inc., personal communication, 2008). Both the fluctuation of the water table and an overall interaction with water were almost certainly the primary cause for the total destruction of Caswell's skeletal remains within the grave.

A covering, such as a shroud, clothing, or coffin, can slow down the rate of decomposition by limiting meso- and microorganisms, insects, and other environmental elements from gaining access to the corpse. Undoubtedly, Caswell's coffin and shroud reduced the rate of decomposition (Keith, 1952, vol. 1). Paradoxically, wooden coffins, which can aid in the overall preservation of the individual, can also be detrimental to preservation. The accumulation of water, moisture, or body decomposition liquids within the coffin can accelerate the decomposition of the submerged remains and of the coffin (Garland and Janaway, 1989; McKeown and Owsley, 2002; Forbes, 2008). Saturated coffin walls and lids, if constructed of wood, increase the moisture content in the enclosed coffin and therefore speed up skeletal degradation (McKeown and Owsley, 2002). Also, if the wood itself is acidic, as in the case of Caswell's pine coffin, it can contribute to skeletal degradation (Matternes, personal communication, 2008).

Clothed individuals buried for an extended period of time in moist, permeable soil in the presence of bacteria typically produce a preservative known as adipocere, or grave wax, a lipid mixture of primarily the fatty acids (palmitic, hydrostearic, stearic, myristic, and oleic), with a waxlike consistency (Evans, 1963; Nawrocki, 1995; Bereuter et al., 1996; Janaway, 1996; Pfeiffer et al., 1998; Forbes et al., 2005; Connor, 2007; Carter and Tibbett, 2008; Forbes, 2008). It is produced by the breakdown of neutral fats into fatty acids in adipose tissue and manifests itself in areas of fatty tissue or lipids on the exterior and internal surfaces of the decomposing individual. Adipocere has been discovered in moist environments; damp, warm, anaerobic environments; dry climates; and cool-water immersion (Garland and Janaway, 1989; Mellen et al., 1993; Forbes et al., 2005).

Not only can soil composition alter the preservation of buried human remains, but it is also altered by the decomposing remains. Bone diagenesis can directly impact the surrounding soil matrix when the remains have decomposed beyond observable existence, as in the excavated grave at the Red House cemetery. This completely decayed organic material, notably phosphorous, produces dark stains or deposits within the grave known as a soil silhouette or pseudomorph (Biek, 1963; Bethell, 1989; Janaway, 1996; Beard et al., 2000; Killam, 2004; Connor, 2007).

The lack of both skeletal material and any soil silhouette within the excavated grave meant that organic chemistry soil analyses were necessary to identify whether a human had decomposed within the grave. The presence of the water table within the grave shaft excluded the more traditional analysis of trace elements in favor a total carbon and total organic carbon ratio analyses and a lipids test, performed under the supervision of Dr. Siddhartha Mitra at East Carolina University's Organic Chemistry Lab and the University of California, Davis, Stable Isotope Facility. Samples were taken from the grave shaft at 70, 130, and 170 cm below the surface (cmbs) of the eastern profile wall and grave soil from approximately 5 feet below the ground surface and from the sump area below the grave at 210 cmbs. The grave soil sample was obtained from the dark sandy soil lying above the wooden coffin planks at a depth approximating 5 feet.

Only recently has grave soil surrounding decomposing human remains, and therefore the presence of carbon and nitrogen isotopes, gained the attention of forensic researchers (Hopkins et al., 2000; Van Nest, 2000; Benninger et al., 2008; Carter and Tibbett, 2008; Forbes, 2008). These isotopes are useful indicators of human remains since, in conjunction with oxygen and hydrogen, they are the most abundant and essential elements for all organic tissue (Sandford, 1993). Also, the organic component of bone is resistant to isotopic exchange during decomposition (Hopkins et al., 2000).

Stable carbon and nitrogen isotope ratios are preserved within organic bone collagen and are represented by $^{13}C/^{12}C$ ($\delta^{13}C$) and $^{15}N/^{14}N$ ($\delta^{15}N$), respectively, and are expressed as delta values in parts per mil (thousand), or ‰ in relation to international standards. Carbon isotopes are measured against the international standard Pee Dee belemnite, and nitrogen is measured against the ambient inhalable reservoir (Cox and Sealy, 1997). These isotopes are a consequence of the individual's dietary protein intake over a period of years (Larsen et al., 1992; Houdek et al., 2000; Privat and O'Connell, 2002; Ambrose et al., 2003; Schulting et al., 2008).

The stable carbon and nitrogen analysis revealed that the soil samples from the shaft above the grave soil had such low organic matter content that they could not be measured. These samples included six total carbon and six total organic carbon samples, one in each category from the eastern profile wall at depths of 70, 130, and 170 cmbs. The low organic matter content in these samples prohibited measurement; however, it does support the hypothesis of a body having decomposed within the grave. In other words, all of the carbon and nitrogen were concentrated in the four grave samples and the four samples from the bottom of the sump trench at 210 cmbs. Total carbon and nitrogen concentrations and mean concentrations were higher than total organic and nitrogen concentrations in all of the 210-cmbs sump trench samples compared to the grave samples, which can probably be attributed to the presence of inorganic carbon and nitrogen in the total carbon and nitrogen samples. Likewise, all 210-cmbs sump trench sample concentration and mean concentration results for total organic carbon and nitrogen displayed an increase over the grave sample concentration results (Figure 7A,B). The increased 210-cmbs results could be due to the trench soil being composed of an impermeable layer of clay, or the water table could have transported isotopes out of the grave soil, not only decreasing the amount of grave soil isotopes but possibly also raising the amount in the trench.

Two grave and four above-grave soil samples were analyzed for the adipocere unsaturated fatty acids (palmitoleic and oleic) and saturated fatty acids (lauric, myristic, palmitic, hydrostearic, and stearic) using gas chromatography combined with mass spectrometry (GC-MS) (Bereuter et al., 1996; Forbes et al., 2005a; Vane and Trick, 2005; Connor, 2007; Carter and Tibbett, 2008). The use of GC-MS is a documented technique for the detection of adipocere in soil associated with decomposing human or animal fat tissue (Forbes et al.,

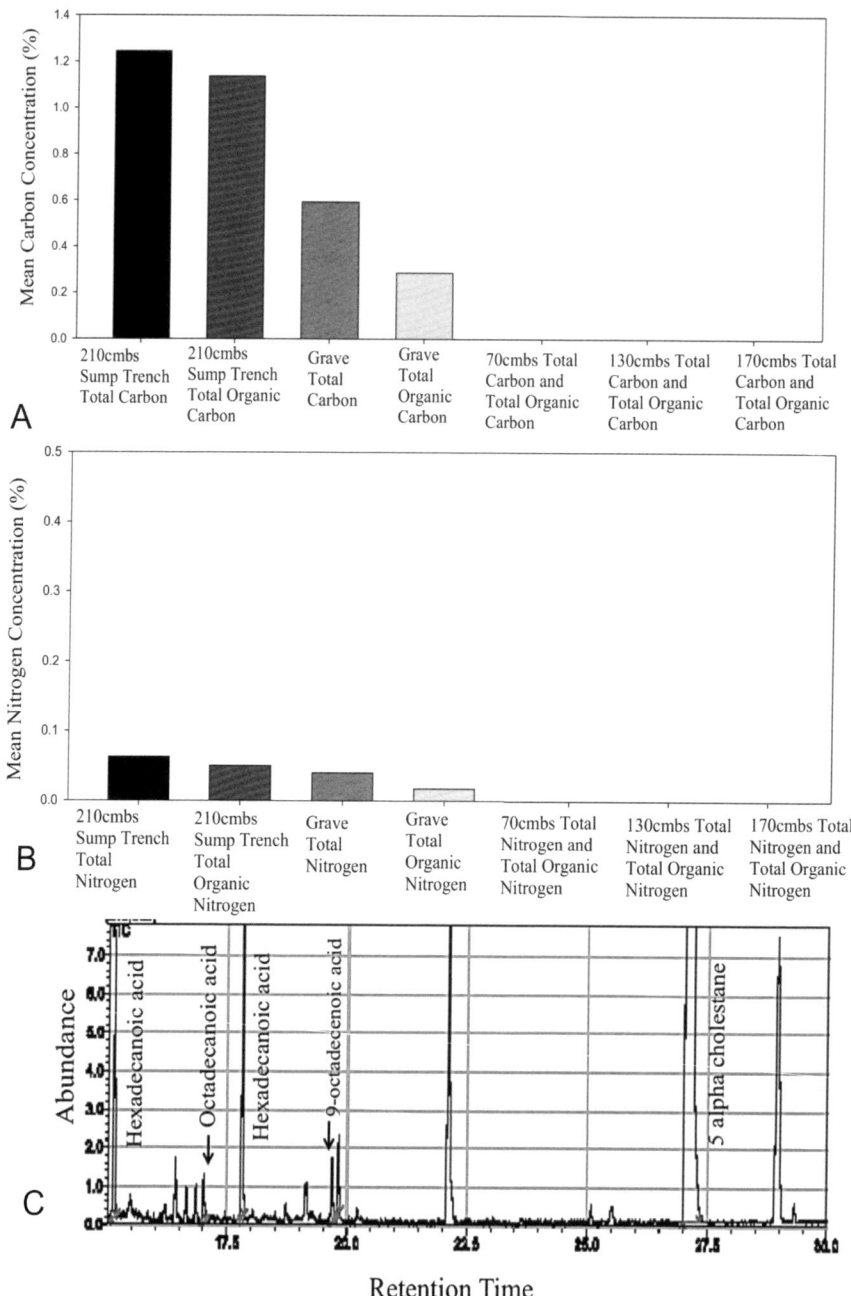

FIGURE 7. Analysis of soils in the grave revealed in May 2008. (A) Mean carbon concentration (%) in soil samples in micrograms. (B) Mean nitrogen concentration (%) in soil samples in micrograms. (C) Total ion chromatograph of sample 24 (grave soil) from a retention time of 15 to 30 minutes.

2002, 2003; Vane and Trick, 2005). The GC-MS detects any fatty acids, both unsaturated and saturated, and displays them (Figure 7C) as peaks in a total ion chromatograph.

The eastern profile wall sample displays palmitic acid, a fatty acid associated with adipocere, but it is also found in the two grave samples. Additional fatty acids found in the grave samples but not in the eastern profile wall samples include octadecanoic acid (stearic acid) and 9-octadecenoic acid (oleic acid). All three fatty acids can be attributed to adipocere from decomposing human remains with confidence because those fatty acids associated with flora, fauna, or fungi would be insignificant at such deep depths (Forbes et al., 2003). Through the application of organic chemistry analyses, specifically stable carbon and nitrogen and a lipids analysis, it was determined with some confidence that a body had decomposed in the grave.

Conclusions

Governor Richard Caswell was a monumental figure within North Carolina's eighteenth-century history whose repose was lost to that history (Figure 5B). The initial fieldwork conclusively demonstrated high-status burials that were not Caswell, although putative identifications can now be proposed following genealogical and archaeological study. The combination of documentary research with geophysical, archaeological, and organic soil chemistry techniques demonstrates that a fully interdisciplinary approach to the study of historic burials can repay great dividends. Our tentative identification of Caswell's grave at the Red House cemetery, using data from many disciplines combined in a sensitive manner, will allow North Carolina to commemorate an individual who figured so highly in its early history. The evidence is enough to bestow Governor Richard Caswell peace at long last.

References

Alexander, C. B. 1946. Richard Caswell's Military and Later Public Services. *North Carolina Historical Review*, 23(3):287–312.

Alexander, C. B. 2007. *The First of Patriots and Best of Men: Richard Caswell in Public Life*. Ed. and annot. W. Keats Sparrow. Kinston, N.C.: Lenoir County Colonial Commission.

Ambrose, S., J. Buikstra, and H. W. Krueger. 2003. Status and Gender Differences in Diet at Mount 72, Cahokia, Revealed by Isotopic Analysis of Bone. *Journal of Anthropological Archaeology*, 22:217–226.

American Advocate. 1859a. Hon. Edward Everett in Newbern. 21 April.

American Advocate. 1859b. "B" Sketches of Eastern North Carolina. 19 May.

Beard, L., J. Hillard, and G. Akridge. 2000. Historical and Chemical Traces of an Ozark Cemetery for Enslaved Africa-Americans: A Study of Silhouette Burials in Benton County, Arkansas. *North American Archaeologist*, 21(4):323–349.

Benninger, L. A., D. O. Carter, and S. L. Forbes. 2008. The Biochemical Alteration of Soil Beneath a Decomposing Carcass. *Forensic Science International*, 180:70–75.

Bereuter, T. L., E. Lorbeer, C. Reiter, H. Seidler, and H. Unterdorfer. 1996. "Post-Mortem Alterations of Human Lipids—Part I: Evaluation of Adipocere Formation and Mummification by Desiccation." In *Human Mummies: A Global Survey of Their Status and the Techniques of Conservation*, ed. K. Sprindler, H. Wilfing, E. Rastbichler-Zissering, D. zur Nedden, and H. Nothdurfter, pp. 265–274. New York: Springer.

Bethell, P. 1989. "Chemical Analysis of Shadow Burials." In *Burial Archaeology: Current Research, Methods, and Developments*, ed. C. A. Roberts, F. Lee, and J. Bintliff, pp. 205–214. BAR British Series 211. Oxford: British Archaeological Reports.

Bevan, B. W. 1991. The Search for Graves. *Geophysics*, 56(9):1310–1319.

Biek, L. 1963. "Soil Silhouettes." In *Science in Archaeology; A Comprehensive Survey of Progress and Research.* ed. D. R. Brothwell and E. Higgs, pp. 118–123. New York: Basic Books.

Bourdas-Smith, S. 2000. Woman Thinks She Found Caswell's Grave Years Ago. *Kinston Free Press*, August.

Bromberg, F. W., and S. J. Shephard. 2006. The Quaker Burying Ground in Alexandria, Virginia: A Study of Burial Practices of the Religious Society of Friends. *Historical Archaeology,* 40(1):57–88.

Bromberg, F. W., S. J. Shephard, B. H. Magid, P. J. Cressy, T. Dennee, and B. K. Means. 2000. *"To Find Rest from All Trouble": The Archaeology of the Quaker Burying Ground, Alexandria, Virginia.* Alexandria, Va.: Alexandria Archaeology, Office of Historic Alexandria.

Bybee, A. 2003. "Bioanthropological Investigations of Historic Cemeteries: What Can We Learn from Biological, Cultural, and Mortuary Remains?" Paper presented at the 5th Annual Council for West Virginia Archeology Spring Workshop, Charleston, W.Va.

Carter, D. O., and M. Tibbett. 2008. "Cadaver Decomposition and Soil: Processes." In *Soil Analysis in Forensic Taphonomy: Chemical and Biological Effects of Buried Remains,* ed. M. Tibbett and D. O. Carter, pp. 203–223. Boca Raton, Fla.: CRC Press.

Connor, M. 2007. *Forensic Methods: Excavation for the Archaeologist and the Investigator.* Lanham, Md.: Altamira Press.

Cox, G., and J. Sealy. 1997. Investigating Identity and Life Histories: Isotopic Analysis and Historical Documentation of Slave Skeletons Found on the Cape Town Foreshore, South Africa. *International Journal of Historical Archaeology,* 1(3):207–224.

Evans, W. E. D. 1963. *The Chemistry of Death.* Springfield, Ill.: Charles Thomas.

Fayetteville Observer. 1863. "From the North Carolina Soldiers." Correspondence of the Fayetteville Observer. March.

Fletcher, I. n.d. Life, Character, Services, and Death of Richard Caswell, First Governor of North Carolina under the Constitution. Manuscript, collection 21, Inglis Fletcher Papers. East Carolina Manuscript Collection, J. Y. Joyner Library, East Carolina University, Greenville, N.C.

Forbes, S. L. 2008. "Decomposition Chemistry in a Burial Environment." In *Soil Analysis in Forensic Taphonomy: Chemical and Biological Effects of Buried Remains,* ed. M. Tibbett and D. O. Carter, pp. 203–223. Boca Raton, Fla.: CRC Press.

Forbes, S. L., J. Keegan, B. H. Stuart, and B. B. Dent. 2003. A Gas Chromatography-Mass Spectrometry Method for the Detection of Adipocere in Grave Soils. *European Journal of Lipid Science and Technology,* 105(12):761–768.

Forbes, S. L., B. H. Stuart, and B. B. Dent. 2002. The Identification of Adipocere in Grave Soils. *Forensic Science International,* 127:225–230.

Forbes, S. L., B. H. Stuart, and B. B. Dent. 2005. The Effect of Burial Environment of Adipocere Formation. *Forensic Science International,* 152:24–34.

Garland, A. N., and R. C. Janaway. 1989. "The Taphonomy of Inhumation Burials." In *Burial Archaeology: Current Research, Methods, and Developments,* ed. C. Roberts, F. Lee, and J. Bintliff, pp. 82–127. BAR British Series 211. Oxford: British Archaeological Reports.

Geddes, G. E. 1981. *Welcome Joy: Death in Puritan New England.* Ann Arbor, Mich.: University Microfilms International.

Habenstein, R. W., and W. M. Lamers. 1962. *History of American Funeral Directing.* Milwaukee, Wisc.: National Funeral Directors Association of the United States.

Haglund, W. D., and M. H. Sorg. 1997. "Method and Theory for Forensic Taphonomy Research." In *Forensic Taphonomy: The Postmortem Fate of Human Remains,* ed. W. D. Haglund and M. H. Sorg, pp. 13–26. Boca Raton, Fla: CRC Press.

Henderson, J. 1987. "Factors Determining the State of Preservation of Human Remains." In *Death, Decay, and Reconstruction: Approaches to Archaeology and Forensic Science*, ed. A. Boddington, A. Garland, and R. Janaway, pp. 43–54. Manchester: Manchester University Press.

Hopkins, D. W., P. E. J. Wiltshire, and B. D. Turner. 2000. Microbial Characteristics of Soil from Graves: An Investigation at the Interface of Soil Microbiology and Forensic Science. *Applied Soil Ecology*, 14:283–288.

Houdek, D., J. E. Buikstra, and C. Stojanowski. 2000. "Osteological Analysis." In *Never Anything So Solemn: An Archaeological, Biological, and Historical Investigation of the Nineteenth-Century Grafton Cemetery*, ed. J. E. Buikstra, J. A. O'Gorman, and C. Sutton, pp. 91–114. Kampsville Studies in Archaeology and History 3. Kampsville, Ill.: Center for American Archeology.

Janaway, R. C. 1996. "The Decay of Buried Human Remains and Their Associated Artifacts." In *Studies in Crime: An Introduction to Forensic Archaeology*, ed. J. Hunter, C. Roberts, and A. Martin, pp. 58–85. New York: Routledge.

Keith, A., ed. 1952. *The John Gray Blount Papers*. Raleigh, N.C.: State Department of Archives and History.

Killam, E. W. 2004. *The Detection of Human Remains*. 2nd ed. Springfield, Ill.: Charles C. Thomas.

Larkin, J. 1988. *The Reshaping of Everyday Life: 1790–1840*. New York: Harper and Row.

Larsen, C. S., M. J. Schoeninger, N. J. van der Merwe, K. M. Moore, and J. A. Lee-Thorp. 1992. Carbon and Nitrogen Stable Isotope Signatures of Human Dietary Change in the Georgia Bight. *American Journal of Physical Anthropology*, 89(2):197–214.

LeeDecker, C. 2001. The Coffin Maker's Craft: Treatment of the Dead in Rural Eighteenth Century Delaware. *Journal of Middle Atlantic Archaeology*, 17:1–14.

LeeDecker, C. H., J. Bloom, I. Wuebber, and M.-L. Pipes. 1995. *Final Archaeological Excavations at a Late 18th-Century Family Cemetery for the U.S. Route 113 Dualization, Milford to Georgetown, Sussex County, Delaware*. With K. R. Rosenberg. DelDOT Archaeology Series 134. Dover: Delaware Department of Transportation.

Lenoir County Register of Deeds. 1929. John R. and Rachel L. Brown Watford to the Moseley-Bright Chapter of the Daughters of the American Revolution of Kinston. Deed in Trust. Book 105:164.

Litten, J. 1991. *The English Way of Death: The Common Funeral Since 1450*. London: R. Hale.

McKeown, A., and D. Owsley. 2002. In Situ Documentation of Historic Period Burials for Bioarchaeology. *Journal of Middle Atlantic Archaeology*, 18:77–95.

Mellen, P. F. M., M. Lowry, and M. S. Micozzi. 1993. Experimental Observations on Adipocere Formation. *Journal of Forensic Sciences*, 38(1):91–93.

Mellett, J. S. 1992. "Location of Human Remains with Ground-Penetrating Radar." Paper presented at the Fourth International Conference on Ground Penetrating Radar, Rovaniemi, Finland, 8–13 June.

Moore, C. R. 2007. Ground Penetrating Radar Investigations of an Historic Unmarked Cemetery in Boone, North Carolina. Unpublished paper, presented to Dr. Thomas R. Whyte, Department of Anthropology, Appalachian State University, Boone, N.C., 16 August.

Nawrocki, S. P. 1995. "Taphonomic Processes in Historic Cemeteries." In *Bodies of Evidence: Reconstructing History through Skeletal* Analysis, ed. A. L. Grauer, pp. 49–66. New York: Wiley & Son.

North Carolina Collection Clipping File. n.d. Joyner Library, East Carolina University.

North Carolina Society Daughters of the American Revolution. 1998. *North Carolina Society Daughters of the American Revolution, Inc: The First One Hundred Years, 1898–1998*. Monroe: North Carolina Society Daughters of the American Revolution.

O'Reilly, N., D. C. Bosse, and R. W. Karrow Jr. 1987. *Civil War Maps: A Graphic Index to the Atlas to Accompany the Official Records of the Union and Confederate Armies.* Chicago: Newberry Library.

Owsley, D., K. Bruwelheidi, S. Foote, A. Aufderheidi, C. Cartmell, and L. Burgess. 2006. North Carolina Iron Coffin Notes. Manuscript on file. Washington, D.C.: Smithsonian Institution, National Museum of Natural History, Department of Anthropology.

Owsley, D., and B. Compton. 1997. "Preservation in Late-Nineteenth-Century Iron Coffin Burials." In *Forensic Taphonomy: Post Mortem Fate of Human Remains,* ed. W.D. Haglund and M. H. Sorg, pp. 511–526. Boca Raton, Fla.: CRC Press.

Parrington, M., D. G. Roberts, S. A. Pinter, and J. C. Wideman. 1989. The First African American Baptist Church Cemetery: Bioarchaeology, Demography, and Acculturation of Early Nineteenth Century Blacks. 3 vols. Report submitted to the Redevelopment Authority of the City of Philadelphia. West Chester, Pa.: John Milner Associates.

Pfeiffer, S., S. Milne, and R. M. Stevenson. 1998. The Natural Decomposition of Adipocere. *Journal of Forensic Sciences,* 43(2):368–370.

Privat, K. L., and T. C. O'Connell. 2002. Stable Isotope Analysis of Human and Faunal Remains from the Anglo-Saxon Cemetery at Berinsfield, Oxfordshire: Dietary and Social Implications. *Journal of Archaeological Science,* 29:779–790.

Riordan, T. B. 2000. *Dig a Grave Both Wide and Deep: An Archaeological Investigation of Mortuary Practices in the 17th-Century Cemetery at St. Mary's City, Maryland.* St. Mary's City Archaeology Series 3. St. Mary's City, Md.: Historic St. Mary's City.

Riordan, T. B. 2009. "Carry Me to You Kirk Yard": An Investigation of Changing Burial Practices in the Seventeenth-Century Cemetery at St. Mary's City, Maryland. *Historical Archaeology,* 43(1):81–92.

Rodriguez, W. C. 1997. "Decomposition of Buried and Submerged Bodies." In *Forensic Taphonomy: The Postmortem Fate of Human Remains,* ed. W. D. Haglund and M. H. Sorg, pp. 13–26. Boca Raton, Fla.: CRC Press.

Sampley, T. 1999. Richard Caswell's Grave. Searching for Richard Caswell's Grave: The Evidence. *Olde Kinston Gazette,* March. http://ncccha.blogspot.co.uk/2007/10/richard-caswells-grave.html (accessed 10 August 2016).

Sandford, M. K. 1993. "Understanding the Biogenic-Diagenetic Continuum: Interpreting Elemental Concentrations of Archaeological Bone." In *Investigations of Ancient Human Tissue: Chemical Analyses in Anthropology,* ed. M. K. Sandford, pp. 3–57. Langhorne, Pa.: Gordon and Breach.

Schulting, R. J., S. M. Blockley, H. Bocherens, D. Drucker, and M. Richards. 2008. Stable Carbon and Nitrogen Isotope Analysis on Human Remains from the Early Mesolithic Site of La Vergne (Charente-Maritime, France). *Journal of Archaeological Science,* 35:763–772.

Sloane, D. C. 1991. *The Last Great Necessity: Cemeteries in American History.* Baltimore: Johns Hopkins University Press.

Sprague, R. 2002. China or Prosser Button Identification and Dating. *Historical Archaeology,* 36(2):111–127.

Vane, C. H., and J. K. Trick. 2005. Evidence of Adipocere in a Burial Pit from the Foot and Mouth Epidemic of 1967 Using Gas Chromatography-Mass Spectrometry. *Forensic Science International,* 154:19–23.

Van Nest, J. 2000. "A Report on the Analysis of Soil Samples from the Historic Grafton Cemetery Site, Jersey County, Illinois." In *Never Anything So Solemn: An Archaeological, Biological, and Historical Investigation of the Nineteenth-Century Grafton Cemetery,* ed. J. E. Buikstra, J. A. O'Gorman, and C. Sutton, pp. 91–114. Kampsville Studies in Archaeology and History 3. Kampsville, Ill.: Center for American Archeology.

Conclusions

CHAPTER 15

Where Now? Future Agendas in Historic Mortuary Culture Studies

Harold Mytum and Laurie Burgess

The chapters in this volume reveal how far the subject of mortuary culture studies has developed since the early work of Litten (1991) and Reeve and Adams (1993) in Britain, and Hacker-Norton and Trinkley (1985), Garrow (1987), and Bell (1990) in North America. It is clear, however, that there is also much still to do, and many of the issues are similar whether in America, Australia, or the British Isles. It is therefore useful to review the major challenges both to the practice of mortuary archaeology, which considers the cultural aspects of historic communities, and to the exciting new interpretive directions that our existing and expanded data could allow. These initiatives would contribute to our wider understanding within historical archaeology and, indeed, form part of an interdisciplinary understanding of historic death ways. That the cultural materials we study can so often be linked directly to particular communities, families, and, often, specific named individuals and their remains provides unique opportunities for highly contextualized analysis.

Various constraints have thus far impeded appreciation of cultural mortuary data beyond a restricted group of researchers, most of whom are represented in this volume. Integration within wider archaeological, anthropological, and historical debates should be the ambition in the next phase of research. The purpose of this chapter is to indicate some of the potential developments, considering first data collection in the field, which will assist in the second—the creation of more robust, representative, and accessible data sets. The ultimate ambitions are interpretive; they can immediately move on from the state of the art as expressed here, but they can be more powerful and extensive if an enhanced resource base is created during the numerous, although often opportunistic, fieldwork interventions.

Policies and Practices in Data Collection in the Field

Although there are important professional statements regarding the excavation, treatment, storage, and reinterment of human remains (Advisory Panel on the Archaeology of Burials in England, 2013), at least in Britain (there is nothing comparable in the United States), there has been far less attention paid to standards and methodologies for the recording of artifacts associated with historic burials. A similar lack of protocols applies to sampling procedures for retention of whole or fragments of artifacts. A number of contractors have developed their own recording procedures, but it would be desirable for the various professional archaeological bodies to set standards in this regard, recognizing that some burial clearance operations are largely outside the control of heritage professionals. However, the existence of such professionally accredited method statements would strengthen provision of archaeological conditions on the cultural dimension of exhumation and also assist in the planning of such work to limit any impediments to clearance logistics. Agreed recording protocols with varying scales of detail, from minimum to ideal, can match external circumstances, and advice on techniques to be applied will create data sets that will be to known standards, which will enable comparison and also contribute to the combined data available for comparative study.

Curation policies for coffin hardware have never been developed, in part because in many cases the prospect of retention has not even been considered. However, there is now sufficient experience of dealing with the often fragile state of such items that advice could be produced to indicate what can be sensibly retained and what requires field recording but cannot be conserved in the long term. This should apply not only to individual items of hardware but also to sampling or retention of coffin wood and textiles, as well as the relatively rare but steadily noted associated artifacts such as coins, buttons, ceramics, and other personal items found within the coffins.

Nondestructive investigation of burial grounds and vaults forms part of existing fieldwork but could be encouraged. Geophysical survey, notably magnetometry, has been successful in North America in locating interments and can be used to differentiate and locate those with iron coffins or large amounts of coffin furniture (King et al., 1993). Vaults and brick-lined shafts can also be located by this method but may also be identified using resistivity (Ellwood, 1990) or ground-penetrating radar (Bevan, 1991; Conyers, 2006). Although geophysical survey still cannot confidently identify the full extent of historic cemeteries, as some backfilled earth-dug graves are so similar in their characteristics to undisturbed subsoil that they can be hard to identify even with excavation, it can provide a minimum extent and density and should be used more frequently. Unfortunately, in long-lived churchyard situations in Britain, only shafts and vaults can often be located, although ground-penetrating radar has been successfully used in church interiors, and recent fieldwork in external graveyard areas without intense historic reuse have produced promising results (Hansen et al., 2014).

One of the main components of mortuary investment was the construction of spaces in which to safely house coffins. The investigation of burial shafts, crypts, and family vaults has already produced important assemblages of well-preserved cultural remains, and these areas should continue to be targeted (Figure 1). This type of investigation could take place not only when development poses a threat but also when access can be granted for noninterventionist recording and study. Litten (1999, 2009) has demonstrated that mere visual examination and recording can be extremely informative. Earth graves can provide excellent data on coffin forms and decoration, but only in the most benign of soil conditions; the unpredictability of the data quality makes these important assemblages hard to recover efficiently. The challenge of obtaining earth grave samples, which reflect wider sections of society, remains dependent upon opportunities during development and burial clearance that can be seized by having the necessary recovery protocols designed and ready to be implemented when necessary.

The range of vault and shaft construction designs has been considered in only a few locations, and given that they are probably dependent on local building traditions and materials, they should reveal significant spatial variation over both time and space. This regionality is visible in church building and in burial monuments, so it would be informative

FIGURE 1. Neatly maintained barrel vault, Congressional Cemetery, Washington, D.C., with an iron coffin to the left of the steps. Photo by Laurie Burgess, courtesy of Smithsonian Institution.

to add the belowground structures to the evidence base. Understanding the structural characteristics of these voids is also important in building conservation and would contribute to solving problems such as building subsidence and damp. Mortsafes and other structural components such as aboveground mausoleums are intimately linked to interments, and how they relate to belowground data requires further consideration. The investment in all aspects of the mortuary process—from mourning jewelry and clothing and funerary meals, through the coffin, its fittings, and contents, to the grave structure, setting, and, finally, any commemorative monument—should be considered as a whole. Past actors decided how to apportion resources at various stages of the grieving process to these socially and emotionally important investments, and the more stages we can consider, the more robust our conclusions will be.

The speed with which many fieldwork operations have to be conducted should be addressed in part by developing new techniques of data recovery. It would be beneficial if commercial projects could collaborate with researchers in the development of on-site recording regarding both improved protocols and the use of innovative equipment. There is clear potential for the use of portable X-ray equipment, reflectance transformation imaging, and physical sampling of coffin furniture for later chemical analysis of materials and study of the manufacturing process, as well as having the recording protocols on handheld devices so data can be input electronically in the field. The relationships between contractors and researchers need to be developed ahead of any potential project, so that the collaboration can be planned into the project design without impeding completion on time and within budget. This collaboration could also enable experimentation within the inevitable health and safety constraints often at the fore in projects associated with historic human remains.

Providing a Robust Data Set

The provision of effective protocols and the development of collaborative teams and research designs can incorporate the wide range of necessary recording and analytical methods. This enhancement of practice should all help to create more comprehensive and defined data sets, as indicated by the example of coffin hinges outlined by Sprague (this volume). At a higher level, however, there are clear biases in our samples. For some periods and regions, such as for eighteenth-century middle-class London or the seventeenth-century Chesapeake, relatively sophisticated questions may now be tackled. In contrast, for most regions and periods there are, at present, no or too little data to make any generalizing statements. Some of these lacunae can be easily identified and can be considered first geographically and socially and then chronologically. These samples will not often be available through planned research investigations, but in response to calls for mitigation strategies in advance of development. Given the relatively short time scales often involved and also the need to educate heritage managers so that the potential of such sites can be built into the planning control process, it is incumbent on those of us with an interest and understanding of the potential of mortuary data to have set out in advance what is required for greater understanding and how that can be obtained. Only then can the appropriate conditions be placed on any archaeological intervention. In England, Historic England's revision of their regional research framework documents provides an opportunity for this relevant data collection to be stated, but how this can be done varies greatly according to legislative, funding, and cultural factors.

Geographical and Social Spread

In Britain, the intensity of London's development, combined with the increased social outreach of its inner-city churches, has led to the destruction of a significant number of historic burial contexts. In recent years this has increasingly been at least in part mitigated by archaeological interventions. City churches have taken on social roles such as supporting the homeless and, in order to maintain their existing liturgical roles in their buildings, have often converted their underground crypts from repositories for the dead to resources for the living. In addition, many burial grounds that were either in institutional grounds or already built over have been redeveloped, and clearance has been necessary with the more substantial belowground impact of modern construction, whether for buildings or infrastructure.

There is now a formidable assemblage of data available regarding the London dead (Figure 2), but in contrast, other cities have experienced few or even no major projects of this kind, with small-scale work far more common. In one respect this is positive, in that the resource remains undisturbed, but it is also the case that the high expense of archaeological removal and study is such that only those London sites with prime land values allow archaeological strategies to be fully employed. Elsewhere, work is either limited because of expense or is avoided by development being placed in less costly locations. The result is that our understanding of the geographical spread of funerary customs, styles, and practices is extremely limited, with only a few relatively small urban assemblages and a restricted number of small town and rural populations having been investigated. Some of these have revealed highly important data, notably the various Quaker and other nonconformist burial grounds, but there are still not enough data to separate out regional from

FIGURE 2. Examples of breastplates from early nineteenth-century middle-class graves, St. Pancras, London. Copyright HS1 Ltd/Ramboll UK Limited.

denominational preferences confidently (bearing in mind also class, chronology, and differential preservation). The existing assemblages are insufficient to consider in detail regional, urban versus rural, class, or religious variation. There are some indications of sexual distinctions regarding a few items of coffin fittings (see Loe and Boston, this volume), but this finding requires further investigation with larger samples to be conclusive.

The North American situation is also geographically constrained, with some cities such as New York, Philadelphia, and Dallas having a few substantial excavated assemblages, but they are insufficient for wider comparative analysis of urban patterns. The same issues of land values and intensity of development, particularly in older cities with more abandoned and often already built-over burial grounds, apply as much to some East Coast cities as to London, but in North America burial clearance of cemeteries has generally been a far more frequent occurrence than in Britain. The importance of including an archaeological dimension to clearance needs to be emphasized in the development control process on private city locations.

Rural burial data are often recovered from farmstead and small, now abandoned community cemeteries in the face of government infrastructure schemes. In North America many rural cemeteries, especially family cemeteries, are characterized by "low archaeological visibility," with graves that are no longer marked. Their excavation can provide valuable information on rural lifeways (LeeDecker et al., 1995:124). Unlike that of their urban counterparts, where the excellent preservation of the contents of elite vaults and mausoleums can provide information on social strata, the excavations of rural cemeteries, on a regional or broader level, could help balance our understanding of death ways across wider segments of society. There are indications that denomination might affect choice of coffin fittings (most notably identified thus far for Roman Catholics); this finding clearly requires further exploration.

Perhaps reflecting greater archaeological interest but also possibly revealing how such modern development is differentially planned across the continent, more published and accessible gray literature reports seem to detail investigations in the South and southeast than in the Midwest or the West. In North America in general, a wealth of burial information is likely contained in gray literature, which, in the case of reports deriving from contract archaeology, also referred to as cultural resource management in the United States, is generally not in the public domain in the interest of protecting sites. However, each state's State Historic Preservation Office generally maintains a library of archaeological reports for their state. The largest body of citations for reports is housed online at the Digital Archaeological Record (tDAR), which incorporated the National Park Service's National Archeological Database with over 300,000 report citations; tDAR is overseen by Digital Antiquity, a group of universities and organizations dedicated to tDAR's long-term support. For Britain, the Archaeological Data Service at the Department of Archaeology, University of York, holds the online Library of Unpublished of Fieldwork Reports, which contains over 38,000 reports, with more being added. Notably, full PDFs of reports are available. Gray literature represents a significant and relatively untapped data source to help frame and answer broader questions about death ways on both sides of the Atlantic.

In all cases, however, given the areas involved, the total amount of recovered evidence is geographically very thin, and where present, it is difficult to generalize on a spatial level. Numerous ethnic identities are represented in the style and content of commemorative monuments (Meyer, 1993), but how far this also applied to coffin design and choice of hardware is not known. Separating ethnicity and religious affiliation might be difficult in some cases, but these various aspects of identity and influences on cultural practice are well worth teasing out.

In both Britain and North America the industrial production of coffin hardware was concentrated in relatively few centers and distributed through choices made from catalogs (Figure 3) and then delivered by the ever-increasing railway network (Springate, 2015; Mytum, 2016). In that regard the patchy geographical representation might be seen as irrelevant, but it is in the combination of availability through catalogs and their relative popularity in purchase and use that geographic and social factors came into play. These regional trends in consumer choice have yet to be addressed, and only further data sets will enable them to be considered. It is important, therefore, that the potential of new coffin assemblages (and, indeed, forms of burial structure such as vaults) be emphasized in any project designs. These sample selections all have implications regarding regional and local identities, practices, and attitudes, even if many of the components used to create such funerary repertoires were mass-produced.

Chronological Spread

Contemporary attitudes toward the dead affect what excavations might take place, and in North America now abandoned burial grounds of some of the earliest European settlers feed into a set of pioneering nationalist tropes that facilitate their investigation. Notably, these investigations have been at early sites of English origin, as opposed to equally early sites of Spanish origin, like Santa Fe or St. Augustine, since the history of English settlements played into the narrative of the dominant culture in North America for the past several centuries as well as today. For this reason, there have been relatively more investigations—often with a high research component—in such contexts in states such as

FIGURE 3. The Beaumont fittings set in the Ingal, Parsons Clive & Company catalog, the major UK supplier at the turn of the twentieth century. Courtesy of the Beamish Museum.

Virginia and Maryland. Postemancipation to early twentieth-century rural burial grounds in the South have often been subject to clearance and investigation during development, although in these cases often because of poor official documentation or assigning low cultural significance by planning authorities rather than archaeologists' priorities. In contrast, eighteenth- and earlier nineteenth-century burials have not attracted such attention, and although some notable urban assemblages have been recovered, generally, they are proportionally less well represented. In particular, crypt and vault burials of this period, where intact coffins with all their fittings and relatively well preserved human and material contents are available for study, have rarely been investigated. The result is that the early period when coffins were less adorned and most were placed in earth graves is relatively well understood, but the next century and beyond has insufficient samples to assess the popularity and range of coffin hardware, coffin types, and other aspects of funerary rituals and practices. For part of this period catalogs indicate what was available but not what was selected. In the later nineteenth and twentieth centuries the combination of catalog and excavated data has produced a rich and highly contextualized opportunity for research, analysis, and interpretation (see Trinkley and Hacker, this volume; Pye, this volume).

The British situation is paradoxically almost the reverse of that in North America. Intact seventeenth-century burials in large numbers have not been recovered, mainly because churchyards where they were placed have been overburied for many generations, and in the later eighteenth and nineteenth centuries graves were dug deeper than previously, thus increasing the degree of disturbance even though ground levels gradually rose in intensively used burial grounds. At present the best evidence for British earth burial practices comes from the Chesapeake! For the eighteenth and early nineteenth centuries, however, a large amount of data, including substantial assemblages from both communal church crypts and family vaults, has been recovered in the last three decades. From the middle of the nineteenth century, however, burial within churches and their crypts was no longer possible except in a few family vaults, and urban graveyards were closed. Interment shifted to newly established cemeteries, and these burial locations are rarely available for excavation. Small-scale development around rural churches, such as with additions of toilets and parish rooms, can lead to the recovery of small numbers of later nineteenth- and early twentieth-century burials. However, these are rare as development is designed, where possible, to leave them in situ. Only the relatively small number of catalogs known from this period indicate what was on offer.

In arguing for investment in archaeological mitigation and analysis, these chronological biases need to be borne in mind, alongside regional and social factors. Gradually, the chronological range of coffin hardware use is becoming clear, but the creation of online resources—both digitally available catalogs from producers on both sides of the Atlantic and typologies of excavated artifacts and burial assemblages—will assist in the dissemination of existing knowledge and its expansion and refinement. Integration of already recovered data now languishing in gray literature across the globe would be an essential part of this process. The creation of an online database similar to the highly successful Digital Archaeological Archive of Comparative Slavery, a collaboration between archaeologists and a range of institutions with funding from the Mellon Foundation and others, would provide a way to make both the scholarly and gray literature data broadly accessible.

Research Questions

Collecting data may be all that is possible in some of the rushed and underfunded mitigation situations, but the accumulated data can be used to study important cultural questions relevant not only to historical archaeology but also to the wider fields of anthropological, sociological, historical and thanatological research. Systematic data collection should enable researchers and those on large well-funded development-inspired projects to integrate data sets with highly contextualized and often closely dated and personalized assemblages. Some suggestions are offered here of the types of research issues that could be addressed; using mortuary data should also be promoted alongside other types of information in the investigation of wider cultural questions linked to the themes of gender, class, and identity and to cultural change brought about by industrialization, secularization, and changes in attitude to the body.

Style

Coffin fittings were produced by manufacturers making many other items for domestic and industrial use, so aspects of their style naturally sat within the broad aesthetic preferences of the time. However, particular motifs and themes may relate to the function of the items, which has been considered more for commemorative monuments than for coffin furniture (Mytum, 2004). Memorials have often been thought to have a significant religious element in their symbolism and their textual content, although some motifs such as cherubs could have obtained their popularity as much because of wider cultural preferences as ideological ones (Heinrich, 2014). However, motifs can carry more than one meaning at once, so fashionable choices could still convey other implications. Springate (2015) notes that the relationship between above- and belowground styles deserves further consideration, and a long-running investigation in Britain has produced preliminary results (Mytum, "Explaining Stylistic Change in Mortuary Material Culture," this volume). Despite similarities in style and symbolic content across the range of mortuary and commemorative material culture, the coffin fittings were far more conservative, whereas monuments were more susceptible to change. The subject requires further investigation even in Britain, although obtaining comparative samples of sufficient size in terms of date, region, and social status is not easy. The issue has not yet been addressed in any detail in North America.

Clear changes in style of fittings, their arrangement on the coffin, and the shape and surface treatment of the coffin occur over time, as indicated by many chapters here. How these changes interrelated and whether coffins had sets as sold in catalogs or partial or mixed sets require further study. The catalogs often show a variety of styles available at any one time; the trends of selection require further analysis. The order and coherence of sets of coffin fittings seen in catalogs may not be replicated on actual coffins; indeed, there is evidence of some coffins having very mixed collections of items, not the sets as illustrated in print.

The ways in which style operates on coffin furniture in relation to wider taste and symbolism in society have, as yet, received limited attention. Mytum notes the conservatism of coffin fitting styles compared with those of memorials, but otherwise, the material is seen as an isolated phenomenon. Memorials have been placed within the wider trends of architectural revivals—classical, Gothic, Egyptian—although most focus has been on the larger monuments. These styles, together with art nouveau, art deco, modernism, and brutalism, all may be relevant to shaping popular taste, which, perhaps largely unconsciously, influences changes in coffin fitting styles, combined with the form and finish of the coffin or casket. In addition, religious affiliation may be relevant; crucifixes were manufactured for Roman Catholics (Figure 4), and other patterns of choice may be manifested among various denominations, as has been demonstrated for aboveground memorials. Mortuary studies must begin to integrate more fully with the wider dialogues of archaeology, anthropology, and cultural history, rather than be an inward-looking archaeological specialism alone, and in the case of study of style this is particularly important.

Craft and Industry

The study of mortuary culture offers insights into a range of craft and industrial practices, some of which were dedicated to the funerary trade but many of which were part of a wider portfolio of production or service provision. As the undertaking industry became more specialized and as the treatment of the corpse moved from the deceased's abode to the funeral home, the social and body treatment practices, material culture used, and the wider meanings of the preburial stages of the funeral all changed in significant ways. The material evidence recovered archaeologically can be highly informative with regard to body treatment and viewing and what was placed within the coffin. Body treatment can be discerned in some cases, although it is clear that body position can be highly influenced by taphonomic processes, which can lead many parts of the body to move. This consideration

FIGURE 4. Crucifix lid motif on the coffin of Elizabeth O'Bryan, died 1806, aged 70. St. Pancras, London. Copyright HS1 Ltd/Ramboll UK Limited.

of post-depositional processes, including bodily decay and movement of skeletal parts, in itself requires study to understand what might indicate past cultural practices and what is caused by decay processes.

The coffins and caskets may be discerned in terms of shape and size by fittings and stains even if no wood survives. The chronology of viewing windows, always very rare in Britain but with a clear rise in popularity in parts of North America, needs to be mapped and then understood—the increase in embalming and the beautification of death may not be the only factors to consider here (Figure 5).

FIGURE 5. Glass viewing plate in coffin lid; human remains still visible beneath. Photo by Laurie Burgess, courtesy of Smithsonian Institution.

Many large-scale excavations reveal a minority of coffins containing items personal to the deceased and, in some cases, other items such as ceramic plates, flowers, or those placed by mourners (see Cherryson, this volume). Some seem to be sentimentally associated with the deceased, whereas others, such as plates possibly used for salt, may in some examples be associated with African traditions (McCarthy, 1998), but many of the British examples suggest a wider practice (Miles and Connell, 2012). In contexts such as burial shafts, vaults, and crypts and some waterlogged or highly desiccated environments, a wide range of materials can be represented.

The large number of catalogs reveals the diversity of choice, used to particularly good effect in both Trinkley and Hacker (this volume) and Pye (this volume), but these sources can be combined with the archaeology to reveal what was actually selected and used. How marketing across countries and, indeed, the globe was advanced through catalogs but then mediated through undertakers and selected by clients underpins several of the other chapters here for coffin fittings (Garrow, this volume; Mytum, "Explaining Stylistic Change in Mortuary Material Culture," this volume; Springate and Maclean, this volume). This integration of trade sources with undertaker and consumer choices revealed through the archaeology offers exciting opportunities for local and regional studies.

Crafts and industries that served undertakers as part of their marketing include plumbers creating complete lead coffins in the seventeenth century and contributing to the multiple shell coffins of the eighteenth and nineteenth centuries. The details of coffin construction have not been analyzed beyond relatively simple site-based classifications. Linked to this, identification of timber species and, where well preserved, surface treatments (including pigments and cloth coverings) should be the focus of study when such evidence is available. The textiles that survive in many coffins—both those clothing the deceased (which may be their own clothes or those specially purchased for the funeral) and that within and covering the coffin—can be linked to wider consumer fashions and textile production technologies, as seen in Pye's study here.

Builders and bricklayers used their local skills and traditions in the design and construction of family vaults and burial shafts, and only once sufficient detailed study of these structures is achieved will they be able to be placed within the wider local vernacular traditions. In Britain these structures are largely belowground, although in parts of Ireland and across many states in North America they are semisubterranean structures that were constructed to withstand weathering. Locations of such features, even without any visible surface remains, are now likely to be identified using ground-penetrating radar or other geophysical prospection methods.

Mortsafes were produced by a few foundries in some numbers, but most were locally made by blacksmiths as ad hoc solutions to the problem of body snatching (Mytum and Webb, this volume), again reflecting local skills and traditions but requiring further contextual analysis. Magnetometry would locate mortsafes or iron coffins very easily and with highly distinctive signatures.

Scientific analysis of coffin fittings and understanding the technology of production of these items can offer important insights into not only coffin hardware but the wider technological development of metal trades in both Britain and North America. Analysis of metal content of fittings is noted by Loe and Boston (this volume), and a preliminary study of a small sample of breastplates from Kellington church, North Yorkshire, has indicated the potential for a more systematic study (Byrne-Sweeney, 2012). Here, two brass (copper-zinc alloys) plates and a tin plate were examined, as well as three tin-dipped iron plates that suggested the use of both wrought and possibly ingot iron. Organic coatings, probably shellac, which could create different color finishes, were identified on some coffin plates from St. Pancras (Doub, 2011), again indicating the potential for scientific analysis. Because many of the fittings will not be permanently preserved given their condition and potential conservation costs, both destructive and nondestructive methods may be more applicable to this category of material culture than many of those found on settlement sites.

Taphonomy and Burial Management

Some studies have already indicated the potential for understanding decay processes in various conditions. The close dating of many interments allows close correlation of time and other factors such as soil chemistry and the interaction of different material in the ground. It is notable that survival is extremely unpredictable and also variable by material; a coffin may survive almost intact, but the textiles and skeleton within may be poorly preserved. Study of such processes requires an interdisciplinary team and substantial resources for postexcavation analysis, but it has implications for other aspects of archaeology and contemporary social uses of our discipline such as forensic archaeology.

Coffin fittings provide key chronological and social information that contributes to the understanding of burial site management—who is buried where, when, and with whom. The three-dimensional analysis at sites such as St. Pancras, London, reveals the complexities of these patterns (Figure 6) and how careful archaeological excavation, analysis, and illustration can reveal the patterns within these large data sets. Here, the excavations have indicated the potential for understanding the filling up of intensely occupied urban

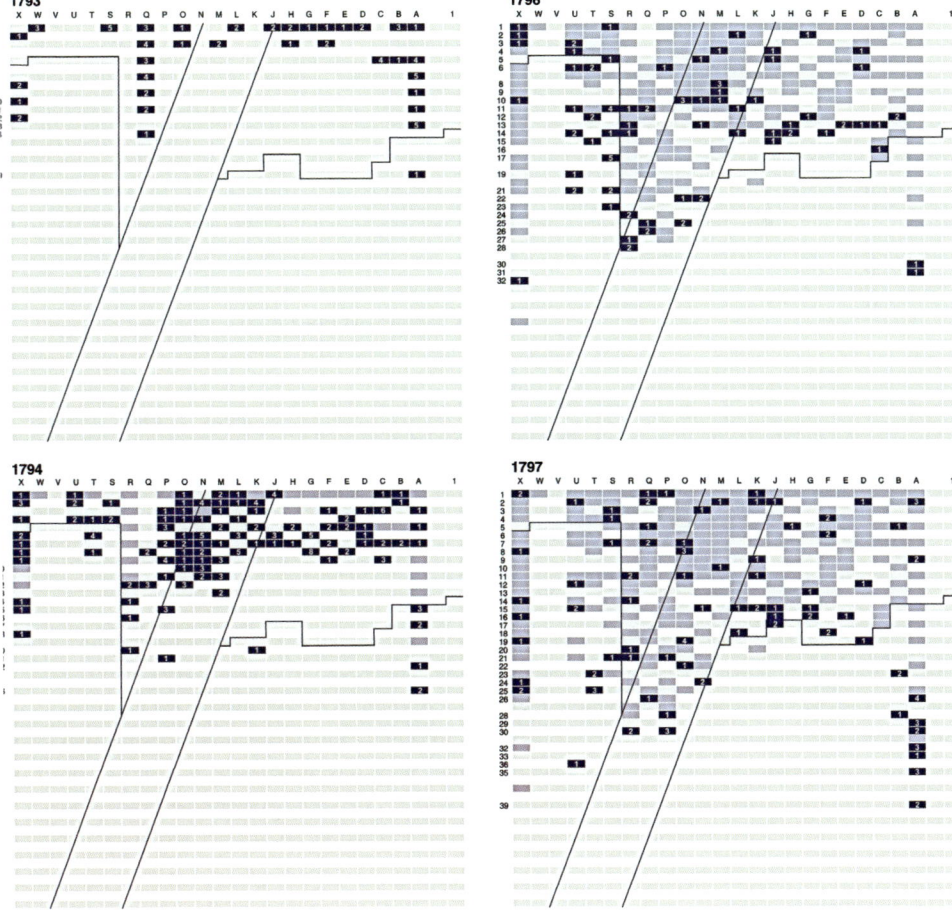

FIGURE 6. Part of the graveyard of St. Pancras, London. Dark shading indicates plots used that year; light shading shows already used plots. Note the spread of use but also continued placement of interments in plots already containing coffins. Copyright HS1 Ltd/Ramboll UK Limited, drawing by Carlos Lemos.

graveyards in not just two but three dimensions (Emery and Wooldridge, 2011), and although some important phasing has been recognized elsewhere, there has been little wider consideration of the decision-making behind the patterns so produced and the ways in which urban graveyard overcrowding was mitigated beyond particular site-specific issues. The frequently documented periodic reuse of burial space in crowded nineteenth-century urban churchyards, which should create distinct phases of burial on each zone of the burial ground, has not yet been clearly demonstrated.

The human element in taphonomy—creating different environments for the enclosure of the body and its container—from the earth grave through the brick- or stone-lined shaft to the family or communal vault is an important factor in the preservation of the materials we wish to study, but even within each of these types, the ways in which these spaces were managed varied. Earth burials may be left untouched or overburied and may become disarticulated, with any coffin fittings displaced also; family vaults may be managed with care and respect with all coffins laid out carefully, or they may have times when coffins are swept to one side to make room for new arrivals. The Spitalfields evidence revealed complex patterns of stacking, rearranging, and blocking off of sections of the crypt below the church (Reeve and Adams, 1993), but the data could no doubt reveal more about crypt management if also considered with evidence from other sites. Moreover, family vaults used over a long period of time have been researched in terms of individual burials but not as complex structures that have their own biographies.

The spatial development of earth-cut graveyards with limited intercutting can be challenging unless many have fittings with dates, but some aspects of phasing based on hardware typologies are possible. In Britain, stratigraphic sequences can often be determined with numerous intercut graves (Figure 7), even if the integrity of many of the interments has suffered from this process; as yet the various site sequences have not been considered comparatively.

The analysis of soils within coffins might support analyses of the skeletal remains, with discoveries such as adipocere and lipids, as investigated on the project reported here by Ewen and Crane. Soils can also provide indications of the changing environments within the grave and coffin and also the presence of now decayed items such as floral tributes or vegetation packed within the coffin. Soil chemistry has a profound effect on the survival and condition of coffin fittings, and the recording of such data would also be valuable in assisting in planning for subsequent excavations in similar conditions.

Relating the Past to the Present

Understanding how descendant families and communities relate to disturbance of burial grounds requires its own dedicated research program, linking historical archaeology with wider issues of contemporary ideology and politics at the level of race, ethnicity, and class. The projects may be in the context of maintenance and conservation works, on the one hand, and cemetery removal, on the other. Some chapters here reveal the complex dynamics between present and past in particular cases (Burgess and Owsley, this volume; Emery, this volume; Ewen and Crane, this volume), but many other investigations do not include this element in their project design. It often surfaces during late stages of planning and during implementation, by which time either conflicts emerge or opportunities for collaboration and mutual learning and understanding cannot be maximized. Understanding the complex and at times incompatible views regarding death and burial in the past

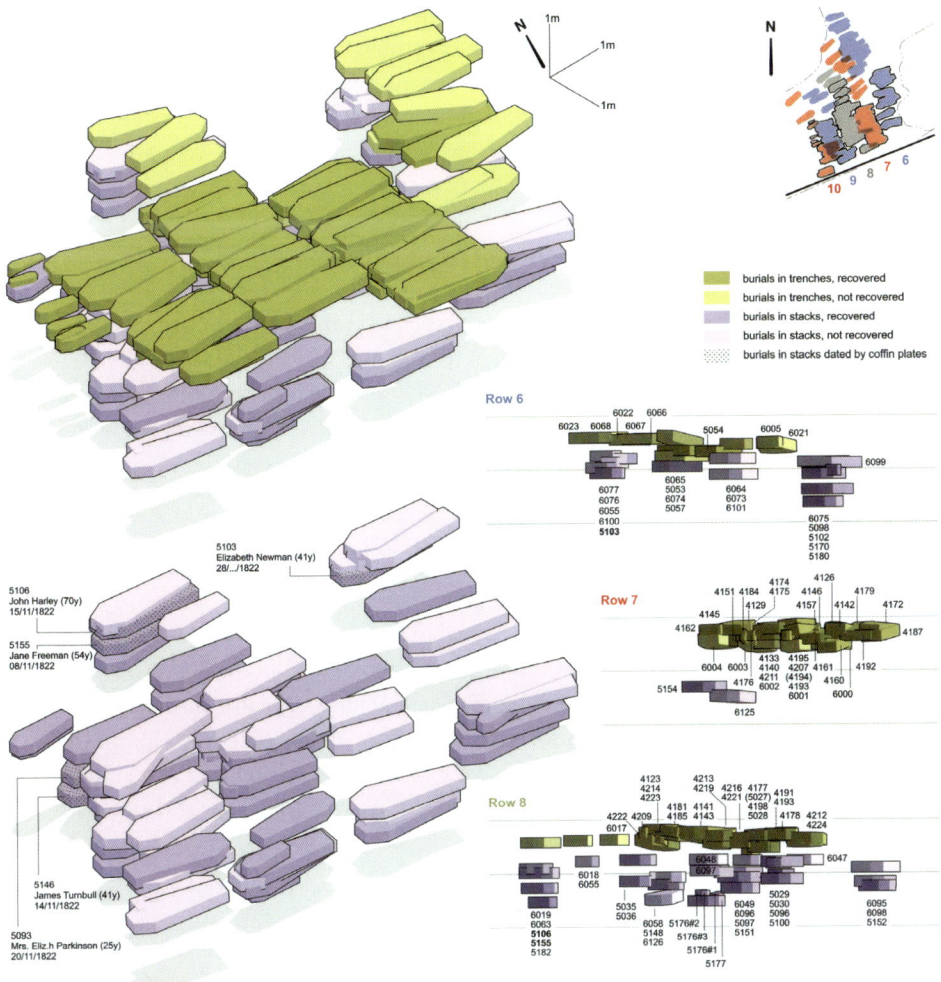

FIGURE 7. Isometric projection of coffin stacks, together with schematic cross sections, showing the rows of burials in St. Pancras churchyard, London. Note the level of recording even though not all graves could be archaeologically excavated but were removed by a commercial exhumation company. Copyright HS1 Ltd/Ramboll UK Limited, drawing by Carlos Lemos.

(see Tarlow, this volume) helps contextualize the emotional turmoil often caused by cemetery clearance in the present. Research questions about the past need to be intertwined with those of relevance to the descendant communities today, and ideally, they should be explored during the earliest planning stages of the project. The opportunities for education, collaboration, and celebration of lives and communities past and present can be one of the greatest outcomes from our fieldwork in this often emotionally draining form of archaeology.

Conclusions

All policies and practices have to be contextually designed within the ethical and legislative frameworks of the jurisdiction where the work is planned, but many aspects of this type of archaeological fieldwork and research would benefit from an international comparative perspective, as this volume demonstrates. The establishment of a network of interested professionals and researchers would be a valuable medium through which experiences could be shared and solutions to common problems sought, even if these have to be adapted to local circumstances. Indeed, such a network would also help to highlight where there are excellent data and where they should be enhanced. There is a danger that some fieldwork associated with clearance will, in time, begin to recover data that are, in effect, redundant and would not require such a level of investment; instead, different data should be collected that augment our understanding in productive ways, potentially linking protocols to data quality and quantity, and to research questions worth asking.

We have reached a point where a basic chronology is being worked out for at least some periods and places, and we see that there is considerable support from descendant groups for the cultural study of mortuary data as well as the biological dimension. The mortuary archaeology discussed throughout this volume has a bright future, building on the foundations of the pioneer scholars, with a new generation also represented here, and we all hope yet more scholars will be inspired by what this volume contains.

Acknowledgments

The editors thank all the contributors for their encouragement in developing this book and pushing forward the subject of historic mortuary material culture. The volume has taken far longer to come to print than was originally intended, but the delays have meant that several younger researchers have also now been included. We are gradually reaching a point where the cultural material associated with historic burial is being more widely recognized as having distinct value, but we all agree that it is important that its significance is further emphasized. Only by following up initiatives such as those suggested in this chapter may its full potential may be realized.

References

Advisory Panel on the Archaeology of Burials in England. 2013. *Science and the Dead: A Guideline for the Destructive Sampling of Archaeological Human Remains for Scientific Analysis.* London: English Heritage Publishing.

Bell, E. L. 1990. The Historical Archaeology of Mortuary Behavior: Coffin Hardware from Uxbridge, Massachusetts. *Historical Archaeology,* 24(3):–78.

Bevan, B. W. 1991. The Search for Graves. *Geophysics,* 56(9):1310–1319.

Byrne-Sweeney, J. 2012. Analysis of Coffin Plates from North Yorkshire by SEM and Light Microscopy. Report submitted as partial fulfilment of a M.A. in archaeology, University of Liverpool.

Conyers, L. B. 2006. Ground-penetrating radar techniques to discover and map historic graves. *Historical Archaeology,* 40(3):64–73.

Doub, N. 2011. "FT-IR Analysis of Organic Coatings on Five Coffin Plates from St. Pancras Burial Ground." In *St. Pancras Burial Ground: Excavations for St. Pancras International, the London Terminus of High Speed 1, 2002–3,* by P. A. Emery and K. Wooldridge, CD-ROM Appendix 3. London: Gifford Monograph, Museum of London Archaeology.

Ellwood, B. B. 1990. Electrical Resistivity Surveys in Two Historical Cemeteries in Northeast Texas: A Method for Delineating Unidentified Burial Shafts. *Historical Archaeology,* 24(1):91–98.

Emery, P. A., and K. Wooldridge. 2011. *St. Pancras Burial Ground: Excavations for St. Pancras International, the London Terminus of High Speed 1, 2002–3.* London: Gifford Monograph, Museum of London Archaeology.

Garrow, P. H. 1987. A Preliminary Seriation of Coffin Hardware Forms in Nineteenth and Twentieth Century Georgia. *Early Georgia*, 15(1/2):19–45.

Hacker-Norton, D., and M. Trinkley. 1985. *Remember Man Thou Art Dust: Coffin Hardware of the Early Twentieth Century*. Chicora Foundation Research Series 2. Columbia, S.C.: Chicora Foundation.

Hansen, J. D., J. K. Pringle, and J. Goodwin. 2014. GPR and Bulk Ground Resistivity Surveys in Graveyards: Locating Unmarked Burials in Contrasting Soil Types. *Forensic Science International*, 237:e14–e29.

Heinrich, A. R. 2014. Cherubs or Putti? Gravemarkers Demonstrating Conspicuous Consumption and the Rococo Fashion in the Eighteenth Century. *International Journal of Historical Archaeology*, 18(1):37–64.

King, J. A., B. W. Bevan, and R. J. Hurry. 1993. The Reliability of Geophysical Surveys at Historic-Period Cemeteries: An Example from the Plains Cemetery, Mechanicsville, Maryland. *Historical Archaeology*, 27(3):4–16.

LeeDecker, C. H., J. Bloom, I. Wuebber, and M.-L. Pipes. 1995. *Final Archaeological Excavations at a Late 18th-Century Family Cemetery for the U.S. Route 113 Dualization, Milford to Georgetown, Sussex County, Delaware*. With K. R. Rosenberg. DelDOT Archaeology Series 134. Dover: Delaware Department of Transportation.

Litten, J. 1991. *The English Way of Death: The Common Funeral Since 1450*. London: Robert Hale.

Litten, J. 1999. Tombs Fit for Kings: Some Burial Vaults of the English Aristocracy and Landed Gentry of the Period 1650–1850. *Church Monuments*, 14:104–128.

Litten, J. 2009. The Anthropomorphic Coffin in England. *English Heritage Historical Review*, 4:73–83.

McCarthy, J. P. 1998. Plates in Graves: An Africanism? *African Diaspora Archaeology Newsletter*, 5(2):3.

Meyer, R. E., ed. 1993. *Ethnicity and the American Cemetery*. Bowling Green, Ohio: Bowling Green State University Popular Press.

Miles, A., and B. Connell. 2012. *New Bunhill Fields Burial Ground, Southwark: Excavations at Globe Academy, 2008*. Archaeology Study Series 24. London: Museum of London Archaeology.

Mytum, H. 2004. *Mortuary Monuments and Burial Grounds of the Historic Period*. New York: Kluwer Academic/Plenum.

Mytum, H. 2016. "The Artefacts of Mortuary Practice: Industrialisation, Choice, and the Individual." In *Nineteenth-Century Material Culture Studies from Britain*, ed. A. Brooks, pp. 274–304. Lincoln: University of Nebraska Press.

Reeve, J., and M. Adams. 1993. *The Spitalfields Project*. Volume 1: *The Archaeology: Across the Styx*. CBA Research Report 85. York: Council for British Archaeology.

Springate, M. E. 2015. *Coffin Hardware in Nineteenth-Century America*. Walnut Creek: Left Coast Press.

About the Contributors

Ceridwen Boston is an experienced independent funerary archaeologist and physical anthropologist, working primarily in Britain, with a D.Phil. from Oxford for her research on trauma patterning in the British Royal Navy (1748–1856). She has worked for ten years in commercial archaeology, mostly for Oxford Archaeology, with particular interests in eighteenth to early-nineteenth century burial practices and physical anthropology. Projects have included small and large churchyard and crypt excavations in which she analysed skeletal assemblages, coffin furniture, and memorials.

Laurie Burgess is associate chair of the Department of Anthropology, National Museum of Natural History, Smithsonian Institution. She is a historical archaeologist whose research focuses on the material culture of historic period North America, with an emphasis on glass trade beads and on mortuary practices.

Annia K. Cherryson was a researcher on the Leverhulme-sponsored "Changing Beliefs about the Human Body" project and is one of the co-authors of *A Fine and Private Place: The Archaeology of Death and Burial in Post-Medieval Britain and Ireland* (2012).

Sheri Crane received an M.A. from East Carolina University in anthropology with a focus on historical archaeology and studied a year at the University of Durham, England. She participated in various archaeological digs along the East Coast, but the closest she comes now to digging is planting her organic vegetable garden. Sheri is currently employed at the University of Virginia in beautiful Charlottesville, Virginia.

Phillip A. Emery is a senior heritage advisor for the Canal & River Trust, previously having worked as a contract archaeologist leading major projects including the excavations at St. Pancras, London. He is a trustee of the Fulham Palace Trust and has co-written two books, *Norwich Greyfriars: Pre-Conquest Town and Medieval Friary* (2007) and *St Pancras Burial Ground: Excavations for St Pancras International, the London Terminus of High Speed 1, 2002–2011*.

Charles R. Ewen is a professor of anthropology and director of the Phelps Archaeology Laboratory at East Carolina University. His research interests focus on the historical archaeology of the Contact and Colonial periods. He is currently undertaking a long-term archaeological study of Brunswick Town, North Carolina. He is the author or editor of six books, including most recently *Pieces of Eight: More Archaeology of Piracy* (2016).

Patrick H. Garrow, RPA, is a retired professional archaeologist who worked in cultural resource management. He has published nine books, most on archaeological projects conducted under his supervision. His interest in cemetery studies dates from 1985, when he directed excavations in the Nancy Creek Primitive Baptist Church Cemetery. Since then he directed delineation and/or removal projects in more than 50 cemeteries across the southeastern United States.

Debi Hacker has more than three decades of experience in Southeastern archaeology and is Chicora's laboratory supervisor and conservator. She was assistant archaeologist at the Charleston Museum, responsible for conducting laboratory analyses and conservation, later serving as conservation administrator with the South Carolina State Museum. She is a member of the International Association of Identification, SC Division, the American Institute for Conservation of Historic and Artistic Works, and the Southeast Regional Conservation Association.

Louise Loe is head of burials at Oxford Archaeology, where she has worked since 2006, previously being a lecturer in biological anthropology at Bournemouth University. She has led large archaeological projects, including of World War I mass graves in Fromelles, Northern France and of a rare Viking-age execution burial from Weymouth, Dorset. Louise has managed and published on many post-medieval and Industrial period cemeteries including crypts, hospitals, Non-conformist and Church of England flat cemeteries, and most recently on burials from Cure's College Almshouse (1587–1831), Southwark, London. She is currently working on the remains from Oxford Radcliffe Infirmary hospital burial ground (c. 1770–1852).

Hilda Maclean has a Ph.D. from the University of Queensland in historical archaeology focusing on Victorian-era burial practices in Brisbane, Queensland. She has developed the Funerary Consumption Model, articulating the purchasing pattern of funerary goods and services by individual, institutional, and intermediary consumers. Hilda examined coffin furniture design in the United Kingdom and the trade route that developed from its source of manufacture in Birmingham to Brisbane.

Harold Mytum is professor of archaeology at the University of Liverpool and director of its Centre for Manx Studies. His research interests include investigating identity and memory through mortuary evidence (seventeenth to twentieth centuries) from not only Britain and Ireland, but also diasporic communities in North America and Australia. His 13 authored and edited books include *Recording and Analysing Graveyards* (2000) and *Mortuary Monuments and Burial Grounds of the Historic Period* (2004).

Douglas W. Owsley is division head of Physical Anthropology at the National Museum of Natural History, Smithsonian Institution. A forensic anthropologist, he has worked on many collaborative projects within historical archaeology, with the most significant in this field being in Washington, D.C., Jamestown and St. Mary's City, Maryland, and those aboard the submarine H. L. Hunley. He is co-author of numerous articles and six books linked to many aspects of forensic anthropology.

Jeremy W. Pye holds a Ph.D. in anthropology from the University of Florida and has more than 14 years of archaeological experience in many regions of the United States. His primary research interests include historic bioarchaeology, archaeo-parasitology, and archaeological geophysics. He is particularly focused on the study of nineteenth and twentieth century mortuary merchandise and burial container construction, amassing a physical and digital comparative library of more than 700 period trade catalogs, 2,000 patent records, and 200 archaeological cemetery relocation reports.

†**Roderick Sprague** was professor emeritus of anthropology and director emeritus of the Laboratory of Anthropology at the University of Idaho after a long career in historical archaeology with a focus on mortuary studies. He received both the J. C. Harrington Medal and the Carol Ruppé Service Award from the Society for Historical Archaeology. His books include *Burial Terminology: A Guide for Researchers* (2005).

Megan E. Springate is a post-doctoral associate with the Department of Anthropology, University of Maryland. A historical archaeologist with extensive experience in academia, museums, and cultural resource management, her research interest in identity formation and expression is what drew her to the study of coffin hardware. She is author of *Coffin Hardware in Nineteenth-Century America* (2014). She received her Ph.D. from the University of Maryland in 2017.

Sarah Tarlow is professor of archaeology at the University of Leicester, with particular interests in emotion, historical mortuary practice, and past attitudes to the human body. She is currently leading a Wellcome Trust–funded project, Harnessing the Power of the Criminal Corpse. She has written and co-edited a number of books, including *Thinking through the Body: Archaeologies of Corporeality* (2001), *Ritual, Belief, and the Dead in Early Modern Britain and Ireland* (2011), and *The Oxford Handbook of the Archaeology of Death and Burial* (2013).

Michael Trinkley has more than 40 years of experience in southeastern archaeology and graduate degrees from the University of North Carolina at Chapel Hill. He served as a senior archaeologist with the State of South Carolina prior to assuming the directorship of Chicora Foundation in 1983, a position he has held since. He is also active in public outreach programs, speaking to teachers, historical organizations, and museums, and is a leader in cemetery conservation. Dr. Trinkley is a registered consultant with numerous state and international agencies. He has published numerous scholarly studies with Chicora Foundation, University of Alabama Press, and others.

Katie Webb was a Masters student at the University of York with particular interest in historical archaeology. She took part in fieldwork in the United Kingdom and in Ireland before carrying out field research on Scottish mortsafes.

Index

Page numbers in *italic* text indicate figures and tables

Aberdeen Medico-Chirurgical Society, 228
Aberdour Mortsafe Association, 231
Abingdon, Oxfordshire, cemeteries, 26, 40, *44*, 45
African Americans
    archaeological investigations and clearance of burial ground, 2–3, 5–6
    descendants interests in information from clearance operations, 5–6
    disinterment of remains for cadavers, 11, 229, 244
    Hopewell Baptist Church cemetery burial of, 114–15
    illegal examination of cadavers found at medical schools, 230
    sick but live slaves sold to medical schools, 229
African Burial Ground, New York, 2, 5–6, 170, *170*, *186*, 198–99
Alameda-Stone Cemetery, Tucson, 180–81, *186*, 188, 199, 211, 212
alarm (signal) coffins, 123
All Saints, Church, Pavement, 42
Anatomy Act, 32, 65, 228, 232, 234, 235, 245–46
anatomy as a meditation upon the divine, 29–31
ancestors, importance of burial in same place as, 28
angels
    coffin fittings, 87–88, *133*, 138, 140, 146, 148, 165, 170, 171, *171*
    headstone/monument symbols, *84*
Anstruther Mortsafe Society, 231, 234
anthropomorphic coffin shapes, 9
Archaeology Data Service, 83, 129, 290
archaeology/historical archaeology
    challenges of incompatible methods and aims of cemetery clearance and research, 5–6, 68–69, 285–86
    crypt clearance activities and investigations, 5
    descendants interests in information from investigations, 5–6, 267
    ethics and field practices, 4–6
    osteological studies, 64–65, 68–69
    sampling strategies for research, 61–62, 68–69
    scope of burial grounds research, 1
    sensitivity in the treatment of human remains, 5, 69
    sensitivity to descendant families and communities feelings about projects, 298–99
Arrit, Mary, 62
Ashmolean Museum, 32
asylums, bodies of deceased as cadavers, 229

Atlantic Coffin & Casket Company, *99*
Auchtertool Mortsafe Association, 231–34, 238, 240
Auferderheide, Arthur, 269
Auferderheide, Mary, 269
Australia
    coffin furniture in, 165, 166–69, *168*, *169*, *170*, 173
    cultural factors in attitudes toward death, the body, containment, and disposal, 14–15
    documentation of locations of burial grounds, 8
    exile of sympathizers to revolutionary France, 67
    mortuary data from, 3
    protection and conservation of burial grounds in, 5

Backchurch Lane burial ground, 48
Balmerino Abbey, 29
Barnard, Anna, 48
Beautification of Death Movement, 98, 173, 208, 252, 256
Becky Wright Cemetery, *186*
Becon, Thomas, 23, 25
Beconsall, Thomas, 25
Belbeuf, Pierre-Augustin Godart de, 67, 69, 70–71
Belleville, Ontario, 3
black/carbon black pigments/paints, 102, *183*, 184, 185–89, *186–87*, 212
Blandford parish church vault, 27
blue pigments/paints, 181–82, *183*, 184–88, *186–87*, 212
body protection
    British practices for, 11, 32, 227–28, 245–46
    burial grounds overcrowding and body and grave protection, 227
    cultural and social factors in attitudes toward human remains and, 11, 228, 245–46
    development of to prevent body snatching, 228
    equipment and structures for, 228, 230–46, *236*, *237*, *239*, *242*, *244*
    mortsafe and watching societies, 230, 231–34
    North American practices for, 11, 227, 228–29, 243–44, 245
    See also mortsafes
body snatching
    archaeological evidence for, 229–30, 245–46
    British concern about and prevention of, 11, 32, 227–28, 245–46
    lucrative business of, 228, 234
    method used by, 228

body snatching (*continued*)
- North American concern about and prevention of, 11, 227, 228–29, 243–44, 245
- organizations to obtain bodies for medical students, 228
- protection of body from (*see* body protection)
- punishment for offense of, 228
- resurrection men or resurrectionists term for, 227

Bond Street Congregational Chapel burial ground, *45*, 48
bonnets and caps, 40, 42, 46, 47, 275
Bourdas-Smith, Stephanie, 265, 267
Bow Baptist Church Burial Ground, *44*, 48
box corners/clip, *7*
Boyd, Zacharie, 23, 27–28
Boyertown Burial Casket Company, *99*
breastplates/coffin plaques
- costs/prices of, 105–7, *106*
- description of, *7*
- metals used for, *142*, *143*, *144*, 149
- St. George's Church examples, 132–33, *142*, *143*, *144*, *147*, *150–54*
- St. Luke's church examples, 132, *133*, *142*, 143, *144*, 147, *150–54*
- St. Pancras examples, 62, *63*, 67, *289*
- seriation research in Georgia, *116*, 118
- trends in and designs and symbols on, *10*, 11, 86–88, *86*, *88*, 89–90, 146–47, *147*, *150–54*

Brick Chapel, St. Mary's City, 2, 9
Bristol Manufacturing Company, *99*
broadcloth
- coffin exterior coverings, *190*, 191, *192–93*
- coffin linings, 201–2, *217*
- description of, 191

brocade
- coffin exterior coverings, *192*
- coffin linings, 202, 203, *214*, *216*, *217*, *218*
- description of, 203

brocatelle, 191, *192*, 194
brown pigments/paints, *183*, 212
Bruwelheide, Kari, 269
Bulkeley Tomb, *186*, 199
Bunhill Fields, 26
Bunyan, John, 25
Burgess, Laurie, 269
burial grounds
- archaeological investigations and clearance operations, 5–6, 68–69
- cultural factors in design and management of, 14
- data recovery and analysis from, 1–4, 285–87
- descendants interests in information from investigations, 5–6, 267
- documentation of locations of, 8
- ethical and practical issues related to investigation of, 4–6, 299–300
- excavation of in advance of development, 2, 3, 5–6, 8
- excavations of, 2–3
- laws and church control over location and rites of burial, 6, 8–9
- locations of vaults and plots and social status, 251
- overcrowding of and body and grave protection, 227
- protection and conservation of, 3, 4–5
- reasons for excavation of, 5
- sensitivity to descendant families and communities feelings about projects in, 298–99
- *See also* cemeteries; churchyards

Burial in Woolen Act, 40, 41, 51
burial structures
- craft and industry research recommendation, 296
- protection and conservation of, 4–5
- studies of, 1

buried alive, fear of, 24, 123
Burning Springs Branch Cemetery, *187*
buttons, hooks, and fasteners, 41–42, 43–45, *44–45*, 269, *270*

Cabinetmaker's Society price list, 177–78, *178*
cadavers
- African American remains as, 11, 229, 244
- Anatomy Act and regulation of human remains for medical purposes, 32, 65, 228, 232, 234, 235, 245–46
- anatomy schools/medical training programs and need for bodies for dissection, 11, 227–28, 229, 245
- cost of bodies, 228
- decomposition time before unsuitable for dissection, 231, 232, 233, 234, 235, 238
- ethics of supply and disposal of, 230
- illegal acquisition of, 228, 229
- illegal examination of cadavers found in hospital burial grounds, 229–30
- prisons as source of, 31, 32, 65
- sale of by Burke and Hare, 232, 235, 245
- state-provided, 227–28, 229, 234
- students need to obtain their own, 228
- supply of from body snatchers, 11, 227
- workhouses and hospitals as sources for, 65, 228, 229

Cadia Cemetery, 167
cage mortsafes, 243–44, *244*
Calhoun General Store, 97
cambric, 202, 203
Canada, 173
candied fruit, 25, 33
canton flannel, 200, *201*, 202, 203
caplifters, *7*, 97, 113, 115, *116*, 118, 120, 121, 126, 178
caps and bonnets, 40, 42, 46, 47, 275
Cartmell, Larry, 269
cashmere and cashmere mattresses, *201*, 202, *202*, 203, 208–9, *213–17*
cast-iron coffins, 11, 77, 257
Castle Howard, 6
Caswell, Lewis, 267, 270
Caswell, Mary Mackilwean, 271, *274*
Caswell, Richard
- cemeteries owned by and confusion over location of grave of, 263–65, *264*, 279
- descendants interests in grave project, 267
- examination and analysis of coffins and remains, 268–70, *270*, 273–79, *278*

excavation and removal of coffins, 268, 273, *274*
Governor Richard Caswell Memorial/CSS *Neuse* Historical Site cemetery, 264–65, *264*, 272
life and death of, 263, 274–75
Red House cemetery, 263–65, *264*, 270–79, *271, 272, 274*
reinterment of remains found during grave project, 269
soil analysis, decomposition of bodies, and lack of human remains, 273–79, *278*
Vernon Hall "the Hill" cemetery, 263–68, *264, 266*
water exposure and disintegration of skeletal remains, 268, 275–77
Caswell, Sarah Herritage, 271, *274*
Caswell, Tuscumbia, 267
Caswell Gatlin, Susan, 271, *272, 274*
catches for cloth work, 198, *198*
Catholic Mission of St. Mary and St. Michael, 42, 43, *44*, 48, 49, 50
Catholics
    burial locations and contagious sanctity, 27
    importance of burial location, 28
    rosary found with body of French prisoner of war, 49, *50*
    St. Pancras cemetery burial of, 67
Causten vault, *251*, 253, *253*, 256, 261
Cavendish vault, 39
cemeteries
    archaeological investigations of, 8
    burial site management and reuse of burial space, 297–98, *297, 299*
    cultural factors in design and management of, 14
    data recovery and analysis about, 285–87
    excavation of in advance of development, 3, 8, 109–10, 114–15
    locations of vaults and plots and social status, 251
    sensitivity to descendant families and communities feelings about projects in, 298
    shift from church and churchyard burial to burial in, 8
    See also burial grounds
cenotaphs, 250, 252, 258
ceramics, 120
cerecloth, 25, 275
Chappell, Chase, Maxwell & Company, 181
cherubs
    coffin fittings, 11, 86–88, *86, 88*, 89, 90–91, 132, 133, *133*, 134–35, *134, 135*, 138, 146, 148, 165, 170, 171, *171*
    headstone/monument symbols, 78, 79–80, *81*, 86, 89, 90–91
Chesapeake burial grounds, 3, 9, 288, 292
China gauffer, 202, 204, *218*
chin cloth/jaw cloths, 46, 275
cholera epidemics, 65, 66, 68
Christ Church. *See* Spitalfields Christ Church
churches
    burial locations and contagious sanctity, 27
    burials beneath and within, 26, 27–29
    crypts beneath in North America, 8
    excavations of vaults and crypts in Britain, 2
    excavations of vaults and crypts in North America, 2–3
    laws and church control over location and rites of burial, 6, 8–9
churchyards
    burial in and beliefs about dead bodies, 26, 27–29
    excavations of in Britain, 2, 8
    excavations of in North America, 3
    laws and church control over location and rites of burial, 6, 8–9
    overcrowding of, 68, 227, 297–98, *297, 299*
    plague victims burial in, 26
    prevalence of use of, 8
    security measures at, 230
Cincinnati Coffin Company, 99
Cleveland Burial Case Company, *99*, 181
cloth
    archaeological records of cloth coverings, 191, 196–99, *197, 198*
    archaeological records of cloth linings, 209–11, *210*
    bedding arrangement of coffin sheets, 43, 48, 51
    British guide to to covering a coffin with, 189
    caps and bonnets, 46
    catalog of fabrics and colors for cloth-covered caskets, 190–91, *190*
    catches for cloth work, 198, *198*
    cloth linings descriptions and costs, 201, 213–17
    coffin exterior coverings, 7, 10, 11, 12, 85, *85*, 88, 140, 143, 178, 189–99
    coffin linings, 200–211, *201, 202*
    coffin lining sets, 200, 201, *202*
    data recovery and analysis about, 177
    early records of, 189
    lining tacks to secure, 10, *10*, 12, 189, 196–99, *197*, 200, 209–11, *210*
    paint-fabric combinations, 199, 212
    patent for cloth-covered caskets, 190, 191
    piece dry goods descriptions and costs, 210, 217–20
    pillows, 202, 208–9, *209*, 211
    price list for lining coffins, 200, *201*
    process for lining with, 200–201
    trimmings and secondary components of linings, 201, 206–8, *208, 209*
    types and colors of cloth used for exterior coverings, 140, 143, 189–96, *190, 192–93*
    types and colors of cloth used for linings, 201–11, *202, 209, 213–20*
clothing
    Burial in Woolen Act and requirements for, 40, 41, 51
    buttons, hooks, and fasteners, 41–42, 43–45, *44–45*, 269, *270*
    caps and bonnets, 40, 42, 46, 47, 275
    decomposition of bodies and, 276
    dressing the body for burial, 27, 40–45, 51, 275
    footwear, 43
    frills and ruffles on, 41–42
    gloves and stocking, 42
    shrouds covering day clothes, 43
    social status and surviving textile examples, 42

clothing (*continued*)
    trousers, 43
    See also shrouds
coburg, 202, *202*, 204, 208–9
coffin hardware/furniture/fittings
    Beautification of Death Movement and, 98, 173, 208, 252, 256
    burial context and condition of, 8–9
    catalogs from producers of, 3, 6, 78, 97, 98–101, *99*, *100*, 146, 165–66, 170–71, 173, 290, *291*, 296
    coffins available without, 100–101
    copyright protection of designs, 166, 167
  costs/prices of, 97–98, 104–7, *105*, *106*, 165, 168
    craft and industry research recommendation, 296
    customized hardware, 6
    direct purchase of by the public, 91, 173
    earth burials and condition of, 2, 8–9
    emotional, social, and cultural context of selection of, 75–78, 90–91, 97–98
    export of British-made furniture, 166–69, *168*, 170, *170*, 171, *171*, 173
    furniture hardware use, 6
    handbook on matching hardware to caskets, 105–7
    mass production of, 11, *12*, 14, 75–76, 89, 131, 165–66, 169–73
    numbering of, 83
    popularity of styles/forms of, 120
    St. George's Church research, 129–31, 132–33, 137, *137*, 138, *138*, 140–49, *141*, *142*, *144*, *150–63*
    St. Luke's church research, 129–30, 132, *133*, 134–37, *134*, *135*, *136*, 138, *139*, 140, *142*, 143, *144*, 145–49, *147*, *150–63*
    seriation research in Georgia, 98, 109–21, *111*, *112*, *113*, *116*, *117*, *119*
    sets of, 166, 167–68, *168*
    simplified designs and restrained use of decorations, 12
    Spitalfields investigation and classification, 78, 83, 85–91, *85*, *86*, *87*, *88*, 129, 132, 146, 147, *150–63*
    stamped designs, 89, 131, 149, 165, 166
    status indications from, 97–98, 107, 121, 146, 148–49, 166, 249–50, 251–61, *253*, *255*, *257*, *260*
    studies of, 1, 2, 129
    style and symbolism changes research recommendation, 292–93
    terminology for, British and North American, 6, 7, 123, 165
    trends, symbols, and designs in Britain, 9–15, *10*, *12*, *13*, 145–49, *147*, 165–66, 290
    trends, symbols, and designs in North America, 9–15, 97–101, *99*, *100*, 104–7, *105*, *106*, 171–73, *171*, *172*, 290
coffin lace (decorative metal), 7, *10*, 11, 131, 146, 167
coffin lids
    hinged lids, 11, 12, 14, 76, 121, 123–27, *126*, 201, 206
    text and symbols in pins on, 10, *10*, 85, *85*, 88, 89, 91
    viewing panels in, 11, 14, 76, 113–14, 115, 116, *116*, 118, 120–21, 294, *295*
coffin plates. *See* breastplates/coffin plaques

coffins/caskets
    acquisition of outside the funeral industry, 120
    burial context and condition of, 8–9
    catalogs from producers of, 100–101
    children's coffins, 11, 101–2, 181, 182
    communal coffins, 9
    costs/prices of, 12, 98, 101–4, *102*, *103*, 107
    decisions about and application of hardware by undertaker, 100–101
    decomposition of bodies and, 276
    description of, 7
    emotional, social, and cultural context of selection of, 75–78, 90–91
    handbook on matching hardware to caskets, 105–7
    local makers of, 83, 85
    names for in catalogs, 12
    pall/mortcloth to cover, 76
    power relationships between undertakers and the bereaved and selection of, 75–78, 83, 89–91
    prevalence of use of in early modern Britain, 26–27
    price list of products and services from Cabinet-maker's Society, 177–78, *178*
    replacement of coffins with caskets, 11, 12, 14
    reusable parish coffins, 41, 123, 227
    shapes of, 9, *10*, 11, 85, *85*, 114, 115–16, *116*, 120–21
    shroud burial replacement with interment in, 9, 41, 51, 227
    studies of, 1, 2
    terminology for, British and North American, 7
    trends in, 9–15, *10*, 83, 85–88, *85*, *86*, *87*, *88*
    triple-shell coffins, 42, 67
    See also exterior surface treatments of burial containers; interior surface treatments of burial containers
coffin sheets, 43, 48, 51
coins over eyes, 46, *47*
combs/hair combs, 47–48, 51, 269, *270*
commemoration
    cultural factors in attitudes toward, 14
    power relationships between undertakers and the bereaved and choices about, 75–78, 89–91
communal coffins, 9
community and farmstead burial grounds, 3, 8
Congressional Cemetery
    barrel vault at, *287*
    brick burial vaults in, 249, *250*, 253–56
    Causten vault, *251*, 253, *253*, 256, 261
    cenotaphs at, 250, 252, 258
    coffin hardware found in vaults at, 253, *253*, 254, *255*, 256–58, *257*, 260, 261
    Coombe vault, 253–54, *253*, *255*, 261
    data recovery and analysis from vaults at, 249–50
    excavation activities during preservation and restoration of vaults, 249
    history of, 250–53
    landscaping of, 261
    locations of vaults and plots and social status, 251
    Macomb vault, 253–54, *253*, 258–61, *258*, *260*
    maintenance at and financial support for, 261–62

material culture from, analysis of, 249–50
membership-based dog park at, 261–62
monuments in, 252, 256, *257*, 258–59, 260–61, *260*
preservation and conservation activities at, 249
recoffining of remains at, 256
reinterment of remains after restoration of vault, 249, 259–60, *260*
status and mortuary practices linkage, exploration at, 249–50, 251–61, *253*, *255*, *257*, *260*
subsurface vaults with monuments at, 249, 253, 256–61, *257*, *260*
Wirt vault, 253–54, *253*, 256–58, *257*, 261
Coombe, Griffith, 253
Coombe vault, 253–54, *253*, *255*, 261
Copyright of Designs Act, 166, 167
cords and tassels, 201, 206, 208, *208*, *213*, *214*, *219*
Crane, Breed & Company, 172, *202*, 208, 267
cremation, 1, 15
crepe, *190*, 191, 194, 206
criminals, treatment of bodies of, 31–32
Crooke, Helkiah, 29, *30*, 31
Cross Bones Cemetery, 41, 43, 229
crypts
 affluence and burial in, 8–9, 83
 American data on, 2–3
 archaeological clearance of, 5
 brick crypt found during Caswell grave project, 266–67, *266*, 268
 British data on, 2
 coffin and fittings condition of investigations of, 8–9
 commercial exhumation companies for clearance of, 3, 5
 data recovery and analysis from, 285–87
 increase in number of burials in, 227
 laws and church control over location and rites of burial, 8–9
 prevalence of use of, 8
 reasons for clearance of, 5
Cuthbert, 37

Dail, Roy, 265
Davidson, James, 98, 101, 106, 107
dead bodies/the dead
 Anatomy Act and regulation of use for medical purposes, 32, 65, 228, 232, 234, 235, 245–46
 archaeological evidence of care and treatment of, 25–27
 archaeological evidence of preparation, clothing, and presentation of the corpse at, 37 51, *47*, *50*
 arranging the corpse, 45–48, *46*
 attitudes toward and changing attitudes toward, 14–15, 23–33, 37–38, 41, 51, 69
 beliefs about in early modern Britain, 23–33
 candied fruit analogy, 25, 33
 care and money spent on preparation and disposal of, 25–27, 33
 clothing and shrouding for burial, 27, 40–45, 51, 275
 coins over eyes of, 46, *47*
 criminals, treatment of bodies of, 31–32
 decomposition time before unsuitable for dissection, 231, 232, 233, 234, 235, 238
 display on bed before placing in a coffin, 48
 documented attitudes toward, 27–33
 face appearance and beautification of the corpes, 46, *47*
 fear of being buried alive, 24, 123
 hair, hairstyles, and wigs, 47–48, 269
 jewelry and personal adornment, 48–51, 269, *270*
 microcosmic view of, 29–31
 resurrection of, beliefs about, 23–25, 37–38
 rocks as replacement to simulate correct weight, 228, 229
 sawdust and wood shavings from coffin construction to prevent shifting and absorption of decomposition fluids from, 200–201
 sleeping characterization of, 47–48, 51, 208
 soul and body, distinction between and beliefs about, 23–25, 29–31, 32, 37–38
 theological views of, 23–25, 32, 33, 37–38
 washing of, 25, 37, 38, 45, 275
deadhouses/morthouses, 230–31, 234–37, *237*
dentures and crowns, 46, 51, 65, 67, 269, *270*
depositum plates, 131, 132–33, *142*, 143, 167
Derby Cathedral, Derbyshire, 39
Des Moines Casket Company, *99*
"Dialogue between the Soul and the Body" (Marvell), 29
The Dignity of Man, Both in the Perfections of His Soule and Bodie (Nixon), 29–31
Dillon, Arthur Richard, 67, 69–71, *70*
dog park, 261–62
Don Jail Cemetery, *187*
Dottridge Brothers, 168–69, *170*
Dove Cemetery, *186*
Dunfermline Abbey, 229

earth burials
 American data on, 2
 British data on, 3
 coffin and fittings condition, 2, 8–9
 earth-cut graves, 3, *299*
East Carolina University, Harriot College of Arts and Sciences, Caswell grave project, 265–79
East Carolina University, Organic Chemistry Lab, 277
east-west burial alignment, 26–27, 31, 272, 273, *274*
Ebenezer Chapel, *45*, *46*, *47*
Eddy Cemetery, *186*
Edwards-Attaway cemetery, *112*, 115–19, *116*, *117*, 121
Elizabeth I, Queen, 189
Elmbank Cemetery, *186*
embalming
 beliefs about and acceptance of, 104
 British practices for, 14, 25, 38–40
 costs/prices of, 104
 North American practices for, 14, 104, 114
 treatment of body parts removed during, 39
epidemic, burial of victims of, 26, 45, 65, 66, 68
escutcheons/studs
 description of, 7

escutcheons/studs (*continued*)
   metals used for, *142*, 143, *144*, 145, 149
   St. George's Church examples, 140, *142*, *144*, *160*
   St. Luke's church examples, 138, *142*, 143, *144*, *160*
   seriation research in Georgia, 113, 116, *116*, 118, 120–21
   trends in, 11, 97, 146, *160*
   upholstery and studwork, 140, *142*, 143, *144*, 145, *161–63*
Eubanks, Beth, 269
Evans Cemetery, *187*
Evansville Coffin Company, *197*
exhumation/clearance contractors
   challenges of incompatible methods and aims of cemetery clearance and research, 5–6, 68–69, 285–86
   commercial exhumation companies in Britain, 3, 5
exterior surface treatments of burial containers
   archaeological records of, 180–81, 185–89, *186–87*, 196–99, *197*, *198*
   availability of information about, 212
   cloth, *7*, 10, 11, 12, 140, 143, 177, 178, 189–99, *190*, *192–93*
   combination treatments, 199
   costs of burial container and, 177
   data recovery and analysis about, 177
   oils, 178, 179
   paint, 11, 177, 178, 181–89, *186–87*
   polish, 11, 12
   price list of products and services from Cabinetmaker's Society, 177–78, *178*
   social importance and cultural perceptions of different treatments, 177, 178, 179, 189, 212
   stains, 178, 179, 180–81
   varnish, 178, 179–81, *180*
   waxes/waxing, 178, 179, 180
   wood types and surface treatments, 177–78, *178*, 179
eyes, coins over, 46, *47*

family burial grounds, 2, 8
farmstead and community burial grounds, 3, 8
faunal remains, 65–66
First African Baptist Church Cemetery, *187*
Fisk cast-iron coffins, 11, 267
floral tributes, 62, 269
flowers, foliage, and flowerpots
   coffin fittings, 11, *12*, 87, *87*, 133, *133*, 137, 140, 146, 148, 166, 167, 172, 189
   coffin linings designs, 213–14, *215*, *218*
   headstone/monument symbols, 83, *84*
Foote, Shelly, 269
footwear, 43
France
   exile of sympathizers to revolution in, 67
   rosary found with body of French prisoner of war, 49, *50*
   St. Pancras cemetery burial of émigrés from, 57, 66–67, 68, 69–71, *70*, *71*
Freedman's Cemetery, 3, 8, 98, 101, *187*, 210, 230

fringe, *193*, 201, *202*, 204, 206, 207, 208, *209*, 213–17, 219
funeral industry
   affluence and burial locations, 8–9, 251
   burial locations and funeral process costs, 8–9
   coffin design and supply control by, 120
   cultural shifts in, 15
   funeral home records, 101–4, *102*, *103*, 107
   handbook on matching hardware to caskets, 105–7
   material culture developed for, 6
   power relationships between undertakers and the bereaved, 75–78, 83, 89–91
   social trends in how dead are buries, 261
   style and content of funeral packages, 6
funerals
   costs/prices of, 101–4, *102*, *103*
   cultural factors in attitudes toward, 14, 51
   impression of last view of body during, importance of, 51
   primary function of, 51
   social standing and importance of, 38–39

gabled coffin, 9
Garrow, Pat, 98
Gatlin, Susan Caswell, 271, *272*, *274*
Georgia
   body snatching in, 230
   cemeteries included in seriation research, 109–10, 114–15
   coffin handle seriation research in, 98
   coffin hardware seriation research, 98, 109–21, *111*, *112*, *113*, *116*, *117*, *119*
gimp and gimp tacks, *197*, 201, 206, 207, 210–11, *210*, *213*, *215*, *216*, *217*, *218–19*
Glasgow Cathedral, 29
gloves and stocking, 42
Goldsborough, Louis Malesherbes, 256
Gothic revival monuments, 83, *84*, 90–91
Goulick, Tom, 269
gravediggers, selling of bodies by, 228
graveguards, 244–45
grave robbing. *See* body snatching
graves and grave shafts
   brick-lined shafts, 3, 227
   burial grounds overcrowding and body and grave protection, 227
   burial site management and reuse of burial space, 297–98, *297*, *299*
   Caswell grave excavation project, 265–79, *266*, *270*, *271*, *272*, *274*, *278*
   east-west burial alignment, 26–27, 31, *272*, 273, *274*
   lined graves, 103
   size of shafts and grave chambers and manner in which graves are dug, 118, 121
   soil analysis and decomposition of bodies, 273–79, *278*, 298
   water exposure and disintegration of skeletal remains, 268, 275–77
gravestones/headstones
   commissioning of before a death, 76

data collection and analysis about, 78–83, *80*, *81*, *82*
emotional, social, and cultural context of selection of, 75–78, 90–91
increase in use of, 227
power relationships between stonemason and the bereaved and selection of, 75–78, 89–91
St. Pancras cemetery headstones/memorial stones, 63–64
shapes and styles of, 79, 89
studies of, 1
symbols and motifs and trends in use of, 78, 79–83, *80*, *81*, *82*, *84*, 89, 90–91

Great Britain
archaeological clearance of crypts in, 5
body protection in, 11, 32, 227–28, 245–46
care, preparation, and presentation of the corpse in, 37–51
coffin and fittings studies in, 2
commercial exhumation companies in, 3, 5
criminals, treatment of bodies of, 31–32
cultural factors in attitudes toward death, the body, containment, and disposal, 14–15, 51, 69
dead bodies, beliefs about in, 23–33, 37–38
denial of Christian burial in, 32
documentation of locations of burial grounds, 8
documented attitudes toward the dead, 27–33
earth burials in, 3
excavations of churchyards in, 2, 8
excavations of vaults and crypts in, 2
export of coffin furniture from, 166–69, *168*, 170, *170*, 171, *171*, 173
headstones and memorials data from, 78–83, *80*, *81*, *82*
historic burial excavation in, 2
laws and church control over location and rites of burial, 6, 8–9
mass production of furniture and hardware in, 11, *12*, 14, 75–76, 89, 131, 165–66
material choice trends, 9–15, *10*, *12*, *13*
material culture terminology, 6, *7*, 165
mortuary data from, 3, 14–15, 288–89, 290, 291–92
protection and conservation of burial grounds in, 5

green coffins, 15
green pigments/paints, *183*, 185–88, *186–87*, 212
grip plates/backing plates/lug
description of, 7
mass production of, 11
metals used for, *142*, 143, *144*, 149
St. George's Church examples, 137, *137*, *138*, *142*, *144*, 155–56
St. Luke's church examples, 134–37, *134*, *135*, *136*, *142*, 143, *144*, 155–56
trends in and designs and symbols on, 11, *13*, 86–87, *86*, *87*, 89–90, 146, *155–56*

grips/handles
absence of, 116, 121
catalog listings of, 11, *13*, 98–101, *99*, *100*
costs/prices of, 104–7, *105*, *106*
description of, 7

mass production of, 11
metals used for, *142*, 143, *144*, 149
St. George's Church examples, 137, *137*, *138*, *142*, *144*, 147–48, *157*
St. Luke's church examples, 134–37, *134*, *135*, *136*, *142*, 143, *144*, 147–48, *157*
seriation research in Georgia, 98, 110–13, *111*, *112*, *113*, 115–18, *116*, *117*, 120–21
status indications from, 254, *255*, 256–58, *257*, 261
trends in and designs and symbols on, 10, 11–12, *13*, 86–87, *86*, 147–48, *157*
trends in styles in North America, 97–101, *99*, *100*, 104–7, 170, *170*, 171–72, *171*, *172*

grips/handles types
bail/swing bail handles, 11–12, *13*, 97, 98–101, *99*, *100*, 104–6, *105*, 110–13, *111*, *113*, 115, 116–18, *117*, 120, 170–71, 254, *255*, 256, *257*–58
double-lug handles, 10, 97, 254
drop handles, 11–12, *13*, 171–72, *171*
long/extended bar handles, 11, 14, 98–101, *99*, *100*, 104–6, *106*, 110–13, *112*, *113*, 116–18, *117*, 120, 172
ring bail handles, 98
short bar handles, 11–12, *13*, 97, 98–101, *99*, *100*, 104–6, *105*, 110–13, *111*, *113*, 116–18, *117*, 120, 172, *172*, 256–57, *257*
single-lug handles, 254, *255*, 256–57

Gurnsey, Tracy, 269

Haines, Eliza, 49
hair, hairstyles, and wigs, 47–48, 269
Halifax, Little Dutch Church, 2, 3
Hamilton, Lemmon, Arnold & Company
cloth-covered caskets available from, 191, *192–93*
cloth linings descriptions and costs, 201, 212, *213–17*
lining tacks descriptions and costs, 210–11, *210*
piece dry goods descriptions and costs, *217–20*
pillow types and costs, 209
Hand, Richard Gideon, 43
handles. *See* grips/handles
Hands, John, 167, *168*
Hardy, Thomas, 58, 60
Hart, Ann, 65
Hazelton Coffin and Casket Company, 181
headstones. *See* gravestones/headstones
Hemingford Grey cemetery, 26–27, 40, 43, *44*
Henrietta cloth, 202, 204
hexagonal coffins
Australian example of, 167
availability of, 120
Caswell grave project, 267, 273, *274*, 275
prevalence of use of, 9, 85, 275
seriation research in Georgia, 114, 115–16, *116*, 121
terminology for, British and North American, 7
transition to rectangular form from, 11, 12, 14, 114, 116
hinged coffin lids, 11, 12, 14, 76, 121, 123–27, *126*, 201, 206
hinges
absence of, 123, 126
availability and production of, 123, 124–25

hinges (*continued*)
  dating of, 125–26, *126*
  selection, use, and configuration of, 124–26, *126*
  seriation research in Georgia, 120
  terminology and types of, 124–25
  transition to hinged lids on coffins, 123
  trends in, 97, 123
  use of on signal and parish coffins, 123
Hoffman, Susan Burgess, 267
Hopewell Baptist Church, 109, 114–19, *116*, *117*, 121
Horne, William, 229
hospitals
  archaeological evidence of preparation, clothing, and presentation of the corpse at, 45, *45*
  bodies of deceased as cadavers, 65, 228, 229
  illegal examination of cadavers found in burial grounds of, 229–30
  investigations at burial grounds of, 9
Hudson, Joseph, 67
Huguenot community, 5, 42
human remains
  Anatomy Act and regulation of human remains for medical purposes, 32, 65, 228, 232, 234, 235, 245–46
  archaeological exhumations and clearance operations, 5–6, 68–69
  archaeologist sensitivity in treatment of, 5, 285–87
  cultural and social factors in attitudes toward, 11, 14–15, 51, 69, 228, 245–46, 252, 261
  ethics of exhumation and data recovery, 2, 4–6, 299–300
  insights from study of, 1
  osteological study of, 64–65, 68–69
  reasons for exhumation of, 5
  recoffining of, 256
  skeletal studies, 1
  soil analysis and decomposition of bodies, 273–79, *278*, 298
  study of biological remains, 1
  water exposure and disintegration of skeletal remains, 268, 275–77
Hume, John, 46
Hunt, David, 269
Hunter, John, 66
Hyatt, Sybil, 271

immortality symbols, 165–66
Inchinnan mortsafe society, 232, 234
infectious disease epidemic, burial of victims of, 26, 45, 65, 66, 68
interior surface treatments of burial containers
  archaeological records of cloth linings, 209–11, *210*
  availability of information about, 212
  bare/no treatment, 199
  bedding arrangement of coffin sheets, 43, 48, 51
  cloth linings, 200–211, *201*, *202*, *209*
  combination treatments, 212
  costs of burial container and, 177
  lining tacks to secure cloth linings, 196–98, *197*, 200
  materials to make linings appear fuller, 200
  mattresses, 48, 200, 201, *201*
  painted surfaces, 200, 211–12
  pillows, 48, 200, 208–9, *209*, 211
  price list of products and services from Cabinetmaker's Society, 177–78, *178*
  sawdust and wood shavings from coffin construction, inclusion of in coffin, 200–201
  social importance and cultural perceptions of different treatments, 177, 178, 200, 212
  time and money spent on, 200
  trimmings and secondary components of linings, 201, 206–8, *208*, *209*
interments
  burial locations and funeral process costs, 8–9
  data recovery and analysis related to, 1
  laws and church control over location and rites of, 6, 8–9
  shroud burial replacement with coffined interment, 9, 41, 51, 227
Ireland
  body snatching and body protection in, 230
  denial of Christian burial in, 32
  historic burial excavation in, 2
  medical school enrollment increase and demand for bodies, 228
iron bands, straps, and chains, 229, 238, 240, 241, *241*, *242*, 243
iron coffins
  body protection in, 229
  cast-iron coffin found during Caswell grave project, *266*, 267
  cast-iron coffins, 11, 77, 257
  status and use of, 77, 275
iron mortsafes, 231, 234, 235, 238, *239*, 240, 241, *241*, 243–45, *244*
Italian cloth, 202, 204–5, *214*, *218*

Jamestown, 2, 9
janker, 232, 233, 238, *239*
janker men, 232, 233
janker stone, 231, 233
jaw cloths/chin cloth, 46, 275
jewelry and personal adornment, 48–51, 269, *270*
J. M. Connelley Funeral Home, 101–2
John Marsellus Casket Company, *99*
J. W. McCormick Funeral Home, 101–4, *102*, *103*, 107

King's Lynn Baptist burial ground, *44*, 46
Kinston
  Caswell cemeteries in, 263–65, *264*, 279
  Governor Richard Caswell Memorial/CSS *Neuse* Historical Site cemetery, 264–65, *264*, 272
  Red House cemetery, 263–65, *264*, 270–79, *271*, *272*, *274*
  Vernon Hall "the Hill" cemetery, 263–68, *264*, *266*
Knox, John, 26

lace (coffin-lining trim), 201, *202*, 206, 207, *209*, 213, *215–16*, 220
lace (decorative metal), *7*, *10*, 11, 131, 146, 167

lace tacks, *210*, 211
lacquers, 179, 180
Langenau Manufacturing Company, *198*
The Last Battell of the Soule in Death (Boyd), 27–28
Las Vegas Gravel Pit Cemetery, *186*
Launceston Castle prison burial ground, 43, *44*, 45
lawn, 202, 205, *216*, *217*, 218
laws and church control over location and rites of burial, 6, 8–9
A. L. Calhoun General Store, 97
lead coffins/lead-lined coffins
　earliest examples of, 9
　preservation of remains in, 25–26
　status and use of, 9, 25–26, 33, 46, 77, 256, 259, 260, 275
　text and symbols on lids, 9, 10
　trends in use and shapes of, 9, 85
　triple-shell coffins, 67
Lebanon Cemetery, 229
lid motifs/plates
　description of, 7
　mass production of, 11, *12*
　metals used for, *142*, 143, *144*, 145, 149
　St. George's Church examples, 138, 140, *141*, *142*, *144*, 145, *158–59*
　St. Luke's church examples, 138, *139*, *142*, 143, *144*, *158–59*
　St. Pancras examples, *12*, 67, *294*
　trends in and designs and symbols on, 11, *12*, 86–88, *87*, *88*, *158–59*, 167
life and death, boundaries between, 37–38
Linlithgow Mortsafe Society, 231
Littee, Joseph, 64
Little, Barbara, 98
Little Dutch Church, Halifax, 2, 3
London
　burials within heart of, end to, 57, 68
　cholera epidemics in, 65, 66, 68
　mortuary data from, 288–89
　population growth of, 68
London Hospital burial grounds, 230

Macomb, Alexander, 258–61
Macomb, Catherine, 259, 260
Macomb vault, 253–54, *253*, 258–61, *258*, *260*
Madam Felix/Hettick Cemetery, *186*
Margarot, Maurice, 67
Martin, Thomas, 49
Marvell, Andrew, 29
Maskoll, Rebecca, 62
material culture
　Beautification of Death Movement and, 98, 173, 208, 252, 256
　burial locations and funeral process costs, 8–9
　catalogs from producers of, 3, 6
　craft and industry research recommendation, 293–96
　cultural and social factors in attitudes toward and selection of, 9–15, 252
　descriptive terms for recovered items, 6, 7
　ethical and practical issues related to investigation of, 4–6, 299–300
　fashion and changes in, 75, 87
　mass production and changes in, 75
　patterns of consumption, research on, 75
　power relationships between undertakers and the bereaved and selection of, 75–78, 89–91
　protection and conservation of, 4–5
　reburial or discard of after excavation and analysis, 4
　retention and discard policies for, 4
　status indications from, 97–98, 107, 121, 249–50, 251–61, *253*, *255*, *257*, *260*
　style and content of funeral packages, 6
　terminology for, British and North American, 6, 7, 123, 165
　trends in choices and selections of, 9–15, *10*, *12*, *13*, 75–78
mattresses, 48, 200, 201, *201*
McCarn, Richard, 265
McCormick Funeral Home, 101–4, *102*, *103*, 107
McDougald Funeral Home, 101–2
Meadowlark Cemetery, *186*, 188, 199
Medical College of Georgia, 230
medical schools
　Anatomy Act and regulation of human remains for medical purposes, 32, 65, 228, 232, 234, 235, 245–46
　anatomy schools/medical training programs and need for bodies for dissection, 11, 227–28, 229, 245
　body-snatching organizations to obtain bodies for medical students, 228
　cost of bodies for, 228
　illegal examination of cadavers found at, 230
　increase in enrollment in and demand for bodies for, 228
Melville, James, 28
memorial stones, 63–64
mercury, 39
merino and merino mattresses, 200, *201*, 202, 205, 208–9, *216*, 217
Mesman, Judith, 49
Microcosmographia (Crooke), 29, *30*, 31
Milwaukee Casket Company, *99*
Mitra, Siddhartha, 277
momie cloth, *190*, 191, 194, 201–2, *216*
monuments/memorials
　commissioning of before a death, 76
　at Congressional Cemetery, 252
　conservation of, 5
　data collection and analysis about, 78–83, *80*, *81*, *82*
　emotional, social, and cultural context of selection of, 75–78, 90–91
　power relationships between stonemason and the bereaved and selection of, 75–78, 89–91
　studies of, 1
　symbols and motifs and trends in use of, 78, 79–83, *80*, *81*, *82*, *84*
　See also gravestones/headstones
mortality symbols, 78, 79, *80*, 90, 165–66, 246

morthouses/deadhouses, 230–31, 234–37, *237*
mortsafe and watching societies, 230, 231–34, 245–46
mortsafes
   archaeological records of, 229
   body protection in, 227, 231, 238
   classification and analysis of data about, 227
   craft and industry research recommendation, 296
   design and types of, 231, *237*, 238–44, *239*, *242*, *244*
   janker for moving and removing, 232, 233, 238, *239*
   length of time of protection with, 231, 232, 233, 238
   membership costs and subscriptions to societies responsible for, 231, 232–33
   number kept by societies, 233–34
   permanent, 241, 243
   price of, 233
   shortages of, 234
   societies for purchase and maintenance of, 231–34, 245–46
   studies of, 1
mortstones, 231, 237–38, *237*, 240
mortuary data
   access to and distribution of, 2, 3–4, 285, 288–92
   chronological spread, 290–92
   craft and industry research recommendation, 293–96
   ethical and practical issues related to acquisition of, 1, 2, 4–6, 299–300
   geographical and social spread, 288–90
   methodological advances for recovery of, 2, 286, 287
   network of professionals and researchers for recovery and analysis of, 299–300
   policies and practices in data collection in the field, 285–87
   recovery and analysis of, 1–4
   research question suggestions, 292–300
   style and symbolism changes research recommendation, 292–93
   taphonomy, burial management, and data analysis, 293–94, 297–98, *297*, 299
mortuary practices and culture
   body disposal methods and research on, 1
   complexity of and insights from study of, 3–4
   craft and industry research recommendation, 293–96
   future research recommendations, 4, 285–300
   locations of vaults and plots and social status, 251
   materials aspects of, study of, 1–2
   status and mortuary practices linkage, 249–50, 251–61, *253*, *255*, *257*, *260*
   terminology and precision in description of, 123
   trends across time and space, 3–4
   See also interments
Muir, Thomas, 67
Muirson, Benjamin Woolsey, 63–64
Muirson, George, 64
Murder Act, 32
muslin
   coffin exterior coverings, 199
   coffin linings, 200, *201*, 202, 205, *218*

nails, 123
Nancy Creek Primitive Baptist Church, 98, 109–14, 115–18, *116*, *117*, 119, 121
National Casket Company, *99*, 181, 190–91, *190*, 200, *201*
National Cemetery Administration (NCA), 258, 259
National Foundation of Funeral Service, 97
National Museum of Natural History, Smithsonian Institution
   Caswell grave project, 267–70
   Congressional Cemetery vault preservation and restoration project, 249–62
National Park Service, Historic Preservation Training Center (HPTC), 258, 259, 260
Native American Graves Protection and Repatriation Act (NAGRPA), 2
Newbattle mortsafe society, 231
New Bunhill Fields, 41, 42
Newburn mortsafe society, 231–34
Newcastle Infirmary burial ground, *45*, 229–30
New Churchyard, 26
Nixon, Anthony, 29–31
nonconformist burial grounds, 2, 6, 8, 45, 46, 80, 288–89. *See also* Quaker burial grounds
North America
   body snatching and body protection in, 11, 227, 228–29, 243–44, 245
   coffin and fittings studies in, 2
   crypts beneath churches in, 8
   cultural factors in attitudes toward death, the body, containment, and disposal, 14–15
   documentation of locations of burial grounds, 8
   earth-cut graves in, 3
   excavations of vaults and crypts in, 2–3
   historic burial excavation in, 2–3
   laws and church control over location and rites of burial, 8–9
   mass production of furniture and hardware in, 169–73
   material choice trends, 9–15
   material culture terminology, 6, *7*, 165
   medical school enrollment increase and demand for bodies, 228
   mortuary data from, 3, 14–15, 289–92
   protection and conservation of burial grounds in, 5
   status indications from mortuary practices, 97–98, 107
North Brisbane Burial Grounds, 167
North Carolina Museum of History, 270–71

Old Branham Cemetery, *186*
Ornamental Design Act, 166
osteological studies, 64–65, 68–69
Owen, Richard, 65–66
Owsley, Douglas, 267–68, 269
Oxford Castle, 31–32

paint
   archaeological records of painting, 185–89, *186–87*

catalog examples of painted exteriors and paint colors, 181, 182, *183*
children's coffins, 11, 181, 182
coffin exterior surfaces, 178, 181–89
coffin interior surfaces, 200, 211–12
colors commonly used, 102, 181–85, *183*, 212
data recovery and analysis about, 177
Munsell color chart for color identification, 189
paint-fabric combinations, 199, 212
pigment, 181
preservation of, 177
social importance and cultural perceptions of different treatments, 189
vehicle, 181
white paint, 181, 182–84, 185–88, *186–87*
Palmer, Thomas Fyshe, 67
parish coffins, 41, 123, 227
Parker, Erastus A., 270–71
Paxson, Comfort & Company, 181, 207, 208–9, *208*
Peerman Burial Company, *99*
Pennsylvania funeral home data, 104
pillows, 48, 200, 208–9, *209*, 211
pink pigments/paint, 102, 188, 212
pins/tacks
　cloth exterior coverings secured with, 10, *10*, 12, 85, *85*, 88, 189, 196–99, *197*
　cloth linings secured with lining tacks, 196–98, *197*, 200, 209–11, *210*
　description of, 7
　discontinuation of use of, 12
　replacement with lace, 11
　text and symbols on lids, 10, *10*, 85, *85*, 88, 89, 91, 198–99
　trends in, 10, *10*
piqué
　coffin exterior coverings, *190*, 191, *192–93*, 194–95, 199
　coffin linings, 201–2, *215*, *217*, *218*
　description of, 194–95
plague, burial of victims of, 26
Plume, Sable, 189
plush, *190*, 191, 195, 199
poor
　burial practices for, 26, 83, 98
　winding sheet shroud for burial, 275
Portchester Castle prisoner burial ground, 49, *50*
prisons
　bodies of deceased as cadavers, 31, 32, 65
　clothing and buttons from burial grounds of, 43, 45, *45*
　criminals, treatment of bodies of, 31–32
　rosary found with body of prisoner of war, 49, *50*
ProMark, 265
Providence Baptist Church Cemetery, *187*
Prynne, William, 23, 24

Quaker burial grounds
　archaeological evidence of preparation, clothing, and presentation of the corpse at, 40, 42, 43, *44*, 48
　data recovery and analysis from, 2
　establishment of as alternatives to state denomination laws regarding burial, 6
　status and material culture choices of Quakers, 252
Quaker Burying Ground, Virginia, *187*
Quantico Corporate Center Tract Burials, *187*

railway projects and St. Pancras cemetery exhumation projects, 57–60, *58*, *59*, 63, *64*, 71
Rasberry, Mattie, 269
Red House cemetery, 263–65, *264*, 270–79, *271*, *272*, *274*
red pigments/paints, 181–82, *183*, 185–88, *186–87*, 212
resurrection, beliefs about, 23–25, 37–38
resurrection men/resurrectionists, 227. *See also* body snatching
Reynolds Cemetery, *187*
rings and jewelry, 48–51, 269, *270*
rosaries, 49, *50*
rosemary, 269
Royal College of Surgeons, 227
Rudley, Moss, 259
Rural Cemetery movement, 256, 261–62

St. Andrew cemetery, 46
St. Bartholomew's, Penn, Wolverhampton, *133*, *150–63*
St. Benet Sherehog burial ground, 43, *44*
St. Bride's church, 26, 229
St. George's Church, Bloomsbury
　breastplate examples, 132–33, *142*, 143, *144*, *150–54*
　breastplates examples, 147, *147*
　coffin and coffin fittings design investigation, 78, 86, 88, 129–31, 145–49
　dentures recovered from burial at, 46
　escutcheon examples, 140, *142*, *144*, *160*
　grip and grip plate examples, 137, *137*, *138*, *142*, *144*, 147–48, *155–57*
　lid motif examples, 138, 140, *141*, *142*, *144*, 145, *158–59*
　status and social and religious backgrounds of burial population, 129–31, 146, 148–49
　types of metals used for coffin fitting, 143–45, *144*, 149
　upholstery and studwork examples, 140, *142*, 143, *144*, 145, *161–63*
St. Giles burial ground, 63
St. Louis Coffin Company, 181
St. Luke's church, Islington
　breastplate examples, 132, *133*, *142*, 143, *144*, 147, *150–54*
　coffin and coffin fittings design investigation, 78, 86, 88, 129–30, 145–49
　escutcheon examples, 138, *142*, 143, *144*, *160*
　grip and grip plate examples, 134–37, *134*, *135*, *136*, *142*, 143, *144*, 147–48, *155–57*
　jewelry recovered from burial at, 50
　lid motif examples, 138, *139*, *142*, 143, *144*, *158–59*
　mercury at base of coffin in vault under, 39
　status and social and religious backgrounds of burial population, 129–30, 146, 148–49

St. Luke's church, Islington (*continued*)
    types of metals used for coffin fitting, *142*, 143, *144*, 149
    upholstery and studwork examples, 140, *142*, 143, *144*, *161–63*
St. Magnus Cathedral, 29
St. Mark's Church, Lincoln, 43
St. Martins-in-the-Bullring, Birmingham, *45*, 46, 47, 48, 49, 50, 146, 147
St. Marylebone Church, *44*, 46, 50, 146
St. Mary's Church, Little Ilford, 39
St. Mary's church, South Stoneham, 83
St. Mary's City, Brick Chapel, 2, 9
St. Mary by the Bourne, Marylebone, 88
St. Mary the Virgin, Potton, 79, 89, 90
St. Nicholas Church, Bathampton, 41, 42, 43, 46, 48, 50
St. Nicholas Church, Forest Hill, 43, *44*
St. Nicholas Church, Sevenoaks, 42, 46
St. Pancras Burial Ground, 57
St. Pancras cemetery
    archaeological evidence of preparation, clothing, and presentation of the corpse at, 46
    breastplate examples, 62, *63*, 67, *289*
    burial patterns and reuse of burial space, 297–98, *297*, *299*
    burial population, 57, 64–65
    Catholicism association with, 67
    coffin fittings examples, 62, 78
    coffin types found at, 62, 67, 78
    descendants interests in, 5
    excavation methodologies, 60–66, *61*, *64*
    exhumation procedures and archaeological recording of remains, 5, 57–58, *58*, 60–66, *61*, *64*
    faunal remains found in coffins from, 65–66
    French émigrés buried at, 57, 66–67, 68, 69–71, *70*, *71*
    headstones/memorial stones at, 63–64
    lid motif examples, *12*, 67, *294*
    location of, *59*, 67–68
    osteological study of remains from, 64–65, 68–69
    population growth of parish, 68
    quality of preservation of remains and material culture at, 62
    railway projects and exhumation of remains from, 57–60, *58*, *59*, 63, *64*, 71
    reinterment of remains from, 5, 69–71, *70*, *71*
    sampling decisions and number of burials included for analysis, 61–62, 68–69
    sensitivity in the treatment of human remains at, 57–58, 60
    status and social and religious backgrounds of burial population, 62, 63–69
St. Pancras Smallpox Hospital, 65
St. Peter's Church, Barton-upon-Humber, Lincolnshire, 38, 49, 50
St. Peter's Church, Wolverhampton, 39, 50
St. Philip's Cathedral, Birmingham, 41
St. Saviour's burial ground, 85–86, 87–88

sateen
    coffin exterior coverings, *190*, 191, 195
    coffin linings, 201–2, *202*, 213–14, *215*, *217*, *218*
    description of, 195
    pillows, 208–9
satin
    coffin exterior coverings, *190*, 191, *193*, 195, 199
    coffin linings, *201*, *202*, 211, *213–18*
    description of, 191
    pillows, 208–9, *209*
Scotland
    body snatching and body protection in, 227–28, 230, 245–46
    burials within and under churches in, 26, 28–29
    laws and church control over location and rites of burial, 6
    morthouses in, 230–31, 234–37, *237*
    mortsafe and watching societies in, 231–34, 245–46
    mortsafes in, 238–44, *239*, *242*, *244*
    mortstones in, 237–38, *237*
screw caps/covers, 7
screw plates/washers, 7
screws/thumbscrews/tacks
    description of, 7
    seriation research in Georgia, 113, 115–16, *116*, 118, 119–21, *119*
    trends in, 97
Seccombe Lake Cemetery, *186*
serge, 202, 205, 206, *215*, *218*
Seven Rivers Cemetery, *186*
Sheffield Cathedral, *45*, 50
shellac, 179, 180
Sherlock, William, 23–24
shield design, 87–88, *88*, 132, 133, *133*, 146–47, *147*, 167
shroud pins, 40
shrouds
    British practices for use of, 40–41, 275
    Burial in Woolen Act and woolen shrouds, 40, 41, 51
    changes in form of, 40–41, 51
    characteristics and size of, 40, 275
    clothing covered by, 43
    coffined interments replacement of shroud burials, 9, 41, 51, 227
    decomposition of bodies and, 276
    frills and ruffles on, 41–42
    pins, ties, and sewn seams for closing, 40, 41–42, 43
    plague victims burial in, 26
    preparation for burial in, 40–41, 275
    winding sheet for burial, 48, 275
signal (alarm) coffins, 123
silk
    coffin exterior coverings, *190*, *193*, 199
    coffin linings, 202, *202*, 206, 211, *213–17*, *219*
    pillows, 208–9
Singer, A. Michael, 269
Skirving, William, 67
sleeping characterization of the dead, 47–48, 51, 208
Smith, John, 168

soil analysis and decomposition of bodies, 273–79, *278*, 298
soul and body, distinction between and beliefs about, 23–25, 29–31, 32, 37–38
"The Soule's Complaint against the Body" (Prynne), 23, 24
South Carolina
    coffin fittings research, 97–98
    funeral home records from, 101–4, *102*, *103*, 107
    mortality rates for children, 101–2
Southwark Cathedral, *45*
Spanish satin, *201*, 204, *213*, *214*, *215*, *216–17*, *218*
Spitalfields Christ Church
    affluence and burial in crypt at, 83
    archaeological clearance of crypts, 5, 83
    archaeological evidence of preparation, clothing, and presentation of the corpse at, 38, 39, 41, 42–43, 46, 48, 49, 50
    archaeological justification of the clearance of the crypt of, 5
    body protection at, 229
    body snatching evidence at, 229
    burial pattern in, 298
    coffin and coffin fittings design investigation, 78, 83, 85–88, *86*, *87*, *88*, 89–90, 129, 132, 146, 147, *150–63*
    descendants interests in, 5
    publication of report about, 83
    studies of vaults and crypts, 2, 129
Spring Street Presbyterian Church, New York City, 3, 230
stains, 178, 179, 180–81
Stein Manufacturing Company and Samuel Stein, 190–91, 209, *209*
stockings and gloves, 42
studs. *See* escutcheons/studs
suicides, burial after, 32
Sumter Casket Company, 97
surface treatments of burial containers
    availability of information about, 177, 212
    costs of burial container and, 177
    data recovery and analysis about, 177, 212
    physical preservation of, 177, 212
    price list of products and services from Cabinetmaker's Society, 177–78, *178*
    social importance and cultural perceptions of different treatments, 177, 178, 212
    See also exterior surface treatments of burial containers; interior surface treatments of burial containers
Sussex City Cemetery, *186*

tacks. *See* pins/tacks
Talbot County cemetery, 109, 110–11, *113*, 114, 115, *116*, 117, *117*, 118
taphonomy, burial management, and data analysis, 293–94, 297–98, *297*, *299*
tassels and cords, 201, 206, 208, *208*, 213, *214*, 219
Traquair Watching Society, 232, 233
Trinity College Dublin, Herb Garden, 230
2-4 Church Street, Chelsea, 43, *44*

United States Casket Company, *99*
University of California, Davis, Stable Isotope Facility, 277
upholstery and studwork
    St. George's Church examples, 140, *142*, 143, *144*, 145, *161–63*
    St. Luke's church examples, 140, *142*, 143, *144*, *161–63*
    trends in, 146
urns
    coffin fittings, 11, *12*, 67, 87–88, *87*, *88*, 89–91, 138, *139*, 140, 146, 148, 167, 170, *253*
    headstone/monument symbols, 79–80, *82*, 89, 90–91
Uxbridge Almshouse burial grounds, 98, *119*, 126, 252

varnish, 178, 179–81, *180*
vaults
    affluence and burial in, 8–9
    British data on, 2
    coffin and fittings condition of investigations of, 8–9
    costs/prices of, 103, 104
    data recovery and analysis from, 285–87
    design of family vaults, 235
    increase in number of burials in, 227
    materials for, 103, 104
    morthouses compared to, 235
    North American data on, 2–3, 102–3, 104
    prevalence of use of, 8
    studies of, 1, 2
velvet
    coffin exterior coverings, *190*, 191, *192–93*, 196, 199
    coffin linings, 201–2, 211, *215*, *217*
    description of, 196
Vernon Hall "the Hill" cemetery, 263–68, *264*, *266*
Voegtly Cemetery, *187*, 189, 198

walrus bones, 65–66
washing the corpse, 25, 37, 38, 45, 275
Washington, Louisa Hernandez, 270
watchhouses, 230, 233, 235
watching and mortsafe societies, 227, 230, 231–34, 245–46
watchtowers, 230
water exposure and disintegration of skeletal remains, 268, 275–77
Watford, John R., 272
Watford, Rachel L. Brown, 272
waxes/waxing, 178, 179, 180
wedding rings, 49, 269, *270*
Weir Family Cemetery, 171, *171*, 252
west-east burial alignment, 26–27, 31, 272, 273, *274*
white paint/zinc white/zinc oxide, 102, 181, 182–84, 185–88, *186–87*, 212
wills and attitudes toward the body, 27
Wirt, Agnes, 256
Wirt, William, 256
Wirt vault, 253–54, *253*, 256–58, *257*, 261
witches, burial of, 32
Wolfe, Linda, 269

Index   319

wooden coffins
- names for in catalogs, 12
- pine coffin found during Caswell grave excavation project, 273, 275, 276
- pitch for sealing, 200
- preservation of human remains and use of, 276
- price list of products and services from Cabinetmaker's Society, 177–78, *178*
- pricing of, 12
- St. Pancras examples, 62, 67
- sawdust and wood shavings from making, inclusion of in coffin, 200–201
- shapes and forms of, 9, 275
- status and use of, 275
- types of wood and surface treatments, 177–78, *178*, 179
- types of wood for, 11, 12, 275

See also exterior surface treatments of burial containers

Woodforde, Alicia, 24
Woodforde, Samuel, 24
workhouses
- bodies of deceased as cadavers, 65, 228, 229
- coffin hardware found in burials grounds of, 252
- coffins for interment of, 227
- investigations at burial grounds of, 9

yellow/yellow ochre pigments/paints, 181–82, *183*, 185–88, *186–87*
York Prison, 43, 45, *45*

zinc white/zinc oxide, 102, 181, 182–84, 185–88, *186–87*
Zoological Society of London, 65–66